The Evolution of
Political Parties, Campaigns, and Elections

The Evolution of Political Parties, Campaigns, and Elections

Landmark Documents, 1787–2007

❧ ❧

Randall E. Adkins, Editor

University of Nebraska at Omaha

CQ PRESS

A Division of Congressional Quarterly Inc.

Washington, D.C.

CQ Press
2300 N Street, NW, Suite 800
Washington, DC 20037

Phone: 202-729-1900; toll-free, 1-866-4CQ-PRESS (1-866-427-7737)

Web: www.cqpress.com

Cover design: Jeffrey M. Hall/ION Graphic Design Works
Composition: BMWW
Photo Credits:
Civil Rights Movement Veterans Web site (www.crmvet.org): 262–265
Courtesy of the Library of Congress: 68, 160
Courtesy of the University of Nebraska at Omaha: 127–128
Federal Election Commission Web site: 288–290
Susan Stocker/South Florida Sun-Sentinel: 313
The Granger Collection: 102 (top and bottom)
Used with permission. Democratic National Committee: 250 (left and right)

♾ The paper used in this publication exceeds the requirements of the American National Standard for Information Sciences—Permanence of Paper for Printed Library Materials, ANSI Z39.48-1992.

Printed and bound in the United States of America

12   11   10   09   08   1   2   3   4   5

Library of Congress Cataloging-in-Publication Data
The evolution of political parties, campaigns, and elections: landmark documents, 1787–2007 / Randall E. Adkins, editor.
    p. cm.
ISBN 978-0-87289-578-2 (alk. paper)
    I. United States—Politics and government—Sources.   I. Adkins, Randall E.
II. Title.
E183.E86   2008
973—dc22   2007050648

To my parents

❧ ❧

who have traveled together to the polling place
for more than 45 years to cancel out each other's vote.

Contents

Preface

A User's Guide to *The Evolution of Political Parties, Campaigns, and Elections*

Primary source materials are well-established tools for engaging student learning that can be easily integrated into most instructional styles. These materials are valuable to instruction because they bring a subject to life for students, they expose students to the perspectives of actual participants, and they develop stronger analytical skills in students. First, primary sources create a direct link between the student and the issue. Documentary materials on political parties, campaigns, and elections are very appealing, ranging from eighteenth-century campaign circulars written by party officials to televised campaign advertisements from the twentieth century. Second, working with primary sources allows students to participate in important events that were observed and then documented in many different formats, including cartoons, transcribed debates, legislative actions, letters, photographs, regulations, reports, and published speeches. Third, working directly with primary sources should lead students to ask better questions, develop more intelligent interpretations, and draw more reasoned conclusions.

Primary sources can be difficult to research without knowledge of the historical, political, and social contexts of a time period. Many students have discovered that although the Internet offers a wealth of information, it is often overwhelming and unreliable. The purpose of this book is to make primary sources accessible to students of political parties, campaigns, and elections by weaving the contextual conditions of a period together with the documents. This book includes fifty documents that span more than two centuries—from the Constitutional Convention of 1787 to the Price-Herman Commission Report of 2005. Each document starts with an introduction that presents students with the circumstances surrounding the event in question. For example, the introduction to the letters of John Beckley to William Irvine explains Beckley's relationship to Thomas Jefferson and why he assumed the role of Jefferson's campaign manager in the 1796 and 1800 presidential campaigns. Some documents are printed in their entirety, but most have been edited to highlight the importance of the document to political parties, campaigns, and elections. Whenever possible, an Internet link to the unedited document has been included. Students should be aware, however, that the Internet is dynamic. Documents may not always continue to be available at the sites listed.

Instructors of classes on political parties, campaigns, and elections will find two features of this book especially helpful. First, discussion questions are included at the beginning of each document to help guide students through the reading. Instructors should feel free to use these questions or develop their own. Second, documents are listed chronologically, but a topical guide is included on pages 361–365 to offer suggestions to instructors for how documents might be grouped together in a course on political parties, campaigns, and elections. For example, when teaching a unit on campaign finance reform one might want to use the following documents:

- 25, The Tillman Act
- 27, The Publicity Act
- 34, The Taft-Hartley Act
- 41, *Buckley v. Valeo* (1976)
- 47, Russ Feingold's Speech Supporting the Bipartisan Campaign Reform Act and Mitch McConnell's Speech Opposing the Bipartisan Campaign Reform Act

Further, some documents obviously apply to multiple units, such as Alexander Hamilton's letter to Edward Carrington, which could be read in relation to units on the origin and history of political parties, the party in government, and the parties and the press. Each document is marked in the topical guide to indicate the units to which it applies.

Finally, librarians and researchers will find this book to be an excellent collection of the most historically important documents concerning political parties, campaigns, and elections. Included here are documents from various sources, including the Constitutional Convention, the office of the president, Congress, the Supreme Court, the Democratic Party, the Republican Party, other major parties such as the Federalists and the Whigs, third parties, the press, and the states. The documents vary in format and style and consist of amendments to the Constitution, campaign advertisements or circulars, court cases, transcribed debates, governmental reports, legislative actions, letters, magazine and newspaper articles and editorials, memoranda, party platforms, party reports, presidential addresses and messages to Congress, radio addresses, and speeches.

Overall, this book provides students, faculty, librarians, and researchers with a solid understanding of both the broader evolution of political parties, campaigns, and elections and how each document fits within the historical, political, and social contexts of a period.

Acknowledgments

I wish to express my heartfelt gratitude to the many people who encouraged me to tackle this project.

First, I want to thank my colleagues and students at the University of Nebraska at Omaha, all of whom were very accommodating. Loree Bykerk and Shelton Hendricks supported my request for a Faculty Development Fellowship, which provided the time necessary to complete the manuscript in the fall of 2007. Jody Neathery-Castro made sure that I concentrated on this project by taking over as the interim chair of our graduate program while I was on leave. Mary Dunn and James Shaw were instrumental in assisting me with the procurement and reproduction of many of the documents contained in this book. And Steve Bullock and Carson Holloway were always willing to listen to my ideas and provide thoughtful feedback.

Second, I deeply appreciate the dedication of the staff of CQ Press. Charisse Kiino, the chief acquisitions editor for the College Division, recognized the potential of this project and provided valuable advice during every stage of the publication process. Allison McKay, the editorial assistant, and Lorna Notsch, the project editor, proved to be very devoted professionals. Their brilliance rescued me from many errors that I would have otherwise made. I also wish to extend thanks to Steve Pazdan, managing editor; Paul Pressau, production manager; and Margot Ziperman, manager, print and art production, for helping to ensure that this book became a reality. Additionally, thanks to BMWW for their careful composition of the text and attention to its various elements.

Credit is due to the public figures who documented the evolution of political parties, campaigns, and elections, and to those who so graciously provided permission to reprint the primary sources included in this book. I also wish to thank those who reviewed the prospectus of the book: William Binning, Youngstown State University; Matthew Eshbaugh-Soha, University of North Texas; Robin Kolodny, Temple University; Scott Paine, University of Texas; Arnold Shober, Lawrence

University; and Rick Valelly, Swarthmore College. Their comments proved very constructive and encouraged me to make a number of revisions that improved the book considerably.

My wife, Natalie, and my sons, Ross and Ryan, deserve special thanks. Their love is unconditional, their joy endless, and their patience without limit. They are my fortress and my refuge.

Finally, I hope that you, the reader, will get as much pleasure from reading this book as I did researching and writing it.

Omaha, Nebraska
December 2007

❧ I ❧

The Constitution:

*Provisions Concerning Elections**

(1787)

1. How do the amendments to the Constitution supplement the provisions laid out in that document? What has been the impact of these amendments on electoral politics?
2. How did changes in America's political and social cultures lead to amendments to the Constitution? What impact have these changes had on political parties?

MORE THAN A DECADE AFTER it was created, the government under the Articles of Confederation was generally regarded as weak and ineffective. In response to the mounting criticism, the Congress of the Confederation passed a resolution on February 21, 1787, calling for "a Convention of delegates who shall have been appointed by the several states to be held in Philadelphia for the sole and express purpose of revising the Articles of Confederation." That convention met from May 25 to September 17, 1787. Those present were, with a few notable exceptions who were serving abroad, the most important and influential leaders in the country. Their meeting has come to be known as the Constitutional Convention, and instead of revising the existing system of government, the attendees submitted to the Congress of the Confederation a draft for a new plan of government to replace the Articles of Confederation. The plan hinged upon approval by nine of the thirteen states. The Constitution was ratified by the ninth state on June 21, 1788, and took effect on March 4 of the following year.

The purpose of the Constitution was to create a stronger national government that was elected by and responsive to the people. Specifically, convention delegates decided that the House of Representatives should be elected directly by the people. The Constitution's architects did not agree with giving the public such an influential voice in the selection of

*www.senate.gov/civics/constitution_item/constitution.htm

I

all federal officials, however. So the design of the new government featured means to insulate officeholders from the direct will of the people. First, senators were to be chosen by state legislatures (this was later amended by the Seventeenth Amendment). Second, the public chose presidential "electors," who were tasked with choosing the president.

Elections to the House of Representatives were held in late 1788 and early 1789. January 7, 1789, was the date set for choosing presidential electors, and these electors met to select a president on February 4. The first session of Congress convened on March 4, 1789. This was also to be the president's inauguration day, unfortunately, only thirteen of fifty-nine representatives and eight of twenty-two senators had arrived in New York (the U.S. capital until 1790). A quorum was finally attained in both chambers on April 6. When the two houses met to count the electoral vote, George Washington was elected president and John Adams was elected vice president. Washington and Adams were sworn into office on April 30, 1789.

To settle the dispute over how representatives were to be allocated, the nation's founders had created a bicameral legislature composed of a House of Representatives and a Senate. Article I, Section 2 of the Constitution details the qualifications, method of selection, and apportionment of House members. Article I, Section 3 describes the number, qualifications, and method of selection of senators.

Article II, Section 2 addresses the qualifications, method of selection, and what occurs in the event that the president of the United States is disabled. Specifically, it establishes what has become known as the Electoral College system. Delegates at the Constitutional Convention could not agree on whether to select the president by direct popular election or allow Congress to choose. The Electoral College was a compromise that put selection in the hands of a special group of electors chosen for the sole purpose of selecting the president. The method of determining electors was left to the states, but today almost all states choose electors by popular vote.

Since the Constitution took effect in 1789, several constitutional amendments have been passed that have altered the process of electing federal officials. In the bitter election of 1800 Thomas Jefferson and his running mate, Aaron Burr, tied in the balloting, which threw the selection of the president to the House of Representatives. From this was born the Twelfth Amendment, which requires separate ballots for presidential and vice presidential candidates. In the early twentieth century, stalemates in state legislatures often left states without two senators for extended periods of time. The Seventeenth Amendment requires that senators be elected directly by the people. The Twentieth Amendment changed the date that congressional and presidential terms started from March to January. More important, however, the amendment mandated that if no candidate had a majority of the electoral vote, the incoming—not the outgoing—House of Representatives would be charged with selecting the new president. After Franklin Roosevelt was elected to the presidency for a record fourth term in 1944, the Twenty-second Amendment limited the number of terms that a president could serve to two. After Roosevelt's sudden death in 1945 and the assassination of John Kennedy in 1963, the Twenty-fifth Amendment clarified language about presidential succession and provided for a process to select a new vice president should the need arise.

A number of other constitutional amendments have expanded the right to participate in the election process. Following the Civil War, the Fifteenth Amendment was passed in 1870 to protect the voting rights of African Americans. Women's suffrage varied from state to state until the Nineteenth Amendment, passed in 1920, standardized voting rights for women. In 1961, the Twenty-third Amendment gave residents of the District of Columbia the right to vote in presidential elections, since the city now included a substantial population who did not work for the federal government. The turbulence of the 1960s led to the passage of two other constitutional amendments. The Twenty-fourth Amendment prohibited poll taxes, which were still being used to keep African Americans from voting. The voting age was lowered to eighteen by the Twenty-sixth Amendment, primarily in response to criticism that men could be drafted into military service at the age of eighteen, but could not vote for the leaders who sent them into battle until they were twenty-one.

Article 1

SECTION 2. The House of Representatives shall be composed of Members chosen every second Year by the People of the several States, and the Electors in each State shall have the Qualifications requisite for Electors of the most numerous Branch of the State Legislature.

No Person shall be a Representative who shall not have attained to the Age of twenty five Years, and been seven Years a Citizen of the United States, and who shall not, when elected, be an Inhabitant of that State in which he shall be chosen.

[Representatives and direct Taxes shall be apportioned among the several States which may be included within this Union, according to their respective Numbers, which shall be determined by adding to the whole Number of free Persons, including those bound to Service for a Term of Years, and excluding Indians not taxed, three fifths of all other Persons.][1] The actual Enumeration shall be made within three Years after the first Meeting of the Congress of the United States, and within every subsequent Term of ten Years, in such Manner as they shall by Law direct. The Number of Representatives shall not exceed one for every thirty Thousand, but each State shall have at Least one Representative; and until such enumeration shall be made, the State of New Hampshire shall be entitled to chuse three, Massachusetts eight, Rhode-Island and Providence Plantations one, Connecticut five, New-York six, New Jersey four, Pennsylvania eight, Delaware one, Maryland six, Virginia ten, North Carolina five, South Carolina five, and Georgia three.

When vacancies happen in the Representation from any State, the Executive Authority thereof shall issue Writs of Election to fill such Vacancies. . . .

SECTION 3. The Senate of the United States shall be composed of two Senators from each State, [chosen by the Legislature thereof,] for six Years; and each Senator shall have one Vote.

Immediately after they shall be assembled in Consequence of the first Election, they shall be divided as equally as may be into three Classes. The Seats of the Senators of the first Class shall be vacated at the Expiration of the second Year, of the second Class at the Expiration of the fourth Year, and of the third Class at the Expiration of the sixth Year, so that one third may be chosen every second Year; [and if Vacancies happen by Resignation, or otherwise, during the Recess of the Legislature of any State, the Executive thereof may make temporary Appointments until the next Meeting of the Legislature, which shall then fill such Vacancies.][2]

No Person shall be a Senator who shall not have attained to the Age of thirty Years, and been nine Years a Citizen of the United States, and who shall not, when elected, be an Inhabitant of that State for which he shall be chosen. . . .

SECTION 4. The Times, Places and Manner of holding Elections for Senators and Representatives, shall be prescribed in each State by the Legislature thereof; but the Congress may at any time by Law make or alter such Regulations, except as to the Places of chusing Senators. . . .

SECTION 5. Each House shall be the Judge of the Elections, Returns and Qualifications of its own Members, and a Majority of each shall constitute a Quorum to do Business; but a smaller Number may adjourn from day to day, and may be authorized to compel the Attendance of absent Members, in such Manner, and under such Penalties as each House may provide. . . .

Article II

SECTION 1. . . . Each State shall appoint, in such Manner as the Legislature thereof may direct, a Number of Electors, equal to the whole Number of Senators and Representatives to which the State may be entitled in the Congress: but no Senator or Representative, or Person holding an Office of Trust or Profit under the United States, shall be appointed an Elector.

[The Electors shall meet in their respective States, and vote by Ballot for two Persons, of whom one at least shall not be an Inhabitant of the same State with themselves. And they shall make a List of all the Persons voted for, and of the Number of Votes for each; which List they shall sign and certify, and transmit sealed to the Seat of the Government of the United States, directed to the President of the Senate. The President of the Senate shall, in the Presence of the Senate and House of Representatives, open all the Certificates, and the Votes shall then be counted. The Person having the greatest Number of Votes shall be the President, if such Number be a Majority of the whole Number of Electors appointed; and if there be more than one who have such Majority, and have an equal Number of Votes, then the House of Representatives shall immediately chuse by Ballot one of them for President; and if no Person have a Majority, then from the five highest on the List the said House shall in like Manner chuse the President. But in chusing the President, the Votes shall be taken by States, the Representatives from each State having one Vote; a quorum for this Purpose shall consist of a Member or Members from two thirds of the States, and a Majority of all the States shall be necessary to a Choice. In every Case, after the Choice of the President, the Person having the greatest Number of Votes of the Electors shall be the Vice President. But if there should remain two or more who have equal Votes, the Senate shall chuse from them by Ballot the Vice-President.][3]

The Congress may determine the Time of chusing the Electors, and the Day on which they shall give their Votes; which Day shall be the same throughout the United States.

No Person except a natural born Citizen, or a Citizen of the United States, at the time of the Adoption of this Constitution, shall be eligible to the Office of President; neither shall any person be eligible to that Office who shall not have attained to the Age of thirty five Years, and been fourteen Years a Resident within the United States.

[In Case of the Removal of the President from Office, or of his Death, Resignation, or Inability to discharge the Powers and Duties of the said Office, the Same shall devolve on the Vice President, and the Congress may by Law provide for the Case of Removal, Death, Resignation or Inability, both of the President and Vice President, declaring what Officer shall then act as President, and such Officer shall act accordingly, until the Disability be removed, or a President shall be elected.] . . .[4]

Amendment XII
(Ratified June 15, 1804)

The Electors shall meet in their respective states and vote by ballot for President and Vice-President, one of whom, at least, shall not be an inhabitant of the same state with themselves; they shall name in their ballots the person voted for as President, and in distinct ballots the person voted for as Vice-President, and they shall make distinct lists of all persons voted for as President, and of all persons voted for as Vice-President, and of the number of votes for each, which lists they shall sign and certify, and transmit sealed to the seat of the government of the United States, directed to the President of the Senate;—The President of the Senate shall, in the presence of the Senate and House of Representatives, open all the certificates and the votes shall then be counted;—The person having the greatest Number of votes for President, shall be the President, if such number be a majority of the whole number of Electors appointed; and if no person have such majority, then from the persons having the highest numbers not exceeding three on the list of those voted for as President, the House of Representatives shall choose immediately, by ballot, the President. But in choosing the President, the votes shall be taken by states, the representation from each state having one vote; a quorum for this purpose shall consist of a member or members from two-thirds of the states, and a majority of all the states shall be necessary to a choice. [And if the House of Representatives shall not choose a President whenever the right of choice shall devolve upon them, before the fourth day of March next following, then the Vice-President shall act as President, as in the case of the death or other constitutional disability of the President—][5] The person having the greatest number of votes as Vice-President, shall be the Vice-President, if such number be a majority of the whole number of Electors appointed, and if no person have a majority, then from the two highest numbers on the list, the Senate shall choose the Vice-President; a quorum for the purpose shall consist of two-thirds of the whole number of Senators, and a majority of the whole number shall be necessary to a choice. But no person constitutionally ineligible to the office of President shall be eligible to that of Vice-President of the United States.

Amendment XV
(Ratified on February 3, 1870)

SECTION 1. The right of citizens of the United States to vote shall not be denied or abridged by the United States or by any State on account of race, color, or previous condition of servitude.

SECTION 2. The Congress shall have power to enforce this article by appropriate legislation.

Amendment XVII
(Ratified on April 8, 1913)

The Senate of the United States shall be composed of two Senators from each State, elected by the people thereof, for six years; and each Senator shall have one vote. The electors in each State shall have the qualifications requisite for electors of the most numerous branch of the State legislatures.

When vacancies happen in the representation of any State in the Senate, the executive authority of such State shall issue writs of election to fill such vacancies: Provided, That the legislature of any State may empower the executive thereof to make temporary appointments until the people fill the vacancies by election as the legislature may direct.

This amendment shall not be so construed as to affect the election or term of any Senator chosen before it becomes valid as part of the Constitution.

Amendment XIX
(Ratified on August 18, 1920)

The right of citizens of the United States to vote shall not be denied or abridged by the United States or by any State on account of sex.

Congress shall have power to enforce this article by appropriate legislation.

Amendment XX
(Ratified on January 23, 1933)

SECTION 1. The terms of the President and Vice President shall end at noon on the 20th day of January, and the terms of Senators and Representatives at noon on the 3d day of January, of the years in which such terms would have ended if this article had not been ratified; and the terms of their successors shall then begin.

SECTION 2. The Congress shall assemble at least once in every year, and such meeting shall begin at noon on the 3d day of January, unless they shall by law appoint a different day.

SECTION 3. If, at the time fixed for the beginning of the term of the President, the President elect shall have died, the Vice President elect shall become President. If a President shall not have been chosen before the time fixed for the beginning of his term, or if the President elect shall have failed to qualify, then the Vice President elect shall act as President until a President shall have qualified; and the Congress may by law provide for the case wherein neither a President elect nor a Vice President elect shall have qualified, declaring who shall then act as President, or the manner in which one who is to act shall be selected, and such person shall act accordingly until a President or Vice President shall have qualified.

SECTION 4. The Congress may by law provide for the case of the death of any of the persons from whom the House of Representatives may choose a President whenever the right of choice shall have devolved upon them, and for the case of the death of any of the persons from whom the Senate may choose a Vice President whenever the right of choice shall have devolved upon them.

SECTION 5. Sections 1 and 2 shall take effect on the 15th day of October following the ratification of this article.

SECTION 6. This article shall be inoperative unless it shall have been ratified as an amendment to the Constitution by the legislatures of three-fourths of the several States within seven years from the date of its submission.

Amendment XXII
(Ratified on February 27, 1951)

SECTION 1. No person shall be elected to the office of the President more than twice, and no person who has held the office of President, or acted as President, for more than two years of a term to which some other person was elected President shall be elected to the office of the President more than once. But this Article shall not apply to any person holding the office of President, when this Article was proposed by the Congress, and shall not prevent any person who may be holding the office of President, or acting as President, during the term within which this Article becomes operative from holding the office of President or acting as President during the remainder of such term.

SECTION 2. This article shall be inoperative unless it shall have been ratified as an amendment to the Constitution by the legislatures of three-fourths of the several States within seven years from the date of its submission to the States by the Congress.

Amendment XXIII
(Ratified on March 29, 1961)

SECTION 1. The District constituting the seat of Government of the United States shall appoint in such manner as the Congress may direct:

A number of electors of President and Vice President equal to the whole number of Senators and Representatives in Congress to which the District would be entitled if it were a State, but in no event more than the least populous State; they shall be in addition to those appointed by the States, but they shall be considered, for the purposes of the election of President and Vice President, to be electors appointed by a State; and they shall meet in the District and perform such duties as provided by the twelfth article of amendment.

SECTION 2. The Congress shall have power to enforce this article by appropriate legislation.

Amendment XXIV
(Ratified on January 23, 1964)

SECTION 1. The right of citizens of the United States to vote in any primary or other election for President or Vice President for electors for President or Vice President, or for Senator or Representative in Congress, shall not be denied or abridged by the United States or any State by reason of failure to pay any poll tax or other tax.

SECTION 2. The Congress shall have power to enforce this article by appropriate legislation.

Amendment XXV
(Ratified on February 10, 1967)

SECTION 1. In case of the removal of the President from office or of his death or resignation, the Vice President shall become President.

SECTION 2. Whenever there is a vacancy in the office of the Vice President, the President shall nominate a Vice President who shall take office upon confirmation by a majority vote of both Houses of Congress.

SECTION 3. Whenever the President transmits to the President pro tempore of the Senate and the Speaker of the House of Representatives his written declaration that he is unable to discharge the powers and duties of his office, and until he transmits to them a written declaration to the contrary, such powers and duties shall be discharged by the Vice President as Acting President.

SECTION 4. Whenever the Vice President and a majority of either the principal officers of the executive departments or of such other body as Congress may by law provide, transmit to the President pro tempore of the Senate and the Speaker of the House of Representatives their written declaration that the President is unable to discharge the powers and duties of his office, the Vice President shall immediately assume the powers and duties of the office as Acting President.

Thereafter, when the President transmits to the President pro tempore of the Senate and the Speaker of the House of Representatives his written declaration that no inability exists, he shall resume the powers and duties of his office unless the Vice President and a majority of either the principal officers of the executive department or of such other body as Congress may by law provide, transmit within four days to the President pro tempore of the Senate and the Speaker of the House of Representatives their written declaration that the President is unable to discharge the powers and duties of his office. Thereupon Congress shall decide the issue, assembling within forty-eight hours for that purpose if not in session. If the Congress, within twenty-one days after receipt of the latter written declaration, or, if Congress is not in session, within twenty-one days after Congress is required to assemble, determines by two-thirds vote of both Houses that the President is unable to discharge the powers and duties of his office, the Vice President shall continue to discharge the same as Acting President; otherwise, the President shall resume the powers and duties of his office.

Amendment XXVI
(Ratified on July 1, 1971)

SECTION 1. The right of citizens of the United States, who are eighteen years of age or older, to vote shall not be denied or abridged by the United States or by any State on account of age.

SECTION 2. The Congress shall have power to enforce this article by appropriate legislation.

NOTES

1. Superseded by the 13th and 14th Amendments.
2. Superseded by the 17th Amendment.
3. Superseded by the 12th Amendment.
4. Superseded by the 25th Amendment.
5. Superseded by the 20th Amendment, section 3.

The Federalist Papers, No. 10*

(1787)

1. How can Madison's definition of a faction be applied to political organizations today? Do political parties fit this description? Why or why not?
2. Was Madison overreacting when he characterized factions as a "disease" for which there must be a "proper cure"? Does this description apply to political parties today? If so, how? If not, why not?

WHILE IT IS HARD today to imagine disagreement over the adoption of the Constitution, there were interested parties in every state who opposed it at the time it was written. After the framers approved the document and submitted it to the states for ratification in September 1787, proponents and opponents emerged to point out its strengths and weaknesses. Those who supported the new system of government were known as Federalists; their opponents were, suitably enough, the Anti-Federalists.

The publicity generated by the Anti-Federalists caused the Federalists to mount a public relations campaign in favor of ratification. Newspapers published essays written by prominent citizens on each side of the debate. The best-known arguments were a series of eighty-five essays published in newspapers in New York under the pseudonym *Publius*. The anonymous authors were actually Alexander Hamilton, James Madison, and John Jay who each wrote on a selection of topics. Given that the Federalists won the ratification argument and that Hamilton and Madison were the principal architects of the document, the *Federalist Papers* are generally considered among the most authoritative interpretations of the intent of the framers.

James Madison authored Federalist 10. During the American Revolution, he had served as a member of Virginia's state legislature and later was a member of the Continental Congress. While serving in the Virginia legislature, Madison was alarmed at the frailty of the new government created under the Articles of Confederation. When the Constitutional

*http://thomas.loc.gov/home/histdox/fed_10.html

Convention was called in Philadelphia in 1787, Madison was chosen as a delegate. He then engineered the Virginia Plan, which proposed abolishing the Articles in favor of a new constitution and which fellow Virginia delegate Edmond Randolph introduced at the convention.

While most of the essays written by Hamilton, Jay, and Madison appeared in the *Independent Journal* or the *New York Packet,* Federalist 10 was first printed in the *Daily Advertiser* on November 22, 1787. Although not as widely distributed as many other Federalist or Anti-Federalist materials, Federalist 10 is generally viewed as the most important of the *Federalist Papers.*

Opponents of the Constitution argued that the country was too large to be ruled by a single government because the large number of "factions" discouraged policy agreement. In Federalist 10, Madison also expressed concern over the "mischief" of factions, but he went on to argue that the republican government created under the Constitution allowed each faction the freedom to express its views and attempt to influence policy while giving due regard to the opposition. Madison's interpretation of republicanism was pretty much ignored when it was written, but it became a central part of the pluralist interpretation of American politics in the twentieth century. Pluralist theorists attribute the success of the American political system to the decentralized government created by the Constitution, which encourages all interests to attempt to influence policy.

Given the concerns by both Federalists and Anti-Federalists over the disruptive nature of factions in the political process, Federalist 10 is frequently cited as a definitive explanation of how and why the framers wished to discourage the new government from becoming partisan in nature.

❦

Friday, November 23, 1787.

To the People of the State of New York:

AMONG the numerous advantages promised by a well-constructed Union, none deserves to be more accurately developed than its tendency to break and control the violence of faction. The friend of popular governments never finds himself so much alarmed for their character and fate, as when he contemplates their propensity to this dangerous vice. He will not fail, therefore, to set a due value on any plan which, without violating the principles to which he is attached, provides a proper cure for it. The instability, injustice, and confusion introduced into the public councils, have, in truth, been the mortal diseases under which popular governments have everywhere perished; as they continue to be the favorite and fruitful topics from which the adversaries to liberty derive their most specious declamations. The valuable improvements made by the American constitutions on the popular models, both ancient and modern, cannot certainly be too much admired; but it would be an unwarrantable partiality, to contend that they have as effectually obviated the danger on this side, as was wished and expected. Complaints are everywhere heard from our most considerate and virtuous citizens, equally the friends of public and private faith, and of public and personal liberty, that our governments are too unstable, that the public good is disregarded in the conflicts of rival parties, and that measures are too often decided, not according to the rules of justice and the rights of the minor party, but by the superior force of an interested and overbearing majority. However anxiously we may wish that these complaints had no foundation, the evidence, of known facts will not permit us to deny that they are in some degree true. It will be found, indeed, on a candid review of our situation, that some of the distresses under which we labor have been erroneously charged on the operation of our governments; but it will be found, at the same time, that other causes will not alone account for many of our heaviest misfortunes; and, particularly, for that prevailing and increasing distrust of public engagements, and alarm for private rights, which are echoed from one end of the continent to the other. These must be chiefly, if not wholly, effects of the unsteadiness and injustice with which a factious spirit has tainted our public administrations.

By a faction, I understand a number of citizens, whether amounting to a majority or a minority of the whole, who are united and actuated by some common impulse of passion, or of interest, adversed to the rights of other citizens, or to the permanent and aggregate interests of the community.

There are two methods of curing the mischiefs of faction: the one, by removing its causes; the other, by controlling its effects.

There are again two methods of removing the causes of faction: the one, by destroying the liberty which is essential to its existence; the other, by giving to every citizen the same opinions, the same passions, and the same interests.

It could never be more truly said than of the first remedy, that it was worse than the disease. Liberty is to faction what air is to fire, an aliment without which it instantly expires. But it could not be less folly to abolish liberty, which is essential to political life, because it nourishes faction, than it would be

to wish the annihilation of air, which is essential to animal life, because it im-
parts to fire its destructive agency.

The second expedient is as impracticable as the first would be unwise. As
long as the reason of man continues fallible, and he is at liberty to exercise it,
different opinions will be formed. As long as the connection subsists between
his reason and his self-love, his opinions and his passions will have a reciprocal
influence on each other; and the former will be objects to which the latter will
attach themselves. The diversity in the faculties of men, from which the rights
of property originate, is not less an insuperable obstacle to a uniformity of interests. The protection of these faculties is the first object of government. From
the protection of different and unequal faculties of acquiring property, the possession of different degrees and kinds of property immediately results; and
from the influence of these on the sentiments and views of the respective pro-
prietors, ensues a division of the society into different interests and parties.

The latent causes of faction are thus sown in the nature of man; and we see
them everywhere brought into different degrees of activity, according to the
different circumstances of civil society. A zeal for different opinions concerning
religion, concerning government, and many other points, as well of speculation
as of practice; an attachment to different leaders ambitiously contending for
pre-eminence and power; or to persons of other descriptions whose fortunes
have been interesting to the human passions, have, in turn, divided mankind
into parties, inflamed them with mutual animosity, and rendered them much
more disposed to vex and oppress each other than to co-operate for their common good. So strong is this propensity of mankind to fall into mutual animosi-
ties, that where no substantial occasion presents itself, the most frivolous and
fanciful distinctions have been sufficient to kindle their unfriendly passions and
excite their most violent conflicts. But the most common and durable source of
factions has been the various and unequal distribution of property. Those who
hold and those who are without property have ever formed distinct interests in
society. Those who are creditors, and those who are debtors, fall under a like
discrimination. A landed interest, a manufacturing interest, a mercantile interest, a moneyed interest, with many lesser interests, grow up of necessity in civilized nations, and divide them into different classes, actuated by different sentiments and views. The regulation of these various and interfering interests
forms the principal task of modern legislation, and involves the spirit of party
and faction in the necessary and ordinary operations of the government.

No man is allowed to be a judge in his own cause, because his interest
would certainly bias his judgment, and, not improbably, corrupt his integrity.
With equal, nay with greater reason, a body of men are unfit to be both judges
and parties at the same time; yet what are many of the most important acts of

legislation, but so many judicial determinations, not indeed concerning the rights of single persons, but concerning the rights of large bodies of citizens? And what are the different classes of legislators but advocates and parties to the causes which they determine? Is a law proposed concerning private debts? It is a question to which the creditors are parties on one side and the debtors on the other. Justice ought to hold the balance between them. Yet the parties are, and must be, themselves the judges; and the most numerous party, or, in other words, the most powerful faction must be expected to prevail. Shall domestic manufactures be encouraged, and in what degree, by restrictions on foreign manufactures? are questions which would be differently decided by the landed and the manufacturing classes, and probably by neither with a sole regard to justice and the public good. The apportionment of taxes on the various descriptions of property is an act which seems to require the most exact impartiality; yet there is, perhaps, no legislative act in which greater opportunity and temptation are given to a predominant party to trample on the rules of justice. Every shilling with which they overburden the inferior number, is a shilling saved to their own pockets.

It is in vain to say that enlightened statesmen will be able to adjust these clashing interests, and render them all subservient to the public good. Enlightened statesmen will not always be at the helm. Nor, in many cases, can such an adjustment be made at all without taking into view indirect and remote considerations, which will rarely prevail over the immediate interest which one party may find in disregarding the rights of another or the good of the whole.

The inference to which we are brought is, that the CAUSES of faction cannot be removed, and that relief is only to be sought in the means of controlling its EFFECTS.

If a faction consists of less than a majority, relief is supplied by the republican principle, which enables the majority to defeat its sinister views by regular vote. It may clog the administration, it may convulse the society; but it will be unable to execute and mask its violence under the forms of the Constitution. When a majority is included in a faction, the form of popular government, on the other hand, enables it to sacrifice to its ruling passion or interest both the public good and the rights of other citizens. To secure the public good and private rights against the danger of such a faction, and at the same time to preserve the spirit and the form of popular government, is then the great object to which our inquiries are directed. Let me add that it is the great desideratum by which this form of government can be rescued from the opprobrium under which it has so long labored, and be recommended to the esteem and adoption of mankind.

By what means is this object attainable? Evidently by one of two only. Either the existence of the same passion or interest in a majority at the same time must be prevented, or the majority, having such coexistent passion or interest, must be rendered, by their number and local situation, unable to concert and carry into effect schemes of oppression. If the impulse and the opportunity be suffered to coincide, we well know that neither moral nor religious motives can be relied on as an adequate control. They are not found to be such on the injustice and violence of individuals, and lose their efficacy in proportion to the number combined together, that is, in proportion as their efficacy becomes needful.

From this view of the subject it may be concluded that a pure democracy, by which I mean a society consisting of a small number of citizens, who assemble and administer the government in person, can admit of no cure for the mischiefs of faction. A common passion or interest will, in almost every case, be felt by a majority of the whole; a communication and concert result from the form of government itself; and there is nothing to check the inducements to sacrifice the weaker party or an obnoxious individual. Hence it is that such democracies have ever been spectacles of turbulence and contention; have ever been found incompatible with personal security or the rights of property; and have in general been as short in their lives as they have been violent in their deaths. Theoretic politicians, who have patronized this species of government, have erroneously supposed that by reducing mankind to a perfect equality in their political rights, they would, at the same time, be perfectly equalized and assimilated in their possessions, their opinions, and their passions.

A republic, by which I mean a government in which the scheme of representation takes place, opens a different prospect, and promises the cure for which we are seeking. Let us examine the points in which it varies from pure democracy, and we shall comprehend both the nature of the cure and the efficacy which it must derive from the Union.

The two great points of difference between a democracy and a republic are: first, the delegation of the government, in the latter, to a small number of citizens elected by the rest; secondly, the greater number of citizens, and greater sphere of country, over which the latter may be extended.

The effect of the first difference is, on the one hand, to refine and enlarge the public views, by passing them through the medium of a chosen body of citizens, whose wisdom may best discern the true interest of their country, and whose patriotism and love of justice will be least likely to sacrifice it to temporary or partial considerations. Under such a regulation, it may well happen that the public voice, pronounced by the representatives of the people, will be more consonant to the public good than if pronounced by the people themselves, convened for the purpose. On the other hand, the effect may be inverted. Men of factious tempers, of local prejudices, or of sinister designs, may, by intrigue, by corruption, or by other means, first obtain the suffrages, and then betray the interests, of the people. The question resulting is, whether small or extensive republics are more favorable to the election of proper guardians of the public weal; and it is clearly decided in favor of the latter by two obvious considerations:

In the first place, it is to be remarked that, however small the republic may be, the representatives must be raised to a certain number, in order to guard against the cabals of a few; and that, however large it may be, they must be limited to a certain number, in order to guard against the confusion of a multitude. Hence, the number of representatives in the two cases not being in proportion to that of the two constituents, and being proportionally greater in the small republic, it follows that, if the proportion of fit characters be not less in the large than in the small republic, the former will present a greater option, and consequently a greater probability of a fit choice.

In the next place, as each representative will be chosen by a greater number of citizens in the large than in the small republic, it will be more difficult for unworthy candidates to practice with success the vicious arts by which elections are too often carried; and the suffrages of the people being more free, will be more likely to centre in men who possess the most attractive merit and the most diffusive and established characters.

It must be confessed that in this, as in most other cases, there is a mean, on both sides of which inconveniences will be found to lie. By enlarging too much the number of electors, you render the representatives too little acquainted with all their local circumstances and lesser interests; as by reducing it too much, you render him unduly attached to these, and too little fit to comprehend and pursue great and national objects. The federal Constitution forms a happy combination in this respect; the great and aggregate interests being referred to the national, the local and particular to the State legislatures.

The other point of difference is, the greater number of citizens and extent of territory which may be brought within the compass of republican than of democratic government; and it is this circumstance principally which renders factious combinations less to be dreaded in the former than in the latter. The smaller the society, the fewer probably will be the distinct parties and interests composing it; the fewer the distinct parties and interests, the more frequently will a majority be found of the same party; and the smaller the number of individuals composing a majority, and the smaller the compass within which they are placed, the more easily will they concert and execute their plans of oppression. Extend the sphere, and you take in a greater variety of parties and interests; you make it less probable that a majority of the whole will have a common motive to invade the rights of other citizens; or if such a common motive exists, it will be more difficult for all who feel it to discover their own strength, and to act in unison with each other. Besides other impediments, it may be remarked that, where there is a consciousness of unjust or dishonorable purposes, communication is always checked by distrust in proportion to the number whose concurrence is necessary.

Hence, it clearly appears, that the same advantage which a republic has over a democracy, in controlling the effects of faction, is enjoyed by a large over a small republic,—is enjoyed by the Union over the States composing it. Does the advantage consist in the substitution of representatives whose enlightened views and virtuous sentiments render them superior to local prejudices and schemes of injustice? It will not be denied that the representation of the Union will be most likely to possess these requisite endowments. Does it consist in the greater security afforded by a greater variety of parties, against the event of any one party being able to outnumber and oppress the rest? In an equal degree does the increased variety of parties comprised within the Union, increase this security. Does it, in fine, consist in the greater obstacles opposed to the concert and accomplishment of the secret wishes of an unjust and interested majority? Here, again, the extent of the Union gives it the most palpable advantage.

The influence of factious leaders may kindle a flame within their particular States, but will be unable to spread a general conflagration through the other States. A religious sect may degenerate into a political faction in a part of the Confederacy; but the variety of sects dispersed over the entire face of it must secure the national councils against any danger from that source. A rage for paper money, for an abolition of debts, for an equal division of property, or for any other improper or wicked project, will be less apt to pervade the whole body of the Union than a particular member of it; in the same proportion as such a malady is more likely to taint a particular county or district, than an entire State.

In the extent and proper structure of the Union, therefore, we behold a republican remedy for the diseases most incident to republican government. And according to the degree of pleasure and pride we feel in being republicans, ought to be our zeal in cherishing the spirit and supporting the character of Federalists.

❧ 3 ❧
Alexander Hamilton's Letter
to Edward Carrington*
(1792)

1. How did the decision of Jefferson to recruit Philip Freneau to work in the State Department institutionalize the partisan press in the United States? What impact did this have on political parties?
2. Did Hamilton's interpretation of Jefferson's and Madison's actions as "subversive to the principles of good government and dangerous to the union, peace, and happiness of the country" foster a partisan political environment?

O N DECEMBER 13, 1790, secretary of the Treasury Alexander Hamilton submitted a report to Congress recommending the establishment of a national bank. Both houses passed the bill and submitted it to President Washington on February 14, 1791, for his signature. Given the controversy over the bill that surrounded the constitutionality of creating a national bank, Washington decided to ask secretary of state Thomas Jefferson and attorney general Edmund Randolph for their written opinions on whether he should sign the bill. Jefferson's and Randolph's opinions were both negative. Washington asked Hamilton to respond to their opinions, which he did on February 23, 1791. Washington sided with Hamilton and, as a consequence, enmity between Hamilton and Jefferson grew steadily.

Within days of Washington's decision to sign the bill Jefferson took the first steps to creating an opposition newspaper that would be sympathetic to the Republican point of view. Jefferson's desire was to counterbalance the Federalist-leaning *Gazette of the United States.* On February 28, he wrote to Philip Freneau, a friend who was an assistant editor of the *New York Daily Advertiser.* Jefferson offered him a position in

*Reprinted in *The Papers of Alexander Hamilton,* vol. XI, February 1792–June 1792, ed. Harold Syrett (New York: Columbia, 1966), 426–445.

19

Philadelphia as a translator for the State Department and was quick to point out that while the pay was low, there was so little work that it would certainly not interfere with "any other calling the person may choose. . . ." Although Freneau's initial reaction was to turn down the undemanding position, he was eventually persuaded to take it after meeting with Jefferson's principal ally, James Madison.

The limited demands as a State Department translator provided Freneau the perfect opportunity to start the Republican newspaper that Jefferson envisioned. First published on October 31, 1791, *The National Gazette* became a vehicle to criticize the Federalists. Many Republicans, including Jefferson and Madison, contributed articles written under pseudonyms. In particular, the *Gazette* published highly derogatory articles about Hamilton and his views on fiscal policy.

The *Gazette* was distinctive among newspapers in early America for two reasons. First, it was highly critical of Washington's administration and voiced strong opposition to it. It is no surprise then that Washington was not a fan of the *Gazette* or Freneau. Second, the *Gazette* was supported by a prominent administration official in the person of Jefferson. While the State Department continued to pay Freneau for his services as a translator, Jefferson gave him access to State Department records and resources that other newspapers did not have.

On May 26, 1792, Hamilton wrote his friend Edward Carrington a very long letter that expressed his alarm at the hostility of Jefferson and Madison, the state of political parties, and the rise of the partisan press. He believed that Jefferson and Madison were the leaders of a new political party hostile to Washington's administration in general and Hamilton in particular. He thought Madison was primarily responsible for conducting the negotiations that brought Freneau to Philadelphia to create the *Gazette,* and he was certain that the newspaper's principle purpose was to promote the ambitions of Jefferson and oppose the actions of Hamilton. Eventually, Hamilton made his criticism public by condemning Freneau as a tool of the Secretary of State. On July 25, 1792, Freneau's dual role as newspaper editor and translator for the State Department was exposed in the *Gazette of the United States* by someone writing under the pseudonym *T. L.* Other newspapers were quick to condemn the impropriety.

26 May 1792

My Dear Sir

Believing that I possess a share of your personal friendship and confidence and yielding to that which I feel towards you—persuaded also that our political creed is the same on *two essential points,* 1st the necessity of *Union* to the respectability and happiness of this Country and 2. the necessity of an *efficient* general government to maintain that Union—I have concluded to unbosom myself to you on the present state of political parties and views. . . .

When I accepted the Office I now hold, it was under a full persuasion, that from similarity of thinking, conspiring with personal goodwill, I should have the firm support of Mr. Madison, in the *general course* of my administration. Aware of the intrinsic difficulties of the situation and of the powers of Mr. Madison, I do not believe I should have accepted under a different supposition.

I have mentioned the similarity of thinking between that Gentleman and myself. This was relative not merely to the general principles of National Policy and Government but to the leading points which were likely to constitute questions in the administration of the finances. I mean 1 the expediency of *funding* the debt 2 the inexpediency of *discrimination* between original and present holders 3 the expediency of *assuming* the state debts. . . .

Under these circumstances, you will naturally imagine that it must have been a matter of surprize to me when I was apprised, that it was Mr. Madison's intention to oppose my plan on both the last mentioned points.

Before the debate commenced, I had a conversation with him on my report, in the course of which I alluded to the calculation I had made of his sentiments and the grounds of that calculation. He did not deny them, but alledged in his justification that the very considerable alienation of the debt, subsequent to the periods at which he had opposed a discrimination, had essentially changed the state of the question—and that as to the assumption, he had contemplated it to take place *as matters stood at the peace.* . . .

At this time and afterwards repeated intimations were given to me that Mr. Madison, from a spirit of rivalship or some other cause had become personally unfriendly to me; and one Gentleman in particular, whose honor I have no reason to doubt, assured me that Mr. Madison in a conversation with him had made a pretty direct attempt to insinuate unfavorable impressions of me.

Still I suspended my opinion on the subject. I knew the malevolent officiousness of mankind too well to yield a very ready acquiescience to the suggestions which were made, and resolved to wait 'till time and more experience should afford a solution.

It was not 'till the last session that I became unequivocally convinced of the following truth—"*That Mr. Madison cooperating with Mr. Jefferson is at the head of a faction decidedly hostile to me and my administration, and actuated by views in my judgment subversive of the principles of good government and dangerous to the union, peace and happiness of the Country."*

These are strong expressions; they may pain your friendship for one or both of the Gentlemen whom I have named. I have not lightly resolved to hazard them. They are the result of a *Serious alarm* in my mind for the public welfare, and of a full conviction that what I have alledged is a truth, and a truth, which ought to be told and well attended to, by all the friends of Union and efficient National Government. The suggestion will, I hope, at least awaken attention, free from the bias of former prepossessions.

This conviction in my mind is the result of a long train of circumstances; many of them minute. To attempt to detail them all would fill a volume. I shall therefore confine myself to the mention of a few.

First—As to the point of opposition to me and my administration.

Mr. Jefferson with very little reserve manifests his dislike of the funding system generally, calling in question the expediency of funding a debt at all. Some expressions which he has dropped in my own presence (sometimes without sufficient attention to delicacy) will not permit me to doubt on this point, representations, which I have had from various respectable quarters. I do not mean, that he advocates directly the undoing of what has been done, but he censures the whole on principles, which, if they should become general, could not but end in the subversion of the system.

In various conversations with *foreigners* as well as citizens, he has thrown censure on my *principles* of government and on my measures of administration. He has predicted that the people would not long tolerate my proceedings & that I should not long maintain my ground. Some of those, whom he *immediately* and *notoriously* moves, have *even* whispered suspicions of the rectitude of my motives and conduct. In the question concerning the Bank he not only delivered an opinion in writing against its constitutionality & expediency; but he did it *in a style and manner* which I felt as partaking of asperity and ill humour towards me. As one of the trustees of the sinking fund, I have experienced in almost every leading question opposition from him. When any turn of things in the community has threatened either odium or embarrassment to me, he has not been able to suppress the satisfaction which it gave him.

A part of this is of course information, and might be misrepresentation. But it comes through so many channels and so well accords with what falls under my own observation that I can entertain no doubt.

I find a strong confirmation in the following circumstances. *Freneau* the present Printer of the National Gazette, who was a journeyman with Childs &

Swain at New York, was a known anti-federalist. It is reduced to a certainty that he was brought to Philadelphia by Mr. Jefferson to be the conductor of a News Paper. It is notorious that cotemporarily with the commencement of his paper he was a Clerk in the department of state for foreign languages. Hence a clear inference that his paper has been set on foot and is conducted under the patronage & not against the views of Mr. Jefferson. What then is the complexion of this paper? Let any impartial man peruse all the numbers down to the present day; and I never was more mistaken, if he does not pronounce that it is a paper devoted to the subversion of me & the measures in which I have had an Agency; and I am little less mistaken if he do not pronounce that it is a paper of a tendency *generally unfriendly to the Government of the U States.* . . .

With regard to Mr. Madison—the matter stands thus. I have not heard, but in the one instance to which I have alluded, of his having held language unfriendly to me in private conversation. But in his public conduct there has been a more uniform & persevering opposition than I have been able to resolve into a sincere difference of opinion. I cannot persuade myself that Mr. Madison and I, whose politics had formerly so much the *same point of departure,* should now diverge so widely in our opinions of the measures which are proper to be pursued. The opinion I once entertained of the candour and simplicity and fairness of Mr. Madison's character has, I acknowledge, given way to a decided opinion that *it is one of a peculiarly artificial and complicated kind.*

For a considerable part of the last session, Mr. Madison lay in a great measure *perdu.* But it was evident from his votes & a variety of little movements and appearances, that he was the prompter of Mr. Giles & others, who were the open instruments of opposition. . . .

My overthrow was anticipated as certain and Mr. Madison, *laying aside his wonted caution,* boldly led his troops as he imagined to a certain victory. He was disappointed. Though, *late* I became apprized of the danger. Measures of counteraction were adopted, & when the Question was called, Mr. Madison was confounded to find character voting against him, whom he had counted upon as certain. . . .

Towards the close of the Session, another, though a more covert, attack was made. It was in the shape of a proposition to insert in the supplementary Act respecting the public Debt something by way of instruction to the Trustees "to make their purchases of the debt at the *lowest* market price." In the course of the discussion of this point, Mr. Madison dealt much in *insidious insinuations* calculated to give an impression that the public money under my particular direction had been unfaithfully applied to put undue advantages in the pockets of speculators, & to support the debt at an *artificial* price for their benefit.

The whole manner of this transaction left no doubt in any ones mind that Mr. Madison was actuated by *personal* & political animosity. . . .

. . . As to the tendency of the views of the two Gentlemen who have been named.

Mr. Jefferson is an avowed enemy to a funded debt. Mr. Madison disavows in public any intention to *undo* what has been done; but in a private conversation with Mr. Charles Carroll (Senator), this Gentlemans name I mention confidentially though he mentioned the matter to Mr. King & several other Gentlemen as well as myself; & if any chance should bring you together you would easily bring him to repeat it to you, he favoured the sentiment in Mr. Mercers speech that a Legislature had no right to *fund* the debt by mortgaging permanently the public revenues because they had no right to bind posterity. The inference is that what has been unlawfully done may be undone.

The discourse of partizans in the Legislature & the publications in the party news-papers direct their main battery against the *principle* of a funded debt, & represent it in the most odious light as a perfect *Pandora's box*. . . .

In almost all the questions great & small which have arisen, since the first session of Congress, Mr. Jefferson & Mr. Madison have been found among those who were disposed to narrow the Federal authority. The question of a National Bank is one example. The question of bounties to the Fisheries is another. Mr. Madison resisted it on the ground of constitutionality 'till it was evident, by the intermediate questions taken, that the bill would pass & he then under the wretched subterfuge of a change of a single word "bounty" for "allowance" went over to the Majority & voted for the bill. In the Militia bill & in a variety of minor cases he has leaned to abridging the exercise of federal authority, & leaving as much as possible to the States & he has lost no opportunity of *sounding the alarm* with great affected solemnity at encroachments meditated on the rights of the States, & of holding up the bugbear of a faction in the Government having designs unfriendly to Liberty. . . .

In respect to our foreign politics the views of these Gentlemen are in my judgment equally unsound & dangerous. *They have a womanish attachment to France and a womanish resentment against Great Britain.* They would draw us into the closest embrace of the former & involve us in all the consequences of her politics, & they would risk the peace of the country in their endeavours to keep us at the greatest possible distance from the latter. This disposition goes to a length particularly in Mr. Jefferson of which, till lately, I had no adequate Idea. Various circumstances prove to me that if these Gentlemen were left to pursue their own course there would be in less than six months *an open War between the U States & Great Britain*. . . .

Another circumstance has contributed to widening the breach. 'Tis evident beyond a question, from every movement, that Mr. Jefferson aims with ardent desire at the Presidential Chair. This too is an important object of the party-politics. It is supposed, from the nature of my former personal & political connexions, that I may favour some other candidate more than Mr. Jefferson when the Question shall occur by the retreat of the present Gentleman. My influence therefore with the Community becomes a thing, on ambitious & personal grounds, to be resisted & destroyed.

You know how much it was a point to establish the Secretary of State as the Officer who was to administer the Government in defect of the President & Vice President. Here I acknowledge, though I took far less part than was supposed, I run counter to Mr. Jefferson's wishes; but if I had had no other reason for it, I had already *experienced opposition* from him which rendered it a measure of *self defense.*

It is possible too (for men easily heat their imaginations when their passions are heated) that they have by degrees persuaded themselves of what they may have at first only sported to influence others—namely that there is some dreadful combination against State Government & republicanism; which according to them, are convertible terms. But there is so much absurdity in this supposition, that the admission of it tends to apologize for their hearts, at the expense of their heads.

Under the influence of all these circumstances, the attachment to the Government of the U States, originally weak in Mr. Jeffersons mind, has given way to something very like dislike; in Mr. Madisons, it is so counteracted by personal feelings, as to be more an affair of the head than of the heart—more the result of a conviction of the necessity of Union than of cordiality to the thing itself. I hope it does not stand worse than this with him.

In such a state of mind, both these Gentlemen are prepared to hazard a great deal to effect a change. Most of the important measures of every Government are connected with the Treasury. To subvert the present head of it they deem it expedient to risk rendering the Government itself odious; perhaps foolishly thinking that they can easily recover the lost affections & confidence of the people, and not appreciating as they ought to do the natural resistance to Government which in every community results from the human passions, the degree to which this is strengthened by the *organized rivality* of State Governments, & the infinite danger that the National Government once rendered odious will be kept so by these powerful & indefatigable enemies. . . .

A word on another point. I am told that serious apprehensions are disseminated in your state as to the existence of a Monarchical party meditating the destruction of State & Republican Government. If it is possible that so absurd an idea can gain ground it is necessary that it should be combatted. I assure you on my *private faith* and *honor* as a Man that there is not in my judgment a shadow of foundation of it. A very small number of men indeed may entertain theories less republican than Mr. Jefferson & Mr. Madison; but I am persuaded there is not a Man among them who would not regard as both *criminal & visionary* any attempt to subvert the republican system of the Country. Most of these men rather *fear* that it may not justify itself by its fruits, than feel a predilection for a different form; and their fears are not diminished by the factions & fanatical politics which they find prevailing among a certain set of Gentlemen and threatening to disturb the tranquillity and order of the Government.

As to the destruction of State Governments, the *great* and *real* anxiety is to be able to preserve the National from the too potent and counteracting influence of those Governments. As to my own political Creed, I give it to you with the utmost sincerity. I am *affectionately* attached to the Republican theory. I desire *above all things* to see the *equality* of political rights exclusive of all *hereditary* distinction firmly established by a practical demonstration of its being consistent with the order and happiness of society.

As to State Governments, the prevailing byass of my judgment is that if they can be circumscribed within bounds consistent with the preservation of the National Government they will prove useful and salutary. If the States were all of the size of Connecticut, Maryland or New Jersey, I should decidedly regard the local Governments as both safe & useful. As the thing now is, however, I acknowledge the most serious apprehensions that the Government of the U States will not be able to maintain itself against their influence. I see that influence already penetrating into the National Councils & perverting their direction.

Hence a disposition on my part towards a liberal construction of the powers of the National Government and to erect every fence to guard it from depredations, which is, in my opinion, consistent with constitutional propriety.

As to the combination to prostrate the State Governments, I disavow and deny it. From an apprehension lest the Judiciary should not work efficiently or harmoniously I have been desirous of seeing some rational scheme of connection adopted as an amendment to the constitution; otherwise I am for maintaining things as they are, though I doubt much the possibility of it, from a tendency in the nature of things towards the preponderancy of the State Governments.

I said that I was *affectionately* attached to the Republican theory. This is the real language of my heart which I open to you in the sincerity of friendship; & I add that I have strong hopes of the success of that theory; but in candor

I ought also to add that I am far from being without doubts. I consider its success as yet a problem.

It is yet to be determined by experience whether it be consistent with that *stability* and *order* in Government which are essential to public strength & private security and happiness. On the whole, the only enemy which Republicanism has to fear in this Country is in the Spirit of faction and anarchy. If this will not permit the ends of Government to be attained under it—if it engenders disorders in the community, all regular & orderly minds will wish for a change—and the demagogues who have produced the disorder will make it for their own aggrandizement. This is the old Story.

If I were disposed to promote Monarchy & overthrow State Governments, I would mount the hobby horse of popularity—I would cry out usurpation—danger to liberty &c., &c.—I would endeavour to prostrate the National Government—raise a ferment—and then "ride in the Whirlwind and direct the Storm." That there are men acting with Jefferson & Madison who have this in view I verily believe. I could lay my finger on some of them. That Madison does *not* mean it I also verily believe, and I rather believe the same of Jefferson; but I read him upon the whole thus—"A man of profound ambition & violent passions."

You must be by this time tired of my epistle. Perhaps I have treated certain characters with too much severity. I have however not meant to do them injustice—and from the bottom of my soul believe I have drawn them truly and that it is of the utmost consequence to the public weal they should be viewed in their true colors. I yield to this impression. I will only add that I make no clandestine attacks on the gentlemen concerned. They are both apprized indirectly from myself of the opinion I entertain of their views. With the truest regard and esteem.

✤ 4 ✤

George Washington's Letter
to Thomas Jefferson*
(1792)

Jefferson's Response to Washington**
(1792)

1. Was Washington's request for Hamilton and Jefferson to put aside their differences in the best interest of the country? Would the absence of political partisanship have fostered better government policy?
2. How did Jefferson respond to Washington's deep disappointment over the dispute between Hamilton and Jefferson? What does his response suggest about the development of political partisanship?

OPPOSING FACTIONS led by Secretary of the Treasury Alexander Hamilton and Secretary of State Thomas Jefferson developed within the administration of George Washington. Newspapers became very important in expressing political issues, as the two factions evolved into political parties. Two of the most important political newspapers in the early years of Washington's administration were the *Gazette of the United States* and the *National Gazette.* John Fenno edited the *Gazette of the United States,* which supported Hamilton and the Federalists. Philip Freneau edited the *National Gazette,* which backed Jefferson and the Republicans. Hamilton, Jefferson, and other prominent government officials were active in both financing and writing articles (typically published under pseudonyms). Although the circulation of each newspaper was never that high, individual news stories and editorials frequently

*http://etext.virginia.edu/etcbin/toccer-new2?id=WasFi32.xml&images=images/modeng
&data=/texts/english/modeng/parsed&tag=public&part=107&division=div1

**Reprinted in *The Papers of Thomas Jefferson,* vol. 24, June 1 to December 31, 1792, ed. John Catanzariti (Princeton, N.J.: Princeton University Press, 1990), 351–360.

were copied by newspapers in other cities. As a result, pieces were often widely circulated to readers in major cities across the country.

During the summer of 1792 the public was exposed to the animosity between Hamilton and Jefferson through a bitter newspaper battle led by the editors of the *Gazette of the United States* and the *National Gazette.* President Washington was deeply disturbed by the controversy and wrote a confidential letter to Jefferson on August 23, 1792, and to Hamilton on August 26, 1792. The language in both letters was similar, calling for each to put aside their dissension for the national good. On September 9, 1792, Jefferson replied to Washington's concern over divisions within the administration by explaining his differences with Hamilton and the reasoning behind them.

❦

George Washington's Letter to Thomas Jefferson

Mount Vernon, August 23, 1792

My dear Sir:

Your letters of the 12th. and 13th came duly to hand, as did that enclosing Mr. Blodgets plan of a Capitol. The latter I forwarded to the Commissioners, and the enclosures of the two first are now returned to you. . . .

How unfortunate, and how much is it to be regretted then, that whilst we are encompassed on all sides with avowed enemies and insidious friends, that internal dissensions should be harrowing and tearing our vitals. The last, to me, is the most serious, the most alarming, and the most afflicting of the two. And without more charity for the opinions and acts of one another in Governmental matters, or some more infalible criterion by which the truth of speculative opinions, before they have undergone the test of experience, are to be forejudged than has yet fallen to the lot of fallibility, I believe it will be difficult, if not impracticable, to manage the Reins of Government or to keep the parts of it together: for if, instead of laying our shoulders to the machine after measures are decided on, one pulls this way and another that, before the utility of the thing is fairly tried, it must, inevitably, be torn asunder. And, in my opinion the fairest prospect of happiness and prosperity that ever was presented to man, will be lost, perhaps for ever!

My earnest wish, and my fondest hope therefore is, that instead of wounding suspicions, and irritable charges, there may be liberal allowances, mutual forebearances, and temporising yieldings on all sides. Under the exercise of these, matters will go on smoothly, and, if possible, more prosperously. Without them every thing must rub; the Wheels of Government will clog; our enemies will triumph, and by throwing their weight into the disaffected Scale, may accomplish the ruin of the goodly fabric we have been erecting.

I do not mean to apply these observations, or this advice to any particular person, or character. I have given them in the same general terms to other Officers of the Government; because the disagreements which have arisen from difference of opinions, and the Attacks wch. have been made upon almost all the measures of government, and most of its Executive Officers, have, for a long time past, filled me with painful sensations; and cannot fail I think, of producing unhappy consequences at home and abroad. . . .

I pray you to note down, or rather to frame into paragraphs or sections such matters as may occur to you as fit and proper for general communication at the opening of the next Session of Congress, not only in the Department of State, but on any other subject applicable to the occasion, that I may, in due time, have everything before me. With sincere esteem and friendship I am &c.

Jefferson's Response to Washington

Monticello, September 9, 1792

Dear Sir,

I received on the 2d inst the letter of Aug 23, which you did me the honor to write me; but the immediate return of our post, contrary to his custom, prevented my answer by that occasion. . . .

I now take the liberty of proceeding to that part of your letter wherein you notice the internal dissentions which have taken place within our government, and their disagreeable effect on it's movements. That such dissentions have taken place is certain, and even among those who are nearest to you in the administration. To no one have they given deeper concern than myself; to no one equal mortification at being myself a part of them. Tho' I take to myself no more than my share of the general observations of your letter, yet I am so desirous ever that you should know the whole truth, and believe no more than the truth, that I am glad to seize every occasion of developing to you whatever I do or think relative to the government; and shall therefore ask permission to be more lengthy now than the occasion particularly calls for, or could otherwise perhaps justify.

When I embarked in the government, it was with a determination to intermeddle not at all with the legislature, and as little as possible with my codepartments. The first and only instance of variance from the former part of my resolution, I was duped into by the Secretary of the treasury and made a tool for forwarding his schemes, not then sufficiently understood by me; and of all the errors of my political life, this has occasioned me the deepest regret. It has ever been my purpose to explain this to you, when, from being actors on the scene, we shall have become uninterested spectators only. The second part of my resolution has been religiously observed with the war department; and as to that of the Treasury, has never been farther swerved from, than by the mere enunciation of my sentiments in conversation, and chiefly among those who, expressing the same sentiments, drew mine from me. If it has been supposed that I have ever intrigued among the members of the legislature to defeat the plans of the Secretary of the Treasury, it is contrary to all truth. As I never had the desire to influence the members, so neither had I any other means than my friendships, which I valued too highly to risk by usurpations on their freedom of judgment, and the conscientious pursuit of their own sense of duty. That I have utterly, in my private conversations, disapproved of the system of the Secretary of the treasury, I acknolege & avow: and this was not merely a speculative difference. His system flowed from principles adverse to liberty, and was calculated to undermine and demolish the republic, by creating an influence of his department over the members of the legislature. I saw this influence actually produced, and it's first fruits to be the establishment of the great outlines of his project by the votes of the very persons who, having swallowed his bait were laying themselves out to profit by his plans: and that had these persons withdrawn, as those interested in a question ever should, the vote of the disinterested majority was clearly the reverse of what they made it. These were no longer the votes then of the representatives of the people, but of deserters from the rights and interests of the people: and it was impossible to consider their decisions, which had nothing in view but to enrich themselves, as the measures of the fair majority, which ought always to be respected.—If what was actually doing begat uneasiness in those who wished for virtuous government, what was further proposed was not less threatening to the friends of the constitution. For, in a Report on the subject of manufactures, (still to be acted on) it was expressly assumed that the general government has a right to exercise all powers which may be for the *general welfare,* that is to say, all the legitimate powers of government: since no government has a legitimate right to do what is not for the welfare of the governed. There was indeed a sham-limitation of the universality of this power *to cases where money is to be employed.* But about what is it that money cannot be employed? Thus the object of these plans taken together is to draw all the powers of government into the hands of the general legislature, to establish means for corrupting a sufficient corps in that legislature to divide the honest votes and preponderate, by their own, the scale which suited, and to have that corps under the command of the Secretary of the Treasury for the purpose of subverting step by step the principles of the constitution, which he has so often declared to be a thing of nothing which must be changed. Such views might have justified something more than mere expressions of dissent, beyond which, nevertheless, I never went.—Has abstinence from the department committed to me been equally observed by him? To say nothing of other interferences equally known, in the case of the two nations with which we have the most intimate connections, France and England, my system was to give some satisfactory distinctions to the former, of little cost to us, in return for the solid advantages yielded us by them; and to have met the English with some restrictions which might induce them to abate their severities against our commerce. I have always supposed this coincided with your sentiments. Yet the Secretary of the treasury, by his cabals with members of the legislature, and by high toned declamation on other occasions, has forced down his own system, which was exactly the reverse. He undertook, of his own authority, the conferences with the ministers of those two nations, and was, on every consultation, provided with some report of a conversation with the one or the other of them, adapted to his views. These views thus made to prevail, their execution fell of course to me; and I can safely appeal to you, who have seen all my letters and proceedings, whether I have not carried them into execution as sincerely as if they had been my own, tho' I ever considered them as inconsistent with the honor and interest of our country. That they have been inconsistent with our interest is but too fatally proved by the stab to our navigation given by the French.—So that if the question be By whose fault is it that Colo. Hamilton and myself have not drawn together? the answer will depend on that to two other questions; whose principles of administration best justify, by their purity, conscientious adherence? and Which of us has, notwithstanding, stepped farthest into the controul of the department of the other?

To this justification of opinions, expressed in the way of conversation, against the views of Colo. Hamilton, I beg leave to add some notice of his late charges against me in Fenno's gazette: for neither the stile, matter, nor venom of the pieces alluded to can leave a doubt of their author. Spelling my name and character at full length to the public, while he conceals his own under the signature of 'an American' he charges me 1. with having written letters from Europe to my friends to oppose the present constitution while depending. 2. with a desire of not paying the public debt. 3. with setting up a paper to decry and slander the government. 1. The first charge is most false. No man in the U.S., I suppose, approved of every title in the constitution: no one, I believe approved more of it than I did: and more of it was certainly disapproved by my accuser than by me, and of it's parts most vitally republican. Of this the few letters I wrote on the subject (not half a dozen I believe) will be a proof: and for my own satisfaction and justification, I must tax you with the reading of them when I return to where they are. You will there see that my objection to the constitution was that it wanted a bill of rights securing freedom of religion, freedom of the press, freedom from standing armies, trial by jury, and a constant Habeas corpus act. Colo. Hamilton's was that it wanted a king and house of lords. The sense of America has approved my objection and added the bill of rights, not the king and lords. I also thought a longer term of service, insusceptible of renewal, would have made a President more independant. My country has thought otherwise, and I have acquiesced implicitly. He wished the general government should have power to make laws binding the states in all cases whatsoever. Our country has thought otherwise: has he acquiesced? . . . 2. The second charge is equally untrue. My whole correspondence while in France, and every word, letter, and act on the subject since my return, prove that no man is more ardently intent to see the public debt soon and sacredly paid off than I am. This exactly marks the difference between Colo. Hamilton's views and mine, that I would wish the debt paid tomorrow; he wishes it never to be paid, but always to be a thing wherewith to corrupt and manage the legislature. 3. I have never enquired what number of sons, relations and friends of Senators, representatives, printers or other useful partisans Colo. Hamilton has provided for among the hundred clerks of his department, the thousand excisemen, customhouse officers, loan officers &c. &c. &c. appointed by him, or at his nod, and spread over the Union; nor could ever have imagined that the man who has the shuffling of millions backwards and forwards from paper into money and money into paper, from Europe to America, and America to Europe, the dealing out of Treasury-secrets among his friends in what time and measure he pleases, and who never slips an occasion of making friends with his means, that such an one I say would have brought forward a charge against me for having appointed the poet Freneau translating clerk to my office, with a salary of 250. dollars a year. That fact stands thus. While the government was at New York I was applied to on behalf of Freneau to know if there was any place within my department to which he could be appointed. I answered there were but four clerkships, all of which I found full, and continued without any change. When we removed to Philadelphia, Mr. Pintard the translating clerk, did not chuse to remove with us. His office then became vacant. I was again applied to there for Freneau, & had no hesitation to promise the clerkship for him. I cannot recollect whether it was at the same time, or afterwards, that I was told he had a thought of setting up a newspaper there. But whether then or afterwards, I considered it as a circumstance of some value, as it might enable me to do, what I had long wished to have done, that is, to have the material parts of the Leyden gazette brought under your eye and that of the public, in order to possess yourself and them of a juster view of the affairs of Europe than could be obtained from any other public source. This I had ineffectually attempted through the press of Mr. Fenno while in New York, selecting and translating passages myself at first, then having it done by Mr. Pintard the translating clerk. But they found their way too slowly into Mr. Fenno's papers. Mr. Bache essayed it for me in Philadelphia, but his being a dayly paper, did not circulate sufficiently in the other states. He even tried at my request, the plan of a weekly paper of recapitulation from his daily paper, in hopes that that might go into the other states, but in this too we failed. Freneau, as translating clerk, and the printer of a periodical paper likely to circulate thro' the states (uniting in one person the parts of Pintard and Fenno) revived my hopes that the thing could at length be affected. On the establishment of his paper therefore, I furnished him with the Leyden gazettes, with an expression of my wish that he could always translate and publish the material intelligence they contained; and have continued to furnish them from time to time, as regularly as I received them. But as to any other direction or indication of my wish how his press should be conducted, what sort of intelligence he should give, what essays encourage, I can protest in the presence of heaven, that I never did by myself or any other, directly or indirectly, say a syllable, nor attempt any kind of influence. I can further protest, in the same awful presence, that I never did by myself or any other, directly or indirectly, write, dictate or procure any one sentence or sentiment to be inserted *in his, or any other gazette,* to which my name was not affixed, or that of my office.—I surely need not except here a thing so foreign to the present subject as a little paragraph about our Algerine captives, which I put once into Fenno's paper.—Freneau's proposition to publish a paper, having been about the time that the writings of Publicola, and the discourses on Davila had a good deal excited the public attention, I took for granted from Freneau's character, which had been marked as that of a good whig, that he would give free place to pieces written against the aristocratical and monarchical principles these papers had inculcated. This having been in my mind, it is likely enough I may have expressed it in conversation with others; tho' I do not recollect that I did. To Freneau I think I could not, because I had still seen him but once, & that was at a public table, at breakfast, at Mrs. Elsworth's, as I passed thro' New York the last year. And I can safely declare that my expectations looked only to the chastisement of the aristocratical and monarchical writers, and not to any criticisms on the proceedings of government: Colo. Hamilton can see no motive for any appointment but that of making a convenient partizan. But you Sir, who have received from me recommendations of a Rittenhouse, Barlow, Paine, will believe that talents and science are sufficient motives with me in appointments to which they are fitted: and that Freneau, as a man of genius, might find a preference in my eye to be a translating clerk, and make good title to the little aids I could give him as the editor of a gazette, by procuring subscriptions to his paper, as I did some, before it appeared, and as I have with pleasure done for the labours of other men of genius. . . . As to the merits or demerits of his paper, they certainly concern me not. He and Fenno are rivals for the public favor. The one courts them by flattery, the other by censure: and I believe it will be admitted that the one has been as servile, as the other severe. But is not the dignity, and even decency of government committed, when one of it's principal ministers enlists himself as an anonymous writer or paragraphist for either the one or the other of them?—No government ought to be without censors: and where the press is free, no one ever will. If virtuous, it need not fear the fair operation of attack and defence. Nature has given to man no other means of sifting out the truth either in religion, law, or politics. I think it as honorable to the government neither to know, nor notice, it's sycophants or censors, as it would be undignified and criminal to pamper the former and persecute the latter. . . .

I confide that yourself are satisfied that, as to dissensions in the newspapers, not a syllable of them has ever proceeded from me; and that no cabals or intrigues of mine have produced those in the legislature, and I hope I may promise, both to you and myself, that none will receive aliment from me during the short space I have to remain in office, which will find ample employment in closing the present business of the department. . . . In the mean time and ever I am with great and sincere affection & respect, dear Sir, your most obedient and most humble servant

TH: JEFFERSON

Thomas Jefferson's Letter to Philip Mazzei*
(1796)

George Washington's Letter to Jefferson**
(1796)

1. How did Jefferson's private criticism of Washington and the Federalist Party reinforce developing partisan preferences? How is this similar to partisan politics today?
2. Washington chose not to respond to the publication of Jefferson's criticism. How would this affect electoral politics today if the president did not respond to similar criticism in the press?

O N APRIL 24, 1796, Thomas Jefferson wrote his friend Philip Mazzei in Tuscany, Italy. A merchant and physician, Mazzei had lived near Jefferson in Virginia. The letter was primarily about Mazzei's business affairs in Virginia, but one paragraph discussed the rise of an aristocratic political party (that is, the Federalists) that Jefferson felt desired to force the United States to return to a form of government that closely mirrored that of Britain. More specifically, Jefferson references the president's administration as being corrupted by these views. The scandal that erupted over the publication of this paragraph of the letter plagued Jefferson for the rest of his political career.

The letter was, of course, a private piece of correspondence Jefferson intended for Mazzei alone. Unfortunately for Jefferson, Mazzei copied the relevant paragraph on politics and sent it to more than one of his friends. Thus, without Jefferson's knowledge the political paragraph,

*www.princeton.edu/~tjpapers/mazzei/transcription.html
**memory.loc.gov/cgi-bin/query/r?ammem/mgw:@field(DOCID+@lit(gw350086))

along with an editorial commentary that was very critical of U.S. foreign policy, was published in the *Gazette Nationale ou Le Moniteur Universel* on January 25, 1797. A little more than three months after it was printed in Paris, the letter surfaced in the American press. On May 2, 1797, a translation of the letter (from French back to English) appeared in *The Minerva,* a newspaper published by Noah Webster that was aligned with the Federalists. Most other Federalist newspapers also printed the story shortly thereafter. While some included only the paragraph from Jefferson's letter, many included the French newspaper's editorial commentary.

The controversy surrounding the letter's publication turned out to be highly partisan, and Jefferson was attacked intensely by the Federalists. Jefferson was, of course, an easy target for Federalist propaganda: by the time the letter had been published in the United States, Jefferson was both vice president and leader of the Republican opposition. At one time John Adams had asserted that Jefferson and the Republicans were more loyal to France than to the United States. Federalist newspapers repeated this claim and depicted the Republicans and their leader, Vice President Jefferson, as dangerous. Of course, Republican newspapers soon came to his defense, claiming that while Jefferson's description of partisan conflict in the United States was unfortunate, it was to a large extent true.

One of the most pointed criticisms in Jefferson's letter was his reference to "Sampsons in the field and Solomons in the Council," which was generally understood as an attack on the outgoing president. Jefferson publicly criticized President Washington's policies in 1794 and 1795 for favoring the British and not the French, but he had refrained at that time from attacking Washington's reputation. After the Mazzei letter was reprinted in the press Washington made no public comment, but prior to its publication he wrote Jefferson to politely share his thoughts about the eruption of party politics and how to improve farming.

The critique that Jefferson shared with Mazzei continued to haunt him for the remainder of his political career. Since it had prompted such intense personal attacks, Jefferson became more closed in his correspondence in later years and even warned people to whom he wrote to be cautious and to keep the content of his letters out of the public eye.

Thomas Jefferson's Letter to Philip Mazzei

Monticello Apr. 24 1796.

My Dear Friend,

. . .The aspect of our politics has wonderfully changed since you left us. In place of that noble love of liberty and republican government which carried us triumphantly thro' the war, an Anglican, monarchical and aristocratical party has sprung up, whose avowed object is to draw over us the substance as they have already done the forms of the British government. The main body of our citizens however remain true to their republican principles, the whole landed interest is with them, and so is a great mass of talents. Against us are the Executive, the Judiciary, two out of three branches of the legislature, all of the officers of the government, all who want to be officers, all timid men who prefer the calm of despotism to the boisterous sea of liberty, British merchants and Americans trading on British capitals, speculators and holders in the banks and public funds a contrivance invented for the purposes of corruption and for assimilating us in all things, to the rotten as well as the sound parts of the British model. It would give you a fever were I to name to you the apostates who have gone over to these heresies, men who were Samsons in the field and Solomons in the council, but who have had their heads shorn by the harlot England. In short we are likely to preserve the liberty we have obtained only by unremitting labors and perils. But we shall preserve them, and our mass of weight and wealth on the good side is so great as to leave no danger that force will ever be attempted against us. We have only to awake and snap the Lilliputian cords with which they have been entangling us during the first sleep which succeeded our labors. . . . While it remains however my heart will be warm in it's friendships and among these will always foster the affection with which I am Dear Sir Your friend & servant

TH: JEFFERSON

George Washington's Letter to Jefferson

Mount Vernon, July 6, 1796.

Dear Sir:

When I inform you, that your letter of the 19th. Ulto. went to Philadelphia and returned to this place before it was received by me; it will be admitted, I am persuaded, as an apology for my not having acknowledged the receipt of it sooner.

If I had entertained any suspicions before, that the queries, which have been published in Bache's Paper, proceeded from you, the assurances you have given of the contrary, would have removed them; but the truth is, I harboured none. I am at no loss to *conjecture* from what source they flowed; through what channel they were conveyed; and for what purpose they and similar publications, appear. They were known to be in the hands of Mr. Parker, in the early part of the last Session of Congress; They were shown about by Mr. Giles during the Cession, and they made their public exhibition about the close of it.

Perceiving, and probably, hearing, that no abuse in the Gazettes would induce me to take notice of anonymous publications, against me; those who were disposed to do me *such friendly Offices,* have embraced without restraint every opportunity to weaken the confidence of the People; and, by having the *whole* game in their hands, they have scrupled not to publish things that do not, as well as those which do exist; and to mutilate the latter, so as to make them subserve the purposes which they have in view.

As you have mentioned the subject yourself, it would not be frank, candid, or friendly to conceal, that your conduct has been represented as derogatory from that opinion I had conceived you entertained of me. That to your particular friends and connexions you have described, and they have denounced me, as a person under a dangerous influence; and that, if I would listen *more* to some *other* opinions, all would be well. My answer invariably has been, that I had never discovered any thing in the conduct of Mr. Jefferson to raise suspicions, in my mind, of his insincerity; that if he would retrace my public conduct while he was in the Administration, abundant proofs would occur to him, that truth and right decisions, were the *sole* objects of my pursuit; that there were as many instances within his *own* knowledge of my having decided *against,* as in *favor* of the opinions of the person evidently alluded to; and moreover, that I was no believer in the infallibility of the politics, or measures of *any man living.* In short, that I was no party man myself, and the first wish of my heart was, if parties did exist, to reconcile them.

To this I may add, and very truly, that, until within the last year or two ago, I had no conception that Parties would, or even could go, the length I have been witness to; nor did I believe until lately, that it was within the bonds of probability; hardly within those of possibility, that, while I was using my utmost exertions to establish a national character of our own, independent, as far as our obligations, and justice would permit, of every nation of the earth; and wished, by steering a steady course, to preserve this Country from the horrors of a desolating war, that I should be accused of being the enemy of one Nation, and subject to the influence of another; and to prove it, that every act of my administration would be tortured, and the grossest, and most insidious misrepresentations of them be made (by giving one side *only* of a subject, and that too in such exaggerated and indecent terms as could scarcely be applied to a

Nero; a notorious defaulter; or even to a common pick-pocket). But enough of this; I have already gone farther in the expression of my feelings, than I intended.

... Mrs. Washington begs you to accept her best wishes, and with very great esteem etc.

⋈ 6 ⋊

John Beckley's Letters to William Irvine[*]

(1796)

1. How were the campaign techniques developed by Beckley and his Republican contemporaries innovative? How did they compensate for the Federalist Party's advantage of controlling a larger newspaper network?
2. How was negative advertising in the campaigns of Adams and Jefferson different from that found in recent presidential elections?

JOHN JAMES BECKLEY was an important force in Virginia politics and Thomas Jefferson's political adviser. While Beckley is best known as the first Clerk of the House of Representatives and the first Librarian of the Congress, his most important political role was in Jefferson's 1796 and 1800 presidential campaigns. His work on behalf of Jefferson became the foundation upon which presidential campaigns were modeled the early years of the party system.

Jefferson and Beckley forged their political partnership during the Revolutionary War. Beckley was born in 1757 in London to impoverished parents and was sent to Virginia as an indentured servant at the age of twelve. Since he was literate, Beckley was employed as a scribe at a mercantile firm and eventually graduated from the College of William and Mary. He used politics as his principal means of advancement, serving as the mayor of Richmond, Virginia, from 1783 to 1784 and from 1788 to 1789. In 1789, James Madison sponsored him to become the

---

[*]Reprinted in *Justifying Jefferson: Political Writings of John James Beckley,* ed. Gerard Gawalt (Washington, D.C.: Library of Congress, 1995).

Clerk of the House of Representatives (1789–1797). After Jefferson's election to the presidency, Beckley was reappointed to the position (1801–1807) and shortly thereafter he was appointed the first Librarian of Congress (1802–1807).

In the early 1790s, the administration of George Washington split into two factions led by Alexander Hamilton and Jefferson. As partisan voting blocs emerged in Congress, Madison's alliance with Jefferson developed into the Republican Party. During this time, Beckley collaborated with Jefferson and Madison to vigorously oppose the policies of Hamilton and the Federalists. The new political parties quickly got involved in the selection of the presidential candidates, and each constructed its own network of newspapers to editorialize on its behalf. The Federalists, however, controlled a greater number of newspapers—an advantage during elections.

The disparity steadily decreased between 1796 and 1800, but Beckley and the Republicans nevertheless invented many new campaign techniques to compensate for the Federalist advantage in the press. Beckley was among the first to support the use of negative advertising and was very successful at it. By 1792 he was responsible for the organization, publication, and distribution of propaganda throughout state capitols and other major cities that attacked Hamilton and other Federalists. Some even assign Beckley the responsibility of destroying Hamilton's political career. In the election of 1796, Beckley managed Jefferson's campaign in the state of Pennsylvania and introduced the mass distribution of pamphlets and handwritten "tickets" (printed ballots were not used at that time). That year the Republicans blanketed parts of the state with 30,000 of these tickets. Such techniques generated unprecedented levels of grassroots support for Jefferson and his allies.

When Jefferson lost the 1796 election, the Federalists removed Beckley as the House Clerk, but Republicans found employment for him—once again in Pennsylvania—and he continued to campaign for Jefferson until the election of 1800. That year, Beckley became the first person to write a campaign biography to promote a presidential candidate. In the following letters, Beckley corresponds with William Irvine, a Republican member of Congress from Pennsylvania, in regard to the implementation of Jefferson's strategy for winning the state.

Philadelphia 15th September 1796.

Dear General,

    . . . The president has at last concluded to decline a reelection, and has forwarded on to the Governor of each State a notification thereof, to be published in each State at the same time, so that we may expect to see it published here about the 1st of next month. You will readily perceive that this short Notice is designed to prevent a fair Election, and the consequent choice of Mr. Jefferson. It will not however produce that effect, if your State make but a reasonable exertion—the general sentiment is in favor of Jefferson, and I think a little exertion by a few good active republicans in each county would bring the people out, and defeat the influence of your little rotten towns such as Carlisle, Lancaster, York &c. A Silent, but certain Cooperation among the country people may do much. In my next I will send you a list of the republican Electors, that have been agreed upon for this State, and hope you will be able to scatter a few copies thro' some proper hands. It will not be forgotten that no ticket must be printed. From Georgia, No. Carolina, South Carolina, Virginia, Kentuckey, & Tennessee we expect a unanimous Vote—half Maryland, & Delaware—some in New Jersey, and several to the Eastward. So that if Pennsylvania do well the Election is safe. In the City & County we expect to carry the republican ticket by a large Majority. Have you any western friends that you can drop a line to, to assist us? What seemed to be the sentiment, if any, in the Country you passed thro'? Cannot an effectual Exertion be made? It is now or never for the republican cause. . . . Our joint love to all your family. Your sincere friend,

                                                              John Beckley

Philadelphia, 22nd September 1796.

Dear General,

    . . . By this mail you will receive the presidents address of declension to serve again, and I enclose you a list of the Electors agreed to here, just before the Assembly adjourned. Governor Mifflin's name being added in the room of Mr. Rittenhouse, deceased; the Governor is as fully eligible as Judge McKean, and it is believed his name will greatly assist the ticket. I shall decline, until I have the pleasure to see you, any remarks on the presidents address, and only say that we have every assurance of success in favour of Mr. Jefferson to the Southward. How it will be to the Eastward I am not yet informed. Your state must decide it, and I hope every exertion will be made. A few copies of the lists of the Electors with the names plainly written, dispersed in a few judicious hands in the Country, and copies of them scattered about in different neigh-bourhoods, would do great good, if the people are warned of the day, and a few popular men will endeavor to bring them out. By next post I will endeavor to send you some handbills, by way of address to the people of Pennsylvania, shewing the strong reasons there is for this States having a Southern rather than an Eastern president. . . .

Maria joins me in affectionate regards to Mrs. Irvine, Nancy, &c. all your family, as do all of ours. With the truest regards, I am, dear General, Yr. friend & Servant

John Beckley.

P.S. The Governor declines being put on the ticket of Electors. No name is yet concluded on in his room; it will be either Charles Biddle, or Thomas Bar-clay. tomorrow it will be decided & by Tuesday mail I will inform you. . . .

Philadelphia, 30th September 1796.

Dear Sir,

I enclose you a complete list of the ticket of Electors, and by next mail or before, I will forward you a dozen or two hand bills on the same subject. By every information we can get Mr. Jefferson will have a unanimous Vote in every Southern State, except Maryland, and there about half. To the Eastward of the North river, we count certain on Eight votes, perhaps more. Rhode Is-land will be with us, two in New Hampshire—three or 4 in Massachusetts, and one or two in Vermont and Connecticut. If Pennsylvania stirs the business is safe. . . .

With our joint regards. We are dear Sir,   Yours truly,
J Beckley

Philadelphia, 4th October 1796.

Dear General,

. . . Inclosed are 6 copies of an address to the people of Pennsylvania—by next mail on friday, or by first certain opportunity will forward you 100 more. It would be most advisable however to push them on over the Mountain, be-fore they are circulated below, which will prevent any counter address—1000 Copies are struck & will be dispersed in such manner that they may appear first above, before they can come back to the City. Mr. Jefferson, has explicitly de-clared that if elected he will serve, and Mr. Patrick Henry, of Virginia, has as explicitly that he neither wishes nor would accept the office. I am this moment advised by a Letter from New York, that Mr. Hamilton publickly declares, that he thinks it would be best on the score of conciliation & expediency to elect Mr. Jefferson, president, since he is the only man in America that could secure us the affections of the French republic. Will it not be advisable to throw this paragraph into the Carlisle paper?

It is too late now to make a change in the Electors. The Aristocrats say themselves that the Republican ticket is by far the best, and believe it will carry. Many of them prefer Pinkney to Adams, and there will be great Schism amongst them. Our accounts South & East, look Well, and we have hopes in New Jersey. By Fridays mail I will write you again. . . . Our affectionate regards to every body.

Yours truly,
John Beckley

Philadelphia, 17th October 1796.

Dear General,

By old Doctor Nesbit, I have forwarded to you a packet with hand bills, which I must tax your goodness to put under way for the Western Country, so as to reach it before the Election for Electors. You best know what characters to address them to. In a few days a select republican friend from the City will call upon you with a parcel of tickets to be distributed in your County. Any assistance and advice you can furnish him with, as to suitable district & characters, will I am sure be rendered. He is one of two republican friends, who have undertaken to ride thro' all the middle & lower counties on this business, and bring with them 6 or 8 thousand tickets. It is necessary at the same time to aid the common object by getting all our friends to write as many tickets as they can, in their respective families, before the Election. The great victory obtained here, over the united & combined force of the British & Aristocrats, gives us great confidence, and is presage of success in the choice of Electors; to rule out Muhlenberg, who gave the casting vote for the British treaty, and elect Blair McClanahan, in his room, who recommended to kick the treaty to hell, and to reelect Swanwick against the most violent exertions ever made in this City, are sufficient to Shew that republicanism [remains] firm here. I hope you are and will be as firm and zealous in Cumberland. I [received] letters from Virginia which assure me that notwithstanding every Exertion of the Aristo[crats the] republicans count with certainty on an unanimous vote in favor of Jefferson [there]. Have you heard of Findley & Gallatins Elections, how did they go? Who succeeded in Cumberland? I hope they trimmed the trimmer Gregg, as they did Christie in Maryland. We continue in great hopes of several Votes in the Eastern States for Jefferson, since it begins to be suspected that Pinkney & not Adams is designed by Hamilton for president. Perhaps their intrigues may benefit us.

Pennsylvania Republican State Committee Election Circular, 1796

Philadelphia
Sept. 25, 1796

Sir, The republican members of the State Legislature and of congress from this State, before their late adjournment had a meeting to frame a ticket fo[r] electors of the President and Vice President. They at the same time appointed a committee to communicate to the citizens of Pennsylvania any information of importance on the subject of the election, which might come to their knowledge at the seat of Government.

By the Death of *David Rittenhouse,* from the City of Philadelphia, a chasm has occurred, and the committee after obtaining every information in their power and consulting with some friends from different counties have agreed to recommend *James Boyd* of Chester County to complete the ticket as it would prove an injury to it had a blank remained.

They greatly lament in common with their Republican friends throughout the State, that the advocates for fair election in the last Legislature were unable to prevail in districting the State, for the choice of electors; they are sensible of the inconvenience of the mode adopted. It was no doubt adopted to promote the views of the antirepublicans by giving full scope to their talents at intrigue and combination; but since it has been forced upon us, let us defeat their designs by union and activity.

The present is an important crisis. The citizen who now fills the station of chief executive magistrate of the Union has officially declined a re-election and the contest for that important office will lie between two men of very dissimilar politics, indeed—*Thomas Jefferson* and *John Adams.* It remains with the Citizens of Pennsylvania to decide, in which they will repose confidence,—the uniform advocate of equal rights among citizens, or the champion of rank, titles and hereditary distinctions;—the steady supporter of our present republican constitution; or the warm panegryrist of the British Monarchical form of Government, one who has unqualifiedly declared as hazardous and dangerous, our departure from this model of excellence, the British constitution, in making our Executives and Senates elective. No comment upon opinions so subversive of the basis upon which our free governments rest, need be addressed to Americans; they will meet in the minds of every one impressions and self-evident truths, that must repel with abhorrence such doctrines.

The issue of the approaching election of President and Vice President from the best information we are able to procure is likely to depend altogether upon exertions which shall be made in this state in the choice of electors. It is calculated, that the States to the North and South of this will be nearly balanced, so that the casting voice remains with Pennsylvania. No greater spur to unremitting exertions can exist. The first executive magistrate of the Union is to be chosen, the contest is between a tried republican and an avowed aristocrat, the balance is in our hands.

Aaron Burr of New-York and *Thomas Pinckney* of South Carolina will be the principal, if not only, candidates for the Vice Presidency; the former will be supported by the republican interest.

Should any further information occur worth communicating we shall immediately impart it. Any information from you in return on the great objects which should now engage our undivided attention will be thankfully received.

In behalf of the Committee.

> *M. Leib,*
> Chairman.

Republican Ticket

Thomas M'Kean,	Chief Justice of Pennsylvania, Philadelphia,
Jacob Morgan	Philadelphia County,
James Boyd	Chester,
Jonas Hartsel,	Northampton,
Peter Muhlenberg,	Montgomery,
Joseph Heister,	Berks,
Wm. M'Clay,	Dauphin,
James Hanna,	Bucks,
John Whitehill,	Lancaster,
William Irwin,	Cumberland,
Abraham Smith,	Franklin,
William Brown,	Mifflin,
John Piper,	Bedford,
John Smilie,	Fayette,
James Edgar,	Washington.

A number of republican Citizens of the County of Cumberland convened in their Borough of Carlisle, and having the subject of the preceding letter under their consideration, unanimously agreed, that the ticket therein mentioned, be recommended to their fellow citizens and request that you and all those who retain republican sentiments urge their fellow citizens to turn out to the election on the 4th day of November next, in order that our united endeavors may have the happy effect of having a President and Vice-President of the republican sentiments elected.

Signed by order of the meeting

> *William Brown*
> Chairman.

October 15th 1796.

SOURCE: Reprinted in Arthur Schlesinger, *History of U.S. Political Parties* (New York: Chelsea House, 1973).

I enclose you a few copies of the ticket to disperse among such good friends, as will exert themselves, to get as many copies before the Election as they can. . . . Yrs. [truly].

John Beckley

Philadelphia, 2d November 1796.

Dear General,

. . . We are all busily engaged in the Election and are sanguine in our hopes of success for Jefferson. The other side are equally active and equally sanguine. I think however that including the City and County of Philadelphia, we shall carry a Majority for the Jefferson ticket. We hope the Counties below the Mountains will be nearly divided and that the Western Counties will carry the Election for us. I send yo. a copy of the last Address of the Republicans to the people. Cumberland & Mifflin we rely will be generally in our favor. As soon as the result of our poll is known I will inform yo. of it, and beg the same favour from you. . . .

With joint & affectionate regards, I am dear General, Yrs. Sincerely,

John Beckley

❧ 7 ❧

George Washington's Farewell Address*
(1796)

1. Proponents of political parties argue that parties have contributed to the overall stability and health of the U.S. government. Is this assessment correct? Why or why not?
2. How might politics in the United States be different if Washington's contemporaries had heeded his warning about the dangers of political parties?

GEORGE WASHINGTON was the unanimous choice to serve as the first president of the United States. As chief of state he turned out to be a very capable leader who provided a careful precedent on which to model the new government. He chose to retire after his first term and,

*www.access.gpo.gov/congress/senate/farewell/sd106-21.pdf

with the help of James Madison, started preparing an address to the nation that would summarize the accomplishments of his administration, the challenges he saw on the political landscape, and his vision of how the United States could become a truly great nation. Members of his cabinet eventually persuaded Washington to serve a second term, but in September 1796 he publicly declared that he would not be willing to serve a third term. Based on Madison's earlier draft, Alexander Hamilton assisted Washington in revising his Farewell Address. In the address Washington counseled Americans to unite for the common good. He feared that the stability of the new Constitution was under threat from the influence of geographic sectionalism, political factionalism, and the interference of other nations in the domestic affairs of the United States. Washington's Farewell Address was published in the Philadelphia *Daily American* on September 19, 1796, and later appeared in other papers across the country. In honor of President Washington's birthday, the U.S. Senate reads his Farewell Address each year and has done so since 1893.

Washington's fear of political parties was one of the principal reasons that he drafted a farewell address. Like many of his contemporaries, Washington disliked political parties and feared that the factionalism from which they were created could very well sow the seeds of destruction for the young republic. He did not recognize the role they would eventually play in the political process as the principal vehicle through which public policy is debated and public issues resolved.

Political parties started forming during Washington's administration in response to the major issues of the day. The two parties that developed were the Federalists and the Republicans. The Federalists were led by Hamilton. The Republicans were led by Thomas Jefferson, the first secretary of state. In domestic policy the Federalists supported the policies of the Washington administration, which advocated a larger role for the federal government in banking, tax, and tariff policy that would hopefully promote manufacturing. The Republicans opposed such policies and favored a more agrarian future for the young nation. In foreign policy both parties promoted neutrality in controversies between European powers, but the Federalists tended to side with the British and the Republicans with the French.

Friends and Fellow-Citizens:

[. . .]In contemplating the causes which may disturb our union it occurs as matter of serious concern that any ground should have been furnished for characterizing parties by *geographical discriminations—northern* and *southern, Atlantic* and *western*—whence designing men may endeavor to excite a belief that there is a real difference of local interests and views. One of the expedients of party to acquire influence within particular districts is to misrepresent the opinions and aims of other districts. You can not shield yourselves too much against the jealousies and heartburnings which spring from these misrepresentations; they tend to render alien to each other those who ought to be bound together by fraternal affection. . . .

To the efficacy and permanency of your union a government for the whole is indispensable. No alliances, however strict, between the parts can be an adequate substitute. They must inevitably experience the infractions and interruptions which all alliances in all times have experienced. Sensible of this momentous truth, you have improved upon your first essay by the adoption of a Constitution of Government better calculated than your former for an intimate union and for the efficacious management of your common concerns. This Government, the offspring of our own choice, uninfluenced and unawed, adopted upon full investigation and mature deliberation, completely free in its principles, in the distribution of its powers, uniting security with energy, and containing within itself a provision for its own amendment, has a just claim to your confidence and your support. Respect for its authority, compliance with its laws, acquiescence in its measures, are duties enjoined by the fundamental maxims of true liberty. The basis of our political systems is the right of the people to make and to alter their constitutions of government. But the constitution which at any time exists until changed by an explicit and authentic act of the whole people is sacredly obligatory upon all. The very idea of the power and the right of the people to establish government presupposes the duty of every individual to obey the established government.

All obstructions to the execution of the laws, all combinations and associations, under whatever plausible character, with the real design to direct, control counteract, or awe the regular deliberation and action of the constituted authorities are destructive of this fundamental principle and of fatal tendency. They serve to organize faction, to give it an artificial and extraordinary force; to put, in the place of the delegated will of the nation, the will of a party, often a small but artful and enterprising minority of the community; and, according to the alternate triumphs of different parties, to make the public administration the mirror of the ill concerted and incongruous projects of faction, rather than the organ of consistent and wholesome plans digested by common councils, and modified by mutual interests. However combinations or associations of the above description may now and then answer popular ends, they are likely, in the course of time and things, to become potent engines, by which cunning, ambitious and unprincipled men will be enabled to subvert the power of the people, and to usurp for themselves the reins of Government; destroying afterwards the very engines which have lifted them to unjust dominion. . . .

I have already intimated to you the danger of parties in the State, with particular reference to the founding of them on geographical discriminations. Let me now take a more comprehensive view, and warn you in the most solemn manner against the baneful effects of the spirit of party, generally.

This spirit, unfortunately, is inseparable from our nature, having its root in the strongest passions of the human mind. It exists under different shapes in all governments, more or less stifled, controlled, or repressed; but in those of the popular form it is seen in its greatest rankness and is truly their worst enemy.

The alternate domination of one faction over another, sharpened by the spirit of revenge, natural to party dissention, which in different ages and countries has perpetrated the most horrid enormities, is itself a frightful despotism. But this leads at length to a more formal and permanent despotism. The disorders and miseries which result gradually incline the minds of men to seek security and repose in the absolute power of an individual, and sooner or later the chief of some prevailing faction, more able or more fortunate than his competitors, turns this disposition to the purposes of his own elevation, on the ruins of public liberty.

Without looking forward to an extremity of this kind (which nevertheless ought not to be entirely out of sight), the common and continual mischiefs of the spirit of party are sufficient to make it the interest and duty of a wise people to discourage and restrain it.

It serves always to distract the public councils and enfeeble the public administration. It agitates the community with ill founded jealousies and false alarms; kindles the animosity of one part against another; foments occasionally riot and insurrection. It opens the door to foreign influence and corruption, which finds a facilitated access to the government itself through the channels of party passion. Thus the policy and the will of one country are subjected to the policy and will of another.

There is an opinion that parties in free countries are useful checks upon the administration of the government, and serve to keep alive the spirit of liberty. This within certain limits is probably true; and in governments of a monarchical cast patriotism may look with indulgence, if not with favor, upon the spirit of party. But in those of the popular character, in governments purely elective, it is a spirit not to be encouraged. From their natural tendency it is certain there will always be enough of that spirit for every salutary purpose; and there being constant danger of excess, the effort ought to be by force of public opinion to mitigate and assuage it. A fire not to be quenched, it demands a uniform vigilance to prevent its bursting into a flame, lest, instead of warming, it should consume. . . .

> George Washington
> United States
> 19th September 1796

⊰ 8 ⊱

Thomas Jefferson's First Inaugural Address*

(1801)

1. After a bitter election in 1800, the Federalists chose to peacefully turn the government over to the Jeffersonian Republicans. How does this transfer of power compare to that following the election of 2000?
2. Presidents often appeal to the minority party for unity following divisive elections. Under what circumstances, if any, can a president expect such appeals to be effective?

THE RETIREMENT OF George Washington led to the first contested presidential election in U.S. history. The Federalists nominated Vice President John Adams, the Republicans former secretary of state Thomas Jefferson. Adams emerged victorious in the presidential election of 1796 by three electoral votes. The Constitution, however, required that the runner-up become vice president. Thus, for the first and only time in U.S. history the president and vice president were from different political parties. Over the next four years, Jefferson used his position as vice president to attack the Federalist policies of Adams's administration.

*www.yale.edu/lawweb/avalon/presiden/inaug/jefinau1.htm

The presidential election of 1800 was again a vicious contest between Adams and Jefferson. While Jefferson clearly won at the polls, an unanticipated consequence of the constitutional procedure for selecting the president led to the election being thrown to the House of Representatives. Clearly, the framers had anticipated that the candidate with the greatest number of electoral votes would become president. They had not expected, however, that the bond of political parties would become so strong. Since the Constitution called for presidential electors to cast two votes for president instead of separate ballots for president and vice president, loyal Republican electors cast their ballots for Jefferson and his vice presidential running mate, Aaron Burr. Each received seventy-three votes, and the House of Representatives was called upon for the first time to decide the outcome of an election.

The Federalist Party controlled the lame-duck Congress, which meant that the debate turned out to be just as acrimonious as the election. In the hope of denying Jefferson the presidency, many state delegations controlled by the Federalists chose to cast votes for Burr. After a number of ballots, Jefferson finally achieved a majority and became the third president of the United States.

The election of 1800 was very bitter, and many political observers were surprised that the United States did not enter into a civil war. The Federalists, however, peacefully surrendered the reins of government to the Republicans. As a result, the precedent for the peaceful transition of government from one party to another was established.

All of this led Congress to propose the Twelfth Amendment to the Constitution, which was approved on December 9, 1803, and was ratified by the required number of state legislators on June 15, 1804. It requires electors to cast distinct ballots for president and vice president.

***

March 4, 1801

FRIENDS AND FELLOW-CITIZENS,

. . . During the contest of opinion through which we have passed the animation of discussions and of exertions has sometimes worn an aspect which might impose on strangers unused to think freely and to speak and to write what they think; but this being now decided by the voice of the nation, announced according to the rules of the Constitution, all will, of course, arrange themselves under the will of the law, and unite in common efforts for the common good. All, too, will bear in mind this sacred principle, that though the will of the majority is in all cases to prevail, that will to be rightful must be reasonable; that the minority possess their equal rights, which equal law must protect, and to violate would be oppression. Let us, then, fellow-citizens, unite with one heart and one mind. Let us restore to social intercourse that harmony and affection without which liberty and even life itself are but dreary things. And let us reflect that, having banished from our land that religious intolerance under which mankind so long bled and suffered, we have yet gained little if we countenance a political intolerance as despotic, as wicked, and capable of as bitter and bloody persecutions. During the throes and convulsions of the ancient world, during the agonizing spasms of infuriated man, seeking through blood and slaughter his long-lost liberty, it was not wonderful that the agitation of the billows should reach even this distant and peaceful shore; that this should be more felt and feared by some and less by others, and should divide opinions as to measures of safety. But every difference of opinion is not a difference of principle. We have called by different names brethren of the same principle. We are all Republicans, we are all Federalists. If there be any among us who would wish to dissolve this Union or to change its republican form, let them stand undisturbed as monuments of the safety with which error of opinion may be tolerated where reason is left free to combat it. I know, indeed, that some honest men fear that a republican government can not be strong, that this Government is not strong enough; but would the honest patriot, in the full tide of successful experiment, abandon a government which has so far kept us free and firm on the theoretic and visionary fear that this Government, the world's best hope, may by possibility want energy to preserve itself? I trust not. I believe this, on the contrary, the strongest Government on earth. I believe it the only one where every man, at the call of the law, would fly to the standard of the law, and would meet invasions of the public order as his own personal concern. Sometimes it is said that man can not be trusted with the government of himself. Can he, then, be trusted with the government of others? Or have we found angels in the forms of kings to govern him? Let history answer this question.

Let us, then, with courage and confidence pursue our own Federal and Republican principles, our attachment to union and representative government. Kindly separated by nature and a wide ocean from the exterminating havoc of one quarter of the globe; too high-minded to endure the degradations of the others; possessing a chosen country, with room enough for our descendants to the thousandth and thousandth generation; entertaining a due sense of our equal right to the use of our own faculties, to the acquisitions of our own industry, to honor and confidence from our fellow-citizens, resulting not from birth, but from our actions and their sense of them; enlightened by a benign religion, professed, indeed, and practiced in various forms, yet all of them inculcating honesty, truth, temperance, gratitude, and the love of man; acknowledging and adoring an overruling Providence, which by all its dispensations proves that it delights in the happiness of man here and his greater happiness hereafter—with all these blessings, what more is necessary to make us a happy and a prosperous people? Still one thing more, fellow-citizens—a wise and frugal Government, which shall restrain men from injuring one another, shall leave them otherwise free to regulate their own pursuits of industry and improvement, and shall not take from the mouth of labor the bread it has earned. This is the sum of good government, and this is necessary to close the circle of our felicities.

About to enter, fellow-citizens, on the exercise of duties which comprehend everything dear and valuable to you, it is proper you should understand what I deem the essential principles of our Government, and consequently those which ought to shape its Administration. I will compress them within the narrowest compass they will bear, stating the general principle, but not all its limitations. Equal and exact justice to all men, of whatever state or persuasion, religious or political; peace, commerce, and honest friendship with all nations, entangling alliances with none; the support of the State governments in all their rights, as the most competent administrations for our domestic concerns and the surest bulwarks against antirepublican tendencies; the preservation of the General Government in its whole constitutional vigor, as the sheet anchor of our peace at home and safety abroad; a jealous care of the right of election by the people—a mild and safe corrective of abuses which are lopped by the sword of revolution where peaceable remedies are unprovided; absolute acquiescence in the decisions of the majority, the vital principle of republics, from which is no appeal but to force, the vital principle and immediate parent of despotism; a well-disciplined militia, our best reliance in peace and for the first moments of war till regulars may relieve them; the supremacy of the civil over the military authority; economy in the public expense, that labor may be lightly burthened; the honest payment of our debts and sacred preservation of the public faith; encouragement of agriculture, and of commerce as its handmaid; the diffusion of information and arraignment of all abuses at the bar of the public reason; freedom of religion; freedom of the press, and freedom of person under the protection of the habeas corpus, and trial by juries impartially selected.

Republican State Manager of Connecticut, Instructions to County Managers

Middletown, Nov. 1, 1805.

Sir, As you are appointed, by the general meeting of Republicans, sole manager for the county of Middlesex, and have pledged yourself for the faithful performance of your trust, I take early occasion to address you on the subject of elections, and on the services which are expected from you.

A majority can relax its exertions occasionally without hazard: a minority must exert its full strength constantly. A majority can afford to lose a thousand votes; but a minority ought never to lose a single vote, to which it is fairly entitled.

We have many obstacles to encounter: every republican ought to do his best toward overcoming them. Those, who talk against federalism through the year, and yet neglect to attend proxies, do worse than nothing. Those, who profess to be republicans, and yet vote for federalists on any occasion, do us irreparable mischief. Federalism cannot be talked down or flattered down; *it must be voted down.*

If we succeed to gain over a small majority, that will soon become a large majority. There is a great number of men in the state, who will always float with the tide. If we can gain a governor or lieutenant governor, or even one in the nomination for congress, all the rest will soon follow. This has been the case in New-Hampshire and in other states, where our cause has prevailed.

By the last returns of nomination for council it appears that we give 8 votes to every 11 votes of the federalists. With such exertions as we might have made, several of the highest on our ticket would have stood on the nomination next spring. *We can and ought to do better.*

In the discharge of your trust you will notice in all the towns of your county the causes of deficiency, and exert yourself to remove them. In some very republican towns we ought to gain an addition of at least 100 votes. In towns nearly balanced the absence of one or two republicans has lost for us an election, and even our friends, who were disappointed, have left the meeting, without voting for higher offices. In towns, where there are few republicans, our friends are remiss, because they cannot carry the representatives.—This is all idle: every vote, given for the higher offices, is important to us; but a little negligence or some paltry excuse costs us too dear. *There must be an end of such indifference.*

For this purpose, I ask you, immediately after the receipt of this, to appoint in each town of your county, an active, influential, republican

---

These instructions convey some of the animosity held by members of the Republican Party toward those with Federalist leanings. The feeling often was mutual, which is why many around the world feared that a transfer of power from one party to the other would not go smoothly.

manager, who will assure you verbally or in writing, that he will faithfully discharge his trust.

The duties of a *Town-Manager* will be,

1st. To appoint a district manager in each district or section of his town, obtaining from each an assurance that he will faithfully do his duty.

2d. To copy from the list of his town the names of all male inhabitants, who are taxed.

3d. To call together his district managers, and with their assistance to ascertain,

1st. The whole number of males, who are taxed.

2d. How many of the whole number are freeman.

3d. How many of the freemen are decided republicans.

4th. How many—decided federalists.

5th. How many—doubtful.

6th. How many republicans who are not freemen, but who may be qualified at the next proxies.

4th. The next duty of the town manager will be to furnish each district manager with the names of all those republicans, who are within the limits of his district. The list of male inhabitants and all proceedings in each town are to be kept by the town manager in a book, from which all his returns are to be made, as herein after directed.

It will be the duty of the *district manager* to exert himself to cause young republicans to be qualified for the oath; also to bring forward the republican freemen in his district at freemen's meetings and other town meetings, as occasion may require: also to furnish them with votes. The list of candidates, as agreed on at the general meetings, will be sent seasonably into every town. The representatives, to be set up in each town, and other town officers will be nominated in such way, as the town and district managers shall agree. . . .

At every Freemen's Meeting it shall be the duty of the Town and District-Managers to assist the republican applicants for the oath, also to notice all objections to admit republicans—also to know the state of the votes for all classes of candidates. They shall also notice what republicans are present, and see that each stays and votes, till the whole business is ended. And each District-Manager shall report to the Town-Manager the names of all republicans absent, and the cause of absence, if known to him, which reports shall be entered in the book for a memorial. . . .

At the general meeting of republicans in May next, it will be my duty to report the whole number of male persons in the state, who are taxed—the whole number of freemen—of republicans—of federalists and of doubtful men. I must also report what hindrances have been given to our cause in any part of the state, either by false reports, by political sermons, by official influence, by refusals to admit freemen, by federal tricks at elections, or by *negligence of republicans*. I must also report the conduct of each class of managers.

On each County Manager I must rely for correct information under each of these heads: they must rely on Town-Managers, and these last on District-Managers. With the last the returns must begin and must be punctual.

As I have power to remove County-Managers and supply vacancies, they have power to do the same in respect to Town-Managers, and these last to do to the same as District-Managers. Formerly responsibility was too much divided: now each one knows the part assigned to him, and if he has the least idea of neglecting it, he must refuse his appointment at once.

I have pointed out some general and indispensible outlines on duty. All subordinate things are left to discretion. The town and district manager will begin their work directly, and will be particular to see that all deeds, left for record, to be relied on for qualification, be actually recorded before the 7th of December next, because in four months from the day, viz. on the 7th of April next, proxies will come, whether we are sleeping or waking.

You will be supplied with newspapers for every town, which the town manager will distribute to the district managers, and these will circulate them among the republicans and federalists in their districts. A correct knowledge of our cause and of our objects will go a great way towards removing the prejudices, which the devices of our enemies have produced on the honest, laborious and most useful part of the community.

The federalists have priests and deacons, judges and justices, sheriffs and surveyors, with a host of corporations and privileged orders, to aid their elections. Let it be shewn that plain men, without titles or hopes of offices, can do better than the mercenary troops of federalism.

Your appointment of each Town-Manager will be accompanied with a few printed copies of this for his use and that of the District-Managers. These will serve as a guide for the opening of business, and you will give additional instructions afterwards as occasion may require. Prompt services and punctual returns are indispensable.

Alexander Wolcott,
State-Manager.

SOURCE: Reprinted in Arthur Schlesinger, *History of U.S. Political Parties* (New York: Chelsea House, 1973).

These principles form the bright constellation which has gone before us and guided our steps through an age of revolution and reformation. The wisdom of our sages and blood of our heroes have been devoted to their attainment. They should be the creed of our political faith, the text of civic instruction, the touchstone by which to try the services of those we trust; and should we wander from them in moments of error or of alarm, let us hasten to retrace our steps and to regain the road which alone leads to peace, liberty, and safety.

I repair, then, fellow-citizens, to the post you have assigned me. With experience enough in subordinate offices to have seen the difficulties of this the greatest of all, I have learnt to expect that it will rarely fall to the lot of imperfect man to retire from this station with the reputation and the favor which bring him into it. Without pretensions to that high confidence you reposed in our first and greatest revolutionary character, whose preeminent services had entitled him to the first place in his country's love and destined for him the fairest page in the volume of faithful history, I ask so much confidence only as may give firmness and effect to the legal administration of your affairs. I shall often go wrong through defect of judgment. When right, I shall often be thought wrong by those whose positions will not command a view of the whole ground. I ask your indulgence for my own errors, which will never be intentional, and your support against the errors of others, who may condemn what they would not if seen in all its parts. The approbation implied by your suffrage is a great consolation to me for the past, and my future solicitude will be to retain the good opinion of those who have bestowed it in advance, to conciliate that of others by doing them all the good in my power, and to be instrumental to the happiness and freedom of all.

Relying, then, on the patronage of your good will, I advance with obedience to the work, ready to retire from it whenever you become sensible how much better choice it is in your power to make. And may that Infinite Power which rules the destinies of the universe lead our councils to what is best, and give them a favorable issue for your peace and prosperity.

The Tennessee General Assembly's Protest
Against the Caucus System*
(1823)

1. Republicans won each presidential election from 1800 to 1820. How did Republican presidential nominee, William H. Crawford, come in fourth in the election of 1824?
2. Critics of the congressional nominating caucus argued that those congressional districts or states unable to elect their party's representative were effectively not represented in the caucus. How did national nominating conventions differ?

AFTER GEORGE WASHINGTON decided not to seek a third term as president, members of Congress began to meet (or "caucus") to decide who to nominate for president and vice president. In 1796, John Adams was the consensus candidate for the Federalist Party. Thomas Jefferson was the candidate of choice for the Republican Party, and that year Republican members of Congress met informally to discuss who should run with Jefferson as vice president.

Before the election of 1800, members of both parties caucused to formally nominate their respective party slates. The Federalists chose Adams to run for reelection and Charles Pinckney as his running mate. The Republicans chose Jefferson to challenge Adams and Aaron Burr as Jefferson's vice president.

The congressional nominating caucus was continued with mixed results. After their loss in 1800 and their decline in congressional membership, the Federalists were unsuccessful in nominating a candidate who could win the presidency. The Republicans, on the other hand, quickly emerged as the majority party and exerted incredible influence in presidential elections—because the candidates who they nominated,

*Reprinted in *The Evolving Presidency,* 3e., ed. Michael Nelson (Washington, D.C.: CQ Press, 2008), 81–86.

won. The Republicans nominated Jefferson in 1796, 1800, and 1804. In 1808 and 1812 they nominated James Madison, and in 1816 and 1820 James Monroe received their nomination.

Both parties initially tried to keep the caucuses an internal affair, but in 1804 proceedings of the Republican caucus were printed in the press. That was also the first year that the parties effectively formed the first national party committees by appointing a group to promote the election of their respective nominees for president. By 1808 the caucuses were so important that they were characterized by intense competition and political maneuvering.

The nominating caucuses provoked intense protest from those who disapproved of the caucuses' choices. The caucus became known as "King Caucus," primarily because its power was perceived as undemocratic. In effect, any congressional district or state unable to elect its party's representative or senator to Congress was not represented. Further, the downfall of the Federalist Party meant that the Republican congressional nominating caucus essentially chose the new president.

In 1823 the system began to break down when conflicts between eastern and western states emerged. Those who supported a candidate not chosen by the caucuses were forced to take their campaign directly to the people. Late that year the General Assembly of Tennessee passed a resolution criticizing the caucus because it appeared unlikely that its favorite son, Gen. Andrew Jackson, would be nominated for president. Other states soon articulated their own grievances. As a result of the division, there was no means for concentrating a majority of electoral support behind one candidate. Thus, the Republican nominee in 1824, William H. Crawford of Georgia, finished fourth. When no candidate gained an electoral majority, the House of Representatives chose John Quincy Adams.

This episode effectively ended the role of Congress as the machinery for choosing presidential nominees. Nominating caucuses were replaced with national presidential nominating conventions. The first convention was held in Baltimore, Maryland, by the Anti-Masonic Party in 1831 to choose a candidate for the 1832 election. Jacksonian Democrats and Republicans soon followed suit.

The General Assembly of the state of Tennessee has taken into consideration the practice which, on former occasions, has prevailed at the city of Washington, of members of the Congress of the United States meeting in caucus, and nominating persons to be voted for as President and Vice-President of the United States; and, upon the best view of the subject which this General Assembly has been able to take, it is believed that the practice of congressional nominations is a violation of the spirit of the Constitution of the United States.

That instrument provides that there shall be three separate and distinct departments of the government, and great care and caution seems to have been exercised by its framers to prevent any one department from exercising the smallest degree of influence over another; and such solicitude was felt on this subject, that, in the 2nd Section of the 2nd Article, it is expressly declared, "That no senator or representative, or person holding an office of trust or profit under the United States, shall be appointed an elector." From this provision, it is apparent that the Convention intended that the members of Congress should not be the principal and primary agents or actors in electing the President and Vice-President of the United States; so far from it, they are expressly disqualified from being placed in a situation to vote for these high officers.

Is there not more danger of undue influence to be apprehended when the members of Congress meet in caucus and mutually and solemnly pledge themselves to support the individuals who may have the highest number of votes in such meeting than there would be in permitting them to be eligible to the appointment of electors? In the latter case, a few characters rendered ineligible by the Constitution might succeed; but, in the former, a powerful combination of influential men is formed, who may fix upon the American people their highest officers against the consent of a clear majority of the people themselves; and this may be done by the very men whom the Constitution intended to prohibit from acting on the subject.

Upon an examination of the Constitution of the United States, there is but one case in which the members of Congress are permitted to act, which is in the event of a failure to make an election by the Electoral College; and then the members of the House of Representatives vote by states. With what propriety the same men, who, in the year 1825, may be called on to discharge a constitutional duty, can, in the year 1824, go into a caucus and pledge themselves to support the men then nominated, cannot be discerned, especially when it might so happen that the persons thus nominated could not, under any circumstances, obtain a single vote from the state whose members stand pledged to support them. . . .

It has been said that the members of Congress in caucus only recommend to the people for whom to vote, and that such recommendation is not obligatory.

Minutes of Last Congressional Nominating Caucus, 1824

At a meeting of the republican members of Congress, assembled this evening, pursuant to public notice, for the purpose of recommending to the people of the United States suitable persons to be supported at the approaching election, for the offices of president and vice-president of the United States:

On motion of Mr. James Barbour, of Virginia,

Mr. Benjamin Ruggles, a senator from the state of Ohio, was called to the chair, and Mr. Ela Collins, a representative from the state of New York, was appointed secretary.

Resolved, That this meeting do now proceed to designate, by ballot, a candidate for president of the United States.

Determined in the affirmative.

On motion of Mr. Van Buren of New York, it was

Resolved, That the Chairman call up the Republican members of Congress by states, in order to receive their respective ballots.

Whereupon the Chairman proceeded to a call, and it appeared the following members were present. . . .

Mr. Bassett, of Virginia, and Mr. Cambrelong, of New York, were appointed tellers, and, on counting the ballots, it appeared that William H. Crawford had sixty-four votes; John Quincy Adams, two votes; Andrew Jackson, one vote, and Nathaniel Macon, one vote.

Mr. Dickinson, of New Jersey, then submitted the following resolution, which was agreed to:

Resolved, That this meeting do now proceed to designate, by ballot, a candidate for the office of Vice President of the United States.

Mr. Van Buren, of New York, then stated that he was authorized to say that the Vice President having, some time since, determined to retire from public life, did not wish to be regarded by his friends as a candidate for re-election to that office.

On counting the ballots, it appeared that Albert Gallatin, of Pennsylvania, had fifty-seven votes; John Q. Adams of Massachusetts, one vote; Samuel Smith of Maryland, one vote; William King, of Maine, one vote; Richard Rush, of Pennsylvania, one vote; Erastus Root, of New York, two votes; John Tod, of Pennsylvania, one vote; and Walter Lowrie, of Pennsylvania, one vote.

And, thereupon, Mr. Clark of New York submitted the following resolution, to wit:

Resolved, As the sense of this meeting that William H. Crawford, of Georgia, be recommended to the people of the United States as a proper candidate for the office of President, and Albert Gallatin, of Pennsylvania, for the office of Vice President of the United States, for four years from the 4th of March 1825.

Resolved, That in making the foregoing recommendation, the members of this meeting have acted in their individual characters, as citizens; that they have been induced to this measure from a deep and settled conviction of the importance of union among Republicans, throughout the United States, and as the best means of collecting and concentrating the feelings and wishes of the people of the Union, upon this important subject. The question being put upon these resolutions, they were unanimously agreed to.

Mr. Holmes of Maine then moved that the proceedings of the meeting be signed by the chairman and secretary, and published, together with an address to the people of the United States, to be prepared by a committee to be appointed for the purpose.

On motion, it was ordered that this committee consist of the chairman and the secretary of the convention, together with the gentlemen whose names were signed to the notice calling the meeting.

On motion, it was further

Resolved, That the chairman and secretary inform the gentlemen nominated for the offices of President and Vice President of their nomination, and learn from them whether they are willing to serve in the said offices, respectively.

BENJAMIN RUGGLES, *Chairman.*
E. COLLINS, *Secretary.*

SOURCE: Reprinted in *Readings in Party Principles and Practical Politics,* ed. Stuart Lewis (New York: Prentice-Hall, 1928).

This is true and clearly proves that it is a matter which does not belong to them—that, in recommending candidates, they go beyond the authority committed to them as members of Congress and thus transcend the trust delegated to them by their constituents. If their acts had any obligatory force, then the authority must be derived from some part of the Constitution of the United States and might be rightfully exercised; but when they say they only *recommend,* it is an admission, on their part, that they are acting without authority and are attempting, by a usurped influence, to effect an object not confided to them and not within their powers, even by implication.

It cannot be admitted that there is any weight in the argument drawn from the fact that both the [Federalist and Democratic-Republican] parties, heretofore contending for the superiority in the United States, have, in former times, resorted to this practice. The actions of public or private men, heated by party zeal and struggling for ascendency and power, ought not to be urged as precedents when circumstances have entirely changed. All political precedents are of doubtful authority and should never be permitted to pass unquestioned,

unless made in good times and for laudable purposes. In palliation of the practice of resorting to caucus nominations in former times, it was said that each
party must of necessity consult together in the best practicable way and select
the most suitable persons from their respective parties so that the united efforts of all those composing it might be brought to bear upon their opponents.
It is to be recollected that there is no danger of a departure from or violation of
the Constitution, except when strong temptations are presented, and this will
seldom occur, except when parties are arrayed against each other and their feelings violently excited.

The state of things, however, in the United States is entirely changed; it is
no longer a selection made by members of Congress of different parties, but it
is an election by the two houses of Congress, in which all the members must
be permitted to attend and vote. It is not difficult to perceive that this practice may promote and place men in office who could not be elected were the
constitutional mode pursued. It is placing the election of the President and
Vice-President of the United States—an election in which all the states have an
equal interest and equal rights—more in the power of a few of the most populous states than was contemplated by the Constitution. This practice is considered objectionable on other accounts: so long as Congress is considered as composed of the individuals on whom the election depends, the executive will is
subjected to the control of that body, and it ceases, in some degree, to be a separate and independent branch of the government; and the expectation of executive patronage may have an unhappy influence on the deliberations of Congress.

Upon a review of the whole question, the following reasons which admit of
much amplification and enlargement, more than has been urged in the foregoing, might be conclusively relied on to prove the impolicy and unconstitution-
ality of the congressional nominations of candidates for the presidency and
vice-presidency of the United States: 1. A caucus nomination is against the
spirit of the Constitution. 2. It is both inexpedient and impolitic. 3. Members
of Congress may become the final electors and therefore ought not to prejudge
the case by pledging themselves previously to support particular candidates.
4. It violates the equality intended to be secured by the Constitution to the
weaker states. 5. Caucus nominations may, in time (by the interference of the
states), acquire the force of precedents and become authoritative and, thereby,
endanger the liberties of the American people.

This General Assembly, believing that the true spirit of the Constitution
will be best preserved by leaving the election of President and Vice-President
to the *people themselves,* through the medium of electors chosen by them, uninfluenced by any previous nomination made by members of Congress, have
adopted the following resolutions:

1. *Resolved,* that the senators in Congress from this state be instructed, and our representatives be requested, to use their exertions to prevent a nomination being made during the next session of Congress, by the members thereof in caucus, of persons to fill the offices of President and Vice-President of the United States.

2. *Resolved,* that the General Assembly will, at its present session, divide the state into as many districts, in convenient form, as this state is entitled to electoral votes, for the purpose of choosing an elector in each to vote for the President and Vice-President of the United States.

3. *Resolved,* that the governor of this state transmit a copy of the foregoing preamble and resolutions to the executive of each of the United States, with a request that the same be laid before each of their respective legislatures.

4. *Resolved,* that the governor transmit a copy to each of the senators and representatives in Congress from this state.

◄⟡ 10 ⟡►

Martin Van Buren's Letter to Thomas Ritchie*
(1827)

1. Why was it important for Van Buren to reach out to influential newspaper editors to support Jackson's candidacy in 1828? Specifically, why was it important to reach out to those in the South?
2. Why was Jackson's victory interpreted as a victory for the Democratic Party?

P RIOR TO HIS ELECTION as president, Martin Van Buren was instrumental in the development and organization of political parties as organizations. His leadership proved critical to constructing a party organization in the state of New York, and by the 1820s he was one of the most important leaders in the Democratic Party.

After his election to the state senate in New York, Van Buren created the Bucktails, a political machine that covered the entire state. The

---

*Reprinted in Arthur Schlesinger, *History of U.S. Political Parties* (New York: Chelsea House, 1973).

Albany Regency led the Bucktails and dominated politics in the state for decades. Its power even stretched well beyond New York. Van Buren was nicknamed the "Little Magician" for his skill at taking advantage of patronage appointments and other public resources in a way that fostered a successful electoral environment for the Bucktails. In 1821 he was rewarded for his diligence by a nomination to the U.S. Senate.

Van Buren was the chief architect of the first political party that reached beyond regionalism or personality differences. He began the operation by reorganizing the remnants of the old Republican Party behind the candidacy of Andrew Jackson. Then, from his political base in New York he reached out to the most prominent Southern politicians, political elites, and newspaper editors, such as Thomas Ritchie of the Richmond *Enquirer,* which was one of the most influential newspapers in the South. Van Buren encouraged Jackson's supporters to engage in a grassroots style of campaigning that energized the public. For example, large groups of volunteers handed out hickory sticks at political rallies and planted hickory trees in honor of Jackson (who gained the nickname "Old Hickory" during the War of 1812). By 1832, the Democrats were ready to hold their first national nominating convention.

After Jackson's election to the presidency in 1828, Van Buren was rewarded for his service by an appointment as Jackson's secretary of state. In 1832 Jackson chose Van Buren as his running mate, and when he retired after two terms Van Buren was handpicked to continue his legacy. So, in May of 1835, the Democrats unanimously nominated Van Buren at their convention in Baltimore. The next year the Democrats only competitor was the Whig Party, the members of which divided their vote among several regional candidates, including William Henry Harrison from the West, Daniel Webster from New England, and Hugh Lawson White from the South. In the press at the time, Van Buren's presidential victory was represented as a broad victory for President Jackson and the Democratic Party.

❦

January 13, 1827

You will have observed an article in the Argus upon the subject of a national convention. That matter will soon be brought under discussion here & I sincerely wish you would bestow upon it some portion of your attention. . . . The following may, I think, justly be ranked among its [the convention's] probable advantages. First, It is the best and probably the only practicable mode of concentrating the entire vote of the opposition & of effecting what is of still greater importance, the substantial reorganization of the Old Republican Party. 2nd Its first result cannot be doubtful. Mr. Adams occupying the seat and being determined not to surrender it except *in extremis* will not submit his pretension to the convention. Noah's real or affected apprehensions upon that subject are idle. I have long been satisfied that we can only get rid of the present, & restore a better state of things, by combining Genl. Jackson's personal popularity with the portion of old party feeling yet remaining. This sentiment is spreading, and would of itself be sufficient to nominate him at the Convention. 3rd The call of such a convention, its exclusive Republican character, & the refusal of Mr. Adams and his friends to become parties to it, would draw anew the old Party lines & the subsequent contest would reestablish them; State nomination alone would fall far short of that object. 4th It would greatly improve the condition of the Republicans of the North & Middle States by substituting *party principle* for *personal preference* as one of the leading points in the contest. The location of the candidates would in a great degree, be merged in its consideration. Instead of the question being between a Northern and Southern man, it would be whether or not the ties, which have heretofore bound together a great political party should be severed. The difference between the two questions would be found to be immense in the elective field. Altho' this is a mere party consideration, it is not on that account less likely to be effectual Considerations of this character not infrequently operate as efficiently as those which bear upon the most important questions of constitutional doctrine. . . . 5th It would place our Republican friends in New England on new & strong grounds. They would have to decide between an indulgence in sectional & personal feelings with an entire separation from their old political friends on the one hand, or acquiescence in the fairly expressed will of the party, on the other. In all the states the division between Republicans and Federalists is still kept up & cannot be laid aside whatever the leaders of the two parties may desire. Such a question would greatly disturb the democracy of the east. . . . 6th Its effects would be highly salutary in your section of the union by the revival of old party distinctions. We must always have party distinctions and the old ones are the best of which the nature of the case admits. Political combinations between the inhabitants of the different states are unavoidable & the most natural &, beneficial to the country is that between the planters of the South and the plain Republicans of the North. The country has once flourished under a party thus constituted & may again. It would take

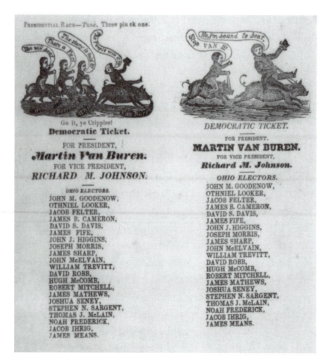

This 1836 Democratic ticket is representative of those found throughout the states prior to the adoption of standardized voting practices. Parties encouraged voters essentially to use these tickets as their ballots and vote the "straight ticket."

longer than our lives (even if it were practicable) to create new party feelings to keep those masses together. If the old ones are suppressed, geographical divisions founded on local interests or, what is worse prejudices between free & slaveholding states will inevitably take their place. Party attachment in former times furnished a complete antidote for sectional prejudices by producing counteracting feelings. It was not until that defense had been broken down that the clamor agt Southern influence and African Slavery could be made effectual in the North. Those in the South who assisted in producing the change are, I am satisfied, now deeply sensible of their errour. . . . Formerly, attacks upon Southern Republicans were regarded by those of the North as assaults upon their political brethren and resented accordingly. This all powerful sympathy has been much weakened, if not, destroyed by the amalgamating policy of Mr. Monroe. It can & ought to be revived and the proposed convention would be eminently serviceable in effecting that object. . . . Lastly, the effect of such a nomination on Genl Jackson could not fail to be considerable. His election, as the result of his military services without reference to party & so far as he alone is concerned, scarcely to principle, would be one thing. His election as the result of a combined and concerted effort of a political party, holding in the main to certain tenets & opposed to certain prevailing principles, might be another and a far different thing.

❊ II ❊

Henry Clay's Speech Concerning the Whig Party*

(1834)

Henry Clay's Letter to the Whig Party Convention**

(1839)

1. How did a coalition of interests opposed to Jackson's policies evolve into a major political party, the Whigs?
2. What role did Clay fill in the development of the Whig Party?

THE WHIG PARTY WAS formed in the early 1830s under the leadership of Henry Clay to oppose the policies of President Andrew Jackson and the Democratic Party. In general, the Whigs saw Jackson as an impediment to their program of modernization and economic development. The principal issue at the time was Jackson's veto of a bill that

---

*Reprinted in *A Century of Lawmaking for a New Nation: U.S. Congressional Documents and Debates, 1774–1875,* 23rd Congress, 1st Session, December 2, 1833, to April 18, 1834; found at http://memory.loc.gov/cgi-bin/ampage?collId=llrd&fileName=016/llrd016.db& recNum=4, images 1311–1315.

**Reprinted in *Proceedings of the Democratic Whig National Convention, which Assembled at Harrisburg, Pennsylvania, on the Fourth of December, 1839, for the Purpose of Nominating Candidates for President and Vice President of the United States* (Harrisburg, Penn.: R. S. Elliott, 1839).

would have extended the charter of the Bank of the United States; this ultimately would become one of the major issues of the 1832 election. After Jackson was handily reelected to the presidency, defeating Sen. Henry Clay of Kentucky, he proceeded to remove the government's deposits from the bank without the consent of Congress, which infuriated his political opponents.

Without a doubt, the bank issue was important, but the Whigs actually were more concerned by Jackson's use (or abuse) of executive power. In 1833 Clay led a majority coalition in the Senate that passed a resolution to censure the president. After a lengthy debate, the Senate voted along party lines to censure Jackson for assuming power not granted to the office by the Constitution. When the Democrats gained the majority in 1837, they expunged the censure resolution from the *Senate Journal*.

It was Clay, in a speech to the U.S. Senate on April 14, 1834, who first used the term "whig" in a partisan sense to mean all persons opposed to the autocratic politics of Jackson and the devastating policies of the Democrats. He borrowed the term from the Whig Party in Great Britain, which historically opposed extending the power of the executive. Initially, the Whigs had rejected developing a strong party organization like the Democrats. They started out as a coalition of Republicans disillusioned with Jackson's policy choices, Southerners who disliked Jackson's use of executive power, and Anti-Masonites, who by this time could no longer rally support for their party on the basis of opposing Freemasons (members of a very old fraternal order) running for public office.

It had taken some time for the Whigs to evolve beyond an alliance of those simply opposed to Jackson. They finally united behind a policy agenda promoted by Clay in a speech to the Senate in early 1832. In it, Clay advocated the creation of an "American System" consisting of three parts: tariffs to protect industry, a national bank that would encourage commerce, and federal subsidies for internal improvements that would make agriculture more profitable.

In 1836 the Whigs chose to support different regional candidates in the hope of denying Democrat Martin Van Buren an electoral majority and sending the election to the House of Representatives. After Van Buren's election, however, they were willing to develop a more effective political organization. The Whigs held their first national nominating convention in late 1839. Clay had served as the principal leader of the party; however, he deferred to the wisdom of the delegates present to nominate a candidate that Whigs from all regions of the country would support. William Henry Harrison, a popular general, was chosen to run for president, and with powerful allies in the press, such as *New York Tribune* editor Horace Greeley, Harrison was successful in defeating incumbent Van Buren.

Henry Clay's Speech Concerning the Whig Party
April 14, 1834

. . . And now, Mr. President I will avail myself of the occasion to say a few words on the subject-matter of these proceedings and memorials, and on the state of the country as we found it at the commencement of the session, and its present state. . . .

Mr. President, it is a question of the highest importance what is to be the issue, what the remedy, of the existing evils. We should deal with the people openly, frankly, sincerely. The Senate stands ready to do whatever is incumbent upon it; but unless the majority in the House will relent; unless it will take heed of and profit by recent events, there is no hope for the nation from the joint action of the two Houses of Congress at this session. Still, I would say to my countrymen, Do not despair. You are a young, brave, intelligent and as yet a free people. A complete remedy for all that you suffer, and all that you dread, is in your own hands. And the events, to which I have just alluded, demonstrate that those of us have not been deceived who have always relied upon the virtue, the capacity, and the intelligence of the people.

I congratulate you, Mr. President, and I hope you will receive the congratulation with the same heartfelt cordiality with which I tender it, upon the issue of the late election in the city of New York. I hope it will excite a patriotic glow in your bosom. I congratulate the Senate, the country, the city of New York, the friends of liberty every where. It was a great victory. It must be so regarded in every aspect. From a majority of more than six thousand, which the dominant party boasted a few months ago, if it retain any, it is a meager and spurious majority of less than two hundred. And the Whigs contended with such odds against them. A triple alliance of State placemen, corporation placemen, and Federal placemen, amounting to about thirty-five hundred, and deriving, in the form of salaries, compensations, and allowances, ordinary and extra, from the public chests, the enormous sum, annually, of near one million of dollars. Marshalled, drilled, disciplined, commanded. The struggle was tremendous; but what can withstand the irresistible power of the votaries of truth, liberty, and their country? It was an immortal triumph—a triumph of the constitution and the laws over usurpation here, and over clubs and bludgeons and violence there.

Go on, noble city! Go on, patriotic whigs! Follow up your glorious commencement, persevere, and pause not until you have regenerated and disenthralled your splendid city, and placed it at the head of American cities devoted to civil liberty, as it now stands pre-eminently the first as the commercial emporium of our common country! Merchants, mechanics, traders, laborers, never cease to recollect that, without freedom, you can have no sure commerce or business; and that without law you have no security for personal liberty, property, or even existence! Countrymen of Tone, of Emmet, of Macneven, and of Sampson, if any of you have been deceived, and seduced into the support of a cause dangerous to American liberty, hasten to review and correct your course! Do not forget that you abandoned the green fields of your native island to escape what you believed the tyranny of a British king! Do not, I adjure you, lend yourselves, in this land of your asylum, this last retreat of the freedom of man, to the establishment here, for you, and for us all, of that despotism which you had proudly hoped had been left behind you, in Europe, forever! There is much, I would fain believe, in the constitutional forms of government: but at last it is its parental and beneficent operation that must fix its character. A government may in form be free, in practice tyrannical; as it may in form be despotic, and in practice liberal and free.

It was a brilliant and signal triumph of the whigs. And they have assumed for themselves, and bestowed on their opponents, a demonination which, according to all the analogy of history, is strictly correct. It deserves to be extended throughout the whole country. What was the origin, among our British ancestors, of those appellations? The tories were the supporters of Executive power, of royal prerogative, of the maxim that the king could do no wrong, of the detestable doctrines of passive obedience and non-resistance. The whigs were the champions of liberty, the friends of the people, and the defenders of the power of their representatives in the House of Commons.

During our revolutionary war, the tories took sides with executive power and prerogative, and with the king, against liberty and independence. And the whigs, true to their principles, contended against royal executive power, and for freedom and independence.

And what is the present but the same contest in another form? The partisans of the present Executive sustain his power in the most boundless extent. They claim for him all Executive authority. They make his sole will the governing power. Every officer concerned in the administration, from the highest to the lowest, is to conform to his mandates. Even the public Treasury, hitherto regarded as sacred and beyond his reach, is placed by them under his entire direction and control. The whigs of the present day are opposing Executive encroachments, and a most alarming extension of Executive power and prerogative. They are ferreting out the abuses and corruptions of an administration, under a Chief Magistrate who is endeavoring to concentrate in his own person the whole powers of Government. They are contending for the rights of the people, for civil liberty, for free institutions, for the supremacy of the constitution and the laws. The contest is an arduous one; but, although the struggle may be yet awhile prolonged, by the blessing of God and the spirit of our ancestors, the issue cannot be doubtful.

The Senate stands in the breach, ready to defend the constitution and to relieve the distresses of the people. But, without the concurrence of another branch of Congress, which ought to be the first to yield it, the Senate alone can send forth no act of legislation. Unaided, it can do no positive good; but it has vast preventive power. It may avert and arrest evil, if it cannot rebuke usurpation. Senators, let us remain steadily by the constitution and the country, in this most portentous crisis: let us oppose, to all encroachments and to all corruption, a manly, a resolute and uncompromising resistance; let us adopt two rules from which we will never deviate, in deliberating upon all nominations. In the first place, to preserve untarnished and unsuspected the purity of Congress, let us negative the nomination of every member for any office, high or low, foreign or domestic, until the authority of the constitution and laws is fully restored. I know not that there is any member of either House capable of being influenced by the prospect of advancement or promotion; I would be the last to make such an insinuation; but suspicion is abroad, and it is best, in these times of trouble and revolution, to defend the integrity of the body against all possible imputations. For one, whatever others may do, I here deliberately avow my settled determination, whilst I retain a seat in this chamber, to act in conformity to that rule. In pursuing it, we but act in consonance with a principle proclaimed by the present Chief Magistrate himself when out of power. But, alas! how little has he respected it in power! How little has he, in office, conformed to any of the principles which he announced when out of office! And, in the next place, let us approve of the original nomination of no notorious brawling partisan and electioneerer; but, especially, of the reappointment of no officer presented to us, who shall have prostituted the influence of his office to partisan and electioneering purposes. Every incumbent has a clear right to exercise the elective franchise. I would be the last to controvert or deny it. But he has no right to employ the influence of his office, to exercise an agency which he holds in trust for the people, to promote his own selfish or party purposes. Here, also, we have the authority of the present Chief Magistrate for this rule; and the authority of Mr. Jefferson. The Senator from Tennessee, (Mr. Grundy,) merits lasting praise for his open and manly condemnation of these practices of official incumbents. He was right, when he declared his suspicion and distrust of the purity of the motives of any officer whom he saw busily interfering in the elections of the people.

Senators! we have a highly responsible and arduous position; but the people are with us, and the path of duty lies clearly marked before us. Let us be firm, persevering and unmoved. Let us perform our duty in a manner worthy of our ancestors—worthy of American Senators—worthy of the dignity of the sovereign States that we represent—above all, worthy of the name of American freemen! Let us "pledge our lives, our fortunes, and our sacred honor," to rescue our beloved country from all impending dangers. And, amidst the general gloom and darkness which prevail, let us continue to present one unextinguished light, steadily burning, in the cause of the people, of the constitution, and of civil liberty. . . .

Henry Clay's Letter to the Whig Party Convention
December 4, 1839

Mr. Banks, of Kentucky, addressed the chair, and declared that however much the friends of the great Statesman of that State might regret that another distinguished patriot had been preferred, they were ready to yield up their preferences for the good of the country, and go for the nominations made by the committee.

Mr. Preston, of the same State, made a similar declaration, and informed the Convention that General Leslie Combs, one of the delegation, had in his possession a letter from the Hon. Henry Clay, which related to the questions presented; and on his motion it was directed to be read: which being done it was

On motion of Mr. Boardman, of Connecticut,

Resolved, That the letter of the Honorable Henry Clay, just read, be, with the consent of the delegation from Kentucky, entered at large on the journals of the proceedings of this Convention.

Which is accordingly done, as follows:

ASHLAND, 20th November, 1839.

Gentleman:—The public use which has been made of my name, in connexion with the office of President of the United States, furnishes the motive as I trust it will form the apology, for this note. I address it to you, because our common residence in the same State appears to me to render you the most appropriate repository and organ of what I wish now to say.

The Convention at Harrisburg to designate candidates of the Opposition to the present Federal Administration, for the offices of President and Vice-President of the United States, has been recommended, and the propriety of it has been generally concurred in by all who agree as to the necessity of a change in the General Administration. It appeared to me to be the best, if not the only practicable method of reconciling and uniting those who, coinciding in the general principle, entertained different views as to the most suitable candidates for those high offices, and I have accordingly frequently expressed, and now repeat the expression of my conviction of the expediency of an entire and cordial acquiescence in the recommendations of the Convention.

In the meantime, appeals directly and indirectly have been made to me by a highly respectable Convention holden in Pennsylvania, and by private individuals, to decline giving my consent to the use of my name, upon the ground that a distinguished citizen of the State of Ohio is the first choice of the Opposition in Pennsylvania, and in the opinion of that Convention would be more likely to conciliate in general support than I should. I have been also addressed by various respectable and intelligent citizens of New York, directly and indirectly, recommending me to decline the contest in behalf of another eminent citizen, who has been distinguished in both the military and civil service of the United States.

Whilst I have been thus urgently but respectfully approached, numerous private citizens and public meetings and conventions in various parts of the United States (one of these conventions, indeed, in Pennsylvania itself) have done me the honor to express their confidence in me, and to intimate their wishes that I might be the candidate of the Opposition for the office of Chief Magistrate.

It is perfectly manifest that I cannot comply with all these conflicting opinions and wishes, nor, I apprehend, with any one of them, without disobliging the others.

Under these embarrassing circumstances, I have thought it most advisable to leave to the Convention at Harrisburg the free selection of candidates, as being the assembly to which, by common consent, that important duty has been referred. Representing, as it probably will, all parts of the United States, bringing together the feelings and views of all, and comparing and weighing the local information which it will derive from every portion, it will be most competent to make a nomination acceptable to the great majority of its constituents. That it will be faithful to the high trust confided to its judgment and patriotism, cannot be doubted; and having a full view of the whole ground, it will be more likely to make a selection agreeable to the great body of the Opposition than any separate convention could do, however enlightened and patriotic it may be. If the Pennsylvania Convention, to which I have just alluded, be right in supposing that the distinguished citizen whom it prefers would be more likely to be successful than any other, he ought to be nominated, and undoubtedly, for that very reason, will be nominated by the Harrisburg Convention, should it entertain the same opinion.

With a just and proper sense of the high honor of being voluntarily called to the office of President of the United States by a great, free and enlightened people, and profoundly grateful to those of my fellow citizens who are desirous to see me placed in that exalted and responsible station, I must, nevertheless, say, in entire truth and sincerity, that if the deliberations of the Convention shall lead them to the choice of another as the candidate of the opposition, far from feeling any discontent, the nomination will have my best wishes, and receive my cordial support.

And, gentlemen, I hope that you, my friends and neighbors, will excuse the liberty I take in expressing to you my anxious desire that, discarding all attachment or partiality to me, and guided solely by the motive of rescuing our country from the dangers which now encompass it, you will heartily unite in the selection of that citizen although it should not be me, who may appear to be most likely, by his election, to bring about a salutary change in the administration of the General Government—a change without which we shall be mocked by the forms, and stript of the substantial benefits of free institutions.

From the tenor of this note, I scarcely need observe that you are at perfect liberty to make such use of it as in your discretion may seem proper.

I am, with high respect, your friend, and obedient servant.

HENRY CLAY

12

Alexis de Tocqueville's
"Parties in the United States"*
(1835)

1. How did de Tocqueville portray the roles of majority and minority political parties in the United States? Was his depiction accurate for the time?
2. How do the political parties de Tocqueville observed differ from political parties found in the United States today?

VISITORS FROM OTHER countries have often highlighted important aspects of American culture and society that even Americans themselves have not noticed. After traveling to the United States, many foreign dignitaries have returned to their native land to write down their impressions of American culture, but none has proven as perceptive or as enduring as that of Alexis de Tocqueville. In 1832, de Tocqueville and his fellow magistrate, Gustave de Beaumont, were sent to the United States by the French government to study the young nation's prison system. After traveling the country for nine months and conducting interviews with more than two hundred people on the topics of law, politics, and social practices, they returned to France to submit their report.

Even before they left France, both de Tocqueville and Beaumont had decided to spend most of their time observing politics in the United States. During his travels de Tocqueville became so fascinated with the dedication of the public to the political process that he decided to write down his observations in a book, *De la démocratie en Amérique.* In preparing the manuscript de Tocqueville drew on the journals he kept during his trip, as well as hundreds of books and other documents that he collected in both the United States and France. *Democracy in America* was published in two volumes. The first was published in Paris on January 23, 1835. De Tocqueville began work on the second volume in the

*http://xroads.virginia.edu/~HYPER/DETOC/1_ch10.htm

fall of 1835, but his political career kept him from completing it as soon as he had expected. It was finally published on April 20, 1840. *Democracy in America* was immediately successful in both the United States and Europe. Numerous editions were published in the nineteenth century, and by the early twentieth century it was considered a classic work in the field of political science.

Given that the United States was such a new nation, most Europeans had only a vague idea of how the American political system worked. De Tocqueville introduced the Old World to the political order of the New World. In the early 1830s the country was undergoing radical economic, geographic, and political transformations. As the economy expanded rapidly and grew more diverse, the country expanded westward. Democrat Andrew Jackson was the newly elected president. His election to that office in 1828 set off the transformation of political parties from local organizations dominated by political elites to mass membership organizations devoted to electing candidates to office at the federal, state, and local levels.

Due to the success of *Democracy in America* de Tocqueville was named a Knight of the Legion of Honour in 1837. The next year he was elected to the Académie des sciences morales et politiques, and in 1841 he was elected to the Académie française.

A great distinction must be made between parties. Some countries are so large that the different populations which inhabit them, although united under the same government, have contradictory interests, and they may consequently be in a perpetual state of opposition. In this case the different fractions of the people may more properly be considered as distinct nations than as mere parties; and if a civil war breaks out, the struggle is carried on by rival states rather than by factions in the same state.

But when the citizens entertain different opinions upon subjects which affect the whole country alike, such, for instance, as the principles upon which the government is to be conducted, then distinctions arise that may correctly be styled parties. Parties are a necessary evil in free governments; but they have not at all times the same character and the same propensities.

The political parties that I style great are those which cling to principles rather than to their consequences; to general and not to special cases; to ideas and not to men. These parties are usually distinguished by nobler features, more generous passions, more genuine convictions, and a more bold and open conduct than the others. In them private interest, which always plays the chief part in political passions, is more studiously veiled under the pretext of the public good; and it may even be sometimes concealed from the eyes of the very persons whom it excites and impels.

Minor parties, on the other hand, are generally deficient in political good faith. As they are not sustained or dignified by lofty purposes, they ostensibly display the selfishness of their character in their actions. They glow with a factitious zeal; their language is vehement, but their conduct is timid and irresolute. The means which they employ are as wretched as the end at which they aim. Hence it happens that when a calm state succeeds a violent revolution, great men seem suddenly to disappear and the powers of the human mind to lie concealed. Society is convulsed by great parties, it is only agitated by minor ones; it is torn by the former, by the latter it is degraded; and if the first sometimes save it by a salutary perturbation, the last invariably disturb it to no good end.

America has had great parties, but has them no longer; and if her happiness is thereby considerably increased, her morality has suffered. When the War of Independence was terminated and the foundations of the new government were to be laid down, the nation was divided between two opinions—two opinions which are as old as the world and which are perpetually to be met with, under different forms and various names, in all free communities, the one tending to limit, the other to extend indefinitely, the power of the people. The conflict between these two opinions never assumed that degree of violence in America which it has frequently displayed elsewhere. Both parties of the Americans were agreed upon the most essential points; and neither of them had to destroy an old constitution or to overthrow the structure of society in order to triumph. In neither of them, consequently, were a great number of private interests affected by success or defeat: but moral principles of a high order, such as the love of equality and of independence, were concerned in the struggle, and these sufficed to kindle violent passions.

The party that desired to limit the power of the people, endeavored to apply its doctrines more especially to the Constitution of the Union, whence it derived its name of Federal. The other party, which affected to be exclusively attached to the cause of liberty, took that of Republican. America is the land of democracy, and the Federalists, therefore, were always in a minority; but they reckoned on their side almost all the great men whom the War of Independence had produced, and their moral power was very considerable. Their cause, moreover, was favored by circumstances. The ruin of the first Confederation had impressed the people with a dread of anarchy, and the Federalists profited by this transient disposition of the multitude. For ten or twelve years, they were at the head of affairs, and they were able to apply some, though not all, of their principles; for the hostile current was becoming from day to day too violent to be checked. In 1801 the Republicans got possession of the government: Thomas Jefferson was elected President; and he increased the influence of their party by the weight of his great name, the brilliance of his talents, and his immense popularity.

The means by which the Federalists had maintained their position were artificial, and their resources were temporary; it was by the virtues or the talents of their leaders, as well as by fortunate circumstances, that they had risen to power. When the Republicans attained that station in their turn, their opponents were overwhelmed by utter defeat. An immense majority declared itself against the retiring party, and the Federalists found themselves in so small a minority that they at once despaired of future success. From that moment the Republican or Democratic Party has proceeded from conquest to conquest, until it has acquired absolute supremacy in the country. The Federalists, perceiving that they were vanquished, without resource, and isolated in the midst of the nation, fell into two divisions, of which one joined the victorious Republicans, and the other laid down their banners and changed their name. Many years have elapsed since they wholly ceased to exist as a party.

The accession of the Federalists to power was, in my opinion, one of the most fortunate incidents that accompanied the formation of the great American Union: they resisted the inevitable propensities of their country and their age. But whether their theories were good or bad, they had the fault of being inapplicable, as a whole, to the society which they wished to govern, and that which occurred under the auspices of Jefferson must therefore have taken place sooner or later. But their government at least gave the new republic time to acquire a certain stability, and afterwards to support without inconvenience the rapid growth of the very doctrines which they had combated. A considerable number of their principles, moreover, were embodied at last in the political creed of their opponents; and the Federal Constitution, which subsists at the present day, is a lasting monument of their patriotism and their wisdom.

Great political parties, then, are not to be met with in the United States at the present time. Parties, indeed, may be found which threaten the future of the Union; but there is none which seems to contest the present form of government or the present course of society. The parties by which the Union is menaced do not rest upon principles, but upon material interests. These interests constitute, in the different provinces of so vast an empire, rival nations rather than parties. Thus, upon a recent occasion the North contended for the system of commercial prohibition, and the South took up arms in favor of free trade, simply because the North is a manufacturing and the South an agricultural community; and the restrictive system that was profitable to the one was prejudicial to the other.

In the absence of great parties the United States swarms with lesser controversies, and public opinion is divided into a thousand minute shades of difference upon questions of detail. The pains that are taken to create parties are inconceivable, and at the present day it is no easy task. In the United States there is no religious animosity, because all religion is respected and no sect is predominant; there is no jealousy of rank, because the people are everything and none can contest their authority; lastly, there is no public misery to serve as a means of agitation, because the physical position of the country opens so wide a field to industry that man only needs to be let alone to be able to accomplish prodigies. Nevertheless, ambitious men will succeed in creating parties, since it is difficult to eject a person from authority upon the mere ground that this place is coveted by others. All the skill of the actors in the political world lies in the art of creating parties. A political aspirant in the United States begins by discerning his own interest, and discovering those other interests which may be collected around and amalgamated with it. He then contrives to find out some doctrine or principle that may suit the purposes of this new association, which he adopts in order to bring forward his party and secure its popularity: just as the imprimatur of the king was in former days printed upon the title page of a volume and was thus incorporated with a book to which it in no wise belonged. This being done, the new party is ushered into the political world.

To a stranger all the domestic controversies of the Americans at first appear to be incomprehensible or puerile, and he is at a loss whether to pity a people who take such arrant trifles in good earnest or to envy that happiness which enables a community to discuss them. But when he comes to study the secret propensities that govern the factions of America, he easily perceives that the greater part of them are more or less connected with one or the other of those two great divisions which have always existed in free communities. The deeper we penetrate into the inmost thought of these parties, the more we perceive that the object of the one is to limit and that of the other to extend the authority of the people. I do not assert that the ostensible purpose or even that the secret aim of American parties is to promote the rule of aristocracy or democracy in the country; but I affirm that aristocratic or democratic passions may easily be detected at the bottom of all parties, and that, although they escape a superficial observation, they are the main point and soul of every faction in the United States. . . .

It sometimes happens in a people among whom various opinions prevail that the balance of parties is lost and one of them obtains an irresistible preponderance, overpowers all obstacles, annihilates its opponents, and appropriates all the resources of society to its own use. The vanquished despair of success, hide their heads, and are silent. The nation seems to be governed by a single principle, universal stillness prevails, and the prevailing party assumes the credit of having restored peace and unanimity to the country. But under this apparent unanimity still exist profound differences of opinion, and real opposition.

This is what occurred in America; when the democratic party got the upper hand, it took exclusive possession of the conduct of affairs, and from that time the laws and the customs of society have been adapted to its caprices. At the present day the more affluent classes of society have no influence in political affairs; and wealth, far from conferring a right, is rather a cause of unpopularity than a means of attaining power. The rich abandon the lists, through unwillingness to contend, and frequently to contend in vain, against the poorer classes of their fellow citizens. As they cannot occupy in public a position equivalent to what they hold in private life, they abandon the former and give themselves up to the latter; and they constitute a private society in the state which has its own tastes and pleasures. They submit to this state of things as an irremediable evil, but they are careful not to show that they are galled by its continuance; one often hears them laud the advantages of a republican government and demo-cratic institutions when they are in public. Next to hating their enemies, men are most inclined to flatter them.

Mark, for instance, that opulent citizen, who is as anxious as a Jew of the Middle Ages to conceal his wealth. His dress is plain, his demeanor unassuming; but the interior of his dwelling glitters with luxury, and none but a few chosen guests, whom he haughtily styles his equals, are allowed to penetrate into this sanctuary. No European noble is more exclusive in his pleasures or more jealous of the smallest advantages that a privileged station confers. But the same individual crosses the city to reach a dark counting-house in the center of traffic, where everyone may accost him who pleases. If he meets his cobbler on the way, they stop and converse; the two citizens discuss the affairs of the state and shake hands before they part.

But beneath this artificial enthusiasm and these obsequious attentions to the preponderating power, it is easy to perceive that the rich have a hearty dislike of the democratic institutions of their country. The people form a power which they at once fear and despise. If the maladministration of the democracy ever brings about a revolutionary crisis and monarchical institutions ever become practicable in the United States, the truth of what I advance will become obvious.

The two chief weapons that parties use in order to obtain success are the newspapers and public associations.

13

The Declaration of Sentiments
and Resolutions from the Seneca Falls
Women's Rights Convention*
(1848)

1. The Nineteenth Amendment was ratified more than seventy years after the Seneca Falls Convention. What cultural, geographical, political, and social reasons suggest why universal women's suffrage took so long to achieve?
2. How did universal women's suffrage affect political parties, campaigns, and elections in the United States in the 1920s? Today?

O N JULY 14, 1848, the *Seneca County Courier* announced a meeting to be held at Wesleyan Chapel in Seneca Falls, New York, on the following Wednesday and Thursday to discuss women's legal and social rights. Approximately three hundred women and men attended the convention held on July 19–20, including prominent abolitionist Frederick Douglas.

On the second day of the convention the group approved what has become known as the Declaration of Sentiments. The document's principal author was Elizabeth Cady Stanton. As a leader in the antislavery movement, Stanton had met other women from antislavery organizations in the Northeast and Midwest. Based on their success fighting slavery, as well as that of the Seneca Falls Convention, many of the women turned their attention to setting an agenda for women's rights.

The Declaration of Sentiments outlined the grievances of women, and the resolutions that were included outlined a plan for reform. To effectively demonstrate how "all men and women were created equal," the declaration was designed to mirror the structure and language of the Declaration of Independence. The document was discussed at length by those in attendance and was approved, signed, and published with few

*www.pinn.net/~sunshine/book-sum/seneca3.html

alterations. Only the resolution regarding voting caused any significant debate, but in the end it was approved by a narrow majority. Stanton later wrote that many of those present feared that demanding the right to vote would, by association, cause the defeat of other measures upon which the general public would find it easier to take action. After approval by the convention, the Declaration of Sentiments and Resolutions was signed by sixty-eight women and thirty-two men.

The convention at Seneca Falls was only the beginning of the formal movement to expand the right to vote to women in the United States. Between 1848 and the early twentieth century, women began winning equal voting rights on a state-by-state basis: in Colorado in 1893; Utah and Idaho in 1896; Washington State in 1910; California in 1911; Oregon, Kansas, and Arizona in 1912; Montana and Nevada in 1914; New York in 1917; and Michigan, South Dakota, and Oklahoma in 1918. It was not until 1920, when the Nineteenth Amendment to the Constitution was ratified, that women were guaranteed the right to vote throughout the United States.

Declaration of Sentiments

When in the course of human events, it becomes necessary for one portion of the family of man to assume among the people of the earth a position different from that which they have hitherto occupied, but one to which the laws of nature and nature's God entitle them, a decent respect to the opinions of mankind requires that they should declare the causes that impel them to such a course.

We hold these truths to be self-evident: that all men and women are created equal; that they are endowed by their Creator with certain inalienable rights; that among these are life, liberty, and the pursuit of happiness; that to secure these rights governments are instituted, deriving their just powers from the consent of the governed. Whenever any form of government becomes destructive of these ends, it is the right of those who suffer from it to refuse allegiance to it, and to insist upon the institution of a new government, laying its foundation on such principles, and organizing its powers in such form, as to them shall seem most likely to effect their safety and happiness. Prudence, indeed, will dictate that governments long established should not be changed for light and transient causes; and accordingly all experience hath shown that mankind are more disposed to suffer while evils are sufferable, than to right themselves by abolishing the forms to which they accustomed. But when a long train of abuses and usurpations, pursuing invariably the same object, evinces a design to reduce them under absolute despotism, it is their duty to throw off such government, and to provide new guards for their future security. Such has been the patient sufferance of women under this government, and such is now the necessity which constrains them to demand the equal station to which they are entitled.

The history of mankind is a history of repeated injuries and usurpations on the part of man toward woman, having in direct object the establishment of an absolute tyranny over her. To prove this, let facts be submitted to a candid world.

He has never permitted her to exercise her inalienable right to the elective franchise.

He has compelled her to submit to laws, in the formation of which she had no voice.

He has withheld from her rights which are given to the most ignorant and degraded men—both native and foreigner.

Having deprived her of this first right of a citizen, the elective franchise, thereby leaving her without representation in the halls of legislation, he has oppressed her on all sides.

He has made her, if married, in the eye of the law, civilly dead.

He has taken from her all right in property, even to wages she earns.

He has made her, morally, an irresponsible being, as she can commit many crimes with impunity, provided they can be done in the presence of her husband. In the covenant of marriage, she is compelled to promise obedience to her husband, he becoming, to all intents and purposes, her master—the law giving him power to deprive her of her liberty, and to administer chastisement.

He has so framed the laws of divorce, as to what shall be the proper causes, and in case of separation, to who, the guardianship of the children shall be given, as to be wholly regardless of the happiness of women—the law, in all cases, going upon a false supposition of the supremacy of man, giving all power into his hands.

After depriving her of all rights as a married woman, if single, and the owner of property, he has taxed her to support a government which recognizes her only when her property can be made profitable to it.

He has monopolized nearly all the profitable employments, and from those she is permitted to follow, she receives but a scanty remuneration. He closes against her all the avenues to wealth and distinction which he considers most honorable to himself. As a teacher of theology, medicine, or law, she is not known.

He has denied her the facilities for obtaining a thorough education, all colleges being closed against her.

He allows her in Church, as well as State, but a subordinate position, claiming Apostolic authority for her exclusion from the ministry, and, with some exceptions, from any public participation in the affairs of the Church.

He has created a false public sentiment by giving to the world a different code of morals for men and women, by which moral delinquencies which exclude women from society, are not only tolerated, but deemed of little account in man.

He has usurped the prerogative of Jehovah himself, claiming it as his right to assign for her a sphere of action, when that belongs to her conscience and to her God.

He has endeavored, in every way that he could, to destroy her confidence in her own powers, to lessen her self-respect and to make her willing to lead a dependent and abject life.

Now, in view of this entire disfranchisement of one-half the people of this country, their social and religious degradation—in view of the unjust laws above mentioned, and because women do feel themselves aggrieved, oppressed and fraudulently deprived of their most sacred rights, we insist that they have immediate admission to all the rights and privileges which belong to them as citizens of the United States.

In entering upon the great work before us, we anticipate no small amount of misconception, misrepresentation, and ridicule; but we shall use every instrumentality within our power to effect our object. We shall employ agents, circulate tracts, petition the State and National legislatures, and endeavor to enlist the pulpit and the press in our behalf. We hope this Convention will be followed by a series of Conventions embracing every part of the county.

Resolutions

Whereas, The great precept of nature is conceded to be, that "man shall pursue his own true and substantial happiness." Blackstone in his Commentaries remarks, that this law of Nature being coeval with mankind, and dictated by God himself, is of course superior in obligation to any other. It is binding over all the globe, in all countries and at all times; no human laws are of any validity if contrary to this, and such of them as are valid, derive their force, and all their validity, and all their authority mediately and immediately from this original; therefore,

Resolved, That all laws which prevent woman from occupying such a station in society as her conscience shall dictate, or which place her in a position inferior to that of man, are contrary to the great precept of nature, and therefore of no force or authority.

Resolved, That woman is man's equal—was intended to be so by the Creator, and the highest good of the race demands that she should be recognized as such.

Resolved, That the women of this country ought to be enlightened in regard to the laws under which they live, that they may no longer publish their degradation by declaring themselves satisfied with their present position, nor their ignorance, by asserting that they have all the rights they want.

Resolved, That inasmuch as man, while claiming for himself intellectual superiority, does accord to woman moral superiority, it is pre-eminently his duty to encourage her to speak and teach, as she has an opportunity, in all religious assemblies.

Resolved, That the same amount of virtue, delicacy, and refinement of behavior that is required of woman in the social state, should also be required of man, and the same transgressions should be visited with equal severity on both man and woman.

Resolved, That the objection of indelicacy and impropriety, which is so often brought against woman when she addresses a public audience, comes with a very ill-grace from those who encourage, by their attendance, her appearance on the stage, in the concert, or in feats of circus.

Resolved, That woman has too long rested satisfied in the circumscribed limits which corrupt customs and a perverted application of the Scriptures have marked out for her, and that it is time she should move in the enlarged sphere which her great Creator has assigned her.

Resolved, That it is the duty of women of this country to secure to themselves their sacred right to the elective franchise.

Resolved, That the equality of human rights results necessarily from the fact of the identity of the race in capabilities and responsibilities.

Resolved, That the speedy success of our cause depends upon the zealous and untiring efforts of both men and women, for the overthrow of the monopoly of the pulpit, and for the securing to women an equal participation with men in the various trades, professions, and commerce.

Resolved, therefore, That, being invested by the creator with the same capabilities, and the same consciousness of responsibility for their exercise, it is demonstrably the right and duty of woman, equally with man, to promote every righteous cause by every righteous means; and especially in regard to the great subjects of morals and religion, it is self-evidently her right to participate with her brother in teaching them, both in private and in public, by writing and by speaking, by any instrumentalities proper to be used, and in any assemblies proper to be held; and this being a self-evident truth growing out of the divinely implanted principles of human nature, any custom or authority adverse to it, whether modern or wearing the hoary sanction of antiquity, is to be regarded as a self-evident falsehood, and at war with mankind.

❧ 14 ❧
Abraham Lincoln's "A House Divided" Speech*
(1858)

1. How did Lincoln's acceptance of the Republican Party's nomination for a U.S. Senate seat place him in a position to become the party's presidential candidate in 1860?
2. How did the issue of slavery promote the Republican Party from minority party to majority party in 1860?

IN THE DECADE preceding the Civil War, the difficulty in resolving the issue of slavery created a realignment of party politics in the United States. Southern legislators blocked legislation necessary to construct a transcontinental railroad until slaveholders were permitted to take their slaves into the new territories. In 1854, Democratic senator Stephen Douglas of Illinois steered the Kansas-Nebraska Act through Congress. The act allowed for slavery in the new territories if approved by the settlers of that territory. In opposition to the Kansas-Nebraska Act, an alliance of Whigs, northern Democrats, and Free-Soilers formed the Republican Party. While this coalition opposed the expansion of slavery into either the territories or new states, those associated also agreed on other issues, such as the modernization of banking, higher education, industry, transportation (particularly railroads), and free homesteads for farmers.

At the Republicans' first national nominating convention, held in 1856 in Philadelphia, John Frémont was chosen as the party's first presidential candidate. Frémont dominated electoral voting in the northeast and northern Midwest that year, but lost to Democrat James Buchanan, who won the remaining parts of the Midwest and the South. The Republican Party quickly grew after this election, as many prominent Democrats were awarded with Republican gubernatorial or Senate nominations for switching parties.

*www.historyplace.com/lincoln/divided.htm

To complicate the slavery issue further, the U.S. Supreme Court's decision in *Dred Scott v. Sanford* (1856) stated that Congress had no power to keep slavery out of the territories. The decision effectively nullified the Kansas-Nebraska Act. After the *Dred Scott* decision was announced, many Northerners began to feel that in order to prevent the expansion of slavery, the institution itself would have to be abolished. The total abolition of slavery, however, scared many moderates within the Republican Party because they believed that Southern states would leave the Union if slavery was threatened. Among the moderates who opposed the expansion, if not the abolition, of slavery was Abraham Lincoln. Lincoln believed the practice would eventually die a natural death.

In 1858, Lincoln was nominated by the Illinois Republican Party to run for the U.S. Senate against incumbent Stephen Douglas. In a speech delivered on June 17 at the close of the Republican State Convention, Lincoln caught the mood of many Republicans across the country who were increasingly concerned about the morality of maintaining the practice of slavery versus the need to maintain the union of the states. The phrase "house divided," which comes from the New Testament book of Mark (3:25) was used frequently, but Lincoln's speech brought a new familiarity to the term. The debates Lincoln and Douglas held that year received national attention and turned Lincoln into a serious threat to win the Republican nomination for president in 1860.

As both candidate and president, Lincoln often disagreed with the "radical" wing of the Republican Party that advocated harsher measures toward the South. He was brilliant, however, in uniting all factions of the party to fight to save the Union. Lincoln successfully persuaded the party to pass major legislation to fulfill many parts of the Republican Party platform in addition to temporary higher taxes and tariffs to finance the war effort.

<hr/>

Springfield, Illinois, June 16, 1858

MR. PRESIDENT AND GENTLEMEN OF THE CONVENTION:

If we could first know where we are, and whither we are tending, we could better judge what to do, and how to do it. We are now far into the fifth year since a policy was initiated with the avowed object, and confident promise, of putting an end to slavery agitation. Under the operation of that policy, that agitation has not only not ceased, but has constantly augmented. In my opinion, it will not cease, until a crisis shall have been reached and passed. "A house divided against itself cannot stand." I believe this government cannot endure permanently half slave and half free. I do not expect the Union to be dissolved—I do not expect the house to fall—but I do expect it will cease to be divided. It will become all one thing, or all the other. Either the opponents of slavery will arrest the further spread of it, and place it where the public mind shall rest in the belief that it is in the course of ultimate extinction; or its advocates will push it forward, till it shall become alike lawful in all the States, old as well as new—North as well as South.

Have we no tendency to the latter condition?

Let any one who doubts, carefully contemplate that now almost complete legal combination—piece of machinery, so to speak—compounded of the Nebraska doctrine, and the Dred Scott decision. Let him consider not only what work the machinery is adapted to do, and how well adapted; but also, let him study the history of its construction, and trace, if he can, or rather fail, if he can, to trace the evidences of design, and concert of action, among its chief architects, from the beginning.

The new year of 1854 found slavery excluded from more than half the States by State Constitutions, and from most of the national territory by Congressional prohibition. Four days later, commenced the struggle which ended in repealing that Congressional prohibition. This opened all the national territory to slavery, and was the first point gained.

But, so far, Congress only had acted; and an indorsement by the people, real or apparent, was indispensable, to save the point already gained, and give chance for more.

This necessity had not been overlooked; but had been provided for, as well as might be, in the notable argument of "squatter sovereignty," otherwise called "sacred right of self-government," which latter phrase, though expressive of the only rightful basis of any government, was so perverted in this attempted use of it as to amount to just this: That if any one man choose to enslave another, no third man shall be allowed to object. That argument was incorporated into the Nebraska bill itself, in the language which follows: "It being the true intent and meaning of this act not to legislate slavery into any Territory or State, nor to exclude it therefrom; but to leave the people thereof perfectly free to form and regulate their domestic institutions in their own way, subject only to the Constitution of the United States." Then opened the roar of loose declamation in favor of "Squatter Sovereignty," and "sacred right of self-government." "But," said opposition members, "let us amend the bill so as to expressly declare that the people of the Territory may exclude slavery." "Not we," said the friends of the measure; and down they voted the amendment.

While the Nebraska bill was passing through Congress, a law case involving the question of a negro's freedom, by reason of his owner having voluntarily taken him first into a free State and then into a Territory covered by the Congressional prohibition, and held him as a slave for a long time in each, was passing through the U.S. Circuit Court for the District of Missouri; and both Nebraska bill and law suit were brought to a decision in the same month of May, 1854. The negro's name was "Dred Scott," which name now designates the decision finally made in the case. Before the then next Presidential election, the law case came to, and was argued in, the Supreme Court of the United States; but the decision of it was deferred until after the election. Still, before the election, Senator Trumbull, on the floor of the Senate, requested the leading advocate of the Nebraska bill to state his opinion whether the people of a Territory can constitutionally exclude slavery from their limits; and the latter answers: "That is a question for the Supreme Court."

The election came. Mr. Buchanan was elected, and the indorsement, such as it was, secured. That was the second point gained. The indorsement, however, fell short of a clear popular majority by nearly four hundred thousand votes, and so, perhaps, was not overwhelmingly reliable and satisfactory. The outgoing President, in his last annual message, as impressively as possible echoed back upon the people the weight and authority of the endorsement. The Supreme Court met again; did not announce their decision, but ordered a reargument. The Presidential inauguration came, and still no decision of the court; but the incoming President in his inaugural address, fervently exhorted the people to abide by the forthcoming decision, whatever it might be. Then, in a few days, came the decision.

The reputed author of the Nebraska bill finds an early occasion to make a speech at this capital indorsing the Dred Scott decision, and vehemently denouncing all opposition to it. The new President, too, seizes the early occasion of the Silliman letter to indorse and strongly construe that decision, and to express his astonishment that any different view had ever been entertained!

At length a squabble springs up between the President and the author of the Nebraska bill, on the mere question of fact, whether the Lecompton Constitution was or was not, in any just sense, made by the people of Kansas; and in that quarrel the latter declares that all he wants is a fair vote for the people, and that he cares not whether slavery be voted down or voted up. I do not understand his declaration that he cares not whether slavery be voted down or voted up, to be intended by him other than as an apt definition of the policy he would impress upon the public mind—the principle for which he declares he has suffered so much, and is ready to suffer to the end. And well may he cling to that principle. If he has any parental feeling, well may he cling to it. That principle is the only shred left of his original Nebraska doctrine. Under the Dred Scott decision "squatter sovereignty" squatted out of existence, tumbled down like temporary scaffolding—like the mould at the foundry served through one blast and fell back into loose sand—helped to carry an election, and then was kicked to the winds. His late joint struggle with the Republicans, against the Lecompton Constitution, involves nothing of the original Nebraska doctrine. That struggle was made on a point—the right of a people to make their own constitution—upon which he and the Republicans have never differed.

The several points of the Dred Scott decision, in connection, with Senator Douglas's "care not" policy, constitute the piece of machinery, in its present state of advancement. This was the third point gained. The working points of that machinery are:

First, That no negro slave, imported as such from Africa, and no descendant of such slave, can ever be a citizen of any State, in the sense of that term as used in the Constitution of the United States. This point is made in order to deprive the negro, in every possible event, of the benefit of that provision of the United States Constitution, which declares that "The citizens of each State, shall be entitled to all privileges and immunities of citizens in the several States."

Secondly, That "subject to the Constitution of the United States," neither Congress nor a Territorial Legislature can exclude slavery from any United States territory. This point is made in order that individual men may fill up the Territories with slaves, without danger of losing them as property, and thus to enhance the chances of permanency to the institution through all the future.

Thirdly, That whether the holding a negro in actual slavery in a free State, makes him free, as against the holder, the United States courts will not decide, but will leave to be decided by the courts of any slave State the negro may be forced into by the master. This point is made, not to be pressed immediately; but, if acquiesced in for awhile, and apparently indorsed by the people at an election, then to sustain the logical conclusion that what Dred Scott's master might lawfully do with Dred Scott, in the free State of Illinois, every other master may lawfully do with any other one, or one thousand slaves, in Illinois, or in any other free State.

Auxiliary to all this, and working hand in hand with it, the Nebraska doctrine, or what is left of it, is to educate and mould public opinion, at least Northern public opinion, not to care whether slavery is voted down or voted up. This shows exactly where we now are; and partially, also, whither we are tending.

It will throw additional light on the latter, to go back, and run the mind over the string of historical facts already stated. Several things will now appear less dark and mysterious than they did when they were transpiring. The people were to be left "perfectly free," "subject only to the Constitution." What the Constitution had to do with it, outsiders could not then see. Plainly enough now, it was an exactly fitted niche, for the Dred Scott decision to afterward come in, and declare the perfect freedom of the people to be just no freedom at all. Why was the amendment, expressly declaring the right of the people, voted down? Plainly enough now: the adoption of it would have spoiled the niche for the Dred Scott decision. Why was the court decision held up? Why even a Senator's individual opinion withheld, till after the Presidential election? Plainly enough now: the speaking out then would have damaged the perfectly free argument upon which the election was to be carried. Why the outgoing President's felicitation on the indorsement? Why the delay of a re-argument? Why the incoming President's advance exhortation in favor of the decision? These things look like the cautious patting and petting of a spirited horse preparatory to mounting him, when it is dreaded that he may give the rider a fall. And why the hasty after-indorsement of the decision by the President and others?

We cannot absolutely know that all these exact adaptations are the result of preconcert. But when we see a lot of framed timbers, different portions of which we know have been gotten out at different times and places and by different workmen—Stephen, Franklin, Roger and James, for instance—and when we see these timbers joined together, and see they exactly make the frame of a house or a mill, all the tenons and mortices exactly fitting, and all the lengths and proportions of the different pieces exactly adapted to their respective places, and not a piece too many or too few—not omitting even scaffolding—or, if a single piece be lacking, we see the place in the frame exactly fitted and prepared yet to bring such a piece in—in such a case, we find it impossible not to believe that Stephen and Franklin and Roger and James all understood one another from the beginning, and all worked upon a common plan or draft drawn up before the first blow was struck.

It should not be overlooked that, by the Nebraska bill, the people of a State as well as Territory, were to be left "perfectly free," "subject only to the Constitution." Why mention a State? They were legislating for Territories, and not for or about States. Certainly the people of a State are and ought to be subject to the Constitution of the United States; but why is mention of this lugged into this merely Territorial law? Why are the people of a Territory and the people of a State therein lumped together, and their relation to the Constitution therein treated as being precisely the same? While the opinion of the court, by Chief Justice Taney, in the Dred Scott case, and the separate opinions of all the concurring Judges, expressly declare that the Constitution of the United States neither permits Congress nor a Territorial Legislature to exclude slavery from any United States Territory, they all omit to declare whether or not the same Constitution permits a State, or the people of a State, to exclude it. Possibly, this is a mere omission; but who can be quite sure, if McLean or Curtis had sought to get into the opinion a declaration of unlimited power in the people of a State to exclude slavery from their limits, just as Chase and Mace sought to get such declaration, in behalf of the people of a Territory, into the Nebraska bill;—I ask, who can be quite sure that it would not have been voted down in the one case as it had been in the other? The nearest approach to the point of declaring the power of a State over slavery, is made by Judge Nelson. He approaches it more than once, using the precise idea, and almost the language, too, of the Nebraska act. On one occasion, his exact language is, "except in cases where the power is restrained by the Constitution of the United States, the law of the State is supreme over the subject of slavery within its jurisdiction." In what cases the power of the States is so restrained by the United States Constitution, is left an open question, precisely as the same question, as to the restraint on the power of the Territories, was left open in the Nebraska act. Put this and that together, and we have another nice little niche, which we may, ere long, see filled with another Supreme Court decision, declaring that the Constitution of the United States does not permit a State to exclude slavery from its limits. And this may especially be expected if the doctrine of "care not whether slavery be voted down or voted up," shall gain upon the public mind sufficiently to give promise that such a decision can be maintained when made.

Such a decision is all that slavery now lacks of being alike lawful in all the States. Welcome, or unwelcome, such decision is probably coming, and will soon be upon us, unless the power of the present political dynasty shall be met and overthrown. We shall lie down pleasantly dreaming that the people of Missouri are on the verge of making their State free, and we shall awake to the reality instead, that the Supreme Court has made Illinois a slave State. To meet and overthrow the power of that dynasty, is the work now before all those who would prevent that consummation. That is what we have to do. How can we best do it?

There are those who denounce us openly to their own friends, and yet whisper us softly, that Senator Douglas is the aptest instrument there is with which to effect that object. They wish us to infer all, from the fact that he now has a little quarrel with the present head of the dynasty; and that he has regularly voted with us on a single point, upon which he and we have never differed.

They remind us that he is a great man, and that the largest of us are very small ones. Let this be granted. But "a living dog is better than a dead lion." Judge Douglas, if not a dead lion, for this work, is at least a caged and toothless one. How can he oppose the advances of slavery? He don't care anything about it. His avowed mission is impressing the "public heart" to care nothing about it. A leading Douglas democratic newspaper thinks Douglas's superior talent will be needed to resist the revival of the African slave trade. Does Douglas believe an effort to revive that trade is approaching? He has not said so. Does he really think so? But if it is, how can he resist it? For years he has labored to prove it a sacred right of white men to take negro slaves into the new Territories. Can he possibly show that it is less a sacred right to buy them where they can be bought cheapest? And unquestionably they can be bought cheaper in Africa than in Virginia. He has done all in his power to reduce the whole question of slavery to one of a mere right of property; and as such, how can he oppose the foreign slave trade—how can he refuse that trade in that "property" shall be "perfectly free"—unless he does it as a protection to the home production? And as the home producers will probably not ask the protection, he will be wholly without a ground of opposition.

Senator Douglas holds, we know, that a man may rightfully be wiser to-day than he was yesterday—that he may rightfully change when he finds himself wrong. But can we, for that reason, run ahead, and infer that he will make any particular change, of which he, himself, has given no intimation? Can we safely base our action upon any such vague inference? Now, as ever, I wish not to misrepresent Judge Douglas's position, question his motives, or do aught that can be personally offensive to him. Whenever, if ever, he and we can come together on principle so that our cause may have assistance from his great ability, I hope to have interposed no adventitious obstacle. But clearly, he is not now with us—he does not pretend to be—he does not promise ever to be.

Our cause, then, must be intrusted to, and conducted by, its own undoubted friends—those whose hands are free, whose hearts are in the work—who do care for the result. Two years ago the Republicans of the nation mustered over thirteen hundred thousand strong. We did this under the single impulse of resistance to a common danger, with every external circumstance against us. Of strange, discordant, and even hostile elements, we gathered from the four winds, and formed and fought the battle through, under the constant hot fire of a disciplined, proud and pampered enemy. Did we brave all then, to falter now?—now, when that same enemy is wavering, dissevered and belligerent? The result is not doubtful. We shall not fail—if we stand firm, we shall not fail. Wise counsels may accelerate, or mistakes delay it, but, sooner or later, the victory is sure to come.

❧ 15 ❧

The Wade-Davis Manifesto*

(1864)

1. With the Republican Party ready to split into factions right before the election of 1864, how did Lincoln keep the party together?
2. How do different factions within political parties manifest themselves in campaigns and elections today?

THE ELECTION OF 1864 was instrumental in determining whether the Republican Party would remain in the majority or splinter. The Civil War was not going well for the Union, and President Lincoln's Republican coalition was in danger of dissolving. The Republican Party even changed its name to the National Union Party to attract the support of Democrats in the North. Lincoln recognized that to win the nomination and the presidency he would need to build support by appeasing numerous factions both inside and outside of his party.

The Republican Nominating Convention was held in June 1864 in Baltimore, Maryland, and many of the president's critics were eager to replace him with another nominee. At first, Treasury Secretary Salmon P. Chase seemed to benefit from the general dissatisfaction with the president's performance. Samuel C. Pomeroy, a senator from Kansas, had published a circular in February of that year that suggested Chase would be a better candidate than Lincoln; however, it failed to bring Chase the type of attention that would draw supporters to his candidacy, and he soon withdrew from consideration. By June Lincoln had secured pledges from a majority of the delegates and won the nomination on the first ballot. Despite Lincoln's nomination, the "radical" wing of the party nominated John Frémont, but he was later persuaded to withdraw his candidacy for the good of Republican unity in November.

While Lincoln was navigating all of this, he was also busy dealing with the politics of Reconstruction in the South after the Civil War. In Decem-

*Reprinted in Arthur Schlesinger, *History of U.S. Political Parties* (New York: Chelsea House, 1973), 1273–1274.

ber 1863 he issued a Proclamation of Amnesty, and many in Congress were unhappy with the provisions of it. Lincoln offered amnesty for all insurgents who were not senior officers in the Confederacy. He also declared that in order for Southern states to be readmitted, 10 percent of the state's electorate would need to sign an oath of loyalty that recognized the authority of both the Emancipation Proclamation and the Confiscation Acts. Critics argued that the 10 percent threshold was too low and pushed a more stringent alternative. Sen. Benjamin Wade of Ohio and Rep. Henry Winter Davis of Maryland, both from the "radical" wing of the party, proposed the Wade-Davis Act of 1864, which required a majority of citizens in each Southern state to swear a loyalty oath.

Both chambers passed the bill on July 2, 1864. For a number of reasons Lincoln feared that the legislation would damage Reconstruction efforts. First, he feared alienating the minority governments still loyal to the Union that controlled Arkansas, Louisiana, and Tennessee. Second, he worried that reaction to the legislation would jeopardize state-level emancipation movements in Maryland and Missouri. Finally, the president was concerned about the effect it would have on the delicate political alliances that he had constructed between moderates in the North and the South. In the end, the bill never took effect because Lincoln killed it with a pocket veto.

On August 4, 1864, Wade and Davis issued a political manifesto that was published the following day in the press. They alleged that the president's decision was based on his own ambitions. By vetoing the Wade-Davis Act, Lincoln's Amnesty Proclamation of 1863 remained in effect. They believed that the lower threshold for readmission meant that there would be a large number of electoral votes from Southern states under the president's direct influence. Although privately many Republicans may have agreed with the manifesto, public reaction to the attack was not positive. As a result, Lincoln survived the assault, reunited the party, and won a landslide victory over the Democrat's nominee, Gen. George McClellan.

<hr/>

We have read without surprise, but not without indignation, the Proclamation of the President of the 8th of July. . . .

The President, by preventing this bill from becoming a law, holds the electoral votes of the rebel States at the dictation of his personal ambition.

If those votes turn the balance in his favor, is it to be supposed that his competitor, defeated by such means, will acquiesce?

If the rebel majority assert their supremacy in those States, and send votes which elect an enemy of the Government, will we not repel his claims?

And is not that civil war for the Presidency inaugurated by the votes of rebel States?

Seriously impressed with these dangers, Congress, *"the proper constituted authority,"* formally declared that there are no State governments in the rebel States, and provided for their erection at a proper time; and both the Senate and the House of Representatives rejected the Senators and Representatives chosen under the authority of what the President calls the free constitution and government of Arkansas.

The President's proclamation *"holds for naught"* this judgment, and discards the authority of the Supreme Court, and strides headlong toward the anarchy his proclamation of the 8th of December inaugurated.

If electors for President be allowed to be chosen in either of those States, a sinister light will be cast on the motives which induced the President to "hold for naught" the will of Congress rather than his government in Louisiana and Arkansas.

That judgment of Congress which the President defies was the exercise of an authority exclusively vested in Congress by the Constitution to determine what is the established government in a State, and in its own nature and by the highest judicial authority binding on all other departments of the Government. . . .

A more studied outrage on the legislative authority of the people has never been perpetrated.

Congress passed a bill; the President refused to approve it, and then by proclamation puts as much of it in force as he sees fit, and proposes to execute those parts by officers unknown to the laws of the United States and not subject to the confirmation of the Senate!

The bill directed the appointment of Provisional Governors by and with the advice and consent of the Senate.

The President, after defeating the law, proposes to appoint without law, and without the advice and consent of the Senate, *Military* Governors for the rebel States!

He has already exercised this dictatorial usurpation in Louisiana, and he defeated the bill to prevent its limitation. . . .

The President has greatly presumed on the forbearance which the supporters of his Administration have so long practiced, in view of the arduous conflict in which we are engaged, and the reckless ferocity of our political opponents.

The Pomeroy Circular

Sir: The movements recently made throughout the country to secure the renomination of President Lincoln, render necessary some counteraction on the part of those unconditional friends of the Union who differ from the policy of his Administration.

So long as no efforts were made to forestall the political action of the people it was both wise and patriotic for all true friends of the Government to devote their influence to the suppression of the rebellion. But when it becomes evident that party machinery and official influence are being used to secure the perpetuation of the present Administration, those who conscientiously believe that the interests of the country and of freedom demand a change in favor of vigor, and purity, and nationality, have no choice but to appeal at once to the people, before it shall be too late to secure a fair discussion of principles.

Those in behalf of whom this communication is made have thoughtfully surveyed the political field, and have arrived at the following conclusions:

1. That even were the reelection of Mr. Lincoln desirable, it is practically impossible against the union of influences which will oppose him.

2. That should he be reelected his manifest tendency toward compromises and temporary expedients of policy will become stronger during a second term than it has been in the first, and the cause of human liberty and the dignity and honor of the nation suffer proportionately; while the war may continue to languish during his whole Administration, till the public debt shall become a burden too great to be borne.

3. That the patronage of the Government, through the necessities of the war, has been so rapidly increased, and to such an enormous extent, and so loosely placed, as to render the application of the "one-term principle" absolutely essential to the certain safety of our Republican institutions.

4. That we find united in Hon. Salmon P. Chase more of the qualities needed in a President during the next four years than are combined in any other available candidate; his record, clear and unimpeachable, showing him to be a statesman of rare ability, and an administrator of the very highest order, while his private character furnishes the surest obtainable guaranty of economy and purity in the management of public affairs.

5. That the discussion of the Presidential question, already commenced by the friends of Mr. Lincoln, has developed a popularity and strength in Mr. Chase unexpected even to his warmest admirers; and, while we are aware that this strength is at present unorganized and in no condition to manifest its real magnitude, we are satisfied that it only needs systematic and faithful effort to develop it to an extent sufficient to overcome all opposing obstacles.

For these reasons the friends of Mr. Chase have determined on measures which shall present his claims fairly and at once to the country. A central organization has been effected, which already has its connections in all the States, and the object of which is to enable his friends everywhere most effectually to promote his elevation to the Presidency. We wish the hearty cooperation of all those in favor of the speedy restoration of the Union upon the basis of universal freedom, and who desire an administration of the Government, during the first period of its new life, which shall, to the fullest extent, develop the capacity of free institutions, enlarge the resources of the country, diminish the burdens of taxation, elevate the standard of public and private morality, vindicate the honor of the Republic before the world, and in all things make our American nationality the fairest example for imitation which human progress has ever achieved.

If these objects meet your approval, you can render efficient aid by exerting yourself at once to organize your section of the country, and by corresponding with the Chairman of the National Executive Committee, for the purpose either of receiving or imparting information.

Very Respectfully,
    S. C. Pomeroy
    Chairman National Executive Committee

SOURCE: Reprinted in Arthur Schlesinger, *History of U.S. Political Parties*, vol. II (New York: Chelsea House, 1973).

But he must understand that our support is of a cause and not of a man; that the authority of Congress is paramount and must be respected; that the whole body of the Union men of Congress will not submit to be impeached by him of rash and unconstitutional legislation; and if he wishes our support, he must confine himself to his executive duties—to obey and execute, not make the laws—to suppress by arms armed rebellion, and leave political reorganization to Congress.

If the supporters of the Government fail to insist on this, they become responsible for the usurpations which they fail to rebuke, and are justly liable to the indignation of the people whose rights and security, committed to their keeping, they sacrifice.

Let them consider the remedy for these usurpations, and, having found it, fearlessly execute it.

Thomas Nast's Cartoons of William "Boss" Tweed*

(1871)

1. Nast's cartoons publicized the corruption of Boss Tweed and Tammany Hall. How does the press today expose political corruption?
2. What role do political cartoons play in campaigns and elections?

EDITORIAL CARTOONIST Thomas Nast drew for *Harper's Weekly* from 1859 until 1886. His rise to national fame came in the early 1870s when his political cartoons were instrumental in arousing public indignation toward the corruption rampant in the New York City political machine led by William M. Tweed. Collectively, Nast's attacks upon Tweed and his cronies are widely considered among the most effective political cartoons in history.

Tweed was the head of Tammany Hall, a Democratic Party political machine established as a social club in the 1780s. By the time Tweed ascended to leadership of the organization, it was the recognized Democratic political machine of New York. Tweed, however, was so influential within Tammany Hall that he became the first recognized "boss" of a political organization in the United States.

If the purpose of a political machine is the perpetuation and precision of the political organization itself, then it is up to the leadership to "lubricate" the machine. To do so, Boss Tweed and his inner circle, known as the "Tweed Ring," engaged in graft. Through their influence over the outcome of elections and the appointment of other public officials, Boss Tweed and his cronies were in a position to award city contracts to the supporters of the Tweed Ring in return for kickbacks to Tammany Hall. Their influence over other public officials also allowed them to avoid disclosure of the machine's fraudulent activities.

*Reprinted in J. Chal Vinson, *Thomas Nast: Political Cartoonist* (Athens: University of Georgia Press, 1967), and Thomas Nast St. Hill, *Thomas Nast: Cartoons and Illustrations* (New York: Dover Publications, 1974).

Who Stole the People's Money? August 19, 1871. The Tweed Ring points the finger of suspicion at the next guy.

The Tammany Tiger Loose—"What Are You Going to Do About It?" November 11, 1871. This political cartoon was published on the eve of the 1871 municipal elections, in which candidates from Tammany Hall were beaten decisively. It is considered one of the most powerful political cartoons of all time.

Boss Tweed was the polar opposite of Thomas Nast in many ways. First, Tweed and Tammany Hall drew most of their popular support from Irish immigrants and Catholics. As a Protestant, Nast's strong nativist and anti-Catholic beliefs often led him to portray immigrants and leaders of the Catholic Church negatively. Second, Nast was an ideological Republican and was horrified that any political party's primary goal would be to perpetuate a political machine. Finally, Nast had a serious distaste for the style of politics practiced by Boss Tweed and the Tweed Ring.

Tweed tried repeatedly to get Nast to stop drawing. He is reported to have said, "I don't care a straw for your newspaper articles, my constituents don't know how to read, but they can't help seeing them damned pictures." His initial attempt to bribe Nast failed: Tweed sent a representative to inform Nast that a group of citizens so admired his work that they wanted to provide $100,000 for him to study art in Europe. When Nast refused, the figure was eventually raised to $500,000. At that point Nast ended the conversation by stating that he preferred to see Tweed and the Tweed Ring in jail first. Nast was so fearful of retaliation from Tweed's machine that he relocated his family from Manhattan to New Jersey. Tweed did later attempt to intimidate Nast's publisher, *Harper's Weekly,* by threatening to cancel New York City's book order. The plan almost worked, but in the end *Harper* chose to support Nast.

Nast escalated his attack on Boss Tweed and the Tweed Ring in anticipation of the municipal elections in November 1871. Tammany lost decisively in the elections, and Tweed was arrested shortly thereafter. He was convicted of forgery and larceny, for which he was sentenced to twelve years in prison. He soon fled to Spain and, ironically, Spanish authorities identified him with the aid of one of Thomas Nast's cartoons. He was extradited to the United States and jailed in New York until his death in 1878.

❧ 17 ❧

Abram Hewitt's "Secret History of the Disputed Election, 1876–77"*

(1878)

1. How was the Republican strategy of contesting the 1876 election successful?
2. Elected presidents often claim a mandate from the voters. Can a president who lost the popular vote claim such a mandate? If so, how?

THE 1876 PRESIDENTIAL ELECTION was among the closest in U.S. history. Of the more than 8.3 million votes cast, 51 percent were cast for Democrat Samuel Tilden, the governor of New York, and almost 48 percent went to Republican Rutherford B. Hayes, the governor of Ohio. The election was also one of the nation's most disputed. Tilden won the popular vote, but eventually Hayes won the Electoral College by a vote of 185 to 184.

The election was accompanied by a number of irregularities: First, the electoral votes of Florida, Louisiana, and South Carolina were disputed. The day after the election it appeared Tilden had won the nineteen electoral votes of these states, but the Republicans also reported that their candidate had won them. As a result, Congress received electoral ballots for each of these states from Democrats and Republicans. The second irregularity was discovered by Lafayette Grover, the Democratic governor of Oregon, who found that a Republican elector from his state was also a U.S. postmaster (by law, federal officials cannot serve as electors). Grover appointed a Democrat to replace him, and again two sets of electoral votes were submitted to Congress. Another important issue, although not necessarily irregular, was Colorado's admittance to the Union on August 1, 1876. Without sufficient time to organize a presidential election the state legislature simply appointed three electors (who voted for Hayes).

*Reprinted in Arthur Schlesinger, *History of U.S. Political Parties* (New York: Chelsea House, 1973), 958–966.

To determine which ballots were valid, Congress created a special electoral commission made up of five members of the House of Representatives, five senators, and four Supreme Court justices. One additional justice was chosen by the four selected by Congress. On every vote the commission sided with Hayes, voting 8–7 along party lines, and Southern Democrats intended to employ a filibuster to block the commission from reporting to the Senate. Ultimately, however, the Republicans compromised with the Southern Democrats on Reconstruction.

The Southern Democrats allowed Hayes to be inaugurated if, in return, the Republicans: (1) removed federal troops from the former Confederate states, (2) appointed at least one Southern Democrat to Hayes's cabinet, (3) funded the construction of a transcontinental railroad through the South, and (4) passed legislation to promote Southern industrialization. Hayes complied with ending Reconstruction, but never made a serious effort to provide federal assistance to construct a new railroad or industrialize the South.

The withdrawal of federal troops from the South effectively ended Reconstruction. African Americans lost political power as a result of troop withdrawal and soon were barred from voting by the passage of grandfather clauses, literacy tests, and poll taxes. Conversely, the Democratic Party regained political power and controlled the "Solid South" until the Civil Rights era of the 1960s.

At the time of the 1876 presidential election, Democrat Abram S. Hewitt was a member of the House of Representatives from New York and chair of the Democratic National Committee. Prominent in the reorganization of Democratic Party politics in New York City after the fall of Boss Tweed and Tammany Hall, he played a pivotal role in organizing the party's efforts to contest the results reported by Republicans in Florida, Louisiana, Oregon, and South Carolina. The "Secret History of the Disputed Election, 1876–77" was first written in 1878; Hewitt significantly revised it in 1895.

The struggle resulted in the triumphant election of Mr. Tilden, not merely by a majority of all votes cast, but by a majority of all the states in the Union. It was not until two days after the election that any doubt was expressed as to the result. The country, however, was then astounded by the claim of the Republican

National Committee that Hayes had secured 185 electoral votes and would therefore be declared President by a majority of one vote. As soon as this claim was made, based upon the votes of South Carolina, Florida, and Louisiana, I caused letters to be sent to the leading men of the North—Democrats and Republicans alike—inviting them to proceed to South Carolina, Florida, and Louisiana for the purpose of seeing that a fair count was made and the returns honestly canvassed. The next day President Grant, who was in Philadelphia, issued a similar request to leading Republicans only, and thus it happened that two sets of "visiting statesmen" repaired to the several states in doubt, one selected by General Grant acting as partisans and the other selected by me for their standing and character without reference to their political affiliation.

The result is known to all men. The returning boards of the several states referred to gave the votes of these states to Hayes, although it was then known and is now universally admitted that the states of Florida and Louisiana were carried for Tilden. In this emergency the state of Oregon seemed to offer an antidote to the fraud thus perpetrated. Oregon had been carried by the Republicans, but one of the electors was disqualified from acting by a Constitutional provision forbidding Federal office holders to act as electors. One of the Republican electors was a postmaster, and hence the Governor, who was a Democrat, refused his certificate and gave it to the highest candidate on the Democratic ticket. Thus one vote was secured for Tilden giving him 185 votes against 184 votes for Hayes, including all the votes from the three Southern states fraudulently secured through corrupt returning boards. . . .

Congress met upon the first Monday in December. It was felt by Democrats and Republicans alike to be necessary to make provision for counting the electoral votes for President and Vice-President. . . .

The question of counting the votes was therefore relegated to the provision of the Constitution that "The President of the Senate shall in the presence of the Senate and the House of Representatives open all the certificates, and the votes shall then be counted."

In view of the claim made by leading Republicans that the President of the Senate under this clause was invested with the authority not only to open the certificates but to count the votes, it was evident that there would be a conflict of authority between the Senate and the House unless some mode of procedure as to the counting of the votes and the declaration of the result should be reached by the two Houses in advance of the date prescribed by the Constitution for the opening of the certificates and the counting of the votes.

Hence, after much consultation and the consideration of the question by a joint caucus of the Democratic members of the Senate and House, the House of Representatives on the 14th December, 1876, appointed a committee of seven to act in conjunction with any similar committee of the Senate

To prepare and report without delay a measure for the removal of difference of opinion as to the proper mode of counting the electoral votes for President and Vice-President which might arise as to the legality and validity of the returns of such votes made by the several states *to the end that the votes should be counted and the result declared by a tribunal whose authority none can question and whose decision all will accept.* . . .

On the 18th of December the Senate resolved to create a special committee of seven Senators "with power to prepare and report without unnecessary delay such a measure either of a legislative or other character as may in their judgment be best calculated to accomplish the counting of the Electoral votes and best disposition of all questions connected therewith and the true declaration of the result." And this committee was instructed to confer and act with the committee of the House of Representatives. . . .

. . . The discussion was long, patient, and thorough; upon one point all the members of the Joint Committee seemed to be agreed and that was that a commission should be appointed which should and would be invested with power to go behind the returns so as to arrive at the true result of the election in the disputed states. . . .

The Joint Committee adjourned without final action, in order to enable the two committees to consider the position in which after the consultation they found themselves to be placed. A resolution, however, was adopted imposing secrecy upon the members of the committees as to the nature of the bill and the discussions which had taken place.

This obligation of secrecy led me to consult with the Democratic members of the House committee as to whether it applied to Mr. Tilden. It was unanimously concluded that we had a superior duty both to the Democratic Party and to him, who was its leader and its elected candidate for President, and that he should be consulted and his approval secured before the House Committee would commit itself to any action whatever. . . .

To this telegram I received from Mr. Tilden through Mr. Cooper the following answer—

New York. January 16th. Be firm and cool, Four Judge Plan will not do perhaps worse than Six—complaints likely to arise of haste and want of consultation with members and embarrassment in exercise of their judgment after plan is disclosed by premature committal of their representatives. There should be more opportunity for deliberation and consultation. Secrecy dangerous, probably a mistake in itself, and if it results in disaster would involve great blame and infinite mischief.

This telegram was the last one which I received from Mr. Tilden through Mr. Cooper or otherwise. It did not reach me until after the Advisory Committee of leading Democrats meeting in the Speakers' room on the evening of Tuesday, January 16th, had approved of the Four Judge Plan which Mr. Tilden thus disapproved. This disapproval gave me great concern and led me to decide at all hazards to get such a modification of the plan as would secure the substance of the Five Judge Plan, which I had originally suggested to Mr. Tilden, and which he had never disapproved either verbally or in any telegram sent to me. On the morning of the 17th of January, therefore, I recommended to the House committee to reject the original Four Senior Justice Plan—Clifford, Swayne, Davis, and Miller—which had been approved at the consultation in the Speakers' room the night before, and to insist upon the plan finally adopted, by which Clifford and Field, Miller and Strong, two Democrats and two Republicans, were named by their districts with the power to choose the fifth judge—it being generally conceded that Davis must be selected, thus securing the original Five Judge Plan except that Strong was substituted for Swayne, to whom Mr. Tilden had expressed to me some personal objection. This suggestion met with the approval of the Democrats on the House committee and was particularly acceptable to the especial friends of Mr. Tilden who were on the spot, as being far more favorable to Mr. Tilden's interests than the Four Judge Plan.

It was accordingly proposed to the Senate committee as an ultimatum, and after some hours of discussion it was adopted on the 17th January against the vigorous opposition and protesting vote of Senator Morton, who said to me that it was equivalent to the abandonment of the contest on the Republican side. . . .

The general feeling, however, was that the victory was won, because no one doubted for a moment that Judge Davis would be selected as the fifth member of the commission.

The report was made both to the Senate and the House at the regular session on the 18th January, and the debate thereon continued for several days in the Senate, where it was adopted on the 25th January by a vote of 47 yeas to 17 nays, the Republicans voting 24 yeas to 16 nays, and the Democrats voting 23 yeas to 1 nay. Absent who were not voting, 9 Republicans and 1 Democrat. . . .

An analysis of the vote proves that the Bill was regarded as a Democratic measure and that a large majority of the Republicans in Congress were opposed to its passage.

I thought at the time, and I still think, that the division of parties on this measure was largely controlled by the conviction that Judge Davis would have the casting vote, and that he could be relied upon to see that the will of the people as expressed in the election of Mr. Tilden should not be thwarted.

The surprise and disappointment, therefore, of the Democrats may be imagined when immediately after the passage of the bill the Democratic members of the legislature of the state of Illinois, reinforced by 7 Republican votes, at once elected Judge Davis to the Senate of the United States without consultation with the National Democratic Committee.

This surprise and disappointment was intensified by the immediate refusal of Judge Davis to be a nominee for the vacant position on the Commission, although his election as Senator in no respect disqualified him for the performance of the duty which he was expected to discharge.

Whether rightly or wrongly, the conviction was general that a bargain had been made by the Republicans by which Judge Davis in consideration of his being made Senator should decline a position upon the Electoral Commission. Certainly if such an arrangement were made it was the last move by which in the long game which had been played between the two parties the final triumph was probably assured to the Republican Party. I can only say that Senator Morton, who had regarded the game as lost, showed as much surprise at this achievement as I felt and could not restrain the expression of his satisfaction.

It now remained to arrange for the choice of the fifth judge, which was limited to Hunt and Bradley because, as stated above, Mr. Tilden advised against the selection of Swayne. . . .

Practically, therefore, the choice was limited to Justice Bradley, whom I had personally known for many years in New Jersey as a very able lawyer and a man of the highest integrity. The confidence which I felt in him was shared by Mr. Tilden, but in order to make assurance doubly sure I requested a mutual friend of Judge Bradley and myself, the late John G. Stevens, of Trenton, N.J., to confer with Judge Bradley and to ascertain whether he felt that he could decide the questions which would come before the commission without prejudice or party feeling. The report of Mr. Stevens was entirely satisfactory. Judge Bradley was therefore selected with the distinct approval of the Democratic representatives, reinforced by the favorable judgment of Judge Clifford and Judge Field, who assured me that absolute reliance could be placed upon the judicial fairness of Judge Bradley. In fact they both stated that it was absurd to fear that any Justice of the Supreme Court would be governed by the partisan feeling or influence, and this was in accordance with the general feeling in Congress and throughout the country.

The other members of the commission under the provisions of the Act consisted of three Republicans and two Democrats from the Senate and three Democrats and two Republicans from the House. The commission, therefore, was composed so far as political preference was concerned of eight Republicans and seven Democrats, practically giving the casting vote to Judge Bradley, in whose freedom from partisan influence absolute confidence was reposed. . . .

This illusion was, however, rudely dispelled when Judge Bradley pronounced his decision in the Florida case by which the vote of this state was unjustly counted for Hayes. The history of this opinion forms an important feature in the final outcome of the electoral count. As stated above, Mr. Stevens was the intimate friend of Judge Bradley. He passed the night previous to the rendition of the judgment in the Florida case at my house. About midnight he returned from a visit to Judge Bradley and reported to General Richard Taylor, who was also staying with me, and to Senator Gibson who was awaiting his return, that he had just left Judge Bradley after reading his opinion in favor of counting the vote of the Democratic electors of the state of Florida. Such a judgment insured the election of Tilden to the Presidency with three votes to spare above the necessary majority. We parted, therefore, with the assurance that all further doubt as to the Presidency was at rest. I attended the delivery of the judgment the next day without the slightest intimation from any quarter that Judge Bradley had changed his mind. In fact, the reading of the opinion, until the concluding paragraphs were reached, was strictly in accordance with the report of Mr. Stevens. The change was made between midnight and sunrise. Mr. Stevens afterward informed me that it was due to a visit to Judge Bradley by Senator Frelinghuysen and Secretary Robeson, made after his departure. Their appeals to Judge Bradley were said to have been reinforced by the persuasion of Mrs. Bradley. Whatever the fact may have been, Judge Bradley himself in a subsequent letter addressed to the Newark *Daily Advertiser* admitted that he had written a favorable opinion which on subsequent reflection he saw fit to modify. . . .

The votes of Louisiana were thus counted for Hayes, and those of South Carolina were also, under the decision of the commission, counted for him and probably justly so in view of the facts afterward developed by the inquiries of the Thompson Committee.

Previously, however, to the South Carolina decision the returns from the state of Oregon had, by the failure of the two Houses to agree, been referred to the commission. No doubt was entertained that the rule in the Florida case required the counting of one vote for Tilden. The commission, however, did not hesitate, but by the invariable vote of eight to seven reversed the precedents created by the commission in the Florida case and counted the three votes of Oregon for Hayes, on the ground that Oregon had undoubtedly given a majority for the Republican ticket. In the Florida case they had refused to go behind the returns and thus gave the four votes of that state to Hayes. In the Oregon case they decided to go behind the returns and thus also gave the three votes of that state to the Republican candidate. This secured the election of Hayes by one majority, and the greatest fraud in the history of the country was thus practically consummated.

18

John McPherson's Speech
Opposing the Pendleton Act*
(1882)

1. What was the effect of the civil service system on political parties? Were parties stronger under a patronage system?
2. Assuming that public accountability is an important value, does a patronage-based bureaucracy or a merit-based bureaucracy best serve the public?

THE SYSTEM THAT evolved for selecting officials to fill positions in the federal bureaucracy in the early nineteenth century was referred to as patronage. Such appointments typically meant that selection to public office was based on personal commitment to president and party and not on professional qualifications or whether an individual already held the position and was qualified to continue doing so. As early as the Washington, Adams, and Jefferson administrations, the winning presidential candidate was hounded by office-seekers hungry for political appointment, often in recognition of support during the campaign. In an effort to quell such actions, Jefferson issued an executive order in 1801 intended to prevent federal employees from participating in electioneering activities.

Many presidents found patronage frustrating, but Andrew Jackson viewed rotation in office as "democratic." In a speech in 1832 New York senator William L. Marcy said of a political appointment by Jackson, "They [Democrats] see nothing wrong in the rule *that to the victor belong the spoils* of the enemy."

The constant turnover created by patronage left the government with little institutional memory and public officials anxious every fourth year because their tenure might end after the election. The situation grew

Congressional Record, 47th Congress, 2nd Sess., December 15, 1882 (Washington, D.C.: Government Printing Office, 1882), 323.

worse as the number of persons on the federal payroll increased and as new government jobs began to require special skills. The notion of a merit-based civil service started gaining public support in the late 1870s, but politicians refused to act until after the assassination of President James Garfield by Charles Guiteau in 1881. Guiteau had reportedly made repeated personal requests to Garfield and Secretary of State James G. Blaine to be appointed as an ambassador and was disappointed at not receiving such a position.

On January 16, 1883, Congress passed the Pendleton Civil Service Reform Act, which established the United States Civil Service Commission. The bipartisan commission was charged with evaluating job candidates using nonpartisan, merit-based criteria. The act, sponsored by Ohio Democrat Sen. George H. Pendleton, was written by Dorman Bridgeman Eaton, an opponent of patronage appointments who became the Civil Service Commission's first chair.

The act effectively marked the end of the patronage system of political appointment. As the White House changed hands from one party to another in the late nineteenth century, outgoing presidents applied the Pendleton Act and transferred those who had supported them into the civil service system. By the turn of the century, most federal employees were classified as civil servants, and patronage was limited to the most senior positions. Thus, a competent, permanent government bureaucracy was created, and the partisan link between the executive and the federal bureaucracy was significantly weakened. It took many years for similar reforms to take hold at the state level. Machine politicians were reluctant to give up their partisan influence over public servants and public policy.

⚜

We have proposed a reform, as it is called, in the civil service. What kind of a reform? Only a method of determining among the applicants for office, who are numbered by thousands and tens of thousands, which one of them is best adapted to take a place where no man should be employed at all. That is what we propose to give to the people in place of the reform which they demand; only a mode by which it may be determined who is the best fitted to fill such a place. So far as that goes I have no objection to it. I have no objection to any reasonable way of determining the fitness of applicants, but I do submit this: Has not the President of the United States all the powers to determine for himself before he makes an appointment to any position of trust or responsibility in this Government as to the qualifications of the particular individual named for it? Why appoint under legislative sanction and authority a commission and send the bill to the President himself for his sanction by which he shall consent to abdicate the powers placed in his hands and for which he is held responsible?

I wish to have it distinctly understood that, so far as I am concerned, I believe in party government; I believe in holding political parties responsible for the management and the administration of the affairs of the Government when intrusted to them. No great reform was ever made in the Government except through one of the great political parties of the country. I do not say this because I wish to delay or prevent any reasonable or proper mode of managing the Government being adopted; but I say it for quite a different reason. I do not know that this bill is in all respects objectionable; yet in some respects it is, to my mind, very objectionable—not objectionable because it will keep Democrats out of office and Republicans in. I am ready at all times to vote for any proper reform in government, whichever political party may be in power. I believe that the iron rule of party despotism today controls too much, both the parties and the people of this country; and I should like to see it thrown down. I should like to see the time come when the rule of either political party will be the rule of patriots; but I can not consent by any vote of mine that a legislative commission shall be appointed, irresponsible to the people, irresponsible in themselves, responsible to no power whatever, and give them all the authority necessary to determine what shall be done in respect to certain offices in this Government.

19

Woodrow Wilson's "Wanted—A Party"*

(1886)

1. What reasons did Wilson provide for suggesting that political parties were in a state of disintegration?
2. What did Wilson suggest parties do to become stronger?

WOODROW WILSON'S path to the presidency was very different than that of his contemporaries. Instead of working his way up the political ladder, he earned a doctorate from Johns Hopkins University and became a professor of government at Princeton University, where he went on to become president of the institution. It was not long after, however, that Wilson entered politics. In 1910 he was elected governor of New Jersey. In 1912, after a deadlocked presidential nominating convention, the Democrats turned to him to take the nomination because he had the support of former presidential nominee William Jennings Bryan.

Early in his career, Wilson was highly critical of the U.S. political system in his academic writings. In his first book, *Congressional Government,* published in 1885, he claimed that political parties failed to provide voters with clear policy alternatives: if the purpose of elections was to determine which direction national policy should take, then political parties needed to offer platforms that charted different courses. Wilson's criticism was rooted in his belief that the separation of powers between the executive branch and the legislature made it difficult for the public to determine which officials to hold accountable. He felt that stronger political parties, like those found in nations with parliamentary systems, could align the interests of the executive and the legislature. If the competing political parties offered clearly different policy directions

*Woodrow Wilson, Wanted—A Party, September 1, 1886, Papers of Woodrow Wilson. Reprinted in Ronald J. Pestritto's *Woodrow Wilson: The Essential Political Writings* (Lanham, Md.: Rowman & Littlefield, 2005).

and the party in power acted upon the agenda endorsed by the public, then voters could hold policymakers accountable in the next election. Wilson thought this could be accomplished if the party machinery allowed stronger leaders to emerge in Congress. Then principled debates over public policy could be carefully scrutinized by the public.

Wilson remained cynical about the future of political parties. While he hoped that parties could be organized along ideological instead of geographical lines, he wrote that political parties remained in decline because, "No leaders, no principles; no principles, no parties." By the time his last scholarly work—*Constitutional Government in the United States* was published in 1908—Wilson had given up on political parties bridging the gap created by the separation of powers. He argued instead that a president should lead a party much like a prime minister led a parliament. In fact, he argued that the presidency would be "as big as and as influential as the man who occupies it."

<hr>

A man must nowadays either belong to a party through mere force of habit or else be puzzled to know what party he belongs to. Party platforms furnish no sort of chart by which he can shape his political course. Unless they are carefully labelled, [h]e cannot tell which party speaks through them, for they all say much the same thing. If voters chose their party instead of happening into it, they would probably choose by the aid of two questions, namely, first, "What policy do we favor?" and, second, "Which party advocates that policy?" Perhaps it is fortunate, therefore, that so many drift to the ballot-box and so few choose; for, otherwise, multitudes would lose their votes before answering the second of these questions. They would practically disfranchise themselves if they waited to answer it. The professions of existing parties do not furnish any satisfactory reply to it; still less do their actions. Does any one favor civil service reform? The present act establishing competitive examinations and a commission was proposed by a democratic senator to a republican senate, was passed by that body and a democratic house, and signed by a republican president. The senator who proposed it was afterward cast aside by his constituency because of his reform sentiments. His measure is now administered, with full sympathy for its purposes, by a democratic president elected because of his record on this question; but it is covertly attacked in a democratic house, and openly sneered at in a republican senate; and the democratic chairman of the house committee on civil service reform fails of a renomination in North Carolina because of his fine reform work on that committee. Which party, then, advocates civil service reform?

Or turn to the question of federal aid to education in the states. Does some voter favor such aid? It was proposed in the senate by a republican, fathered in the house by a democrat, carried in the senate by a complex mixture of republican and democratic votes, and smothered in the house by no one knows whom. Is it the democrats or the republicans that would have national aid to education in the states?

Or, again, is it the tariff that is crucial? Does some new manufacturer in the South want the import duties kept up? Let him examine the record of proceedings in congress. Democratic revenue reformers are kept from even so much as introducing a bill by the opposition of democratic protectionists, and republicans assist both sides. Is the protectionist voter to be a democrat or a republican?

Is the silver question to be made a test? Each party is on both sides. Or labor problems? Which party is on any side with regard to that, except the side of profession which will catch the laborer's vote?

But why extend the perplexing recital? It is sadly confounding to think about so much confusion. And, be it observed, I am not speaking of these things in ridicule of our national parties, or in disgust with our national politics, nor yet in despair of our national institutions. I am simply gathering facts to serve as food for reflection, and in order to state what my own reflections upon them have been. My chief reflection has been, not that our national parties are in a state of disintegration; that is not a reflection. It is a mere patent fact. But that such a course of things is tending, so to say, to *individualize* our politics is a reflection, and one which seems worth exploring somewhat at large.

First, let me explain what I mean by the individualizing of our politics. I mean simply that the voter who exercises any choice at all, is being obliged to choose *men,* particular individuals, to tie to, instead of parties. Of course the conscientious voter always chose between men, between candidates, in voting; both formerly he could choose them as representing parties. Now he must choose them instead of parties. The feeling is: "No party means what it says; some men do seem to mean what they say; we will tie to them when we can." The last presidential election of course furnishes the most striking illustration of the operation of this feeling. The mugwump is the man who has cast loose from parties, which don't mean what they say, and offers to follow men who do speak with a purpose. Mr. Cleveland is a democrat. But he was not elected because he was a democrat, but because the civil service of the country needed re-forming, and he evidently meant to reform it, if given a chance. A man of that sort in the presidential chair would be worth any number of party platforms; a great number of discriminating voters accordingly followed him in preference to any party,—"irrespective of party," to use the orthodox phrase.

Mr. Cleveland's case was only a conspicuous one, however; it was not iso-lated. There is a yearly increasing number of mayors, governors, and congress-men holding their offices because of personal qualities or opinions pleasing to constituencies who do not stop to ask, in choosing them, whether the parties they formally represent possess like qualities or opinions.

Various reasons, historical and others, might be offered to explain this in-teresting but necessarily transitional state of affairs; as, for instance, that the republican party has outlived the purposes for which it was organized, and that the democratic party has ceased to be opposed to it in most matters, except in a Pickwickian sense. The republican party rendered the country some ines-timable services, and the country, in natural gratitude, pensioned it with a quarter of a century of power. Meantime, the democratic party kicked its heels with what philosophy it could command on the cold outside of the offices, comforting itself with dignified repetitions of certain old and important con-stitutional principles which had all of a sudden apparently lost their old power as charms to conjure with. But the republican pension has run out now. It could not reasonably be claimed for a second generation. The pensioners, too, got intolerable as they grew old. We, accordingly, have a president who is a democrat in favor of civil service reform, and a congress which is nothing in particular and in favor of nothing unanimously, save large expenditures of money. The old parties, to put it in the vernacular, have "played out," and we are choosing here a man and there a man who means what he says, while wait-ing for a party which shall mean what *it* says.

The new parties which are hoped for in the future do not form readily or quickly for the same reason that the old parties have not adapted themselves to changed circumstances. Our system of government has supplied no official place, no place of actual authority, for leaders of parties. A party, conse-quently, must be a merely fortuitous concourse of atoms; and we must wait on the atoms. Even after it is formed, any party of ours must keep together rather by grace and enthusiasm than by vital organization. There is no ruling station in the government for its leaders. It must follow them rather for what they eloquently profess than for anything that they can actually do. The most leader-like post in politics is the speakership of the house of representatives, which is the most unsuitable place possible for a party captain. If we did not have a natural talent for forming parties, and it were not the fashion in all popular governments to have parties, it is to be seriously doubted whether we would not approximate that "natural society," of which some philosophers and some anarchists have dreamed, in which everybody would act for himself and nobody act, expect accidentally, or through chance amiability, in concert with his neighbors.

There is, however, another and a better reason why we always have parties, and that is, that we have a splendid habit of all believing in certain great principles of human liberty and self-government, without being tamely all of one mind about the way in which those principles ought to be applied in particular cases. No time was ever bigger than this with unsolved problems as to the best ways in which to make liberty real and government helpful. Labor questions, financial questions, administrative questions must all tax the best thought of the country from this time on, until some clear purpose of reform, of financial reconstruction, or of governmental betterment is conceived by some group of men who mean what they say, who all mean the same thing, and who know how to say it, begin to speak their purpose, so that the nation will wake as at a new voice—a voice which calls with authority to duty and to action. Then a new party will be formed—and another party opposed to it. All that is wanting is a new, genuine and really meant purpose held by a few strong men of principle and boldness. That is a big "all," and it is still conspicuously wanting.

But the generations that really loved the old and now disintegrated parties is fast passing away. It is largely the new generation that wonders that any one ever doubted that the war was over—even sometimes wonders what the war was all about—that is compelling a clearing away of the worn-out formulas of the old dispensation and a hastening of something not stated to determine their politics. With the growth of this new generation we shall unquestionably witness the growth of new parties.

20

The Massachusetts Australian Ballot Law*
(1888)

1. How did the use of party "tickets" strengthen the control of political parties over campaigns and elections?
2. How did the Australian-style ballot weaken party influence in campaigns and elections?

IN THE NINETEENTH century political parties printed "tickets" that listed all of the candidates endorsed by a party for each office in an election. Since the government did not print ballots for elections, voters were responsible for printing their choices by hand on paper. Political parties, however, encouraged voters to use their tickets as ballots. Voters could split their tickets by crossing off the name of a party's nominee and writing in the name of a preferred candidate; however, the parties pushed them to simply vote a straight party ticket.

This use of party tickets made secrecy in voting virtually impossible. Parties typically printed tickets on a distinctive paper to make it easy for observers at the polls to recognize the ballot used by each voter. It was even more difficult in those parts of the country where ballot boxes were made of glass, which did prevent "stuffing" the box, but also made it virtually impossible for voters to hide the color of the ballots they deposited. The bosses of political machines bought votes confidently, knowing their subordinates would observe the balloting. In fact, ballot fraud developed a vocabulary of its own: "repeaters" were those who voted early and often by changing their appearance each time they voted; "colonizers" were groups of voters paid to move from one voting precinct to another to secure an election that was in doubt; and "floaters" were those who moved between parties in each election and cast their ballots in favor of the highest bidder. Such buying and selling votes was facilitated by a lack of voter registration laws in many states.

*Reprinted in John Wigmore, *The Australian Ballot System as Embodied in the Legislation of Various Countries* (Boston: Charles C. Soule, 1889).

One example of the rampant voter fraud taking place occurred in 1888, when the treasurer of the Republican National Committee, William W. Dudley, wrote a circular that instructed the Indiana G.O.P. to: "Divide the floaters into blocks of five and put a trusted man with necessary funds in charge of these five and make him responsible that none get away and that all vote our ticket." Even though the circular was intercepted and leaked to the press near the end of the campaign, the purchase of votes continued. Ballot reform became a major issue after this election after Republican Benjamin Harrison won the Electoral College 233 to 168 over incumbent Grover Cleveland although Cleveland actually won the popular vote by approximately 100,000 votes.

Other democracies also faced apprehension over ballot fraud in the nineteenth century. To combat concerns in Victoria, Australia, the government there approved an innovative type of ballot in 1858 that has since come to be known, unsurprisingly, as the Australian ballot. These ballots are: (1) printed by the government, (2) distributed only at polling places, (3) printed with the names all candidates for office—regardless of party affiliation, and (4) marked by voters in secret. The benefits of the ballot were not immediately obvious when introduced because the system requires the government to absorb the expenses of printing, transporting, and securing the ballots—and spending money is seldom seen by a government as a policy benefit. Today, however, the practice is firmly entrenched in democracies throughout the world.

Ballot reform initiatives swept through the United States after the election of 1888. The changes were inspired by the election results and by an article published in 1883 by economist Henry George in the *North American Review*. George argued that money gave those who donated it special privileges. Since the money was used to print party tickets, it unfairly gave party organizations power over candidates, who were assessed the cost of the tickets, and over voters, who were paid to vote the ticket. If the government printed ballots and voters cast those ballots in secret, the power of political parties to influence elections would be severely weakened.

The first law based on the Australian ballot was adopted by the city of Louisville, Kentucky, in 1888 (the rest of the state used voice voting until 1891). Massachusetts was the first state to adopt the Australian ballot. By the next presidential election in 1892, a number of other states had adopted the Australian ballot, and Grover Cleveland was returned to the Oval Office.

An Act to Provide for Printing and Dist. Ballots at the Public Expense, and to Regulate Voting at State and City Elections.

Be it enacted, etc., as follows:

SECTION 1. All ballots cast in elections for national, state, district, and county officers in cities and towns after the first day of November in the year eighteen hundred and eighty-nine, and all ballots cast in municipal elections in cities after that date, shall be printed and distributed at public expense, as hereinafter provided. The printing of the ballots and cards of instructions to voters shall in municipal elections in cities be paid for by the several cities respectively, and in all other elections the printing of the ballots and cards of instruction, and the delivery of them to the several cities and towns, shall be paid for by the Commonwealth. The distribution of the ballots to the voters shall be paid for by the cities and towns respectively. The term "state election," as used in this act, shall apply to any election held for the choice of a national, state, district, or county officer, whether for a full term or for the filling of a vacancy, and the term "state officer" shall apply to any person to be chosen by the qualified voters at such an election. The term "city election" shall apply to any municipal election so held in a city, and the term "city officer" shall apply to any person to be chosen by the qualified voters at such an election.

Nominations of Candidates.

SECT. 2. Any convention of delegates, and any caucus or meeting of qualified voters, as hereinafter defined, and individual voters to the number and in the manner hereinafter specified, may nominate candidates for public office, whose names shall be placed upon the ballots to be furnished as herein provided.

SECT. 3. Any convention of delegates representing a political party which, at the election next preceding, polled at least three per cent of the entire vote cast in the state, or in the electoral district or division thereof for which the nomination is made, or any convention of delegates who have been selected in caucuses called and held in accordance with a special statute providing therefor, and any caucus so called and held in any such electoral district or division, may for the state or for the district or division for which the convention or caucus is held, as the case may be, by causing a certificate of nomination to be duly filed, make one such nomination for each office therein to be filled at the election. . . .

SECT. 5. All certificates of nomination and nomination papers shall, besides containing the names of candidates, specify as to each, (1) the office for which he is nominated; (2) the party or political principle which he represents, expressed in not more than three words; (3) his place of residence, with street and number thereon, if any. In the case of electors of president and vice-president of the United States, the names of the candidates for president and vice-president may be added to the party or political appellation.

SECT. 6. Certificates of nomination and nomination papers for the nomination of candidates for state offices shall be filed with the secretary of the Commonwealth at least fourteen days previous to the day of the election for which the candidates are nominated. Such certificates and papers for the nomination of candidates for the offices of mayor and of aldermen in cities shall be filed with the city clerks of the respective cities at least ten days previous to the day of such election, and for the nomination of candidates for all other city offices at least six days previous to the day of such election. . . .

Form of Ballots.

SECT. 10. Every general ballot, or ballot intended for the use of all male voters, which shall be printed in accordance with the provisions of this act, shall contain the names, residences, together with street and number, if any, and the party or political designation of all candidates whose nominations for any offices specified in the ballot have been duly made and not withdrawn in accordance herewith, and shall contain no other names. Except that in the case of electors of president and vice-president of the United States the names of the candidates for president and vice-president may be added to the party or political designation. The names of candidates for each office shall be arranged under the designation of the office in alphabetical order, according to surnames, except that the names of candidates for the offices of electors of president and vice-president shall be arranged in groups, as presented in the several certificates of nomination or nomination papers. There shall be left at the end of the list of candidates for each different office as many blank spaces as there are persons to be elected to such office, in which the voter may insert the name of any person, not printed on the ballot, for whom he desires to vote as candidate for such office. Whenever the approval of a constitutional amendment or other question is submitted to the vote of the people, such questions shall be printed upon the ballot after the list of candidates. Special ballots in cities, containing only the names of candidates for the school committee, shall also be prepared in like manner and printed for the use of women qualified according to law to vote for members of the school committee. The ballots shall be printed as to give to each voter a clear opportunity to designate by a cross mark [X] in a sufficient margin at the right of the name of each candidate, his choice of candidates and his answer to the questions submitted, and on the ballot may be printed such words as will aid the voter to do this, as "vote for one," "vote for three," "yes," "no," and the like. The ballot shall be of the length now required by law and two or more times such width. Before distribution the ballots shall be so folded in marked creases that their width and length when folded shall be those of the ballot now required by law. On the back and outside when folded, shall be printed "Official Ballot for," followed by the designation of the polling-place for which the ballot is prepared, the date of the election, and a fac-simile of the signature of the secretary of the Commonwealth or city clerk who has caused the ballot to be printed. The special ballots printed in cities for the use of women qualified to vote for school committee shall contain the additional endorsement that they are for such use only. Except as otherwise herein provided, ballots shall be printed in accordance with the existing provisions of law.

SECT. 11. All ballots when printed shall be folded as hereinbefore provided and fastened together in convenient numbers in books or blocks, in such manner that each ballot may be detached and removed separately. A record of the number of ballots printed and furnished to each polling-place shall be kept and preserved by the secretary of the Commonwealth and the several city clerks. . . .

Information to Voters.

SECT. 13. The secretary of the Commonwealth, in case of a State election, and the several city clerks, in case of city elections, shall prepare full instructions for the guidance of voters at such elections, as to obtaining ballots, as to the manner of marking them, and the method of gaining assistance, and as to obtaining new ballots in place of those accidentally spoiled, and they shall respectively cause the same, together with copies of sections twenty-seven, twenty-eight, twenty-nine, and thirty of this Act to be printed in large, clear type, on separate cards, to be called cards of instructions; and they shall respectively furnish the same and the ballots for use in each such election. They shall also cause to be printed on tinted paper, and without the fac-simile indorsements, ten or more copies of the form of the ballot provided for each voting place at each election therein, which shall be called specimen ballots, and shall be furnished with the other ballots provided for each such voting place.

SECT. 14. The secretary of the Commonwealth shall, six days at least previous to the day of any election of State officers, transmit to the registrars of voters in each city and town in which such election is to be held, printed lists containing the names, residences, and party or political appellations of all candidates nominated as herein provided for such election, and to be voted for at each polling place in each such city and town respectively, substantially in the form of the general ballot to be so used therein; and the registrars of voters shall immediately cause the lists for each town or voting precinct, as the case may be, to be conspicuously posted in one or more public places in such town or voting precinct. The secretary of the Commonwealth shall likewise cause to be published prior to the day of any such election, in at least two newspapers, if there be so many, published in each county, representing, as far as practicable, the political parties which, at the preceding election, cast the largest and next largest number of votes, a list of all the nominations made as herein provided, and to be voted for in such county, so far as may be, in the form in which they shall appear upon the general ballots.

SECT. 15. The city clerk of each city shall four days at least prior to the day of any city election therein, cause to be conspicuously posted in one or more public places in each voting precinct of such city a printed list containing the names, residences, and party or political appellations of all candidates nominated, as herein provided, and to be voted for in such precinct, substantially in the form of the general ballot to be so used therein; and he shall likewise cause to be published, prior to the day of such election in at least two newspapers, if there be so many; published in such city, representing the political parties which cast at the preceding election the largest and next largest number of votes, a list of all the nominations made, as herein provided, and to be voted for in such city, so far as may be, in the form in which they shall appear upon the general ballots.

Delivery of Ballots to Cities and Towns.

SECT. 16. The secretary of the Commonwealth shall send, separately and at different times or by different methods, the two sets of general and special ballots, together with the specimen ballots and cards of instruction printed by him, as herein provided, to the several city and town clerks, so as to be received by them, one set forty-eight hours at least previous to the day of election, and the other set twenty-four hours at least previous thereto. The same shall be sent in sealed packages, with marks on the outside clearly designating the polling-place for which they are intended and the number of ballots of each kind enclosed; and the respective city and town clerks shall on delivery to them of such packages return receipts therefor to the secretary. The secretary shall keep a record of the time when, and the manner in which the several packages are sent, and shall preserve for the period of one year the receipts of the city and town clerks.

SECT. 17. The two sets of ballots, together with the specimen ballots and cards of instruction printed by the city clerks, as herein provided, shall be packed by them in separate sealed packages, with marks on the outside clearly designating the polling precincts for which they are intended, and the number of ballots of each kind enclosed.

SECT. 18. The several city and town clerks shall send to the election officers of each voting-place before the opening of the polls on the day of election one set of ballots so prepared, sealed, and marked for such voting-place, and a receipt of such delivery shall be returned to them from the presiding or senior election officer present, which receipt, with a record of the number of ballots sent, shall be kept in the clerks' office. At the opening of the polls in each polling-place the seals of the packages shall be publicly broken, and the packages shall be opened by the presiding election officer, and the books or blocks of ballots shall be delivered to the ballot officers hereinafter provided for. The cards of instruction shall be immediately posted at or in each voting shelf or compartment provided in accordance with this act for the marking of the ballots, and not less than three such cards and not less than five specimen ballots shall be immediately posted in or about the polling-room, outside the guard-rails. The second set of ballots shall be retained by the respective clerks until they are called for or needed for the purposes of voting, and, upon the requisition in writing of the presiding election officer of any voting-place, the second set of ballots shall be furnished to such voting-place in the manner above provided as to the first set.

SECT. 19. In case the ballots to be furnished to any city or town or voting-place therein, in accordance with the provisions of this act, shall fail for any reason to be duly delivered, or in case after delivery they shall be destroyed or stolen, it shall be the duty of the clerk of such city or town to cause other ballots to be prepared substantially in the form of the ballots so wanting and to be furnished; and upon receipt of such other ballots from him, accompanied by a statement under oath that the same have been so prepared and furnished by him, and that the original ballots have so failed to be received or have been so destroyed or stolen, the election officers shall cause the ballots so substituted to be used in lieu of the ballots wanting, as above. . . .

Voting Shelves or Compartments.

SECT. 21. The officers in each city or town whose duty it is to designate and appoint polling-places therein shall cause the same to be suitably provided with a sufficient number of voting shelves or compartments (*n*), at or in which voters may conveniently mark their ballots, so that in the marking thereof they may be screened from the observation of others, and a guard-rail shall be so constructed and placed that only such persons as are inside said rail can approach within six feet of the ballot-boxes and of such voting shelves or compartments. . . .

Preparations of Ballots.

SECT. 22. Any person desiring to vote shall give his name, and, if requested so to do, his residence, to one of the ballot clerks, who shall thereupon announce the same in a loud and distinct tone of voice, clear and audible, and if such name is found upon the check-list by the ballot officer having charge thereof, he shall likewise repeat the said name, and the voter shall be allowed to enter the space enclosed by the guard-rail as above provided. The ballot clerk shall give him one, and only one, ballot, and his name shall be immediately checked on said list. If the voter is a woman, she shall receive a special ballot containing the names of candidates for school committee only. Besides the election officers, not more than four voters in excess of the number of voting shelves or compartments provided shall be allowed in said enclosed space at one time.

SECT. 23. On receipt of his ballot the voter shall forthwith, and without leaving the enclosed space, retire alone to one of the voting shelves or compartments so provided and shall prepare his ballot by marking in the appropriate margin or place, a cross [X] opposite the name of the candidate of his choice for each office to be filled, or by filling in the name of the candidate of his choice in the blank space provided therefor, and marking a cross [X] opposite thereto; and, in case of a question submitted to the vote of the people, by marking in the appropriate margin or place, a cross [X] against the answer which he desires to give. Before leaving the voting shelf or compartment the voter shall fold his ballot, without displaying the marks thereon, in the same way it was folded when received by him, and he shall keep the same so folded until he has voted. He shall vote in the manner now provided by law before leaving the enclosed space, and shall deposit his ballot in the box with the official endorsement uppermost. He shall mark and deposit his ballot without undue delay and shall quit said enclosed space as soon as he has voted. No such voter shall be allowed to occupy a voting shelf or compartment already occupied by another, nor to remain within said enclosed space more than ten minutes nor to occupy a voting shelf or compartment for more than five minutes in case all of such shelves or compartments are in use, and other voters are waiting to occupy the same. No voter not an election officer whose name has been checked on the list of the ballot officers, shall be allowed to re-enter said enclosed space during said election. It shall be the duty of the presiding election officer for the time being to secure the observance of the provisions of this section. . . .

OFFICIAL BALLOT

FOR

Precinct One, Ward One,

OF CAMBRIDGE,

8th November, 1887.

Henry B. Peirce,

Secretary of the Commonwealth.

[This represents a form of a Ballot, under the Massachusetts Ballot Act of 1888, excepting number and name of street upon it. It contains the names of all candidates voted for in Precinct 1, Ward 1, of Cambridge, on November 8, 1887. The voter places a X on the right-hand side of the name of the person for whom he wishes to vote, or a X against the Yes or No in the vote on the license question. To illustrate how a question may be voted on by the people, the license question as it would appear on the City ballot is added.]

FOR GOVERNOR.

OLIVER AMES, of Easton.
Republican.

WILLIAM H. EARLE, of Worcester.
Prohibition.

HENRY B. LOVERING, of Lynn.
Democrat.

Vote for ONE.

FOR LIEUTENANT–GOVERNOR.

JOHN BLACKMER, of Springfield.
Prohibition.

JOHN Q. A. BRACKETT, of Arlington.
Republican.

WALTER CUTTING, of Pittsfield.
Democrat.

Vote for ONE.

FOR SECRETARY OF THE COMMONWEALTH.

AMOS E. HALL, of Chelsea.
Prohibition.

JOHN F. MURPHY, of Lowell.
Democrat.

HENRY B. PEIRCE, of Abington.
Republican.

Vote for ONE.

FOR TREASURER AND RECEIVER–GENERAL.

ALANSON W. BEARD, of Boston.
Republican.

JOHN L. KILBON, of Lee.
Prohibition.

HENRY C. THACHER, of Yarmouth.
Democrat.

Vote for ONE.

FOR AUDITOR OF ACCOUNTS.

WILLIAM F. COOK, of Springfield.
Democrat.

CHARLES R. LADD, of Springfield.
Republican.

EDMUND M. STONE, of Hudson.
Prohibition.

Vote for ONE.

FOR ATTORNEY–GENERAL.

ALLEN COFFIN, of Nantucket.
Prohibition.

JOHN W. CORCORAN, of Clinton.
Democrat.

ANDREW J. WATERMAN, of Pittsfield.
Republican.

Vote for ONE.

FOR EXECUTIVE COUNCILLOR—Third District.

ROBERT LUCE, of Somerville.
Democrat.

EBENEZER M. McPHERSON, of Boston.
Republican.

JOHN S. PAINE, of Cambridge.
Prohibition.

Vote for ONE.

FOR COUNTY COMMISSIONER.

JOSEPH W. BARBER, of Sherborn.
Prohibition.

J. HENRY READ, of Westford.
Republican.

JAMES SKINNER, of Woburn.
Democrat.

Vote for ONE.

FOR SENATOR—Third Middlesex District.

GEORGE W. GALE, of Cambridge.
Democrat.

CHESTER W. KINGSLEY, of Cambridge.
Republican and Prohibition.

Vote for ONE.

FOR REPRESENTATIVES TO THE GENERAL COURT.
FIRST MIDDLESEX DISTRICT.

WILLIAM H. MARBLE, of Cambridge.
Prohibition.

ISAAC McLEAN, of Cambridge.
Democrat.

GEORGE A. PERKINS, of Cambridge.
Democrat.

JOHN READ, of Cambridge.
Republican.

CHESTER F. SANGER, of Cambridge.
Republican.

WILLIAM A. START, of Cambridge.
Prohibition.

Vote for TWO.

QUESTION SUBMITTED TO THE VOTE OF THE PEOPLE.

Shall Licenses be granted for the Sale of Intoxicating Liquors in this City?

Yes.

No.

Penalties.

SECT. 27. A voter who shall, except as herein otherwise provided, allow his ballot to be seen by any person with an apparent intention of letting it be known how he is about to vote, or who shall make a false statement as to his inability to mark his ballot, or any person who shall interfere, or attempt to interfere with any voter when inside said enclosed space or when marking his ballot, or who shall endeavor to induce any voter before voting to show how he marks or has marked his ballot, shall be punished by fine of not less than five dollars nor more than one hundred dollars; and election officers shall report any person so doing to the police officer in charge of the polls, whose duty it shall be to see that the offender is duly brought before the proper court.

SECT. 28. Any person who shall, prior to an election, wilfully deface or destroy any list of candidates posted in accordance with the provisions of this act, or who, during an election, shall wilfully deface, tear down, remove or destroy any card of instruction or specimen ballot printed or posted for the instruction of voters, or who shall during an election wilfully remove or destroy any of the supplies or conveniences furnished to enable a voter to prepare his ballot, or shall wilfully hinder the voting of others, shall be punished by fine of not less than five dollars nor more than one hundred dollars.

SECT. 29. Any person who shall falsely make or wilfully deface or destroy any certificate of nomination or nomination-paper, or any part thereof, or any letter of withdrawal; or file any certificate of nomination or nomination paper or letter of withdrawal, knowing the same or any part thereof to be falsely made; or suppress any certificate of nomination or nomination paper, or any part thereof which has been duly filed; or forge or falsely make the official endorsement on any ballot; or wilfully destroy or deface any ballot, or wilfully delay the delivery of any ballots, shall be punished by fine not exceeding one thousand dollars, or by imprisonment in the jail not more than one year, or by both such fine and imprisonment.

SECT. 30. Any public officer upon whom a duty is imposed by this act, who shall wilfully neglect to perform such duty (x), or who shall wilfully perform it in such a way as to hinder the objects of this act (x), shall be punished by fine of not less than five nor more than one thousand dollars, or by imprisonment in jail for not more than one year, or by both such fine and imprisonment.

Approved May 29, 1888.

✥ 21 ✥

The Omaha Platform*

(1892)

1. What provisions of the Omaha Platform were later enacted into law by the major political parties? What effect did this have on third parties like the Populist Party?
2. Why did the election of 1892 represent the pinnacle of success for a third party since the Civil War?

THE BASIC BELIEFS of the Populist movement placed the interests of average people such as farmers and laborers against the business interests of bankers, corporations, railroads, and the politicians allied with them. Although the movement can be traced back to the 1880s, the Populist Party, or People's Party, was not formally organized until 1892 in St. Louis. The party's first national nominating convention was held in July of that year in Omaha, Nebraska. At that convention James K. Weaver, a former member of the House of Representatives from Iowa, was nominated as the party's presidential candidate, and James G. Field was its vice presidential candidate. The Populists won only 8.5 percent of the popular vote in the 1892 presidential election, but they secured twenty-two electoral votes in Colorado, Idaho, Kansas, Nevada, and parts of North Dakota and Oregon; captured eleven seats in the House of Representatives; and won control of the governorship and the legislature in several states. The legislative majorities in those states allowed the Populists to select several U.S. senators.

On July 4 at the nominating convention, the party formally adopted what has become known as the Omaha Platform. The platform's preamble was written by a former member of the House of Representatives, Ignatius L. Donnelly, of Minnesota; the platform itself represented a merger of many different agricultural and political interests. A number

---

*The World Almanac, 1893 (New York: World Almanac, 1893), 83–85. Reprinted in A Populist Reader, Selections from the Works of American Populist Leaders, ed. George Brown Tindall (New York: Harper and Row, 1966), 90–96.

of specific initiatives that were part of the Omaha Platform, such as the graduated income tax, an eight-hour workday, and the direct election of senators, were eventually enacted into law during the Progressive era.

The Populists discarded the Omaha Platform in 1896 in order to endorse William Jennings Bryan, the Democratic nominee. However, the accomplishments of Populist Party candidates at the ballot box and their success in achieving many of the goals set forth in the Omaha Platform later in the Progressive era represent the pinnacle of success for a third party in the United States since the Civil War.

National People's Party Platform

Assembled upon the 116th anniversary of the Declaration of Independence, the People's Party of America, in their first national convention, invoking upon their action the blessing of Almighty God, put forth in the name and on behalf of the people of this country, the following preamble and declaration of principles:

Preamble

The conditions which surround us best justify our co-operation; we meet in the midst of a nation brought to the verge of moral, political, and material ruin. Corruption dominates the ballot-box, the Legislatures, the Congress, and touches even the ermine of the bench. The people are demoralized; most of the States have been compelled to isolate the voters at the polling places to prevent universal intimidation and bribery. The newspapers are largely subsidized or muzzled, public opinion silenced, business prostrated, homes covered with mortgages, labor impoverished, and the land concentrating in the hands of capitalists. The urban workmen are denied the right to organize for self-protection, imported pauperized labor beats down their wages, a hireling standing army, unrecognized by our laws, is established to shoot them down, and they are rapidly degenerating into European conditions. The fruits of the toil of millions are boldly stolen to build up colossal fortunes for a few, unprecedented in the history of mankind; and the possessors of those, in turn, despise the republic and endanger liberty. From the same prolific womb of governmental injustice we breed the two great classes—tramps and millionaires.

The national power to create money is appropriated to enrich bondholders; a vast public debt payable in legal tender currency has been funded into gold-bearing bonds, thereby adding millions to the burdens of the people.

Silver, which has been accepted as coin since the dawn of history, has been demonetized to add to the purchasing power of gold by decreasing the value of all forms of property as well as human labor, and the supply of currency is purposely abridged to fatten usurers, bankrupt enterprise, and enslave industry. A vast conspiracy against mankind has been organized on two continents, and it is rapidly taking possession of the world. If not met and overthrown at once it forebodes terrible social convulsions, the destruction of civilization, or the establishment of an absolute despotism.

We have witnessed for more than a quarter of a century the struggles of the two great political parties for power and plunder, while grievous wrongs have been inflicted upon the suffering people. We charge that the controlling influences dominating both these parties have permitted the existing dreadful conditions to develop without serious effort to prevent or restrain them. Neither do they now promise us any substantial reform. They have agreed together to ignore, in the coming campaign, every issue but one. They propose to drown the outcries of a plundered people with the uproar of a sham battle over the tariff, so that capitalists, corporations, national banks, rings, trusts, watered stock, the demonetization of silver and the oppressions of the usurers may all be lost sight of. They propose to sacrifice our homes, lives, and children on the altar of mammon; to destroy the multitude in order to secure corruption funds from the millionaires.

Assembled on the anniversary of the birthday of the nation, and filled with the spirit of the grand general and chief who established our independence, we seek to restore the government of the Republic to the hands of "the plain people," with which class it originated. We assert our purposes to be identical with the purposes of the National Constitution; to form a more perfect union and establish justice, insure domestic tranquillity[sic], provide for the common defence, promote the general welfare, and secure the blessings of liberty for ourselves and our posterity.

We declare that this Republic can only endure as a free government while built upon the love of the whole people for each other and for the nation; that it cannot be pinned together by bayonets; that the civil war is over, and that every passion and resentment which grew out of it must die with it, and that we must be in fact, as we are in name, one united brotherhood of free men.

Our country finds itself confronted by conditions for which there is no precedent in the history of the world; our annual agricultural productions amount to billions of dollars in value, which must, within a few weeks or months, be exchanged for billions of dollars' worth of commodities consumed in their production; the existing currency supply is wholly inadequate to make this exchange; the results are falling prices, the formation of combines and rings, the impoverishment of the producing class. We pledge ourselves that if given power we will labor to correct these evils by wise and reasonable legislation, in accordance with the terms of our platform.

We believe that the power of government—in other words, of the people—should be expanded (as in the case of the postal service) as rapidly and as far as the good sense of an intelligent people and the teachings of experience shall justify, to the end that oppression, injustice, and poverty shall eventually cease in the land.

While our sympathies as a party of reform are naturally upon the side of every proposition which will tend to make men intelligent, virtuous, and temperate, we nevertheless regard these questions, important as they are, as secondary to the great issues now pressing for solution, and upon which not only our individual prosperity but the very existence of free institutions depend; and we ask all men to first help us to determine whether we are to have a republic to administer before we differ as to the conditions upon which it is to be administered, believing that the forces of reform this day organized will never cease to move forward until every wrong is remedied and equal rights and equal privileges securely established for all the men and women of this country.

Platform

We declare, therefore—

First.—That the union of the labor forces of the United States this day consummated shall be permanent and perpetual; may its spirit enter into all hearts for the salvation of the Republic and the uplifting of mankind.

Second.—Wealth belongs to him who creates it, and every dollar taken from industry without an equivalent is robbery. "If any will not work, neither shall he eat." The interests of rural and civic labor are the same; their enemies are identical.

Third.—We believe that the time has come when the railroad corporations will either own the people or the people must own the railroads, and should the government enter upon the work of owning and managing all railroads, we should favor an amendment to the Constitution by which all persons engaged in the government service shall be placed under a civil-service regulation of the most rigid character, so as to prevent the increase of the power of the national administration by the use of such additional government employes[sic].

FINANCE.—We demand a national currency, safe, sound, and flexible, issued by the general government only, a full legal tender for all debts, public and private, and that without the use of banking corporations, a just, equitable, and efficient means of distribution direct to the people, at a tax not to exceed 2 per cent. per annum, to be provided as set forth in the sub-treasury plan of the Farmers' Alliance, or a better system; also by payments in discharge of its obligations for public improvements.

1. We demand free and unlimited coinage of silver and gold at the present legal ratio of 16 to 1.

2. We demand that the amount of circulating medium be speedily increased to not less than $50 per capita.

3. We demand a graduated income tax.

4. We believe that the money of the country should be kept as much as possible in the hands of the people, and hence we demand that all State and national revenues shall be limited to the necessary expenses of the government, economically and honestly administered.

5. We demand that postal savings banks be established by the government for the safe deposit of the earnings of the people and to facilitate exchange.

TRANSPORTATION—Transportation being a means of exchange and a public necessity, the government should own and operate the railroads in the interest of the people. The telegraph, telephone, like the post-office system, being a necessity for the transmission of news, should be owned and operated by the government in the interest of the people.

LAND.—The land, including all the natural sources of wealth, is the heritage of the people, and should not be monopolized for speculative purposes, and alien ownership of land should be prohibited. All land now held by railroads and other corporations in excess of their actual needs, and all lands now owned by aliens should be reclaimed by the government and held for actual settlers only.

Expression of Sentiments

Your Committee on Platform and Resolutions beg leave unanimously to report the following:

Whereas, Other questions have been presented for our consideration, we hereby submit the following, not as a part of the Platform of the People's Party, but as resolutions expressive of the sentiment of this Convention.

1. RESOLVED, That we demand a free ballot and a fair count in all elections and pledge ourselves to secure it to every legal voter without Federal Intervention, through the adoption by the States of the unperverted Australian or secret ballot system.

2. RESOLVED, That the revenue derived from a graduated income tax should be applied to the reduction of the burden of taxation now levied upon the domestic industries of this country.

3. RESOLVED, That we pledge our support to fair and liberal pensions to ex-Union soldiers and sailors.

4. RESOLVED, That we condemn the fallacy of protecting American labor under the present system, which opens our ports to the pauper and criminal classes of the world and crowds out our wage-earners; and we denounce the present ineffective laws against contract labor, and demand the further restriction of undesirable emigration.

5. RESOLVED, That we cordially sympathize with the efforts of organized workingmen to shorten the hours of labor, and demand a rigid enforcement of the existing eight-hour law on Government work, and ask that a penalty clause be added to the said law.

6. RESOLVED, That we regard the maintenance of a large standing army of mercenaries, known as the Pinkerton system, as a menace to our liberties, and we demand its abolition. . . .

7. RESOLVED, That we commend to the favorable consideration of the people and the reform press the legislative system known as the initiative and referendum.

8. RESOLVED, That we favor a constitutional provision limiting the office of President and Vice-President to one term, and providing for the election of Senators of the United States by a direct vote of the people.

9. RESOLVED, That we oppose any subsidy or national aid to any private corporation for any purpose.

10. RESOLVED, That this convention sympathizes with the Knights of Labor and their righteous contest with the tyrannical combine of clothing manufacturers of Rochester, and declare it to be a duty of all who hate tyranny and oppression to refuse to purchase the goods made by the said manufacturers, or to patronize any merchants who sell such goods.

William Jennings Bryan's "Cross of Gold" Speech*

(1896)

1. What was Bryan's strategy for winning the Democratic Party's presidential nomination in 1896? How was his strategy appropriate for winning the nomination at the convention?
2. If Bryan was one of the most dynamic and energetic campaigners in the history of presidential elections, what does his loss to McKinley suggest about the mood of the electorate?

O N JULY 9, 1896, William Jennings Bryan delivered one of the most famous speeches in the history of American politics at the Democratic National Convention in Chicago, Illinois. At that time Bryan was a former member of Congress from Nebraska who desired the Democratic nomination and was shrewdly working behind the scenes to build support for his candidacy.

Bryan's speech was given as part of the debate at the convention over bimetallism. Democrats desired to link the value of the dollar to silver. If this occurred, most people expected that the supply of money would increase substantially since silver was more readily available than gold, and inflation would be the result. This would make it easier for those in debt (such as farmers) to increase their revenue and pay off their debt. Republicans, on the other hand, preferred to link the value of the dollar to gold. They believed that doing so was important to protect the country against runaway inflation, since high inflation would burden banks and other creditors as the interest paid on loans would be effectively devalued.

After several U.S. senators spoke on the subject, Bryan took the floor, and his passionate speech incited the delegates. Much of the speech was

*Official Proceedings of the Democratic National Convention Held in Chicago, Illinois, July 7–11, 1896 (Logansport, Ind., 1896), 226–234. Reprinted in the Annals of America, vol. 12, 1895–1904: Populism, Imperialism, and Reform (Chicago: Encyclopedia Brittanica, 1968), 100–105.

in response to what others had said that day, but his rhetoric clearly placed him in favor of borrowers such as farmers and against creditors such as banks. The speech not only convinced delegates at the convention to nominate him for president the next day on the fifth ballot, but it also cemented his role as the leader of the Populist movement. At thirty-six years of age, Bryan became the youngest person ever nominated to run for president. In addition to the Democratic nomination, Bryan received the nomination of the Populist Party.

Defeated in the general election by Republican William McKinley, the governor of Ohio, Bryan nonetheless is credited with being one of the most energetic campaigners in the history of campaigns and elections. While McKinley campaigned from his front porch in Canton, Ohio, Bryan crisscrossed the country giving hundreds of speeches.

Bryan maintained control of the Democratic Party for more than a decade and was nominated by the Democratic Party to run for president two more times. In 1896, he enthusiastically promoted the silver standard, but was defeated by McKinley. In 1900, he fought for anti-imperialism, but was again defeated by McKinley. In 1908, Bryan was again defeated, this time by Republican vice president William Howard Taft, while calling for Democrats to fight the financial interests in the United States.

Despite his lack of success in gaining the presidency, Bryan's "Cross of Gold" speech became instantly famous, and he repeated it numerous times over the next three decades.

I would be presumptuous, indeed, to present myself against the distinguished gentlemen to whom you have listened if this were but a measuring of ability; but this is not a contest among persons. The humblest citizen in all the land when clad in the armor of a righteous cause is stronger than all the whole hosts of error that they can bring. I come to speak to you in defense of a cause as holy as the cause of liberty—the cause of humanity. When this debate is concluded, a motion will be made to lay upon the table the resolution offered in commendation of the administration and also the resolution in condemnation of the administration. I shall object to bringing this question down to a level of persons. The individual is but an atom; he is born, he acts, he dies; but principles are eternal; and this has been a contest of principle.

Never before in the history of this country has there been witnessed such a contest as that through which we have passed. Never before in the history of American politics has a great issue been fought out as this issue has been by the voters themselves.

On the 4th of March, 1895, a few Democrats, most of them members of Congress, issued an address to the Democrats of the nation asserting that the money question was the paramount issue of the hour; asserting also the right of a majority of the Democratic Party to control the position of the party on this paramount issue; concluding with the request that all believers in free coinage of silver in the Democratic Party should organize and take charge of and control the policy of the Democratic Party. Three months later, at Memphis, an organization was perfected, and the silver Democrats went forth openly and boldly and courageously proclaiming their belief and declaring that if successful they would crystallize in a platform the declaration which they had made; and then began the conflict with a zeal approaching the zeal which inspired the crusaders who followed Peter the Hermit. Our silver Democrats went forth from victory unto victory, until they are assembled now, not to discuss, not to debate, but to enter up the judgment rendered by the plain people of this country.

But in this contest, brother has been arrayed against brother, and father against son. The warmest ties of love and acquaintance and association have been disregarded. Old leaders have been cast aside when they refused to give expression to the sentiments of those whom they would lead, and new leaders have sprung up to give direction to this cause of freedom. Thus has the contest been waged, and we have assembled here under as binding and solemn instructions as were ever fastened upon the representatives of a people.

We do not come as individuals. Why, as individuals we might have been glad to compliment the gentleman from New York [Senator Hill], but we knew that the people for whom we speak would never be willing to put him in a position where he could thwart the will of the Democratic Party. I say it was not a question of persons; it was a question of principle; and it is not with gladness, my friends, that we find ourselves brought into conflict with those who are now arrayed on the other side. The gentleman who just preceded me [Governor Russell] spoke of the old state of Massachusetts. Let me assure him that not one person in all this convention entertains the least hostility to the people of the state of Massachusetts.

But we stand here representing people who are the equals before the law of the largest cities in the state of Massachusetts. When you come before us and tell us that we shall disturb your business interests, we reply that you have disturbed our business interests by your action. We say to you that you have made too limited in its application the definition of a businessman. The man who is employed for wages is as much a businessman as his employer. The attorney in a country town is as much a businessman as the corporation counsel in a great metropolis. The merchant at the crossroads store is as much a businessman as the merchant of New York. The farmer who goes forth in the morning and toils all day, begins in the spring and toils all summer, and by the application of brain and muscle to the natural resources of this country creates wealth, is as much a businessman as the man who goes upon the Board of Trade and bets upon the price of grain. The miners who go 1,000 feet into the earth or climb 2,000 feet upon the cliffs and bring forth from their hiding places the precious metals to be poured in the channels of trade are as much businessmen as the few financial magnates who in a backroom corner the money of the world.

We come to speak for this broader class of businessmen. Ah. my friends, we say not one word against those who live upon the Atlantic Coast; but those hardy pioneers who braved all the dangers of the wilderness, who have made the desert to blossom as the rose—those pioneers away out there, rearing their children near to nature's heart, where they can mingle their voices with the voices of the birds—out there where they have erected schoolhouses for the education of their children and churches where they praise their Creator, and the cemeteries where sleep the ashes of their dead—are as deserving of the consideration of this party as any people in this country.

It is for these that we speak. We do not come as aggressors. Our war is not a war of conquest. We are fighting in the defense of our homes, our families, and posterity. We have petitioned, and our petitions have been scorned. We have entreated, and our entreaties have been disregarded. We have begged, and they have mocked when our calamity came.

We beg no longer; we entreat no more; we petition no more. We defy them!

The gentleman from Wisconsin has said he fears a Robespierre. My friend, in this land of the free you need fear no tyrant who will spring up from among the people. What we need is an Andrew Jackson to stand as Jackson stood, against the encroachments of aggregated wealth.

They tell us that this platform was made to catch votes. We reply to them that changing conditions make new issues; that the principles upon which rest Democracy are as everlasting as the hills; but that they must be applied to new conditions as they arise. Conditions have arisen and we are attempting to meet those conditions. They tell us that the income tax ought not to be brought in here; that is not a new idea. They criticize us for our criticism of the Supreme Court of the United States. My friends, we have made no criticism. We have simply called attention to what you know. If you want criticisms, read the dissenting opinions of the Court. That will give you criticisms.

They say we passed an unconstitutional law. I deny it. The income tax was not unconstitutional when it was passed. It was not unconstitutional when it went before the Supreme Court for the first time. It did not become unconstitutional until one judge changed his mind; and we cannot be expected to know when a judge will change his mind.

The income tax is a just law. It simply intends to put the burdens of government justly upon the backs of the people. I am in favor of an income tax. When I find a man who is not willing to pay his share of the burden of the government which protects him, I find a man who is unworthy to enjoy the blessings of a government like ours.

He says that we are opposing the national bank currency. It is true. If you will read what Thomas Benton said, you will find that he said that in searching history he could find but one parallel to Andrew Jackson. That was Cicero, who destroyed the conspiracies of Cataline and saved Rome. He did for Rome what Jackson did when he destroyed the bank conspiracy and saved America.

We say in our platform that we believe that the right to coin money and issue money is a function of government. We believe it. We believe it is a part of sovereignty and can no more with safety be delegated to private individuals than can the power to make penal statutes or levy laws for taxation.

Mr. Jefferson, who was once regarded as good Democratic authority, seems to have a different opinion from the gentleman who has addressed us on the part of the minority. Those who are opposed to this proposition tell us that the issue of paper money is a function of the bank and that the government ought to go out of the banking business. I stand with Jefferson rather than with them, and tell them, as he did, that the issue of money is a function of the government and that the banks should go out of the governing business.

They complain about the plank which declares against the life tenure in office. They have tried to strain it to mean that which it does not mean. What we oppose in that plank is the life tenure that is being built up in Washington which establishes an office-holding class and excludes from participation in the benefits the humbler members of our society. . . .

Let me call attention to two or three great things. The gentleman from New York says that he will propose an amendment providing that this change in our law shall not affect contracts which, according to the present laws, are made payable in gold. But if he means to say that we cannot change our monetary system without protecting those who have loaned money before the change was made, I want to ask him where, in law or in morals, he can find authority for not protecting the debtors when the act of 1873 was passed when he now insists that we must protect the creditor. He says he also wants to amend this platform so as to provide that if we fail to maintain the parity within a year that we will then suspend the coinage of silver. We reply that when we advocate a thing which we believe will be successful we are not compelled to raise a doubt as to our own sincerity by trying to show what we will do if we are wrong.

I ask him, if he will apply his logic to us, why he does not apply it to himself. He says that he wants this country to try to secure an international agreement. Why doesn't he tell us what he is going to do if they fail to secure an international agreement. There is more reason for him to do that than for us to expect to fail to maintain the parity. They have tried for thirty years—thirty years—to secure an international agreement, and those are waiting for it most patiently who don't want it at all.

Now, my friends, let me come to the great paramount issue. If they ask us here why it is we say more on the money question than we say upon the tariff question, I reply that if protection has slain its thousands the gold standard has slain its tens of thousands. If they ask us why we did not embody all these things in our platform which we believe, we reply to them that when we have restored the money of the Constitution, all other necessary reforms will be possible, and that until that is done there is no reform that can be accomplished.

Why is it that within three months such a change has come over the sentiments of the country? Three months ago, when it was confidently asserted that those who believed in the gold standard would frame our platforms and nominate our candidates, even the advocates of the gold standard did not think that we could elect a President; but they had good reasons for the suspicion, because there is scarcely a state here today asking for the gold standard that is not within the absolute control of the Republican Party.

But note the change. Mr. McKinley was nominated at St. Louis upon a platform that declared for the maintenance of the gold standard until it should be changed into bimetallism by an international agreement. Mr. McKinley was the most popular man among the Republicans; and everybody three months ago in the Republican Party prophesied his election. How is it today? Why, that man who used to boast that he looked like Napoleon, that man shudders today when he thinks that he was nominated on the anniversary of the Battle of Waterloo. Not only that, but as he listens he can hear with ever increasing distinctness the sound of the waves as they beat upon the lonely shores of St. Helena.

Why this change? Ah, my friends. is not the change evident to anyone who will look at the matter? It is because no private character, however pure, no personal popularity, however great, can protect from the avenging wrath of an indignant people the man who will either declare that he is in favor of fastening the gold standard upon this people, or who is willing to surrender the right of self-government and place legislative control in the hands of foreign potentates and powers. . . .

We go forth confident that we shall win. Why? Because upon the paramount issue in this campaign there is not a spot of ground upon which the enemy will dare to challenge battle. Why, if they tell us that the gold standard is a good thing, we point to their platform and tell them that their platform pledges the party to get rid of a gold standard and substitute bimetallism. If the gold standard is a good thing, why try to get rid of it? If the gold standard, and I might call your attention to the fact that some of the very people who are in this convention today and who tell you that we ought to declare in favor of international bimetallism and thereby declare that the gold standard is wrong and that the principles of bimetallism are better—these very people four months ago were open and avowed advocates of the gold standard and telling us that we could not legislate two metals together even with all the world.

I want to suggest this truth, that if the gold standard is a good thing we ought to declare in favor of its retention and not in favor of abandoning it; and if the gold standard is a bad thing, why should we wait until some other nations are willing to help us to let it go?

Here is the line of battle. We care not upon which issue they force the fight. We are prepared to meet them on either issue or on both. If they tell us that the gold standard is the standard of civilization, we reply to them that this, the most enlightened of all nations of the earth, has never declared for a gold standard, and both the parties this year are declaring against it. If the gold standard is the standard of civilization, why, my friends, should we not have it? So if they come to meet us on that, we can present the history of our nation. More than that, we can tell them this, that they will search the pages of history in vain to find a single instance in which the common people of any land ever declared themselves in favor of a gold standard. They can find where the holders of fixed investments have.

Mr. Carlisle said in 1878 that this was a struggle between the idle holders of idle capital and the struggling masses who produce the wealth and pay the taxes of the country; and my friends, it is simply a question that we shall decide upon which side shall the Democratic Party fight. Upon the side of the idle holders of idle capital, or upon the side of the struggling masses? That is the question that the party must answer first; and then it must be answered by each individual hereafter. The sympathies of the Democratic Party, as described by the platform, are on the side of the struggling masses, who have ever been the foundation of the Democratic Party.

There are two ideas of government. There are those who believe that if you just legislate to make the well-to-do prosperous, that their prosperity will leak through on those below. The Democratic idea has been that if you legislate to make the masses prosperous their prosperity will find its way up and through every class that rests upon it.

You come to us and tell us that the great cities are in favor of the gold standard. I tell you that the great cities rest upon these broad and fertile prairies. Burn down your cities and leave our farms, and your cities will spring up again as if by magic. But destroy our farms and the grass will grow in the streets of every city in the country.

My friends, we shall declare that this nation is able to legislate for its own people on every question without waiting for the aid or consent of any other nation on earth, and upon that issue we expect to carry every single state in the Union.

I shall not slander the fair state of Massachusetts nor the state of New York by saying that when citizens are confronted with the proposition, "Is this nation able to attend to its own business?"—I will not slander either one by saying that the people of those states will declare our helpless impotency as a nation to attend to our own business. It is the issue of 1776 over again. Our ancestors, when but 3 million, had the courage to declare their political independence of every other nation upon earth. Shall we, their descendants, when we have grown to 70 million, declare that we are less independent than our forefathers? No, my friends, it will never be the judgment of this people. Therefore, we care not upon what lines the battle is fought. If they say bimetallism is good but we cannot have it till some nation helps us, we reply that, instead of having a gold standard because England has, we shall restore bimetallism, and then let England have bimetallism because the United States have.

If they dare to come out in the open field and defend the gold standard as a good thing, we shall fight them to the uttermost, having behind us the producing masses of the nation and the world. Having behind us the commercial interests and the laboring interests and all the toiling masses, we shall answer their demands for a gold standard by saying to them, you shall not press down upon the brow of labor this crown of thorns. You shall not crucify mankind upon a cross of gold.

·≪ 23 ≫·

Robert LaFollette's
"Peril in the Machine" Speech*

(1897)

1. In what ways did LaFollette expect primary elections to weaken political parties?
2. How have primary elections changed the strategies of candidates seeking a presidential nomination?

FROM THE 1830S until the end of the nineteenth century, national nominating conventions served as the method for selecting the presidential nominees of each party. In most states, delegates to the national party convention were appointed by the delegates to the state party conventions. Since local party "bosses" controlled the selection of delegates to the state party convention, they subsequently influenced the choice of delegates to the national convention, presidential nominees, and nominees for state offices. Selecting party nominees was, therefore, neither transparent nor democratic.

Progressive reformers sought to break the control of the bosses of political machines over party nominees by adopting state laws that required the use of primary elections. The 1912 presidential election was the first to use presidential primaries. Incumbent president William Howard Taft was challenged by Sen. Robert M. LaFollette Sr. of Wisconsin and former president Theodore Roosevelt. While Roosevelt turned out to be the most popular candidate in the primaries, Taft won the Republican nomination. Twelve states used presidential preference primaries that year, but most were considered nonbinding because the delegates to the convention were not obligated by law to vote the will of the people. As a result, local party bosses still controlled the delegates to

*"Peril in the Machine," *Chicago Times-Herald,* February 23, 1897. Reprinted at www.wisconsin history.org/wlhba/articleView.asp?pg=1&id=1995&pn=0.

the convention. Twenty states had adopted presidential primaries by 1920, but as in the past, the results of few of these were binding upon convention delegates. The use of primaries became more widely accepted after reforms in the 1970s.

LaFollette was the leader of progressive reformers who fought to eliminate the power of state and national conventions and adopt primaries nationwide. Known as "Fighting Bob" to his colleagues, LaFollette served in the House of Representatives, as governor, and finally as a senator from Wisconsin. By the early 1890s, he had grown to believe that banking and corporate interests were too influential within the Republican Party. Given this, he often found himself in conflict with political interests in his state and throughout the nation. Initially, his interests were to reform the Republican Party rather than to leave it, although in 1924 he accepted the presidential nomination of the Progressive Party.

Those LaFollette led were known within the party as "Insurgents," and those influenced by corporate interests were "Stalwarts." By the mid-1890s the Stalwarts found themselves challenged by the Insurgents for leadership of the party, and LaFollette campaigned for governor under the Insurgent banner. His speeches were critical of banking and corporate interests, but they also called for direct democracy through the direct election of party nominees in preference primaries. He advocated primaries because he felt that the power of political party machines in government threatened democracy.

On February 22, 1897, LaFollette addressed the faculty and students of the University of Chicago at the invitation of its president. His topic that day was what he referred to in his autobiography as the "Menace of Political Machines." In this speech, he demonstrated how caucuses and conventions tended to lend themselves to manipulation, and he outlined a system by which nation, state, and local political parties could nominate candidates through primary elections held under the same legal provisions that had been adopted for the general election. Over the next decade, LaFollette continued to champion the direction nomination of candidates by the public both within Wisconsin and elsewhere.

In every democracy men will affiliate with one or the other of two great political parties. The ballot must determine which party shall administer government, enact new legislation, adjust the laws to all the complex social relations of life, to all the complicated business transactions of millions of human beings with order and justice. The ballot can achieve the kind of administration desired, establish the economic and financial policies essential, only through the election of men of integrity and ability, embodying the ideas expressed in the ballot. That the voter may be thoroughly informed upon the questions involved and upon the men to be chosen as the representatives of his convictions there should be the widest discussion and the most searching investigation.

The fundamental principle of a republic is individual responsibility. The responsibility is personal at the point in our political system where the citizen comes in direct contact with the system itself. This is the initial point of all legislation, all administration. In all the activities preliminary to the primary, and in the primary itself, the citizen is an elementary force in government. Here the voter can lay his hand directly upon the shoulder of the public servant and point the way he should go. But this ends with the adjournment of the primary or caucus. From that moment the citizen in a representative democracy, under a caucus, delegate and convention system, does not again come in direct personal touch with the work either of legislation or administration. How essential, then, if he is to be a factor in government, that he take part, and intelligently too, in this fundamental work. If there be failure here, there is failure throughout. If through inattention or indifference, through mistake or misrepresentation, through trickery or fraud, or "the work," the minority control caucus, the laws will be made and executed by the agent of the minority, and the first principle of government fails. . . .

It Is Machine Despotism.

The wrongs inflicted by the machine do not end with the appropriation of offices. It does not secure the offices for salaries primarily. The salary is merely an Incident. Government by the machine is machine despotism. It administers the laws, through its subjects, after its own interpretation. It is independent of the people and fears no reckoning. In extreme cases, where it becomes necessary to meet arraignment, it has its own press to parry or soften the blow. Having no constituency to serve, it serves itself. The machine is its own master. It owes no obligation and acknowledges no responsibility.

Its legislatures make the laws by its schedule. It names their committees. Behind the closed doors of its committee-rooms it suppresses bills inimical to its interests. It suppresses debate by a machine role and the ready gavel of a pliant speaker. It exploits measures with reform titles designated to perpetuate machine control. It earns for special interests and takes tribute from its willing subjects, the private corporations.

Grave danger lies not in waiting for this republic, to destroy its life or change its character by force of arms. The shock and heat of collision will ever rouse and solidify patriotic citizenship in defense of American liberty. It is the insidious, creeping, progressive encroachment that presents the greatest peril.

The machine—this invisible empire—does its work so quietly. There is no explosion, no clash of arms, no open rebellion, but a sly covert nullification of the highest law of the land. It incurs none of the risks of armed assault; escapes the personal dangers and swift public retribution—provoked by organized violence and intimidation. So long as the methods were the methods of Boss Tweed it was more notorious but infinitely less dangerous. It would in time go down beneath the overpowering weight of decent, loyal public condemnation. But when adroit, skilled, talented men, schooled in practical politics, devised a system that had in the beginning the semblance of serving its party, but mastered it instead; that openly lauded allegiance to party principle and artfully violated every principle of honor; that had its secret agents in every community and its cunning operatives in every caucus; that fooled the citizen by the tricks of legerdemain; that with a handful of unscrupulous men manipulated caucuses, defeated majorities, debauched politics and drove thousands of good citizens away from the primaries to stay—then, indeed, was the danger to the republic greatly augmented. But more than all this, when they worked into the political thought and life of people by the thousands, young men and old, ignorant men and educated, the pernicious, monstrous doctrine that the violation of the sacred principle of representative government, the spirit and letter of the constitution, is highly commendable. If it is only successful; that the American citizen's ballot, his defense, his power, his hope, his prophecy is the legitimate, rightful spoil and plunder of the political machine—then they corrupted the very springs of national life and poluted [sic] them in their courses as they flow on to meet the coming generations.

Remedy Is Suggested.

What, then, shall we do to be saved?

Waste no more time in vain sermons on the duty of attending the caucus. It is too late for that. Except at long intervals, when in a sort of frenzy the citizen strikes at the machine shackles, men can be no longer drafted into caucus attendance. They have seen the game before. They know the dice are loaded. They are no longer indifferent to their duties, nor ignorant of the situation.

They well understand that their only part in government is to vote the ticket prepared for them and bear the machine rule of their own party, or the machine rule of the other party. They know they do not get the kind of government they vote for, but they do the best they can. They still attend the elections. They are as vitally interested in good government as ever. They are only waiting to find the way to achieve it. Here is our final safety. Here is the ultimate overthrow of the machine. If we provide the same safeguards, the same certainty, the same facility for expressing and executing the will of the people at the primaries as now prevail at the elections, we shall have the same general interest, the same general participation in the one as in the other.

Aye, more than this, if we guarantee the American citizen a full voice in the selection of candidates, and shaping the policy of his party and the administration of government incident thereto, then shall we invest not only the primaries, but the elections as well, with an abiding interest for him, extending beyond the day of the primaries and the day of the election, the weeks of the campaign—indeed, we shall make the primary and the election of vastly deeper significance, appealing in a new way to his deliberate judgment, his patriotism and his personal responsibility.

It is as much the interest and as plainly the duty of the state to as carefully perfect and guard a system of nominating candidates as it perfects and guards the system of electing them.

The caucus, delegate and convention system is inherently bad. It invites to manipulation, scheming, trickery, corruption and fraud. Even if the caucus were fairly conducted, the plan of which it is a part removes the nomination too far from the voter. Every transfer of delegated power weakens responsibility, until finally, by the time it is lodged in the hands of a nominating convention, the sense of responsibility has been lost in transit, unless it has been ticketed through by instructions from its original source. And even then all along the journey, from the primary to the convention, the confidential agents of the machine are introducing delegates to the mysteries of "gold brick" and "three card" political schemes.

The convention under the most favorable conditions is anything but a deliberative body. Its work is hurried and business necessarily transacted in confusion. There is great excitement. It is the storm center of a political tempest. There are rumors and roorbacks, challenges and denials. There is no time for investigation and no opportunity to distinguish the real issue from the false issue. Charges are withheld and "sprung" in the convention purposely to avoid disproval and mislead delegates; and the dark horse is ever in reserve, waiting a favorable opportunity to take the convention unawares. Add to this all the corruption which comes with machine domination of a convention and you have political disaster and political crime as a result.

If, after long suffering and misrepresentation, the people by tremendous and united effort could succeed in defeating and even destroying the machine, the opportunity offered by the caucus and convention plan would simply restore the old or build up a new machine in its place.

Drop Caucus and Convention.

No, no! Beginning the work in the state, put aside the caucus and the convention. They have been and will continue to be prostituted to the service of corrupt organization. They answer no purpose further than to give respectable form to political robbery. Abolish the caucus and the convention. Go back to the first principles of democracy. Go back to the people. Substitute for the caucus and the convention a primary election—held under all the sanctions of law which prevail at the general elections—where the citizen may cast his vote directly to nominate the candidate of the party with which he affiliates and have it canvassed and returned just as he cast it.

Provide a means of placing the candidates in nomination before the primary and forestall the creation of a new caucus system back of the primary election.

Provide a ballot for the primary election and print on it the names of all candidates for nomination who have previously filed preliminary nomination papers with a designated official.

Provide that no candidate for nomination shall be entitled to have his name printed on the primary election ticket who shall not have been called out as a candidate by the written request of a given percentage of the vote cast at the preceding election in the district, county or state in which he is proposed as a candidate in the same manner that judicial candidates are now called out in many states.

Provide for the selection of a committee to represent the party organization and promulgate the party platform by the election at the primary of a representative man from the party for each county in the state.

Under severe penalties for violation of the law prohibit electioneering in or about the election booth, punish bribery and the singular attempt to bribe and protect fully the counting and return of the votes cast.

Do this and the knell of the political machine has sounded in the state.

Then every citizen will share equally in the nomination of the candidates of his party and attend primary elections as a privilege as well as a duty. It will no longer be necessary to create an artificial interest in the general election to induce voters to attend. Intelligent, well-considered judgment will be substituted for unthinking enthusiasm; the lamp of reason for the torchlight. The voter will not have to be persuaded that he has an interest in the election; he will know that he has. The nomination of the party will not be the result of "compromise" or impulse or evil design—the barrel of the machine—but the candidates of the majority honestly and fairly nominated.

To every generation some important work is committed. If this generation will destroy the political machine, will emancipate the majority from its enslavement, will gain place the destinies of this nation in the minds of its citizens, then, "under God this government of the people, by the people and for the people shall not perish from the earth."

❧ 24 ❧

William Riordan's "The Strenuous Life of the Tammany District Leader"*

(1905)

1. How did political machines maintain power? What information does Plunkitt share about Tammany Hall's strategy?
2. How did machine politicians like Plunkitt maintain their close relationships to their constituents? Why were these relationships important?

AT THE TURN OF THE twentieth century, New York's Tammany Hall was still the city's most powerful political organization. One of its leaders, George Washington Plunkitt, first ran for the New York State Assembly in 1866 without the endorsement of the Tammany Hall political machine and lost. In 1868 he became a Tammany Hall candidate, and from then until 1904 held the offices of assemblyman, county supervisor, alderman, police magistrate, deputy commissioner of street

---

*William L. Riordan, *Plunkitt of Tammany Hall: A Series of Very Plain Talks on Very Practical Politics, Delivered by ex-Senator George Washington Plunkitt, the Tammany Philosopher, from his Rostrum— the New York County Court-house Bootblack Stand—and Recorded by William L. Riordon* (New York, McClure, Phillips, 1905). Reprinted in *Plunkitt of Tammany Hall: A Series of Very Plain Talks on Very Practical Politics,* ed. Terrence J. McDonald (Boston: Bedford/St. Martins, 1994).

cleaning, and state senator. In fact, he claimed to have held at least four of the offices simultaneously.

After the downfall of William M. "Boss" Tweed, Tammany Hall's political boss in the early 1870s, the machine became more hierarchical and disciplined. Under the leadership of each boss an executive committee made up of Tammany Hall's elected leaders in the state assembly was responsible for making and enforcing the machine's decisions. Plunkitt served on this committee from 1900 to 1905 while a member of the state assembly. As a traditional practitioner of machine politics, he used patronage appointments and social services to please his voters. The result was that he remained very close to his constituents throughout his career.

William L. Riordan covered city politics for the *Evening Post* (now the *New York Post*). Through his interactions with Tammany Hall, the journalist became familiar with Plunkitt's stories about party politics and often published them as interviews in the *Post* or other local newspapers. Plunkitt, of course, was not hurt by Riordan's publicity of his generosity nor the practical way he approached politics, and Riordan's editors were very interested in entertaining articles that revealed a look at a ward boss behind the scenes. In 1905, Riordan published the stories as a collection in *Plunkitt of Tammany Hall: A Series of Very Plain Talks on Very Practical Politics, Delivered by ex-Senator George Washington Plunkitt, the Tammany Philosopher, from His Rostrum—the New York County Court-house Bootblack Stand—and Recorded by William L. Riordan.*

Strenuous Life of the Tammany District Leader

. . . The life of the Tammany district leader is strenuous. To his work is due the wonderful recuperative power of the organization.

One year it goes down in defeat and the prediction is made that it will never again raise its head. The district leader, undaunted by defeat, collects his scattered forces, organizes them as only Tammany knows how to organize, and in a little while the organization is as strong as ever.

No other politician in New York or elsewhere is exactly like the Tammany district leader or works as he does. As a rule, he has no business or occupation other than politics. He plays politics every day and night in the year, and his headquarters bears the inscription, "Never closed."

Everybody in the district knows him. Everybody knows where to find him, and nearly everybody goes to him for assistance of one sort or another, especially the poor of the tenements.

He is always obliging. He will go to the police courts to put in a good word for the "drunks and disorderlies" or pay their fines, if a good word is not effective. He will attend christenings, weddings, and funerals. He will feed the hungry and help bury the dead.

A philanthropist? Not at all. He is playing politics all the time.

Brought up in Tammany Hall, he has learned how to reach the hearts of the great mass of voters. He does not bother about reaching their heads. It is his belief that arguments and campaign literature have never gained votes.

He seeks direct contact with the people, does them good turns when he can, and relies on their not forgetting him on election day. His heart is always in his work, too, for his subsistence depends on its results.

If he holds his district and Tammany is in power, he is amply rewarded by a good office and the opportunities that go with it. What these opportunities are has been shown by the quick rise to wealth of so many Tammany district leaders. With the examples before him of Richard Croker, once leader of the Twentieth District; John F. Carroll, formerly leader of the Twenty-ninth; Timothy ("Dry Dollar") Sullivan, late leader of the Sixth, and many others, he can always look forward to riches and ease while he is going through the drudgery of his daily routine.

This is a record of a day's work by Plunkitt:

2 A.M.: Aroused from sleep by the ringing of his doorbell; went to the door and found a bartender, who asked him to go to the police station and bail out a saloon-keeper who had been arrested for violating the excise law. Furnished bail and returned to bed at three o'clock.

6 A.M.: Awakened by fire engines passing his house. Hastened to the scene of the fire, according to the custom of the Tammany district leaders, to give assistance to the fire sufferers, if needed. Met several of his election district captains who are always under orders to look out for fires, which are considered great vote-getters. Found several tenants who had been burned out, took them to a hotel, supplied them with clothes, fed them, and arranged temporary quarters for them until they could rent and furnish new apartments.

8:30 A.M.: Went to the police court to look after his constituents. Found six "drunks." Secured the discharge of four by a timely word with the judge, and paid the fines of two.

9 A.M.: Appeared in the Municipal District Court. Directed one of his district captains to act as counsel for a widow against whom dispossess proceed-

ings had been instituted and obtained an extension of time. Paid the rent of a poor family about to be dispossessed and gave them a dollar for food.

11 A.M.: At home again. Found four men waiting for him. One had been discharged by the Metropolitan Railway Company for neglect of duty, and wanted the district leader to fix things. Another wanted a job on the road. The third sought a place on the Subway and the fourth, a plumber, was looking for work with the Consolidated Gas Company. The district leader spent nearly three hours fixing things for the four men, and succeeded in each case.

3 P.M.: Attended the funeral of an Italian as far as the ferry. Hurried back to make his appearance at the funeral of a Hebrew constituent. Went conspicuously to the front both in the Catholic church and the synagogue, and later attended the Hebrew confirmation ceremonies in the synagogue.

7 P.M.: Went to district headquarters and presided over a meeting of election district captains. Each captain submitted a list of all the voters in his district, reported on their attitude toward Tammany, suggested who might be won over and how they could be won, told who were in need, and who were in trouble of any kind and the best way to reach them. District leader took notes and gave orders.

8 P.M.: Went to a church fair. Took chances on everything, bought ice cream for the young girls and the children. Kissed the little ones, flattered their mothers and took their fathers out for something down at the corner.

9 P.M.: At the club-house again. Spent $10 on tickets for a church excursion and promised a subscription for a new church bell. Bought tickets for a base-ball game to be played by two nines from his district. Listened to the complaints of a dozen push-cart peddlers who said they were persecuted by the police and assured them he would go to Police Headquarters in the morning and see about it.

10:30 P.M.: Attended a Hebrew wedding reception and dance. Had previously sent a handsome wedding present to the bride.

12 P.M.: In bed.

That is the actual record of one day in the life of Plunkitt. He does some of the same things every day, but his life is not so monotonous as to be wearisome.

Sometimes the work of a district leader is exciting, especially if he happens to have a rival who intends to make a contest for the leadership at the primaries. In that case, he is even more alert, tries to reach the fires before his rival, sends out runner to look for "drunks and disorderlies" at the police stations, and keeps a very close watch on the obituary columns of the newspapers.

A few years ago there was a bitter contest for the Tammany leadership of the Ninth district between John C. Sheehan and Frank J. Goodwin. Both had had long experience in Tammany politics and both understood every move of the game.

Every morning their agents went to their respective headquarters before seven o'clock and read through the death notices in all the morning papers. If they found that anybody in the district had died, they rushed to the homes of their principals with the information and then there was a race to the house of the deceased to offer condolences, and, if the family were poor, something more substantial.

On the day of the funeral there was another contest. Each faction tried to surpass the other in the number and appearance of the carriages it sent to the funeral, and more than once they almost came to blows at the church or in the cemetery.

On one occasion the Goodwinites played a trick on their adversaries which has since been imitated in other districts. A well-known liquor dealer who had a considerable following died, and both Sheehan and Goodwin were eager to become his political heir by making a big showing at the funeral.

Goodwin managed to catch the enemy napping. He went to all the livery stables in the district, hired all the carriages for the day, and gave orders to two hundred of his men to be on hand as mourners.

Sheehan had never had any trouble about getting all the carriages that he wanted, so he let the matter go until the night before the funeral. Then he found that he could not hire a carriage in the district.

He called his district committee together in a hurry and explained the situation to them. He could get all the vehicles he needed in the adjoining district, he said, but if he did that, Goodwin would rouse the voters of the Ninth by declaring that he (Sheehan), had patronized foreign industries.

Finally, it was decided that there was nothing to do but to go over to Sixth Avenue and Broadway for carriages. Sheehan made a fine turnout at the funeral, but the deceased was hardly in his grave before Goodwin raised the cry of "Protection to home industries," and denounced his rival for patronizing livery-stable keepers outside of his district. The cry had its effect in the primary campaign. At all events, Goodwin was elected leader.

A recent contest for the leadership of the Second district illustrated further the strenuous work of the Tammany district leaders. The contestants were Patrick Divver, who had managed the district for years, and Thomas F. Foley.

Both were particularly anxious to secure the large Italian vote. They not only attended all the Italian christenings and funerals, but also kept a close lookout for the marriage in order to be on hand with wedding presents.

At first, each had his own reporter in the Italian quarter to keep track of the marriages. Later, Foley conceived a better plan. He hired a man to stay all day at the City Hall marriage bureau, where most Italian couples go through the civil ceremony, and telephone to him at his saloon when anything was doing at the bureau.

Foley had a number of presents ready for use and, whenever he received a telephone message from his man, he hastened to the City Hall with a ring or a watch or a piece of silver and handed it to the bride with his congratulations. As a consequence, when Divver got the news and went to the home of the couple with his present, he always found that Foley had been ahead of him. Toward the end of the campaign, Divver also stationed a man at the marriage bureau and then there were daily foot races and fights between the two heelers.

Sometimes the rivals came into conflict at the death bed. One night a poor Italian peddler died in Roosevelt Street. The news reached Divver and Foley about the same time, and as they knew the family of the man was destitute, each went to an undertaker and brought him to the Roosevelt Street tenement.

The rivals and the undertakers met at the house and an altercation ensued. After much discussion the Divver undertaker was selected. Foley had more carriages at the funeral, however, and he further impressed the Italian voters by paying the widow's rent for a month, and sending her half a ton of coal and a barrel of flour.

The rivals were put on their mettle toward the end of the campaign by the wedding of a daughter of one of the original Cohens of the Baxter Street region. The Hebrew vote in the district is nearly as large as the Italian vote, and Divver and Foley set out to capture the Cohens and their friends.

They stayed up nights thinking what they would give the bride. Neither knew how much the other was prepared to spend on a wedding present, or what form it would take; so spies were employed by both sides to keep watch on the jewelry stores, and the jewelers of the district were bribed by each side to impart the desired information.

At last Foley heard that Divver had purchased a set of silver knives, forks, and spoons. He at once bought a duplicate set and added a silver tea service. When the presents were displayed at the home of the bride, Divver was not in a pleasant mood and he charged his jeweler with treachery. It may be added that Foley won at the primaries.

One of the fixed duties of a Tammany district leader is to give two outings every summer, one for the men of his district, and the other for the women and children and a beefsteak dinner and ball every winter. The scene of the outings is, usually, one of the groves along the Sound.

The ambition of the district leader on these occasions is to demonstrate that his men have broken all records in the matter of eating and drinking. He gives out the exact number of pounds of beef, poultry, butter, etc., that they have consumed and professes to know how many potatoes and ears of corn have been served.

According to his figures, the average eating record of each man at the outing is about ten pounds of beef, two or three chickens, a pound of butter, a half peck of potatoes, and two dozen ears of corn. The drinking records, as given out, are still more phenomenal. For some reason, not yet explained, the district leader thinks that his popularity will be greatly increased if he can show that his followers can eat and drink more than the followers of any other district leader.

The same idea governs the beefsteak dinners in the winter. It matters not what sort of steak is served or how it is cooked; the district leader considers only the question of quantity, and when he excels all others in this particular, he feels, somehow, that he is a bigger man and deserves more patronage than his associates in the Tammany Executive Committee.

As to the balls, they are the events of the winter in the extreme East Side and West Side society. Mamie and Maggie and Jennie prepare for them months in advance, and their young men save up for the occasion just as they save for the summer trips to Coney Island.

The district leader is in his glory at the opening of the ball. He leads the cotillion with the prettiest woman present—his wife, if he has one, permitting—and spends almost the whole night shaking hands with his constituents. The ball costs him a pretty penny, but he has found that the investment pays.

By these means the Tammany district leader reaches out into the homes of his district, keeps watch not only on the men, but also on the women and children; knows their needs, their likes and dislikes, their troubles and their hopes, and places himself in a position to use his knowledge for the benefit of his organization and himself. Is it any wonder that scandals do not permanently disable Tammany and that it speedily recovers from what seems to be crushing defeat?

❧ 25 ❧
The Tillman Act*
(1907)

1. McKinley campaigned from his front porch in Canton, Ohio, in 1896, while Bryan campaigned vigorously throughout the United States. How did the campaign strategy managed by Mark Hanna for McKinley compare to that of Bryan and the Democrats?
2. What effect might prohibiting corporations from donating money to candidates have on federal elections?

MONEY HAS ALWAYS been associated with electoral politics—the first legislation regulating campaign finance at the federal level in the United States was passed in 1867 and prohibited federal officials from requesting political contributions from workers in the Navy Yard in Washington, D.C. Serious regulation of campaign finance, however, did not come into fashion until the Progressive era, when the contributions of corporations and individual fat cat donors reached astonishing levels.

In the 1896 and 1900 presidential elections, the Republican Party raised more and spent more funds than the Democrats by very substantial margins. In fact, the comparative advantage of the Republicans over the Democrats in fund-raising during those election cycles alarmed many journalists and Progressive politicians and led them to cry out for reform. The architect of the this fund-raising success was the chair of the Republican National Committee, Ohio governor Mark Hanna. In 1896 Hanna pressured corporate interests to make regular and substantial donations to William McKinley's presidential campaign, arguing that the election of Democrat William Jennings Bryan would be a disaster for business, if only because Bryan supported linking the value of the U.S. dollar to silver instead of gold, which many feared would cause rampant inflation and devalue investments.

*Tillman Act of 1907, 34 Stat. 864 (January 26, 1907). Reprinted at www.brookings.edu/gs/cf/sourcebk/chap2.pdf.

157

While McKinley gave brief remarks to reporters from the front porch of his home in Ohio, Bryan crisscrossed the country promoting his Populist message. To compensate for Bryan's oratorical advantage over McKinley, Hanna changed the nature of political marketing to voters by using the Republicans' fund-raising advantage to saturate the country with McKinley's message through every means of advertisement available at the time, including buttons and circulars. The approach was unprecedented and unparalleled for many years to come, but it foreshadowed changes on the horizon of political campaigns.

The influence of corporate interests in presidential campaigns continued into the next election cycle. In 1904 Alton B. Parker, the Democratic presidential nominee, criticized President Theodore Roosevelt for accepting campaign contributions from corporations. Roosevelt denied the claim, but investigators found that major corporations had made a number of large contributions to his campaign. To save face, Roosevelt forcefully called for election reform in his message to Congress on December 5, 1905, stating, "All contributions by corporations to any political committee or for any political purpose should be forbidden by law."

With public sentiment clearly in favor of reform, the House Committee on Elections began to investigate proposals to limit the influence of corporations on electoral politics. One such proposal had been introduced in an earlier session of Congress and championed by Democratic senator Benjamin "Pitchfork Ben" Tillman of South Carolina. On January 26, 1907, Congress passed the Tillman Act, which forbid corporations and nationally chartered banks from directly contributing to federal candidates. The law, however, was unenforceable because no effective mechanism for maintaining compliance existed. Legislation requiring the reporting of campaign finance was not enacted until 1910 as part of the Federal Corrupt Practices Act.

***

An Act to prohibit corporations from making money contributions in connection with political elections.

Be it enacted, That it shall be unlawful for any national bank, or any corporation organized by authority of any laws of Congress, to make a money contribution in connection with any election to any political office. It shall also be unlawful for any corporation whatever to make a money contribution in connection with any election at which Presidential and Vice-Presidential electors or a Representative in Congress is to be voted for or any election by any State legislature of a United States Senator. Every corporation which shall make any contribution in violation of the foregoing provisions shall be subject to a fine not exceeding five thousand dollars, and every officer or director of any corporation who shall consent to any contribution by the corporation in violation of the foregoing provisions shall upon conviction be punished by a fine of not exceeding one thousand and not less than two hundred and fifty dollars, or by imprisonment for a term of not more than one year, or both such fine and imprisonment in the discretion of the court.

⋅෧ 26 ෨⋅

George Norris's Resolution to Change the Membership of the House Rules Committee*
(1910)

1. The Speaker of the House of Representatives is a powerful position. How did denying the Speaker the chance to serve as the chair of the Rules Committee decrease Cannon's influence?
2. Is it important for the Speaker of the House to maintain party discipline? Why or why not?

THE POWER OF THE Speaker of the House of Representatives grew significantly in the late nineteenth and early twentieth centuries, especially under the leadership of Illinois Republican Joseph Gurney Cannon. At that time the presiding officer of the chamber also served as chair of the powerful Rules Committee. This committee was not only responsible for determining the order and circumstances whereby legislation was brought to the floor, but it also made committee assignments. "Uncle Joe," Speaker from 1903 to 1910, was a firm believer in

*www.archives.gov/exhibits/treasures_of_congress/Images/page_16/53b.html

HRes.
Resolved that the rules of the House be amended as follows:

The Committee on Rules shall consist of fifteen members, nine of whom shall be members of the majority party and six of whom shall be members of the minority party, to be selected as follows: The States of the Union shall be divided, by a committee of three, elected by the House for that purpose, into nine groups, each group containing, as near as may be, an equal number of members belonging to the majority party. The States of the Union shall likewise be divided into six groups, each group containing, as near as may be, an equal number of members belonging to the minority party.

At 10:00 o'clock A. M. of the day following the adoption of the report of said committee, each of said groups shall meet and select one of its ~~members~~ number a member of the Committee on Rules. The place of meeting for each of said groups shall be designated by the said committee of three, in its report. Each of said groups shall report to the House the name of the member selected for membership on the Committee on Rules.

The Committee on Rules shall select its own chairman.

The Speaker shall not be eligible to membership on said Committee.

All rules or parts thereof inconsistent with the foregoing resolutions are hereby repealed.

party discipline and used his power as chair to reward those in his party who carried out his will and punish others who did not.

Later in his tenure as Speaker, the Progressive wing of the Republican Party became frustrated with Cannon's ability to control the agenda and debate in the House. His own economic and social philosophy made Cannon unwilling to yield to the call for Progressive legislation supported by members of Congress from both parties. In response to their criticism he retorted, "I am damned tired of listening to all this babble for reform. America is a hell of a success."

Dissatisfaction with Cannon culminated in the introduction of a resolution by Progressive Republican George Norris of Nebraska on March 17, 1910. Norris and a small group of Progressive Republicans allied with Democrats in challenging Cannon's power as Speaker. The proposal made by Norris was to remove the Speaker from the Rules Committee, which would effectively eliminate Cannon's immeasurable power over the members of the House.

Although Cannon was a master of House rules he opened the door for Norris when he tried to prevent a procedure that allowed committees to call up legislation of their choice, known as Calendar Wednesday. In response, Norris rose to offer his resolution as a matter of constitutional privilege. The Speaker's supporters raised a point of order by arguing that the Norris resolution was not a matter of constitutional privilege. Cannon let the debate over the point of order continue for two days so that his supporters in the House could return from St. Patrick's Day parades—and then he sustained it. Norris and the Progressives appealed his decision to the full chamber, which overturned the Speaker's ruling by a vote of 182–162. The resolution was then adopted by a vote of 191–156.

While Cannon remained Speaker, his power over the House effectively ended, and the power of the Speaker over party members also ended. Years later Norris remembered of his resolution, "I had carried it for a long time, certain, that in the flush of its power, the Cannon machine would overreach itself. The paper upon which I had written my resolution had become so tattered it scarcely hung together."

✧ 27 ✧
The Publicity Act of 1910*
(1910)

1. In principle, how does public disclosure of contributions improve campaigns and elections?
2. The Publicity Act's enforcement provisions were weak. Why might it have taken until the 1970s for Congress to reform campaign finance?

AFTER PASSAGE OF the Tillman Act in 1907, groups like the National Publicity Law Organization (NPLO) continued to lobby for the regulation and disclosure of campaign finances. As a result of their efforts the Publicity Act, officially known as the Federal Corrupt Practices Act, was enacted on June 25, 1910.

As passed, the act required that after each election political parties operating in two or more states had to report all campaign contributions and expenditures made in behalf of candidates for the House of Representatives. The provision affected the national party committees and the congressional campaign committees, and was an attempt on the part of the Republican majority in Congress to appease the critics of the campaign finance system. It did little to deter advocates for reform, however. After winning a majority in the House in 1910 and gaining seats in the Senate, the Democrats sought to strengthen the Publicity Act. Republicans hoped to defeat the bill by including amendments regulating primary elections that would be unacceptable to Southern Democrats who faced stiffer competition in the primaries. Ultimately, their strategy backfired.

On August 19, 1911, the Publicity Act was amended in four ways. First, the requirements of public disclosure were applied to both House and Senate candidates. Second, public disclosure was required of all congressional candidates for both primaries and general elections. Third, public disclosure was required of all congressional candidates before and

*Publicity Act of 1910, 36 Stat. 822 (June 25, 1910). Reprinted at www.brookings.edu/gs/cf/sourcebk/chap2.pdf.

after an election. Finally, limits were set on candidate spending at the lesser of $5,000 for House candidates and $10,000 for Senate candidates or the amount established by state law.

The law came under fire after the Republican primary for the Michigan Senate seat in 1918, when Truman H. Newberry defeated Henry Ford. Newberry's campaign committee reported spending almost $180,000—more than ten times the limit permitted under the Michigan campaign spending law. Newberry was convicted of violating the Federal Corrupt Practices Act. In his appeal to the U.S. Supreme Court, Newberry argued that he had not violated the law because Congress did not have the authority to regulate primary elections. The spending limits ultimately were struck down by the Court in *Newberry v. U.S.* (1921), with the Court holding that Congress did not have the authority to regulate spending limits in party nomination campaigns. The Court later reversed its stance when it ruled in *United States v. Classic* (1941) that Congress did have the authority to regulate primary elections when they were governed under state law or when they effectively determined the outcome of a general election, such as in states dominated by one political party.

The Publicity Act was again amended in 1925. First, the amendments extended the legislation to cover parties and election committees that operated in multiple states. Second, it was changed to mandate that financial disclosure be reported quarterly. Third, it set a requirement that parties and election committees report any contribution of more than $100. Fourth, spending limits on Senate campaigns were raised to $25,000. Compliance with the legislation was still effectively voluntary, however, since Congress had created no provision for enforcement.

It took the Teapot Dome scandal of the 1920s, which involved gifts made to federal officials responsible for granting oil leases on public lands, to once again encourage Congress to reform campaign finance by amending the Publicity Act. The resulting amendments required all political committees operating in more than one state and all House and Senate candidates to file quarterly reports of expenditures and all contributions of more than $100, even in nonelection years. The reporting requirements were later challenged, but upheld by the Supreme Court in *Burroughs v. U.S.* (1934). The act remained in force until the Federal

Election Campaign Act of 1971 took effect. Despite its considerable amendments, the act remained ineffective throughout its tenure, because Congress never created meaningful provisions for its enforcement.

<hr>

An Act providing for publicity of contributions made for the purpose of influencing elections at which Representatives in Congress are elected.

Be it enacted, That the term "political committee" under the provisions of this Act shall include the national committees of all political parties and the national congressional campaign committees of all political parties and all committees, associations, or organizations which shall in two or more States influence the result or attempt to influence the result of an election at which Representatives in Congress are to be elected.

SEC. 2. That every political committee as defined in this Act shall have a chairman and a treasurer. It shall be the duty of the treasurer to keep a detailed and exact account of all money or its equivalent received by or promised to such committee or any member thereof, or by or to any person acting under its authority or in its behalf, and the name of every person, firm, association, or committee from whom received, and of all expenditures, disbursements, and promises of payment or disbursement made by the committee or any member thereof, or by any person acting under its authority or in its behalf, and to whom paid, distributed, or disbursed. No officer or member of such committee, or other person acting under its authority or in its behalf, shall receive any money or its equivalent, or expend or promise to expend any money on behalf of such committee, until after a chairman and treasurer of such committee shall have been chosen.

SEC. 3. That every payment or disbursement made by a political committee exceeding ten dollars in amount be evidenced by a receipted bill stating the particulars of expense, and every such record, voucher, receipt, or account shall be preserved for fifteen months after the election to which it relates.

SEC. 4. That whoever, acting under the authority or in behalf of such political committee, whether as a member thereof or otherwise, receives any contribution, payment, loan, gift, advance, deposit, or promise of money or its equivalent shall, on demand, and in any event within five days after the receipt of such contribution, payment, loan, gift, advance, deposit, or promise, render to the treasurer of such political committee a detailed account of the same, together with the name and address from whom received, and said treasurer shall forthwith enter the same in a ledger or record to be kept by him for that purpose.

SEC. 5. That the treasurer of every such political committee shall, within thirty days after the election at which Representatives in Congress were chosen in two or more States, file with the Clerk of the House of Representatives at Washington, District of Columbia, an itemized, detailed statement, sworn to by said treasurer and conforming to the requirements of the following section of this Act. The statement so filed with the Clerk of the House of Representatives shall be preserved by him for fifteen months, and shall be a part of the public records of his office, and shall be open to public inspection. . . .

SEC. 10. That every person willfully violating any of the foregoing provisions of this Act shall, upon conviction, be fined not more than one thousand dollars or imprisoned not more than one year, or both.

✥ 28 ✥
Theodore Roosevelt's
"Confession of Faith" Speech*
(1912)

1. Given that the Progressive Party was led by former president Theodore Roosevelt, why did it fail to become a major party?
2. Why was Roosevelt's strategy for regaining the Oval Office ineffective?

IN LATE 1911 FORMER president Theodore Roosevelt announced that he would challenge incumbent William Howard Taft for the Republican presidential nomination. Roosevelt had served as president from 1901 to 1909 and had supported Taft to succeed him when leaving office, but later had come to believe that Taft had failed to continue his legacy of championing progressive reform.

The 1912 election was the first to utilize presidential preference primaries in the party nomination process, and Roosevelt won primaries in nine states. His challengers, Sen. Robert LaFollette and Taft, won the

*www.theodore-roosevelt.com/trarmageddon.html

primaries in the remaining three. While Roosevelt was popular with the electorate in those states holding primaries, most states were still using party conventions. Ultimately, Roosevelt was unable to sway the support of the machine politicians who controlled convention delegates from Taft.

When he realized that he would fail to secure the Republican nomination, Roosevelt started the new Progressive Party and urged his supporters to walk out of the Republican Convention and join him. At the Auditorium Theater in Chicago, those who walked out put together the Progressive Party Platform and nominated Roosevelt to be the party's presidential candidate. On August 6, he delivered his "Confession of Faith" as his acceptance speech.

When a reporter suggested that he was no longer fit to hold office, Roosevelt responded, "I'm as fit as a bull moose." In honor of this self-proclaimed strength and vigor, the Progressive Party was often referred to as the Bull Moose Party. While many independents and reformers joined the new Progressive Party, the majority of Republican officeholders refused to switch. Most of Roosevelt's closest political allies simply found leaving the Republican Party too radical and continued to support Taft.

On October 14, 1912, Roosevelt was scheduled to address ten thousand people in Milwaukee, Wisconsin. Unknown to him, New York bartender John Schrank had been following him for three weeks across eight states with the intent of assassinating him. As Roosevelt left the Gilpatrick Hotel to speak at the auditorium, Schrank fired his revolver upon the former president while he was waving to the crowd. Roosevelt was wounded, but the contents of his breast pocked spared his life: the metal case that held his glasses and a bulky copy of his speech absorbed the bullet's force. Police apprehended Schrank, and Roosevelt proceeded to the auditorium to deliver his speech. News of the assassination attempt reached the crowd gathered in the auditorium, but Roosevelt stunned the crowd stating, "It takes more than one bullet to kill a Bull Moose."

On Election Day the Progressive Party actually performed well compared to other third parties: Roosevelt's 27 percent of the popular vote and eighty-eight electoral votes surpassed Taft's 23 percent of the popular vote and eight electoral votes. The split in the Republican Party, however, allowed Democrat Woodrow Wilson to win 435 electoral votes and the presidency with only 42 percent of the popular vote. The Progressive Party performed poorly in the 1914 midterm elections and

effectively disappeared. Most Progressives, including Roosevelt, returned to the Republican Party by 1916.

To you, men and women who have come here to this great city of this great
State formally to launch a new party, a party of the people of the whole Union,
the National Progressive Party, I extend my hearty greeting. You are taking a
bold and a greatly needed step for the service of our beloved country. The old
parties are husks, with no real soul within either, divided on artificial lines,
boss-ridden and privilege-controlled, each a jumble of incongruous elements,
and neither daring to speak out wisely and fearlessly what should be said on
the vital issues of the day. This new movement is a movement of truth, sincerity, and wisdom, a movement which proposes to put at the service of all our
people the collective power of the people, through their Governmental agencies, alike in the Nation and in the several States. We propose boldly to face
the real and great questions of the day, and not skillfully to evade them as do
the old parties. We propose to raise aloft a standard to which all honest men
can repair, and under which all can fight, no matter what their past political
differences, if they are content to face the future and no longer to dwell among
the dead issues of the past. We propose to put forth a platform which shall not
be a platform of the ordinary and insincere kind, but shall be a contract with
the people; and, if the people accept this contract by putting us in power, we
shall hold ourselves under honorable obligation to fulfill every promise it contains as loyally as if it were actually enforceable under the penalties of the law.

No Hope from Old Party Machines

The prime need today is to face the fact that we are now in the midst of a great
economic evolution. There is urgent necessity of applying both common sense
and the highest ethical standard to this movement for better economic conditions among the mass of our people if we are to make it one of healthy evolution and not one of revolution. It is, from the standpoint of our country, wicked
as well as foolish longer to refuse to face the real issues of the day. Only by so
facing them can we go forward; and to do this we must break up the old party
organizations and obliterate the old cleavage lines on the dead issues inherited
from fifty years ago. Our fight is a fundamental fight against both of the old
corrupt party machines, for both are under the dominion of the plunder league
of the professional politicians who are controlled and sustained by the great
beneficiaries of privilege and reaction. How close is the alliance between the
two machines is shown by the attitude of that portion of those Northeastern

newspapers, including the majority of the great dailies in all the Northeastern cities—Boston, Buffalo, Springfield, Hartford, Philadelphia, and, above all, New York—which are controlled by or representative of the interests which, in popular phrase, are conveniently grouped together as the Wall Street interests. The large majority of these papers supported Judge Parker for the Presidency in 1904; almost unanimously they supported Mr. Taft for the Republican nomination this year; the large majority are now supporting Professor Wilson for the election. Some of them still prefer Mr. Taft to Mr. Wilson, but all make either Mr. Taft or Mr. Wilson their first choice; and one of the ludicrous features of the campaign is that those papers supporting Professor Wilson show the most jealous partisanship for Mr. Taft whenever they think his interests are jeopardized by the Progressive movement—that, for instance, any Electors will obey the will of the majority of the Republican voters at the primaries, and vote for me instead of obeying the will of the Messrs. Barnes-Penrose-Guggenheim combination by voting for Mr. Taft. No better proof can be given than this of the fact that the fundamental concern of the privileged interests is to beat the new party. Some of them would rather beat it with Mr. Wilson; others would rather beat it with Mr. Taft; but the difference between Mr. Wilson and Mr. Taft they consider as trivial, as a mere matter of personal preference. Their real fight is for either, as against the Progressives. They represent the allied Reactionaries of the country, and they are against the new party because to their unerring vision it is evident that the real danger to privilege comes from the new party, and from the new party alone. The men who presided over the Baltimore and the Chicago Conventions, and the great bosses who controlled the two Conventions, Mr. Root and Mr. Parker, Mr. Barnes and Mr. Murphy, Mr. Penrose and Mr. Taggart, Mr. Guggenheim and Mr. Sullivan, differ from one another of course on certain points. But these are the differences which one corporation lawyer has with another corporation lawyer when acting for different corporations. They come together at once as against a common enemy when the dominion of both is threatened by the supremacy of the people of the United States, now aroused to the need of a National alignment on the vital economic issues of this generation.

Neither the Republican nor the Democratic platform contains the slightest promise of approaching the great problems of today either with understanding or good faith; and yet never was there greater need in this Nation than now of understanding, and of action taken in good faith, on the part of the men and the organizations shaping our governmental policy. Moreover, our needs are such that there should be coherent action among those responsible for the conduct of National affairs and those responsible for the conduct of State affairs; because our aim should be the same in both State and Nation; that is, to use the Government as an efficient agency for the practical betterment of social and economic conditions throughout this land. There are other important things to be done, but this is the most important thing. It is preposterous to leave a movement in the hands of men who have broken their promises as have the present heads of the Republican organization (not of the Republican voters, for they in no shape represent the rank and file of Republican voters). These men by their deeds give the lie to their words. There is no health in them, and they cannot be trusted. But the Democratic party is just as little to be trusted. The Underwood-Fitzgerald combination in the House of Representatives has shown that it cannot safely be trusted to maintain the interests of this country abroad or to represent the interests of the plain people at home. The control of the various State bosses in the State organizations has been strengthened by the action at Baltimore; and scant indeed would be the use of exchanging the whips of Messrs. Barnes, Penrose, and Guggenheim for the scorpions of Messrs. Murphy, Taggart, and Sullivan. Finally, the Democratic platform not only shows an utter failure to understand either present conditions or the means of making these conditions better, but also a reckless willingness to try to attract various sections of the electorate by making mutually incompatible promises which there is not the slightest intention of redeeming, and which, if redeemed, would result in sheer ruin. Far-seeing patriots should turn scornfully from men who seek power on a platform which with exquisite nicety combines silly inability to understand the National needs and dishonest insincerity in promising conflicting and impossible remedies.

If this country is really to go forward along the path of social and economic justice, there must be a new party of Nationwide and non-sectional principles, a party where the titular National chiefs and the real State leaders shall be in genuine accord, a party in whose counsels the people shall be supreme, a party that shall represent in the Nation and the several States alike the same cause, the cause of human rights and of governmental efficiency. At present both the old parties are controlled by professional politicians in the interests of the privileged classes, and apparently each has set up as its ideal of business and political development a government by financial despotism tempered by make-believe political assassination. Democrat and Republican alike, they represent government of the needy many by professional politicians in the interests of the rich few. This is class government, and class government of a peculiarly unwholesome kind.

The Right of the People to Rule

It seems to me, therefore, that the time is ripe, and overripe, for a genuine Progressive movement, Nationwide and justice-loving, sprung from and responsible to the people themselves, and sundered by a great gulf from both of the old party organizations, while representing all that is best in the hopes, beliefs, and aspirations of the plain people who make up the immense majority of the rank and file of both the old parties.

The first essential in the Progressive programme is the right of the people to rule. But a few months ago our opponents were assuring us with insincere clamor that it was absurd for us to talk about desiring that the people should rule, because, as a matter of fact, the people actually do rule. Since that time the actions of the Chicago Convention, and to an only less degree of the Baltimore Convention, have shown in striking fashion how little the people do rule under our present conditions. We should provide by National law for Presidential primaries. We should provide for the election of United States Senators by popular vote. We should provide for a short ballot; nothing makes it harder for the people to control their public servants than to force them to vote for so many officials that they cannot really keep track of any one of them, so that each becomes indistinguishable in the crowd around him. There must be stringent and efficient corrupt practices acts, applying to the primaries as well as the elections; and there should be publicity of campaign contributions during the campaign. We should provide throughout this Union for giving the people in every State the real right to rule themselves, and really and not nominally to control their public servants and their agencies for doing the public business; all incident of this being giving the people the right themselves to do this public business if they find it impossible to get what they desire through the existing agencies. I do not attempt to dogmatize as to the machinery by which this end should be achieved. In each community it must be shaped so as to correspond not merely with the needs but with the customs and ways of thought of that community, and no community has a right to dictate to any other in this matter. But wherever representative government has in actual fact become nonrepresentative there the people should secure to themselves the initiative, the referendum, and the recall, doing it in such fashion as to make it evident that they do not intend to use these instrumentalities wantonly or frequently, but to hold them ready for use in order to correct the misdeeds or failures of the public servants when it has become evident that these misdeeds and failures cannot be corrected in ordinary and normal fashion. The administrative officer should be given full power for otherwise he cannot do well the people's work; and the people should be given full power over him.

I do not mean that we shall abandon representative government; on the contrary, I mean that we shall devise methods by which our Government shall become really representative. To use such measures as the initiative, referendum, and recall indiscriminately and promiscuously on all kinds of occasions would undoubtedly cause disaster; but events have shown that at present our institutions are not representative—at any rate in many States, and sometimes in the Nation—and that we cannot wisely afford to let this condition of things remain longer uncorrected. We have permitted the growing up of a breed of politicians who, sometimes for improper political purposes, sometimes as a means of serving the great special interests of privilege which stand behind them, twist so-called representative institutions into a means of thwarting instead of expressing the deliberate and well thought-out judgment of the people as a whole. This cannot be permitted. We choose our representatives for two purposes. In the first place, we choose them with the desire that, as experts, they shall study certain matters with which we, the people as a whole, cannot be intimately acquainted, and that as regards these matters they shall formulate a policy for our betterment. Even as regards such a policy, and the actions taken thereunder, we ourselves should have the right ultimately to vote our disapproval of it, if we feel such disapproval. But, in the next place, our representatives are chosen to carry out certain policies as to which we have definitely made up our minds, and here we expect them to represent us by doing what we have decided ought to be done. All I desire to do by securing more direct control of the governmental agents and agencies of the people is to give the people the chance to make their representatives really represent them whenever the Government becomes mis-representative instead of representative.

I have not come to this way of thinking from closet study, or as a mere matter of theory; I have been forced to it by a long experience with the actual conditions of our political life. A few years ago, for instance, there was very little demand in this country for Presidential primaries. There would have been no demand now if the politicians had really endeavored to carry out the will of the people as regards nominations for President. But, largely under the influence of special privilege in the business world, there have arisen castes of politicians who not only do not represent the people, but who make their bread and butter by thwarting the wishes of the people. This is true of the bosses of both political parties in my own State of New York, and it is just as true of the bosses of one or the other political party in a great many States of the Union. The power of the people must be made supreme within the several party organizations.

In the contest which culminated six weeks ago in this city I speedily found that my chance was at a minimum in any State where I could not get an expression of the people themselves in the primaries. I found that if I could appeal to the rank and file of the Republican voters, I could generally win, whereas, if I had to appeal to the political caste—which includes the most noisy defenders of the old system—I generally lost. Moreover, I found, as a matter of fact, not as a matter of theory, that these politicians habitually and unhesitatingly resort to every species of mean swindling and cheating in order to carry their point. It is because of the general recognition of this fact that the words politics and politicians have grown to have a sinister meaning throughout this country. The bosses and their agents in the National Republican Convention at Chicago treated political theft as a legitimate political weapon. It is instructive to compare the votes of States where there were open primaries and the votes of States where there were not. In Illinois, Pennsylvania and Ohio we had direct primaries, and the Taft machine was beaten two to one. Between and bordering on these States were Michigan, Indiana, and Kentucky. In these States we could not get direct primaries, and the politicians elected two delegates to our one. In the first three States the contests were absolutely open, absolutely honest. The rank and file expressed their wishes, and there was no taint of fraud about what they did. In the other three States the contest was marked by every species of fraud and violence on the part of our opponents, and half the Taft delegates in the Chicago Convention from these States had tainted titles. The entire Wall Street press at this moment is vigorously engaged in denouncing the direct primary system and upholding the old convention system, or, as they call it, the "old representative system." They are so doing because they know that the bosses and the powers of special privilege have tenfold the chance under the convention system that they have when the rank and file of the people can express themselves at the primaries. The nomination of Mr. Taft at Chicago was a fraud upon the rank and file of the Republican Party; it was obtained only by defrauding the rank and file of the party of their right to express their choice; and such fraudulent action does not bind a single honest member of the party.

Well, what the National Committee and the fraudulent majority of the National Convention did at Chicago in misrepresenting the people has been done again and again in Congress, perhaps especially in the Senate and in the State legislatures. Again and again laws demanded by the people have been refused to the people because the representatives of the people misrepresented them. Now my proposal is merely that we shall give to the people the power, to be used not wantonly but only in exceptional cases, themselves to see to it that the governmental action taken in their name is really the action that they desire. . . .

Conclusion

Now, friends, this is my confession of faith. I have made it rather long because I wish you to know just what my deepest convictions are on the great questions of today, so that if you choose to make me your standard-bearer in the fight you shall make your choice understanding exactly how I feel—and if, after hearing me, you think you ought to choose some one else, I shall loyally abide by your choice. The convictions to which I have come have not been arrived at as the result of study in the closet or the library. but from the knowledge I have gained through hard experience during the many years in which, under many and varied conditions, I have striven and toiled with men. I believe in a larger use of the governmental power to help remedy industrial wrongs, because it has been borne in on me by actual experience that without the exercise of such power many of the wrongs will go unremedied. I believe in a larger opportunity for the people themselves directly to participate in government and to control their governmental agents, because long experience has taught me that without such control many of their agents will represent them badly. By actual experience in office I have found that, as a rule, I could secure the triumph of the causes in which I most believed, not from the politicians and the men who claim an exceptional right to speak in business and government, but by going over their heads and appealing directly to the people themselves. I am not under the slightest delusion as to any power that during my political career I have at any time possessed. Whatever of power I at any time had, I obtained from the people. I could exercise it only so long as, and to the extent that, the people not merely believed in me, but heartily backed me up. Whatever I did as President I was able to do only because I had the backing of the people. When on any point I did not have that backing, when on any point I differed from the people, it mattered not whether I was right or whether I was wrong, my power vanished. I tried my best to lead the people, to advise them, to tell them what I thought was right; if necessary, I never hesitated to tell them what I thought they ought to hear, even though I thought it would be unpleasant for them to hear it; but I recognized that my task was to try to lead them and not to drive them, to take them into my confidence, to try to show them that I was right, and then loyally and in good faith to accept their decision. I will do anything for the people except what my conscience tells me is wrong, and that I can do for no man and no set of men; I hold that a man cannot serve the people well unless he serves his conscience; but I hold also that where his conscience bids him refuse to do what the people desire, he should not try to continue in office against their will. Our Government system should be so shaped that the public servant, when he cannot conscientiously carry out the wishes of the people, shall at their desire leave his office and not misrepresent them in office; and I hold that the public servant can by so doing, better than in any other way, serve both them and his conscience.

Surely there never was a fight better worth making than the one in which we are engaged. It little matters what befalls any one of us who for the time being stand in the forefront of the battle. I hope we shall win, and I believe that if we can wake the people to what the fight really means we shall win. But, win or lose, we shall not falter. Whatever fate may at the moment overtake any of us, the movement itself will not stop. Our cause is based on the eternal principles of righteousness; and even though we who now lead may for the time fail, in the end the cause itself shall triumph. Six weeks ago, here in Chicago, I spoke to the honest representatives of a Convention which was not dominated by honest men; a Convention wherein sat, alas! a majority of men who, with sneering indifference to every principle of right, so acted as to bring to a shameful end a party which had been founded over half a century ago by men in whose souls burned the fire of lofty endeavor. Now to you men, who, in your turn, have corne [sic] together to spend and be spent in the endless crusade against wrong, to you who face the future resolute and confident, to you who strive in a spirit of brotherhood for the betterment of our Nation, to you who gird yourselves for this great new fight in the never-ending warfare for the good of humankind, I say in closing what in that speech I said in closing: We stand at Armageddon, and we battle for the Lord.

✥ 29 ✥

Franklin Roosevelt's "Commonwealth Club" Speech*

(1932)

1. How did the use of radio revolutionize campaigns and elections?
2. How did Roosevelt criticize his opposition while rarely mentioning President Hoover or the Republican Party by name? Why might he have pursued this strategy?

THE COMMONWEALTH CLUB of California was founded in 1903 and is one of the oldest and largest nonpartisan, nonprofit education organizations in the United States. Since 1924, the club has broadcast its forums on many public radio stations. Historically, it has hosted many

---

*www.americanrhetoric.com/speeches/fdrcommonwealth.htm

political celebrities, allowing them to use the forum to address the nation on major issues of the day. On September 23, 1932, many Americans across the country heard Franklin Roosevelt broadcasting from the Commonwealth Club for the first time.

At that time, Franklin Delano Roosevelt was governor of New York and the Democratic candidate for president. In his Commonwealth Club speech, Roosevelt first introduced his ideas to confront the Great Depression, which had begun with the stock market crash of October 29, 1929. Governor Roosevelt's proposals to energize the economy included various types of recovery, reform, and relief. His plan soon became known to the public as the New Deal.

According to his closest advisers, when Roosevelt first considered running for president he realized that his command of the affairs of the state of New York was considerable, but his understanding of national issues was still rather limited. This meant that he would be at a serious disadvantage relative to his opponent, incumbent president Herbert Hoover. To develop a better understanding of government and economics at the national level, Roosevelt gathered what he called his "Privy Council," publicly known as the "Brains Trust." The Brains Trust initially included three government and economics professors from Columbia University: Raymond Moley, Rexford Tugwell, and Adolf D. Berle Jr. Later, Harvard law professor Felix Frankfurter, Basil O'Connor, Samuel Rosenman, Gen. Hugh Johnson, and others joined the group. Roosevelt met with the Brains Trust at his Hyde Park estate in early 1932, where they offered him insight into how to confront the economic and social impact of the Great Depression. To win the election and combat the Depression, however, Governor Roosevelt needed to make a plan of action. This plan became the foundation of the New Deal.

Roosevelt's speech at the Commonwealth Club permitted the American public to hear firsthand his plan for recovery from the Great Depression. It played an important role in convincing the public to select him as president in 1932 and allowed him to claim a mandate for economic reform that Congress could enact quickly.

I count it a privilege to be invited to address the Commonwealth Club. It has stood in the life of this city and state, and it is perhaps accurate to add, the nation, as a group of citizen leaders interested in fundamental problems of government, and chiefly concerned with achievement of progress in government through non-partisan means. The privilege of addressing you, therefore, in the heat of a political campaign, is great. I want to respond to your courtesy in terms consistent with your policy.

I want to speak not of politics but of government. I want to speak not of parties, but of universal principles. They are not political, except in that larger sense in which a great American once expressed a definition of politics, that nothing in all of human life is foreign to the science of politics. . . .

You are familiar with the great political duel . . . and how Hamilton, and his friends, building towards a dominant centralized power were at length defeated in the great election of 1800, by Mr. Jefferson's party. Out of that duel came the two parties, Republican and Democratic, as we know them today.

So began, in American political life, the new day, the day of the individual against the system, the day in which individualism was made the great watchword of American life. The happiest of economic conditions made that day long and splendid. On the Western frontier, land was substantially free. No one, who did not shirk the task of earning a living, was entirely without opportunity to do so. Depressions could, and did, come and go; but they could not alter the fundamental fact that most of the people lived partly by selling their labor and partly by extracting their livelihood from the soil, so that starvation and dislocation were practically impossible. At the very worst there was always the possibility of climbing into a covered wagon and moving west where the untilled prairies afforded a haven for men to whom the East did not provide a place. So great were our natural resources that we could offer this relief not only to our own people, but to the distressed of all the world; we could invite immigration from Europe, and welcome it with open arms. Traditionally, when a depression came, a new section of land was opened in the West; and even our temporary misfortune served our manifest destiny.

It was the middle of the 19th century that a new force was released and a new dream created. The force was what is called the industrial revolution, the advance of steam and machinery and the rise of the forerunners of the modern industrial plant. The dream was the dream of an economic machine, able to raise the standard of living for everyone; to bring luxury within the reach of the humblest; to annihilate distance by steam power and later by electricity, and to release everyone from the drudgery of the heaviest manual toil. It was to be expected that this would necessarily affect government. Heretofore, government had merely been called upon to produce conditions within which people could live happily, labor peacefully, and rest secure. Now it was called upon to aid in the consummation of this new dream. There was, however, a shadow over the dream. To be made real, it required use of the talents of men of tremendous will, and tremendous ambition, since by no other force could the problems of financing and engineering and new developments be brought to a consummation.

So manifest were the advantages of the machine age, however, that the United States fearlessly, cheerfully, and, I think, rightly, accepted the bitter with the sweet. It was thought that no price was too high to pay for the advantages which we could draw from a finished industrial system. The history of the last half century is accordingly in large measure a history of a group of financial Titans, whose methods were not scrutinized with too much care, and who were honored in proportion as they produced the results, irrespective of the means they used. The financiers who pushed the railroads to the Pacific were always ruthless, we have them today. It has been estimated that the American investor paid for the American railway system more than three times over in the process; but despite that fact the net advantage was to the United States. As long as we had free land; as long as population was growing by leaps and bounds; as long as our industrial plants were insufficient to supply our needs, society chose to give the ambitious man free play and unlimited reward provided only that he produced the economic plant so much desired.

During this period of expansion, there was equal opportunity for all and the business of government was not to interfere but to assist in the development of industry. This was done at the request of businessmen themselves. The tariff was originally imposed for the purpose of "fostering our infant industry", a phrase I think the older among you will remember as a political issue not so long ago. The railroads were subsidized, sometimes by grants of money, oftener by grants of land; some of the most valuable oil lands in the United States were granted to assist the financing of the railroad which pushed through the Southwest. A nascent merchant marine was assisted by grants of money, or by mail subsidies, so that our steam shipping might ply the seven seas. Some of my friends tell me that they do not want the Government in business. With this I agree; but I wonder whether they realize the implications of the past. For while it has been American doctrine that the government must not go into business in competition with private enterprises, still it has been traditional particularly in Republican administrations for business urgently to ask the government to put at private disposal all kinds of government assistance.

The same man who tells you that he does not want to see the government interfere in business—and he means it, and has plenty of good reasons for saying so—is the first to go to Washington and ask the government for a prohibitory tariff on his product. When things get just bad enough—as they did two years ago—he will go with equal speed to the United States government and ask for a loan; and the Reconstruction Finance Corporation is the outcome of it. Each group has sought protection from the government for its own special interest, without realizing that the function of government must be to favor no small group at the expense of its duty to protect the rights of personal freedom and of private property of all its citizens.

In retrospect we can now see that the turn of the tide came with the turn of the century. We were reaching our last frontier; there was no more free land and our industrial combinations had become great uncontrolled and irresponsible units of power within the state. Clear-sighted men saw with fear the danger that opportunity would no longer be equal; that the growing corporation, like the feudal baron of old, might threaten the economic freedom of individuals to earn a living. In that hour, our antitrust laws were born. The cry was raised against the great corporations. Theodore Roosevelt, the first great Republican progressive, fought a Presidential campaign on the issue of "trust busting" and talked freely about malefactors of great wealth. If the government had a policy it was rather to turn the clock back, to destroy the large combinations and to return to the time when every man owned his individual small business.

This was impossible; Theodore Roosevelt, abandoning the idea of "trust busting", was forced to work out a difference between "good" trusts and "bad" trusts. The Supreme Court set forth the famous "rule of reason" by which it seems to have meant that a concentration of industrial power was permissible if the method by which it got its power, and the use it made of that power, was reasonable.

Woodrow Wilson, elected in 1912, saw the situation more clearly. Where Jefferson had feared the encroachment of political power on the lives of individuals, Wilson knew that the new power was financial. He say, in the highly centralized economic system, the depot of the twentieth century, on whom great masses of individuals relied for their safety and their livelihood, and whose irresponsibility and greed (if it were not controlled) would reduce them to starvation and penury. The concentration of financial power had not proceeded so far in 1912 as it has today; but it had grown far enough for Mr. Wilson to realize fully its implications. It is interesting, now, to read his speeches.

What is called "radical" today (and I have reason to know whereof I speak) is mild compared to the campaign of Mr. Wilson. "No man can deny," he said, "that the lines of endeavor have more and more narrowed and stiffened; no man who knows anything about the development of industry in this country can have failed to observe that the larger kinds of credit are more and more difficult to obtain unless you obtain them upon terms of uniting your efforts with those who already control the industry of the country, and nobody can fail to observe that every man who tries to set himself up in competition with any process of manufacture which has taken place under the control of large combinations of capital will presently find himself either squeezed out or obliged to sell and allow himself to be absorbed."

Had there been no World War—had Mr. Wilson been able to devote eight years to domestic instead of to international affairs- we might have had a wholly different situation at the present time. However, the then distant roar of European cannon, growing ever louder, forced him to abandon the study of this issue. The problem he saw so clearly is left with us as a legacy; and no one of us on either side of the political controversy can deny that it is a matter of grave concern to the government.

A glance at the situation today only too clearly indicates that equality of opportunity as we have know[n] it no longer exists. Our industrial plant is built; the problem just now is whether under existing conditions it is not overbuilt. Our last frontier has long since been reached, and there is practically no more free land. More than half of our people do not live on the farms or on lands and cannot derive a living by cultivating their own property. There is no safety valve in the from [sic] of a Western prairie to which those thrown out of work by the Eastern economic machines can go for a new start. We are not able to invite the immigration from Europe to share our endless plenty. We are now providing a drab living for our own people.

Our system of constantly rising tariffs has at last reacted against us to the point of closing our Canadian frontier on the north, our European markets on the east, many of our Latin American markets to the south, and a goodly proportion of our Pacific markets on the west, through the retaliatory tariffs of those countries. It has forced many of our great industrial institutions who exported their surplus production to such countries, to establish plants in such countries within the tariff walls. This has resulted in the reduction of the operation of their American plants, and opportunity for employment.

Just as freedom to farm has ceased, so also the opportunity in business has narrowed. It still is true that men can start small enterprises, trusting to native shrewdness and ability to keep abreast of competitors; but area after area has been preempted altogether by the great corporations, and even in the fields which still have no great concerns, the small man starts with a handicap. The unfeeling statistics of the past three decades show that the independent business man is running a losing race. Perhaps he is forced to the wall;

perhaps he cannot command credit; perhaps he is "squeezed out," in Mr. Wilson's words, by highly organized corporate competitors, as your corner grocery man can tell you.

Recently a careful study was made of the concentration of business in the United States. It showed that our economic life was dominated by some six hundred odd corporations who controlled two-thirds of American industry. Ten million small business men divided the other third. More striking still, it appeared that if the process of concentration goes on at the same rate, at the end of another century we shall have all American industry controlled by a dozen corporations, and run by perhaps a hundred men. Put plainly, we are steering a steady course toward economic oligarchy, if we are not there already.

Clearly, all this calls for a re-appraisal of values. A mere builder of more industrial plants, a creator of more railroad systems, and organizer of more corporations, is as likely to be a danger as a help. The day of the great promoter or the financial Titan, to whom we granted anything if only he would build, or develop, is over. Our task now is not discovery or exploitation of natural resources, or necessarily producing more goods. It is the soberer, less dramatic business of administering resources and plants already in hand, of seeking to reestablish foreign markets for our surplus production, of meeting the problem of under consumption, of adjusting production to consumption, of distributing wealth and products more equitably, of adapting existing economic organizations to the service of the people. The day of enlightened administration has come.

Just as in older times the central government was first a haven of refuge, and then a threat, so now in a closer economic system the central and ambitious financial unit is no longer a servant of national desire, but a danger. I would draw the parallel one step farther. We did not think because national government had become a threat in the 18th century that therefore we should abandon the principle of national government. Nor today should we abandon the principle of strong economic units called corporations, merely because their power is susceptible of easy abuse. In other times we dealt with the problem of an unduly ambitious central government by modifying it gradually into a constitutional democratic government. So today we are modifying and controlling our economic units.

As I see it, the task of government in its relation to business is to assist the development of an economic declaration of rights, an economic constitutional order. This is the common task of statesman and business man. It is the minimum requirement of a more permanently safe order of things.

Every man has a right to life; and this means that he has also a right to make a comfortable living. He may by sloth or crime decline to exercise that right;

but it may not be denied him. We have no actual famine or death; our industrial and agricultural mechanism can produce enough and to spare. Our government formal and informal., [sic] political and economic, owes to every one an avenue to possess himself of a portion of that plenty sufficient for his needs, through his own work.

Every man has a right to his own property; which means a right to be assured, to the fullest extent attainable, in the safety of his savings. By no other means can men carry the burdens of those parts of life which, in the nature of things afford no chance of labor; childhood, sickness, old age. In all thought of property, this right is paramount; all other property rights must yield to it. If, in accord with this principle, we must restrict the operations of the speculator, the manipulator, even the financier, I believe we must accept the restriction as needful, not to hamper individualism but to protect it.

These two requirements must be satisfied, in the main, by the individuals who claim and hold control of the great industrial and financial combinations which dominate so large a pert [sic] of our industrial life. They have undertaken to be, not business men, but princes—princes of property. I am not prepared to say that the system which produces them is wrong. I am very clear that they must fearlessly and competently assume the responsibility which goes with the power. So many enlightened business men know this that the statement would be little more that [sic] a platitude, were it not for an added implication.

This implication is, briefly, that the responsible heads of finance and industry instead of acting each for himself, must work together to achieve the common end. They must, where necessary, sacrifice this or that private advantage; and in reciprocal self-denial must seek a general advantage. It is here that formal government—political government, if you choose, comes in. Whenever in the pursuit of this objective the lone wolf, the unethical competitor, the reckless promoter, the Ishmael or Insull whose hand is against every man's, declines to join in achieving and [sic] end recognized as being for the public welfare, and threatens to drag the industry back to a state of anarchy, the government may properly be asked to apply restraint. Likewise, should the group ever use its collective power contrary to public welfare, the government must be swift to enter and protect the public interest.

The government should assume the function of economic regulation only as a last resort, to be tried only when private initiative, inspired by high responsibility, with such assistance and balance as government can give, has finally failed. As yet there has been no final failure, because there has been no attempt, and I decline to assume that this nation is unable to meet the situation.

The final term of the high contract was for liberty and the pursuit of happiness. We have learnt a great deal of both in the past century. We know that

individual liberty and individual happiness mean nothing unless both are ordered in the sense that one man's meat is not another man's poison. We know
that the old "rights of personal competency"—the right to read, to think, to
speak to choose and live a mode of life, must be respected at all hazards. We
know that liberty to do anything which deprives others of those elemental
rights is outside the protection of any compact; and that government in this
regard is the maintenance of a balance, within which every individual may
have a place if he will take it; in which every individual may find safety if he
wishes it; in which every individual may attain such power as his ability permits, consistent with his assuming the accompanying responsibility. . . .

Faith in America, faith in our tradition of personal responsibility, faith in
our institutions, faith in ourselves demands that we recognize the new terms of
the old social contract. We shall fulfill them, as we fulfilled the obligation of
the apparent Utopia which Jefferson imagined for us in 1776, and which Jefferson, Roosevelt and Wilson sought to bring to realization. We must do so,
lest a rising tide of misery engendered by our common failure, engulf us all.
But failure is not an American habit; and in the strength of great hope we
must all shoulder our common load.

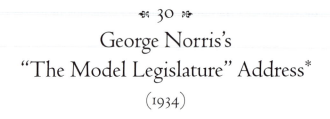

❧ 30 ☙

George Norris's
"The Model Legislature" Address*
(1934)

1. What are the benefits of having a nonpartisan state legislature? If a nonpartisan legislature is beneficial, why haven't additional states adopted it?
2. How might a nonpartisan legislature affect political parties in a state?

NEBRASKA'S STATE legislature is unique for many reasons, not the
least of which is the fact that it is unicameral. The movement to
reform the state's legislature was led in 1934 by Sen. George Norris, a

*Congressional Record, 73rd Congress, 2nd Sess., February 27, 1934 (Washington, D.C.: Gov-
ernment Printing Office, 1934), 3276–3280.

Republican from the party's Progressive wing. In the 1930s Norris supported many of the initiatives of President Franklin Roosevelt and his New Deal.

The drive for a unicameral legislature for Nebraska was not a new one. A commission had been created in 1913 to study the functions of the state's legislature. Among the commission's recommendations was a proposal to establish a unicameral legislature like that found in Canada. Similar proposals were defeated in the legislature in 1917, 1923, 1925, and 1933, and at the state's constitutional convention of 1919–1920.

Like the commission, Senator Norris also believed that it made little sense to have two legislative bodies performing essentially the same duties over the same geographic jurisdiction, so he proposed a unicameral legislature similar to that used by most local governing bodies. But his principal criticism of the bicameral legislature in Nebraska was that conference committees abused their power. Legislative actions were easy to conceal when conference committees met to resolve the differences in legislation passed by the two houses. Further, conference committee votes were not public record in Nebraska because the six appointed members met in secret. Norris believed that such secrecy provided conference committees with too much power and invited lobbyists to exert their influence. A unicameral system could curb these abuses.

Since the state legislature refused to approve the plan, Senator Norris crisscrossed the state, speaking to the electorate about the need for reform and securing the signatures necessary to get the plan on the ballot as an amendment to the state's constitution. Norris was reported to have worn out two sets of automobile tires driving across Nebraska to campaign for the measure. In the end, his efforts paid off: the constitutional amendment to create a unicameral legislature was passed in 1934 by a vote of 286,086 to 193,152.

Besides its being unicameral, Nebraska's legislature is also unique in that it is nonpartisan. Prior to becoming unicameral in 1937, the Nebraska legislature had been very partisan. The 1934 amendment that changed the legislature to a single house also provided for nonpartisan elections. In most states, political parties use primaries to choose candidates who run under a party's label in the general election. In Nebraska, the political party of each candidate for the legislature is not listed on the ballot. The two candidates who receive the most votes in the primary elections, regardless of party, face off in the general election. This makes voting a straight party ticket almost impossible. Norris advocated just such a nonpartisan legislature because he believed that legislators should be free to focus on local interests without the interference or influence of the national political parties. He felt that most local issues had little to do with national political parties and that lawmakers should take action based on the needs of their legislative districts.

The Model Legislature—Address by Senator Norris

. . . In setting up new State institutions under the Federal Government, our forefathers followed the precedents established by the Federal Government in dividing the legislative authority between two houses. In a general way, out of it grew the common and universal rule of a two-branch legislature, usually termed a "senate" and a "house of representatives." The theory back of this kind of a legislature was a beautiful one. The object to be attained was to have one branch of the legislature as a check upon the other. It was a system of checks and balances. But the dominant reason was one which had descended from a time in the history of the world when the common people comprising the government were not sufficiently civilized and sufficiently educated to govern themselves. The Senate of the United States was originally a body elected by the legislatures. This precaution was taken on the theory that this body would be more aristocratic, and would, if thus elected, be more likely to protect the rights of property, than if elected directly by the people. The President of the United States was elected by a college of electors, who, it was assumed, would select the Chief Magistrate with more deliberation than if that official were elected directly by the people. The House of Representatives was elected directly by the people. And thus in the new Government, the only place where the people had a direct voice and vote was in the election of the House of Representatives. This House was intended to represent the people, as against property, and thus the check and balances were completed with the idea that the rights of property should always be safeguarded and protected, and the people themselves should not have a direct voice, either in the selection of Members of the Senate, or in the selection of the President.

But civilization continued to advance. Universal education improved the ability of the people to act more directly in their Government. And again the age-old contest between retaining the power of aristocracy as against the people exhibited itself in our own Government. As civilization advanced and as education increased the people again demanded a change. We provided by amendment to the Federal Constitution for the direct election by the people of the Members of the United States Senate. The electoral college still lingers, but it has been modified to such an extent that, although retained, it is only a body of men pledged to vote for a particular man without regard to deliberation or discussion. The government of the people is gradually being placed in the hands of the people themselves.

Our people are sufficiently civilized and educated to know what kind of government they want and the laws they want enacted to enforce government among themselves. If we can now improve upon our lawmaking bodies, and if we can give to the people a more direct voice in their State governments, why should we not eliminate some of the things which have been found unnecessary and cumbersome, as well as expensive, in these State legislatures? Why should the Legislature of Nebraska have two branches instead of one? We have in this great State one dominating and all-controlling industry—agriculture. Every person in the State, every business in the State, is dependent, for his or its success, upon agriculture. If agriculture is prosperous, the people of our State are happy; if agriculture fails, then the happiness of our people is necessarily taken away. The qualifications of members of both branches of our State legislature are exactly the same. They represent exactly the same idea. The official duties they are to perform are of exactly the same nature. Why should we then have two bodies instead of one, and burden our taxpayers with the necessarily increased expense, to attain the object that can be fully attained by one house instead of two?

Conference Committee

But if we analyze our present Government we find we have 3 Houses instead of 2. We have the conference committee—a necessary adjunct wherever two houses are provided for by the constitution. The conference committee, in reality, constitutes a third house. The members of this "house" are not elected by the people to serve as members of the conference committee. The people have no voice as to who these members shall be. They have nothing to say in regard to their selection. This conference committee is many times, in very important manners of legislation, the most important branch of our legislature. There is no record kept of the workings of the conference committee. Its work is performed, in the main, in secret. No constituent has any definite knowledge as to how members of this conference committee vote, and there is no record to prove the attitude of any member of the conference committee.

When a bill passes one branch of the legislature and passes the other branch in a different form, the matter is referred to the conference committee. This conference committee, arbitrarily selected by the presiding officers of the different branches, takes the dispute and molds it into a law. It then submits the report to the house and to the senate. The conference committee report cannot be amended by either branch. It must be voted up or voted down, as a whole. Members must take what they believe to be bad, in order to get what they believe to be good. If it is rejected entirely, it may mean, and often does mean, the entire defeat of the legislation. If the conference committee does not agree upon a bill then it must necessarily fall in its entirety. As a practical proposition we have legislation then, not by the voice of the members of the senate, not by the members of the house of representatives, but we have legislation by the voice of five or six men. And for practical purposes, in most cases, it is impossible to defeat the legislation proposed by this conference committee. Every experienced legislator knows that it is the hardest thing in the world to defeat a conference report.

Those who are clamoring for a large legislature, those who are asking for a check and balance between the two houses of the legislature, because they claim this represents the voice of the people, do not realize that such a condition results in legislation by a much smaller number of men than is proposed in the contemplated amendment to our constitution. Those who clamor for 133 legislators in our State, because they say that is the only way in which the voice of the people can be heard, forget that in hotly contested matters of legislation, where the most vital issues are at stake, they are, in effect, retaining a legislature of five or six men which enacts the laws that shall govern the entire State.

I am not complaining because of the existence of the conference committee. If we are to have a legislature composed of two branches, the conference committee is an absolute necessity. No man has ever suggested a plan, so far as I know, which would do away with this third branch of the legislature, where the constitution provides for two branches of the legislature. In all the history of the various States of the Union I do not know of an instance where any provision is made, either by the constitution or by the laws, which takes away from this third branch, known as the "conference committee", the power to hold its sessions in secret, the power to hold them without anyone being able to know how the votes are cast, or the power to avoid keeping a record of any of its deliberations or votes.

It would be possible, it is true, to provide by a constitutional amendment that the people themselves should elect a third branch of the legislature to perform the duties of the conference committee, but no one has ever suggested this third branch. If we are to retain the two-branch legislature, it would be a vast improvement to provide by constitutional amendment that the people should elect directly a third branch to take over the jurisdiction and the powers of the conference committee. But no one in this State, so far as I have ever heard, has ever suggested such an amendment. It would be an improvement over present conditions, but would add greatly to the expense and the delay now existing.

It is in conference-committee rooms that jokers frequently creep into our laws, and it is in the conference committee that good things are often taken out of our laws. It seems to me to be sufficient to say that this third branch, under our present two-branch system, is an absolute necessity, and that the people—in the most vital part of this legislative government—are now helpless. If our people are sufficiently educated and sufficiently intelligent to honestly and efficiently govern themselves, then all this machinery can be remodeled and put into the one-branch legislature, and the people, through it, can then secure the kind of laws and the kind of government which they desire. To deny this principle is to deny that the people are qualified to govern themselves. To deny this principle is to deny the theory of democratic government. To deny this principle is to put upon the shoulders of the taxpayers of Nebraska unnecessary expenses and, in addition, to deny them the right to have the kind of government they wish.

One of the necessities is a provision in the constitution which will make it impossible for any member of the legislature to shift responsibility. I can point to an instance of recent history in Nebraska where a majority of both branches were pledged in writing to vote for a bill embodying a particular principle of legislation. Notwithstanding this pledge, the legislature adjourned without enacting any such law. It does not follow from this that any member of this legislature was necessarily dishonest in making this pledge. But whether he was honest about it or not, he could go back to his people and tell them truthfully that he voted for a bill embodying this particular item of legislation. The difficulty there was, and the difficulty is, in such cases, that when the Senate passes a bill on a subject, and the House passes a different bill on the same subject, if the conference committee fails to agree upon a report, the legislation is dead. The bill has died the death that many bills must die in this third branch of the legislature, known as the "conference committee."

A one-house legislature would have made this impossible. It often occurs in the two-house legislature that the senate bill and the house bill are intentionally made different. They die the death in the conference committee that special interests desire them to die. The lobby, composed of experts hired by machine politicians and special interests, is successful in killing legislation before these four or five men who hold their deliberations in secret and who make no record of their proceedings. The present system affords an opportunity to a dishonest legislator which he could not possess in a one-house legislature. It is, therefore, an open invitation to the disreputable man to seek office in the legislature. He is often enabled to introduce bills with the very object of getting something either of a financial or political nature which he otherwise could not get. Such a legislator sometimes introduces bills which he expects to be killed; he wants to be paid for helping to kill them; and he kills them by getting them into a parliamentary tangle where his own record may appear on the surface as perfect. His constituents will therefore perhaps reelect him without knowing his real record. . . .

The Fundamental Idea Is the One-Branch Legislature

The fundamental principle involved in the proposed change of our constitution is to embody the legislative authority in a legislature consisting of one house. Upon this principle there can be no compromise. As to the qualifications of the members of the one-house legislature, as to the number of members, as to their term of office, and as to their salaries, there can well be a difference of opinion. On these subjects, those who believe in a one-house legislature ought to be willing to compromise in order to attain the fundamental object to be achieved. While some of these subjects are of vast importance, yet honest men and women can disagree, and some compromise is going to be necessary in order to attain the fundamental principle which we seek. . . .

Partisanship Would Be Abolished

The proposed amendment to the constitution provides that members of our legislature should be elected on a nonpartisan ballot. Our State ought to be a business institution. Its government should be conducted on business principles. The issues which divide the great political parties in our country should in no way interfere with the business operations of our State. And yet, under present methods, such conditions exist. The Legislature of Nebraska has nothing to do with the tariff; the Legislature of Nebraska, in its official capacity, has nothing to do with shipping on the great oceans. It has no jurisdiction over interstate commerce. It has no official connection with the appointment of postmasters and other official appointments which under our system of government are dealt out to faithful partisan workers. There is no issue involved in the election of a member of the Nebraska Legislature that is the same as the issue involved in the election of a United States Senator or a Member of the House of Representatives. Yet men are often elected as members of a State legislature simply and solely because they are members of a political party pledged to some issue on the tariff, or some other issue of national concern. The citizen who goes into his booth ought not decide the question of the election of his member of the legislature simply because he agrees with the voter on some national question. Neither should he be defeated for the office of member of the State legislature merely because the voter does not agree with him on some question of international importance. We have our State questions and our State institutions, and these should be the guiding star when we come to elect a member of the legislature.

If politics were eliminated, members would be elected to enact our laws according to their qualifications for the State legislature, without being handicapped by any partisan matters. Members of the legislature should be able to give the best that is in them to the welfare of the State. They should be elected on business principles rather than as a result of partisan considerations. Men may disagree as to whether the Federal Government should pay a subsidy to the international mercantile marine, but the Legislature of the State of Nebraska has nothing to do with that question, and its members should neither be elected nor defeated on that issue. Men may disagree as to whether our country should join the League of Nations, but the Legislature of the State of Nebraska has nothing to do with that subject.

Why should we not divorce the business of our State completely from partisan matters affecting only national legislation? We ought to have a legislature entirely divorced from partisan politics—a legislature elected on a business basis, transacting its duties along business lines. We should make of our State a great business institution. We cannot do this unless we eliminate partisan politics.

Moreover, men in the legislature, elected on a partisan political platform, are inclined to follow the bidding and the dictates of party machines and party bosses. We have taken our school officials out of partisan politics. We have done the same thing with our judges. Ask yourself the question, Why? If the divorcing of our judges and our school officials from partisan politics is a good thing, if their official duties have no connection with partisan politics, why not extend the same theory to members of the legislature, whose official duties nowhere, nor in any degree, connect them with partisan politics? Partisanship is one of the great evils of our Government, when carried into avenues and into places where, officially, there is no politics.

For instance, our legislature makes the laws which govern the property and the legal rights of our people. The judges enforce those laws. How inconsistent it is to elect the one on the basis of his belief in the tariff, and yet remove the other from the same category. . . .

Elimination of Corruption

A one-house legislature, composed of a comparatively small number, would be much more free from corrupt influences than would a two-house legislature or a legislature composed of a large number of members. I know many people, at first blush, will not agree with this statement. There was a time in my life when I did not believe it, but I have reached the conviction from my observation that special interests, by unfair and unjustifiable means, are able to influence and corrupt a two-house legislature much more easily than they could a one-house legislature. I have been told by lobbyists that the easiest legislature to control is the one which is large in number. Where the number is large they necessarily have to handle only a few men, who, in turn, do their work with the legislature itself. In a two-house legislature the control of the conference committee is, in fact, for all practical purposes a control of both branches.

There are thousands of ways in which this is done. A conference committee can often be controlled by one man—the man who appoints the conference committee. The control of a large body of men can be handled by the control of two or three men who constitute the committee on rules, or who otherwise have a dominating parliamentary influence in the body.

The smallest legislature, which is now under consideration, may be likened to our judiciary, where the power is vested in one man. We know that our judiciary is comparatively free from such influences. A small legislature such as is suggested would be very similar to our judges. The lobbyist who desires to control the membership does not, as a rule, seek out the individual member, and go through the legislature in that way. He undertakes to deceive men by various methods, mostly of a parliamentary nature. The cases of direct sale of votes are very few. Men in Congress or in the legislature are, as a rule, not bribed individually. They are led astray by placing them in hopeless parliamentary predicaments, in which they are deceived. In fact, the actual cases of honest men being misled are far more numerous than the purchase of dishonest men. If the opportunities for hiding beneath the parliamentary cloak brought about by a two-house legislature were taken away, the dishonest man would not be so likely to become a candidate for the legislature. He would know to begin with that he could not shift responsibility, he could not conceal his vote, or his official conduct, which would have to take place in the open before all the people of the State, and he would, therefore, seek other avenues of enriching himself. In other words, it would have a tendency to eliminate the dishonest man from the legislature, and if you eliminate the dishonest man and make it impossible to deceive the honest man, you have attained as near perfection as is possible in a legislature.

The plan proposed would therefore tend to decrease deception, and the man who tried to practice deception would be almost powerless, and we would then have a legislature which would be untrammeled, and, to a great extent, untainted. The possibility of covering up the tracks of those who wanted to deceive would be practically eliminated, and it would be impossible to place the honest legislator in a false light.

I reach the conclusion, therefore, that the proposed amendment would save money to the taxpayers. It would go far toward the reestablishment of a democratic form of government. It would make it more difficult for dishonest men to get into office and make it more difficult for dishonest men to retain office. It would give the honest legislator an opportunity to have his record known to the people, and it would make it possible for the people of the State to readily ascertain and comprehend the record of the members of the legislature. It would enable the people to reward the honest servants and to defeat the dishonest ones.

There would, of course, always be a possibility of dishonest men getting into office. There would be a possibility of dishonest men who were in office deceiving the people. But these possibilities would be very much minimized. Nothing has ever been said that is truer than the saying that "Eternal vigilance is the price of liberty."

To get a good government, and to retain it, it is necessary that a liberty-loving, educated, intelligent people should be ever watchful, to carefully guard and protect their rights and liberties. The proposed amendment is not offered with the idea that it is perfect. It is not offered with the idea that it will eliminate wrong entirely, or that it will make it unnecessary for the people of the State to always keep a watchful eye upon their servants, but it will help them to know and to find out what is wrong. It will enable them to get better laws enacted and better men into office, and to this extent it will be a guidepost along the road to human advancement and a higher civilization. . . .

✑ 31 ✑

Huey Long's "Every Man a King" Radio Address*

(1934)

1. How did the theme and content of Long's speech further his political ambitions?
2. Why was it important for Long to deliver his speeches over the radio instead of through more traditional printed methods?

H UEY P. LONG'S political career began with his 1918 election to the Louisiana Railroad Commission. He went on to become governor of Louisiana in 1928 and a U.S. senator in 1930. As governor, Long used his political machine to authoritatively rule over Louisiana, but he was also the catalyst for many important reforms, including the construction of new roads, free textbooks, and the abolition of the poll tax. In the Senate, Long's flamboyant rhetorical style and irreverent actions filled the galleries as viewers waited to see what he would say or do next.

On February 23, 1934, Long delivered a radio address to the nation that outlined his solution to the Great Depression, which centered around the redistribution of wealth in the United States. Senator Long was among the first to utilize radio to reach a national audience, and "Every Man a King" was a popular theme he employed. The title of the speech (and his 1933 autobiography) was borrowed from 1896 Democratic presidential candidate William Jennings Bryan. Its substance was based on legislation that Long had introduced in the Senate earlier in his term that was designed to address the economic suffering of the public. He proposed taxing the income of affluent individuals at progressively higher rates and redistributing it. Because his proposals were never taken seriously by his colleagues, Long utilized radio to build support for them (and potentially his own presidential candidacy)

*www.americanrhetoric.com/speeches/hueyplongking.htm

among the public. By early 1935, millions of Americans had accepted his invitation to form local "Share Our Wealth" societies.

Although they may have shared a desire to better the lives of the general public, Long's relationship with President Franklin Roosevelt was never good. The senator did support Roosevelt for the Democratic nomination in 1932 and campaigned for him throughout the Great Plains, but the relationship had grown bitter by 1934. In fact, Roosevelt stated that Huey Long was one of the most dangerous men in the country, and he actively used federal patronage to support Long's rivals in Louisiana. These actions, along with Long's conviction that the New Deal was insufficient to fight the Great Depression, led the ambitious senator to consider how he could defeat Roosevelt, using among other tools, radio.

Whether Long would have challenged Roosevelt in 1936 is unknown, but he clearly wanted to be president: in 1935, he published *My First Days in the White House*. More likely, he could have thrown his support behind a "Share Our Wealth" candidate in 1936, which would have split the Democratic vote and allowed the Republicans to win. Then, assuming the Republicans failed to effectively combat the Great Depression, Long would have been in a position to win the 1940 Democratic nomination. What might have been will never be known, however, as Long was assassinated by a political rival in September 1935 on a trip home to Baton Rouge.

<hr/>

"It Is Necessary to Scale Down the Big Fortunes"

Is that a right of life, when the young children of this country are being reared into a sphere which is more owned by 12 men that is by 120 million people?...

I contend, my friends, that we have no difficult problem to solve in America, and that is the view of nearly everyone with whom I have discussed the matter here in Washington and elsewhere throughout the United States—that we have no very difficult problem to solve.

It is not the difficulty of the problem which we have; it is the fact that the rich people of this country—and by rich people I mean the super-rich—will not allow us to solve the problems, or rather the one little problem that is afflicting this country, because in order to cure all of our woes it is necessary to scale down the big fortunes, that we may scatter the wealth to be shared by all of the people.

We have a marvelous love for this government of ours; in fact, it is almost a religion, and it is well that it should be, because we have a splendid form of government and we have a splendid set of laws. We have everything here that we need, except that we have neglected the fundamentals upon which the American government was principally predicated.

How may of you remember the first thing that the Declaration of Independence said? It said, "We hold these truths to be self-evident, that there are certain inalienable rights for the people, and among them are life, liberty, and the pursuit of happiness"; and it said, further, "We hold the view that all men are created equal."

Now, what did they mean by that? Did they mean, my friends, to say that all men were created equal and that that meant that any one man was born to inherit $10 billion and that another child was to be born to inherit nothing?

Did that mean, my friends, that someone would come into this world without having had an opportunity, of course, to have hit one lick of work, should be born with more than it and all of its children and children's children could ever dispose of, but that another one would have to be born into a life of starvation?

That was not the meaning of the Declaration of Independence when it said that all men are created equal or "That we hold that all men are created equal."

Nor was it the meaning of the Declaration of Independence when it said that they held that there were certain rights that were inalienable—the right of life, liberty, and the pursuit of happiness.

Is that right of life, my friends, when the young children of this country are being reared into a sphere which is more owned by 12 men than it is by 120 million people?

Is that, my friends, giving them a fair shake of the dice or anything like the inalienable right of life, liberty, and the pursuit of happiness, or anything resembling the fact that all people are created equal; when we have today in America thousands and hundreds of thousands and millions of children on the verge of starvation in a land that is overflowing with too much to eat and too much to wear? . . .

"Ten Men Dominate . . . at Least 85 Percent of the Activities that You Own"

Now, ladies and gentlemen, if I may proceed to give you some other words that I think you can understand—I am not going to belabor you by quoting tonight—I am going to tell you what the wise men of all ages and all times, down even to the present day, have all said: that you must keep the wealth of the country scattered, and you must limit the amount that any one man can own. You cannot let any man own $300 billion or $400 billion. If you do, one man can own all of the wealth that the United States has in it.

So, we have in America today, my friends, a condition by which about ten men dominate the means of activity in at least 85 percent of the activities that you own. They either own directly everything or they have got some kind of mortgage on it, with a very small percentage to be excepted. They own the banks, they own the steel mills, they own the railroads, they own the bonds, they own the mortgages, they own the stores, and they have chained the country from one end to the other, until there is not any kind of business that a small, independent man could go into today and make a living, and there is not any kind of business that an independent man can go into and make any money to buy an automobile with; and they have finally and gradually and steadily eliminated everybody from the fields in which there is a living to be made, and still they have got little enough sense to think they ought to be able to get more business out of it anyway. . . .

"These Big-Fortune Holders . . . Own Just as Much as They Did"

Both of these men, Mr. Hoover and Mr. Roosevelt, came out and said there had to be a decentralization of wealth, but neither one of them did anything about it. But, nevertheless, they recognized the principle. The fact that neither one of them ever did anything about it is their own problem that I am not undertaking to criticize; but had Mr. Hoover carried out what he says ought to be done, he would be retiring from the president's office, very probably three years from now, instead of one year ago; and had Mr. Roosevelt proceeded along the lines that he stated were necessary for the decentralization of wealth, he would have gone, my friends, a long way already, and within a few months he would have probably reached a solution of all of the problems that afflict this country today.

But I wish to warn you now that nothing that has been done up to this date has taken one dime away from these big-fortune holders; they own just as much as they did, and probably a little bit more; they hold just as many of the debts of the common people as they ever held, and probably a little bit more; and unless we, my friends, are going to give the people of this country a fair shake of the dice, by which they will all get something out of the funds of this land, there is not a chance on the topside of this God's eternal earth by which we can rescue this country and rescue the people of this country. . . .

"Every Man a King"

Now, we have organized a society, and we call it "Share Our Wealth Society," a society with the motto "every man a king."

Every man a king, so there would be no such thing as a man or woman who did not have the necessities of life, who would not be dependent upon the whims and caprices and *ipsi dixit* of the financial martyrs for a living. What do we propose by this society? We propose to limit the wealth of big men in the country. There is an average of $15,000 in wealth to every family in America. That is right here today.

We do not propose to divide it up equally. We do not propose a division of wealth, but we propose to limit poverty that we will allow to be inflicted upon any man's family. We will not say we are going to try to guarantee any equality, or $15,000 to families. No; but we do say that one third of the average is low enough for any one family to hold, that there should be a guaranty of a family wealth of around $5,000; enough for a home, an automobile, a radio, and the ordinary conveniences, and the opportunity to educate their children; a fair share of the income of this land thereafter to that family so there will be no such thing as merely the select to have those things, and so there will be no such thing as a family living in poverty and distress.

We have to limit fortunes. Our present plan is that we will allow no one man to own more than $50 million. We think that with that limit we will be able to carry out the balance of the program. It may be necessary that we limit it to less than $50 million. It may be necessary, in working out of the plans, that no man's fortune would be more than $10 million or $15 million. But be that as it may, it will still be more than any one man, or any one man and his children and their children, will be able to spend in their lifetimes; and it is not necessary or reasonable to have wealth piled up beyond that point where we cannot prevent poverty among the masses. . . .

"We Have Got to Hit the Root with the Ax"

You cannot solve these things through these various and sundry alphabetical codes. You can have the NRA and PWA and CWA and the UUG and GIN and any other kind of "dadgummed" lettered code. You can wait until doomsday and see twenty-five more alphabets, but that is not going to solve this proposition. Why hide? Why quibble? You know what the trouble is. The man that says he does not know what the trouble is is just hiding his face to keep from seeing the sunlight. . . .

We had these great incomes in this country; but the farmer, who plowed from sunup to sundown, who labored here from sunup to sundown for six days a week, wound up at the end of the time with practically nothing. . . .

Now, my friends, we have got to hit the root with the ax. Centralized power in the hands of a few, with centralized credit in the hands of a few, is the trouble.

Get together in your community tonight or tomorrow and organize one of our Share Our Wealth societies. If you do not understand it, write me and let me send you the platform; let me give you the proof of it.

"Organize Your Share Our Wealth Society"

This is HUEY P. LONG talking, United States Senator, Washington, D.C. Write me and let me send you the data on this proposition. Enroll with us. Let us make known to the people what we are going to do. I will send you a button, if I have got enough of them left. We have got a little button that some of our friends designed, with our message around the rim of the button, and in the center "Every man a king." Many thousands of them are meeting through the United States, and every day we are getting hundreds of hundreds of letters. Share Our Wealth societies are now being organized, and people have it within their power to relieve themselves from this terrible situation. . . .

Organize your Share Our Wealth Society and get your people to meet with you, and make known your wishes to your senators and representatives in Congress. . . .

I thank you, my friends, for your kind attention, and I hope you will enroll with us, take care of your own work in the work of this government, and share or help in our Share Our Wealth Society.

I thank you.

❧ 32 ❧
The *Literary Digest* Poll*
(1936)

1. Why did the *Literary Digest* successfully predict the outcome of presidential elections from 1916 through 1932, but miss the winner of the 1936 election?
2. How is polling used in presidential elections today?

THE 1936 PRESIDENTIAL election inspired new methods of public opinion polling. That year *Literary Digest,* a popular magazine founded in 1890, conducted a poll to ascertain the outcome of the election. Similar polls conducted by the periodical had correctly predicted the winners of the 1916, 1920, 1924, 1928, and 1932 elections, a profitable endeavor in that these successful predictions generated free news coverage and sold subscriptions.

After more than two million postcards of the ten million distributed were returned, the magazine announced just days before the presidential election that Alf Landon, the governor of Kansas, would defeat incumbent President Franklin Roosevelt by winning 57 percent of the popular vote and 370 electoral votes. Despite this declaration, Roosevelt garnered 60.8 percent of the popular vote—a landslide that at the time was the greatest margin of victory in the history of U.S. presidential elections. Roosevelt carried every state except Maine and Vermont, and the Democrats increased their majorities in both the House and the Senate.

Despite its previous successes, the *Literary Digest*'s poll ultimately failed because the polling techniques it employed were unreliable. The magazine did survey an incredibly large sample, but that sample was not representative of the nation's views as a whole. This happened because the magazine first surveyed its own readers and then added to that number the owners of registered automobiles and telephone subscribers. While this strategy had worked in previous election cycles, it

*Literary Digest, October 31, 1936. Reprinted at http://historymatters.gmu.edu/d/5168.

did not create a valid sample during the depths of the Great Depression. During that time most individuals were underemployed or unemployed and barely had (or didn't have) money enough for essentials, much less such luxuries as magazines, cars, and phones. The result was an overrepresentation of individuals who had disposable incomes higher than the national average, and individuals in that economic bracket were inclined to vote for Republicans; hence, Landon's "victory" in the poll.

Whatever the reason, the incorrect prediction of the 1936 election discredited the *Literary Digest* in the eyes of the American public, and by 1938 it had merged with *Time* magazine. Despite the outcome of this particular poll, however, public opinion polling remained an important part of campaigns and elections: George H. Gallup achieved national recognition by correctly predicting Roosevelt would win over Landon with a poll based on a random sample of just five thousand people. Gallup's correct prediction introduced new methodologies to survey research upon which politicians and pundits still rely today.

❧

Landon, 1,293,669; Roosevelt, 972,897

Final Returns in the *Digest*'s Poll of Ten Million Voters

Well, the great battle of the ballots in the poll of 10 million voters, scattered throughout the forty-eight states of the Union, is now finished, and in the table below we record the figures received up to the hour of going to press.

These figures are exactly as received from more than one in every five voters polled in our country—they are neither weighted, adjusted, nor interpreted.

Never before in an experience covering more than a quarter of a century in taking polls have we received so many different varieties of criticism—praise from many and condemnation from many others—and yet it has been just of the same type that has come to us every time a Poll has been taken in all these years.

A telegram from a newspaper in California asks: "Is it true that Mr. Hearst has purchased *The Literary Digest*?" A telephone message only the day before these lines were written: "Has the Republican National Committee purchased *The Literary Digest*?" And all types and varieties, including: "Have the Jews purchased *The Literary Digest*?" "Is the Pope of Rome a stockholder of *The Literary Digest*?" And so it goes—all equally absurd and amusing. We could add more to this list, and yet all of these questions in recent days are but repetitions of what we have been experiencing all own the years from the very first Poll.

Problem—Now, are the figures in this poll correct? In answer to this question we will simply refer to a telegram we sent to a young man in Massachusetts the other day answer to his challenge to us to wager 100,000 on the accuracy of our Poll. We wired him as follows:

For nearly a quarter century, we have been taking Polls of the voters in the forty-eight States, and especially in Presidential years, and we have always merely mailed the ballots, counted and recorded those returned and let the people of the Nation draw their conclusions as to our accuracy. So far, we have been right in every Poll. Will we be right in the current Poll? That, as Mrs. Roosevelt said concerning the President's reelection, is in the "lap of the gods."

We never make any claims before election but we respectfully refer you to the opinion of one of the most quoted citizens today, the Hon. James A. Farley, Chairman of the Democratic National Committee. This is what Mr. Farley said October 14, 1932:

"Any sane person cannot escape the implication of such a gigantic sampling of popular opinion as is embraced in *The Literary Digest* straw vote. I consider this conclusive evidence as to the desire of the people of this country for a change in the National Government. *The Literary Digest* poll is an achievement of no little magnitude. It is a Poll fairly and correctly conducted."

In studying the table of the voters from of the States printed below, please remember that we make no claims at this time for their absolute accuracy. On a similar occasion we felt it important to say:

In a wild year like this, however, many sagacious observers will refuse to bank upon appearances, however convincing. As for *The Digest,* it draws no conclusions from the results of its vast distribution of twenty million ballots. True to its historic non-partizan policy—or "omni-partizan," as some editor described it in 1928—we supply our readers with the facts to the best of our ability, and leave them to draw their own conclusions.

We make no claim to infallibility. We did not coin the phrase "uncanny accuracy" which has been so freely-applied to our Polls. We know only too well the limitations of every straw vote, however enormous the sample gathered, however scientific the method. It would be a miracle if every State of the forty-eight behaved on Election day exactly as forecast by the Poll.

We say now about Rhode Island and Massachusetts that our figures indicate in our own judgment too large a percentage for Mr. Landon and too small a percentage for Mr. Roosevelt, and although in 1932 the figures in these two States indicated Mr. Hoover's carrying both, we announced:

"A study of the returns convinces us that in those States our ballots have somehow failed to come back in adequate quantity from large bodies of Democratic voters."

Our own opinion was that they would be found in the Roosevelt column, and they were. We will not do the same this year; we feel that both States will be found in the Landon column, and we are reaching this conclusion by the same process that lead [sic] to the reverse conclusion in 1932.

Pennsylvania is another State which requires special mention. Four years ago, our figures gave the State to Mr. Roosevelt, and Mr. Hoover carried it on Election day. In comparing our ballot this year with that of 1932, we find that in many cities in Pennsylvania our figures showed a much higher trend toward Mr. Roosevelt than was justified by the election figures on Election day in 1932. In examining the very same cities now we discover the reverse trend, and in cities that in 1932 indicated an approximately 60–40 percent relationship between Roosevelt and Hoover, we now find 60 percent for Landon and 40 percent for Roosevelt.

That's the plain language of it. Many people wonder at these great changes in a State like Pennsylvania, and we confess to wonderment ourselves.

On the Pacific Coast, we find California, Oregon, and Washington all vote for Mr. Landon in our Poll, and yet we are told that the Pacific Coast is "aflame" for Mr. Roosevelt.

State	Electoral Vote	Landon 1936 Total Vote For State	Roosevelt 1936 Total Vote For State	State	Electoral Vote	Landon 1936 Total Vote For State	Roosevelt 1936 Total Vote For State
Ala.	11	3,060	10,082	Nev.	3	1,003	955
Ariz.	3	2,337	1,975	N.H.	4	9,207	2,737
Ark.	9	2,724	7,608	N.J.	16	58,677	27,631
Calif.	22	89,516	77,245	N.M.	3	1,625	1,662
Colo.	6	15,949	10,025	N.Y.	47	162,260	139,277
Conn.	8	28,809	13,413	N.C.	13	6,113	16,324
Del.	3	2,918	2,048	N. Dak.	4	4,250	3,666
Fla.	7	6,087	8,620	Ohio	26	77,896	50,778
Ga.	12	3,948	12,915	Okla.	11	14,442	15,075
Idaho	4	3,653	2,611	Ore.	5	11,747	10,951
Ill.	29	123,297	79,035	Pa.	36	119,086	81,114
Ind.	14	42,805	26,663	R.I.	4	10,401	3,489
Iowa	11	31,871	18,614	S.C.	8	1,247	7,105
Kans.	9	35,408	20,254	S.Dak.	4	8,483	4,507
Ky.	11	13,365	16,592	Tenn.	11	9,883	19,829
La.	10	3,686	7,902				

SOURCE: *Literary Digest*, October 31, 1936.

A State like California is always a difficult State to get an accurate opinion from by the polling method, and we may be far astray, yet every one should remember that in the Gubernatorial campaign a few years ago, we took a Poll of California when it was believed by most of California citizens that Mr. Upton Sinclair would be elected Governor, and the result of our Poll showed that Mr. Sinclair would not be elected Governor and the Poll was correct.

The State of Washington seems to be more favorable to Mr. Landon than either Oregon or California. We cannot in our Poll detect anything that would indicate a reason for this difference.

Seattle—Right here we wish to say that in 1932 our Poll in Seattle gave Mr. Roosevelt 65.43 percent of the vote, and he carried that city by 61.58 percent of the vote. In the current Poll, 1936, Seattle gives Mr. Landon 58.52 percent and Mr. Roosevelt 40.46 percent. Our readers will notice we overestimated Mr. Roosevelt in 1932—are we overestimating Mr. Landon now? We see no reason for supposing so. And the three Pacific Coast States which now show for Mr. Landon and which millions believe will vote for Mr. Roosevelt (they may be right) in 1924, 1928, and 1932 were correctly forecast in *The Literary Digest* Polls.

In the great Empire State, New York the figures for so large a State are what might be called very close. After looking at the figures for New York in the column at the left, remember that in 1932 we gave Mr. Roosevelt 46.1 percent and Mr. Hoover 43.9 percent, even closer than it is to day. And yet we correctly forecast that Mr. Roosevelt would carry the State.

And so we might go on with many States that are very close, and some not so close, but in which local conditions have much to do with results, not in polls such as our Poll but on Election day.

The Poll represents the most extensive straw ballot in the field—the most experienced in view of its twenty-five years of perfecting—the most unbiased in view of its prestige—a Poll that has always previously been correct.

Even its critics admit its value as an index of popular sentiment. As one of these critics, the *Nation,* observes:

"Because it indicates both the 1932 and 1936 vote, it offers the raw material for as careful a prognostication as it is possible to make at this time."

33

Franklin Roosevelt's Message to Congress on the Hatch Act*

(1939)

1. Under what circumstances, if any, should federal employees be permitted to engage in partisan political activities?
2. Why is it important that federal officials not engage in partisan political activities?

THE PARTISAN POLITICAL activities of federal employees continued to be a problem even after the passage of the Pendleton Act in 1883, so much so that in 1907 President Theodore Roosevelt, a former U.S. Civil Service commissioner, demanded action. He ordered that the Civil Service Commission take the necessary steps to prevent civil servants from using their official position to influence election outcomes. Accordingly, over the next three decades, the commission developed rules that distinguished between prohibited partisan political activities and permitted expressions of political opinion.

By the late 1930s the success of President Franklin Roosevelt's New Deal policies had led many Republicans and conservative Democrats to become concerned that the rapidly expanding number of federal employees necessary to implement New Deal programs, such as the Works Progress Administration (WPA), would keep the Democratic Party in power for years to come, as these workers voted with the party that had employed them. Some Republicans were even convinced that WPA employees had used public funds for partisan political purposes, and with their conservative Democrat allies, they sought additional campaign finance reform related to the actions of federal employees during campaigns and elections.

*John Wooley and Gerhard Peters, The American Presidency Project (online) (Santa Barbara: University of California [hosted], Gerhard Peters [database]). Available at www.presidency. ucsb.edu/ws/?pid=15781.

As a result, in 1939 Congress passed "An Act to Prevent Pernicious Political Activities," commonly referred to as the Hatch Act after the chair of the Committee on Privileges and Elections, Democratic senator Carl Hatch of New Mexico. Hatch had sponsored what he called the "Clean Politics Act" in response to what he saw as partisan corruption that should not be tolerated by either Democrats or Republicans. After resisting the efforts of Senator Hatch for months, President Roosevelt signed the legislation into law on August 2 and issued a message to Congress that offered support, but expressed his desire that the act also be applied to state and local employees.

The Hatch Act strengthened the prohibition on political activity by federal employees originally established under the Pendleton Act. That act had sought to reduce the influence of political patronage, and over the years it had been expanded by each presidential administration to cover an increasing number of federal officials. The Hatch Act prohibited federal employees not already covered under the Pendleton Act from engaging in partisan political activities. It also prohibited the use of intimidation or bribery to influence voters and barred the use of federal funds designated for public works for electoral purposes.

Amended in 1940 to include state and local employees paid through federal funds, the act was expanded to incorporate new restrictions on political donations made by individuals. These regulations limited individual contributions to federal candidates to $5,000 per year and $3 million in total. A 1993 amendment to the act now permits many forms of participation by federal employees in partisan political campaigns for federal office as long as they occur outside the scope of an employee's official duties.

<hr/>

To the Congress:

Because there have been so many misrepresentations, some unpremeditated, some deliberate, in regard to the attitude of the Executive Branch of the Government in relation to Senate Bill 1871, "An Act to Prevent Pernicious Political Activities," and because a number of questions have been raised as to the meaning and application of some of its provisions, I deem it advisable at the time of executive approval to make certain observations to the Congress of the United States.

The genesis of this legislation lies in the message of the President of January 5, 1939, respecting an additional appropriation for the Works Progress Administration. I said in that message: "It is my belief that improper political practices can be eliminated only by the imposition of rigid statutory regulations and penalties by the Congress, and that this should be done. Such penalties should be imposed not only upon persons within the administrative organization of the Works Progress Administration, but also upon outsiders who have in fact in many instances been the principal offenders in this regard. My only reservation in this matter is that no legislation should be enacted which will in any way deprive workers on the Works Progress Administration program of the civil rights to which they are entitled in common with other citizens."

Furthermore, in applying to all employees of the Federal Government (with a few exceptions) the rules to which the Civil Service employees have been subject for many years, this measure is in harmony with the policy that I have consistently advocated during all my public life, namely, the wider extension of Civil Service as opposed to its curtailment.

It is worth noting that nearly all exemptions from the Civil Service, which have been made during the past six years and a half, have originated in the Congress itself and not in the Executive.

Furthermore, it is well known that I have consistently advocated the objectives of the present bill. It has been currently suggested that partisan political reasons have entered largely into the passage of the bill: but with this I am not concerned, because it is my hope that if properly administered the measure can be made an effective instrument of good Government. . . .

The Attorney General has advised me that it seems clear that the Federal Government has the power to describe as qualifications for its employees that they refrain from taking part in other endeavors which, in the light of common experience, may well consume time and attention required by their duties as public officials. He points out, however, that such qualifications cannot properly preclude Government employees from the exercise of the right of free speech or from their right to exercise the franchise.

The question of constitutionality being resolved in favor of the bill, our next inquiry relates to the exercise and preservation of these rights. It is obvious that the intent of the bill is to follow broadly the provisions of Civil Service regulations that have existed for many years in regard to political activities of Federal employees.

It is because I have received and will continue to receive so many queries asking what a Government employee may or may not do that it seems appropriate at the outset to postulate the broad principle that if the bill is administered in accord with its spirit, and if it is in the future administered without abuse, oppression or groundless fear, it will serve the purpose intended by the Congress.

For example, I have been asked by employees of the Government whether under this law they would lose their positions if they merely attend political meetings. The answer is, of course, No.

I have been asked whether they would lose their positions if they contributed voluntarily to party or individual campaign funds without being solicited. The answer is, of course, No.

I have been asked whether they would lose their positions if they should merely express their opinion or preference publicly—orally, by radio, or in writing—without doing so as part of an organized political campaign. The answer is No.

I have been asked if citizens who have received loans from the Home Owners' Loan Corporation, from the Farm Credit Administration or its subsidiaries, from the Farm Security Administration, from the Reconstruction Finance Corporation and other Government lending agencies, would be subject to the terms of this bill. The answer is No.

I have been asked whether farmers receiving farm benefits would be bound by the terms of the bill. Again, the answer is No.

I have been asked if Government employees who belong to Young Republican Clubs, Young Democratic Clubs, Civil Service Reform Associations, the League of Women Voters, the American Federation of Labor, the Congress of Industrial Organizations, and similar bodies are subject to the penalties of the measure because of mere membership in these organizations. The answer is No.

There will be hundreds of similar questions raised in the actual administration and enforcement of this bill. Such questions will be asked in most cases by individuals in good faith. And it is only fair that they should receive an answer. I am, therefore, asking the Attorney General to take the necessary steps through the new Civil Liberties unit of the Department of Justice in order that the civil rights of every government employee may be duly protected and that the element of fear may be removed.

I have been asked if the bill applies to veterans—Civil War, Indian Wars, the War with Spain, the World War—retired officers and men of the Army, Navy and Marine Corps who, though not Government employees, are receiving benefits or pensions of one kind or another. The answer is, of course, No.

I have been asked if the Act applies to those who get Government benefits under the Social Security Act in the form of old age pensions or in the form of unemployment compensation. The answer is No.

Finally, I have been asked various questions relating to the right of a Government employee publicly to answered [sic] unwarranted attacks made on him or on his work or on the work of his superiors or on the work of his subordinates, notwithstanding the fact that such attacks or misrepresentations were made for political purposes by newspapers or by individuals as a part of a political campaign.

This raises the interesting question as to whether all Government officials except the President and Vice President, persons in the office of the President,

Summary of Hatch Act Provisions Applicable to Employees of the National Archives

Employees MAY:	Employees may NOT:
• Vote as you choose • Register as a member of a political party • Join and be an active member of a political party or club • Express opinions about candidates and issues • Attend and be active at political rallies, conventions, and meetings • Contribute money to political candidates and organizations • Attend political fund raising functions • Give a speech at a fund raiser so long as the speech does not include an appeal for political contributions • Hold office in political clubs or parties so long as the duties do not involve personal solicitation, acceptance, or receipt of political contributions • Campaign for or against candidates in partisan elections • Campaign for or against referendum questions, ballot initiatives, constitutional amendments, and municipal ordinances • Sign nominating petitions, make nominations, or place a name in a nomination at a nominating caucus • Assist in voter registration drives, including serving in a polling place • Serve as a delegate, alternate, or proxy to a state or national party convention	• Engage in political activity while on duty • Engage in political activity while wearing an official Government uniform or identifying National Archives insignia • Engage in political activity while using a Government vehicle • Engage in political activity in any Government office • Engage in political activity while using Government property, including computers, printers, copiers, fax machines, and telephones • Wear political buttons while on duty • Display items (e.g., posters, signs, stickers) at work that indicate support of or opposition to a political party or a candidate in a partisan election • Run as a candidate for public office in any partisan election, except in jurisdictions specified by OPM • Solicit, accept, or receive political contributions (except in limited circumstances involving certain Federal labor or employee organizations) • Solicit, accept, or receive political contributions from a subordinate employee • Allow your official title to be used in connection with fund raising activities • Host a fund raiser at your home

Continued on next page

Summary of Hatch Act Provisions Applicable to Employees of the National Archives   *(continued)*

Employees MAY:	Employees may NOT:
• Distribute campaign literature in partisan elections • Run as a candidate for public office in nonpartisan elections • Run as an independent candidate in a partisan election in certain, OPM-specified jurisdictions • Manage or otherwise work on a partisan political campaign of a candidate for public office, except for activities involving the direct solicitation, acceptance, or receipt of funds • Serve as poll watcher, election judge, clerk or similar official • Drive voters to polling places for a partisan political candidate	• Use your official authority or influence to interfere with an election • Knowingly solicit or discourage the political activity of any person who has business before the National Archives

SOURCE: www.archives.gov/legal/ethics/hatch-act.html

heads and assistant heads of Executive Departments and policy determining officers appointed by and with the advice and consent of the Senate must remain mute if and when they or the work with which they are concerned are attacked and misrepresented in a political campaign or preliminary thereto.

It will be noted that the language of the bill wholly excludes members or employees of the Legislative Branch of the Government from its operation.

It can hardly be maintained that it is an American way of doing things to allow newspapers, magazines, radio broadcasters, members and employees of the Senate and House of Representatives and all kinds of candidates for public office and their friends to make any form of charge, misrepresentation, falsification or vituperation against the acts of any individual or group of individuals employed in the Executive Branch of the Federal Government with complete immunity against reply except by a handful of high executive officials. That, I repeat, would be un-American because it would be unfair, and the great mass of Americans like fair play and insist on it. They do not stand for any gag act.

It is, therefore, my considered opinion, in which the Attorney General of the United States joins me, that all Federal employees, from the highest to the lowest, have the right publicly to answer any attack or misrepresentation, provided, of course, they do not make such reply as part of active participation in political campaigns.

The same definition of fair and proper administration of the bill applies to the right of any Government employee, from the highest to the lowest, to give to the public factual information relating to the conduct of governmental affairs. To rule otherwise would make it impossible for the people of the United States to learn from those who serve the Government vital, necessary and interesting facts relating to the manifold activities of the Federal Government. To rule otherwise would give a monopoly to originate and disseminate information to those who, primarily for political purposes, unfortunately have been given to the spreading of false information. That again is unfair and, therefore, un-American.

It is, I am confident, the purpose of the proponents of this legislation that the new law be thus administered so that the right of free speech will remain, even to those who serve their Government; and that the Government itself shall have full right to place all facts in its possession before the public. If some future Administration should undertake to administer this legislation to the detriment of these rights, such action would be contrary to the purpose of the Act itself and might well infringe upon the constitutional rights of citizens. I trust that public vigilance will for all time prevent this.

The Attorney General calls my attention to a practical difficulty which should be corrected by additional legislation as soon as possible. For many years there has been an exception to the Civil Service regulation whereby employees permanently residing in the District of Columbia or in municipalities adjacent thereto may become candidates for or hold municipal office in their municipalities. This and a few similar exceptions should, I believe, be maintained.

The other question relates to the fact that the bill does not in any way cover the multitude of State and local employees who greatly outnumber Federal employees and who may continue to take part in elections in which there are candidates for Federal office on the same ballot with candidates for State and local office. It is held by many who have examined the constitutional question that because the Congress, under the Constitution, may maintain the integrity of Federal elections, it has the power to extend the objectives of this bill so as to cover State and local Government employees who participate actively in Federal elections. This is at least worth the study of the Congress at its next session and therefore before the next Federal election.

It is because for so many years I have striven in public life and in private life for decency in political campaigns, both on the part of Government servants, of candidates, of newspapers, of corporations and of individuals, that I regard this new legislation as at least a step in the right direction.

34

The Taft-Hartley Act[*]

(1947)

1. How might labor unions influence campaigns and elections in ways other than making donations to political candidates?
2. How influential are political action committees today?

AFTER CORPORATE TREASURY funds were banned from political campaigns by passage of the Tillman Act in 1907, political donations made by labor unions were next to come under closer scrutiny. Since New Deal legislation had been friendly to labor unions, union membership had grown, and as organized labor grew it became a more important factor in American politics and a more important source of campaign revenue, primarily for Democrats. As a result, Republicans and Southern Democrats (there was considerably less industry in the southern part of the country than in the northern part) in Congress fought to reduce the influence of organized labor.

A major step toward this goal was the passage of the War Labor Disputes Act of 1943 (WLDA), also known as the Smith-Connally Act. This legislation was adopted during World War II to allow the federal government to seize and operate any industry if a labor dispute interfered with the production of materials necessary to wage the war. In addition, the WLDA prohibited labor unions from contributing directly to candidates for federal office. To enact the legislation Congress had to override President Roosevelt's veto, which it did on June 25, 1943. (While Roosevelt believed that it was important to enact legislation that would assist in settling labor disputes, he was not in support of legislation that he believed would weaken labor leaders' relationships with either union members or candidates for office.) Since the WLDA was enacted to facilitate production during World War II only, however, it expired in early 1946, six months after the end of the conflict.

*Taft-Hartley Act of 1947, 61 Stat. 136 (June 23, 1947). Reprinted at www.brookings.edu/gs/cf/sourcebk/chap2.pdf.

Later that year, after the 1946 congressional elections, the Republicans were in the majority in both houses of Congress. Many in the party were eager to overturn parts of the New Deal, and among the first priorities was to amend the National Labor Relations Act (NLRA), also known as the Wagner Act, which had been passed by Congress in 1935. To further that end, Republican senator Robert Taft of Ohio and Republican representative Fred Hartley of New Jersey sponsored the Labor Management Relations Act (LMRA), also known as the Taft-Hartley Act. President Harry Truman vetoed the legislation primarily because he needed the support of organized labor to win the 1948 presidential election, but Congress overrode that veto on June 23, 1947. The LMRA retained many elements of the NLRA in that it placed limitations on industries, but it also added other features that placed limitations on labor unions. One such provision was to make permanent the ban on labor unions donating directly to candidates for federal office.

To circumvent this ban, the Congress of Industrial Organizations (CIO) created the first political action committee (PAC) in 1944. In the United States, a PAC is a private group organized to elect or defeat government officials or to promote legislation. An organization becomes a PAC by receiving contributions or making expenditures of more than $1,000 for the purpose of influencing a federal election. The CIO used its PAC to contribute funds to candidates preferred by unions, and not surprisingly, other unions soon followed its example. By the 1970s businesses were creating their own PACs to balance the strength of unions, and by the 1990s members of Congress were starting leadership PACs to redistribute funds to members of their political party.

An Act to amend the National Labor Relations Act, to provide additional facilities for the mediation of labor disputes affecting commerce, to equalize legal responsibilities of labor organizations and employers, and for other purposes. . . .

SEC. 304. Section 313 of the Federal Corrupt Practices Act, 1925 (U.S.C., 1940 edition, title 2, sec. 251; Supp. V, title 50, App., sect. 1509), is amended to read as follows:

"SEC. 313. It is unlawful for any national bank, or any corporation organized by authority of any law of Congress, to make a contribution or expenditure in connection with any election to any political office, or in connection with any primary election or political convention or caucus held to select candidates for any political office, or for any corporation whatever, or any labor organization to make a contribution or expenditure in connection with any election at which Presidential and Vice Presidential electors or a Senator or Representative in, or a Delegate or Resident Commissioner to Congress are to be voted for, or in connection with any primary election or political convention or caucus held to select candidates for any of the foregoing offices, or for any candidate, political committee, or other person to accept or receive any contribution prohibited by this section. Every corporation or labor organization which makes any contribution or expenditure in violation of this section shall be fined not more than $5,000; and every officer or director of any corporation, or officer of any labor organization, who consents to any contribution or expenditure by the corporation or labor organization, as the case may be, in violation of this section shall be fined not more than $1,000 or imprisoned for not more than one year, or both. For the purposes of this section 'labor organization' means any organization of any kind, or any agency or employee representation committee or plan, in which employees participate and which exists for the purpose, in whole or in part, of dealing with employers concerning grievances, labor disputes, wages, rates of pay, hours of employment, or conditions of work. . . ."

❦ 35 ❧

James Rowe's Memorandum to Harry Truman*

(1947)

1. How does a written strategy benefit a campaign? How did such a strategy benefit the reelection campaign of President Truman?
2. Why was Rowe incorrect in his prediction that the South was safe in Democratic hands? How did this affect the Democratic Party in the short- and long-term?

IN EARLY 1947, the "Monday Night Group," Democrats who were either part of or close to the Truman administration, realized that the Democratic Party lacked a strategy for the 1948 presidential campaign.

*www.trumanlibrary.org/whistlestop/study_collections/1948campaign/large/docs/documents/index.php?documentdate=1947-09-18&documentid=17&studycollectionid=Election&pagenumber=1

Most saw the need to draft a comprehensive campaign plan for the upcoming presidential election, but no one in the group was able to devote the attention necessary to write it.

The task was eventually undertaken by James H. Rowe, an administrative assistant for President Franklin Roosevelt and one of the brightest minds of the New Deal era. Rowe had left the administration in 1945 to become the law partner of another important Roosevelt aide, Thomas "Tommy the Cork" Corcoran. Truman intensely disliked Corcoran, however, which meant that Rowe's counsel was not welcome in the White House either. Rowe was not a fan of Truman, but he did not want the Republicans to win the presidency, so his memorandum regarding strategy for the 1948 campaign was circulated to Truman through surrogates.

The Rowe memorandum was first given to James Webb, director of the Bureau of the Budget, who tried to pass it directly to Truman. When he did so, Truman noticed that it was written by Rowe and suggested that Webb send it to his presidential aide Clark Clifford. Webb then asked another White House aide, Richard E. Neustadt, to hand-deliver the memorandum to Clifford with a cover letter stating, "The President asked me to give this to you for the appropriate action." Clifford rewrote the memorandum, reviewed it with the Monday Night Group, and handed it to Truman on November 19, 1947. According to Clifford, the president adopted the game plan presented in the memorandum as the working strategy of his campaign and kept a copy in his desk in the Oval Office to reference.

The memorandum is widely considered to be one of the most insightful game plans ever produced in preparation for a presidential campaign. In it, Rowe argues that Truman could win if he ran as a progressive liberal. Doing so would allow him to maintain the support of the constituencies of the New Deal coalition. Six of the seven predictions outlined in the memorandum proved correct, including Thomas Dewey's nomination by the Republicans and the third-party candidacy of Henry Wallace. The memorandum, however, assumed that the South was in safe Democratic hands and did not forecast the third-party candidacy of Strom Thurmond.

Throughout the campaign journalists, publishers, pollsters, and even some on Truman's own staff expected he would lose, but his campaign managed to execute a strategy that allowed them to come from behind and secure reelection over Dewey.

The Politics of 1948

. . . The aim of this memorandum is to suggest a course of political conduct for the Administration to follow from September 1947 to the November 1948 elections.

(What suggestions there are on policy are based solely on an appraisal of "the politically advantageous thing to do." In a democracy, what is politically advisable may often accord with the merits of a particular policy; often it does not. This memorandum makes no attempt to evaluate the merits; that is a matter of conscience for the Administration. For working purposes it is assumed here that the politically wise thing to do is also the best policy for the United States.) . . .

. . . [T]he basic premise of this memorandum—that the Democratic Party is an unhappy alliance of Southern conservatives, Western progressives and Big City labor—is very trite; but it is also very true. And it is equally true that the success or failure of the Democratic leadership can be precisely measured by its ability to lead enough members of these three misfit groups to the polls on the first Tuesday after the first Monday of November. . . .

A. The Probabilities.

1. Governor Dewey will be the nominee of the Republican Party. This tentative conclusion is of course based on the usual factors. Among these is the fact that, at least at the present time, a strong candidate is required to defeat President Truman, as the recent Fortune Poll shows. Just as a year ago the probability was that any Republican could defeat him, so the swiftly fluctuating currents of American opinion may again destroy his strong popularity a few months hence if "the breaks"—such as an imminent European crisis which the American government fails to handle smoothly—are against his Administration. But as of September 1947 it takes a strong candidate to defeat him. . . .

It should be assumed, therefore, that the candidate is Dewey (the only man to lead the President in the Fortune Poll); and that, because of his 1944 experience and because of the extremely efficient group of men he has drawn around him, he will be a resourceful intelligent and highly dangerous candidate, even more difficult to defeat than in 1944.

2. President Truman will be elected if the Administration will successfully concentrate on the traditional Democratic alliance between the South and the West. It is inconceivable that any policies initiated by the Truman Administration no matter how "liberal" could so alienate the South in the next year that it would revolt. As always, the South can be considered safely Democratic. And in formulating national policy it can be safely ignored. . . .

The Administration is, for practical purposes, politically free to concentrate on the Winning of the West. If the Democrats carry the solid South and also those Western States carried in 1944, they will have 216 of the required 266 votes. And if the Democratic Party is powerful enough to capture the West it will almost certainly pick up enough of the doubtful Middlewestern and Eastern states to get 50 more votes (e.g. Missouri's 14 votes). They could lose New York, Pennsylvania, Illinois, New Jersey, Ohio, Massachusetts—all the "big" states—and still win.

Therefore, political and program planning demands concentration upon the West and its problems, including reclamation, floods, and agriculture. It is the Number One Priority for the 1948 campaign. The Republican Congress has already done its share to give the West to the Administration.

3. Henry Wallace will be the candidate of a third party. As of September 1947 the majority of informed opinion does not favor this particular hypothesis. Nevertheless, the factors which impel Wallace toward a third party clearly outweigh those which do not. . . .

The casual comment by the professional politicians on third party talk is that it is futile since a third party cannot get on enough state ballots. This is dangerously unrealistic. Wallace is gambling for high stakes. He hopes to defeat President Truman by splitting the Democratic Party and then inherit its leadership so he can be the candidate of 1952. If Wallace can get on the ballots of only a few states and can then draw five or ten per cent of the vote, that vote alone taken from the Democrats in a close election is enough to give the Republicans the electoral vote of those states and therefore national victory. And Wallace can get on the ballot of New York (American Labor Party) and California and other states. . . .

In a close election no votes can be ignored. The only safe working hypothesis is to assume now that Wallace will run on a third party ticket. Every effort must be made now jointly and at one and the same time—although of course by different groups—to dissuade him, and also to identify him and isolate him in the public mind with the Communists.

4. The independent and progressive voter will hold the balance of power in 1948; he will not actively support President Truman unless a great effort is made. The Democratic and Republican Parties each have a minimum, a residue, of voters whose loyalty almost nothing can shake. The independent voter who shifts on the issues comprises a group which today is probably larger than both.

The truth is that the old "party organization" control is gone forever. Better education, the rise of the mass pressure group, the economic depression of the

30's, the growth of government functions—all these have contributed to the downfall of "the organization." . . .

They have been supplanted in large measure by the pressure groups— and the support of these must be wooed since they really control the 1948 election. . . .

(a) The Farmer. The farm vote is in most ways identical with the Winning of the West—the Number One Priority. The farmer is at least at present, favorably inclined toward the Truman Administration. His crops are good, however the high prices may be affecting the rest of the people, they help him more than they hurt him. . . . Whether prosperity makes him the conservative he usually becomes in good times remains to be seen—but, if it does, nothing much can be done about it in terms of more political or economic favors to woo him back to the Democratic Banner.

(b) Labor. President Truman and the Democratic Party cannot win without the active support of organized labor. It is dangerous to assume that labor now has nowhere else to go in 1948. Labor can stay home.

The rank and file of the workers are not yet politically minded; they will not, therefore, vote or work actively unless they are inspired to do so. . . .

(c) The "Liberals". Nor are the liberal and progressive leaders overly enthusiastic about the Administration. . . . This is particularly true of such organizations as Americans for Democratic Action where most of the Roosevelt New Dealers have found haven. . . .

The liberals and progressives need to be fed idealism. They cannot, for the most part, swallow the Wallace brand but they are not adverse to the kind James Roosevelt, politically sensitive to the powerful California "left," gave them on September 5th when he announced in a radio speech he would introduce a limited "redistribution of wealth" plank at the Democratic Convention.

The liberals are numerically small. But, similar to manufacturers and financiers of the Republican Party, they are far more influential than mere numbers entitle them to be. . . .

(d) The Negro. Since 1932 when, after intensive work by President Roosevelt, their leaders strung the Pennsylvania Negro bloc into the Democratic column with the classic remark, "Turn your picture of Abraham Lincoln to the wall—we have paid that debt," the northern Negro has voted Democratic (with the exception of 1946 in New York). A theory of many professional politicians is that the northern Negro voter today holds the balance of the power in Presidential elections for the simple arithmetical reason that the Negroes not only vote in a bloc but are geographically concentrated in the pivotal, large and closely contested electoral states such as New York, Illinois,

Pennsylvania, Ohio and Michigan. This theory may or may not be absolutely true, but it is certainly close enough to the truth to be extremely arguable.

In great measure this explains the assiduous and continuous cultivation of the New York Negro vote by Governor Dewey and his insistence that his controllable legislature pass a state anti-discrimination act. . . .

To counteract this trend, the Democratic Party can point only to the obvious—that the really great improvement in the economic lot of the Negro of the North has come in the last sixteen years only because of the sympathy and policies of a Democratic Administration. The trouble is that this has worn a bit thin with the passage of the years. Unless the Administration makes a determined campaign to help the Negro (and everybody else) on the problems of high prices and housing—and capitalizes politically on its efforts—the Negro vote is already lost. . . .

(e) The Jew. The Jewish vote, insofar as it can be thought of as a bloc, is important only in New York. But (except for Wilson in 1916) no candidate since 1876 has lost New York and won the Presidency, and its 47 votes are naturally the first prize in any election. Centered in New York City, that vote is normally Democratic and, if large enough, is sufficient to counteract the upstate vote and deliver the state to Truman. Today the Jewish bloc is interested primarily in Palestine and somewhat critical of the Truman Administration on that ground. The bungling of the British in the Exodus case is sure to intensify these already complicated and irrational resentments. Unless the Palestine matter is boldly and favorably handled there is bound to be some defection on their part to the alert Dewey. It should not be overlooked, either, that much of this Jewish vote is also the "left" vote and will go to Wallace.

(f) The Catholic. The Catholic vote is traditionally Democratic. But there have been disturbingly consistent and fairly well documented rumors that the Catholic fear of Communism is grown so great that it is actively distrustful and suspicious today of any group which gives even an appearance of neutrality towards foreign or domestic Communists. . . . This particular bloc need very careful watching; the liaisons existing during the Roosevelt Administrations with the Catholic Church must be rebuilt if there are none today. . . .

(g) The Italian. The Italian vote—which has weight in New York, Rhode Island, Massachusetts, California and several minor states because it almost always votes as a solid bloc—is notoriously volatile, swinging easily from party to party. . . . Today the Italian racial leaders are again somewhat unhappy—this time because they regard the peace treaty for Italy as unnecessarily harsh. They were not made any happier by the casual "brush off" by the Administration of their protests (the State Department being the chief offender). . . .

(h) <u>The Alien Group.</u> As of today, the Administration enjoys good standing with the Harrison group interested in expanded immigration quotas. . . .

The immigration leaders today lean to the belief the Democrats are more sympathetic, but they maintain a flexible position.

5. <u>The foreign policy issues of the 1948 campaign will be our relations with the USSR and the Administration's handling of foreign reconstruction and relief.</u> The probability that the foreign affairs of the United States will remain on a basis of "bi-partisan cooperation" is unfortunately remote. The stakes in a Presidential contest are so high that the temptation to make an issue of anything on which there is any segment or group of dissatisfied voters is too irresistible.

There is considerable political advantage to the Administration in its battle with the Kremlin. The best guess today is that our poor relations with Russia will intensify—and will be clarified at the forthcoming meeting of the United Nations in New York. . . .

In a flank attack tied up with foreign policy, the Republicans are trying to identify the Administration with the domestic Communists. . . .

If the third party effort [of Henry Wallace] fizzles, it is quite possible the Communists will try to deliver the unions they dominate to the Republicans. The shoe may conceivably be on the Republican foot by election time—and it will be the Democrats' turn to emphasize the red lining on the opposition banner. . . .

6. <u>The domestic issues of the campaign will be high prices and housing.</u> The High Cost of Living will be the most controversial issue of the 1948 campaign—indeed the <u>only</u> domestic issue. Whichever Party is adjudged guilty of causing it will lose the election. For that reason the presentation of its case by the Democratic Party—the manner, the substance and the effectiveness of its evidence—is of crucial importance. . . .

Both parties will do a great deal of talking about inflation but neither will really do anything about it. Politics will make it impossible in 1948 to touch the farmers; yet farm price support and large food exports abroad are the main reasons for high food prices. In an election year the farmer is everybody's friend. Certainly the Administration is committed to the Marshall Plan which, whatever it means, at the very least means the export of materials and food during the crucial months of the campaign. The resulting smaller supply to meet domestic demand means the other inevitable rise in the price level—just at the worst time from the political point of view.

The big political question is who will be blamed? The Republicans because they removed the OPA controls and refused to subsidize housing? Or the

Democrats because of farm prices, labor "coddling" and "restrictive" tax policies? There is a third possibility—that the public won't "give a damn" who caused it. By November 1948 it may again be in that irritable and irrational mood it found itself in during the Congressional Election of 1946—and vote the "ins" out and the "outs" in. If so, "ins" should be translated to read "the Democratic President"—since the nature of American elections means the spotlight concentrated on the Presidential contest.

How the Administration dramatizes the High Cost of Living, how effective it is in presenting its story to the people—beginning <u>now</u>—can determine the next incumbent of the White House.

7. <u>The conflict between the President and the Congress will increase during the 1948 election.</u> With both major parties making their records for the campaign, and with each trying to claim credit for popular issues and to place the blame for the unpopular ones on the opposition, the political atmosphere will be so pervading that little real "business" will be done. The mutual distrust which such conduct necessarily engenders must result in a continual conflict almost from the beginning of the session.

This probably means the end of "bipartisan cooperation" on foreign policy. In the election year atmosphere it is quite difficult to "compartmentalize" issues. To expect reasonableness and partnership on foreign affairs while guerrilla warfare is going on in domestic matters is to expect that politicians overnight have become more than the mere mortal beings they are.

In so far as it has control of the situation, the Administration should select the issues upon which there will be conflict with the majority in Congress. It can assume it will get no major part of its own program approved. Its tactics therefore must be entirely different than if there were any real point to bargaining and compromise. Its recommendations—in the State of the Union message and elsewhere—must be tailored for the voter, not the Congressmen; they must display a label which reads "no compromises." The strategy on the Taft-Hartley Bill—refusal to bargain with the Republicans and to accept any compromises—paid big dividends. That strategy should be expanded in the next session to include all the <u>domestic</u> issues.

B. <u>The Course of Action.</u>
If the "<u>Probabilities</u>" (as discussed above), or most of them, are correct, there remain the twin problems of how to take advantage of those which are favorable and how to effect changes in those unfavorable.

The action required to achieve this should take place on two levels—the political level and what can be called "the program" level.

1. <u>The Political Level.</u>

(a) <u>"The Party Organization."</u> The one particular upon which all politicians agree is that the leadership of the Democratic organization is moribund. It is hardly important on this late day whether this is anyone's fault. The blunt facts seem to be that the Party has been so long in power it is fat, tired and even a bit senile. Those alert party machines which, beginning with 1932, turned out such huge majorities in the big cities for the Democratic ticket have all through the years of their victories been steadily deteriorating underneath—until in 1944 the Democratic organization found itself rivaled, in terms of money and workers, and exceeded in alertness and enthusiasm by the PAC. . . .

The one essential is to have a new Chairman as soon as possible—working to rebuild the Party organization from the ground up and trying to harmonize such appalling feuds as that in California. The practice of today's Democratic organization in spending almost all its time in raising money and doing favors for "the faithful" may be useful but it does little to rebuild the Democratic Party—and that is what it needs.

(b) <u>Liaisons with Labor and Independents.</u> Just as vital to eventual political success is the renewal of the Administration's working relationship with progressive and labor leaders. Whatever may be the reasons, these seem to have entirely ceased except on a perfunctory basis in the past year. No moment will ever be better for the President to make political capital out of the present frustration of the labor movement.

The leaders of labor must be given the impression that they are once more welcome in the councils of the Administration. . . .

(c) <u>The insulation of Henry Wallace.</u> Wallace should be put under attack whenever the moment is psychologically correct. If it is clear that organizational work is being undertaken by his men in the West either for a third party or for delegates to the Democratic Convention—and that work seems to be taking effect—the Administration must persuade prominent liberals and progressives—<u>and no one else</u>—to move publicly into the fray. They must point out that the core of the Wallace backing is made up of Communists and the fellow-travelers. At the same time some lines should be kept out so that if the unpredictable Henry finally sees the light and can be talked into supporting the Administration, he will have handy rope to climb back on the bandwagon—if he is wanted. . . .

. . . And here is the strong weapon of the President's arsenal—his <u>appointing</u> power. Politicians, like most other people, think of issues in terms of men, not statistics. When the President moves "left" in his appointments he is putting political money in his bank. . . .

The Wallace plan is simplicity itself. It should be—because it has been used before. He merely borrowed it from Fighting Bob LaFollette who received five million votes in 1924 by attacking Coolidge and John W. Davis as "Tweedle-dum and Tweedledee, the messenger boys of Wall Street." And the significance of the LaFollette third party was not its total vote but that the Progressives ran ahead of the Democrats in eleven Western States. The combined Democratic-Progressive vote was larger than the Republican vote in thirteen states, includ-ing President's Truman's own state of Missouri. Democrats who voted for Davis would have voted for any Democrat and the LaFollette Progressive would have voted for any liberal Democrat. In effect, then, this was a present of 86 electoral votes to the Republicans, not enough to change the 1924 election (382 minus 86 equals 292 [sic] votes; 136 plus 86 equals 222); but is more than enough to raise havoc for a close election. Henry Wallace may be fuzzy-minded on many matters, but his mathematics is all right.

Truman must carry the West to win. To carry the West he must be "lib-eral"; he cannot afford to be shackled with the Wall Street label by any so-called progressive movement. And Wallace recalls only too well that the spiri-tual father of the New Deal was not John W. Davis but Bob LaFollette, and that the New Deal came only eight years later. . . .

It is imperative that the President make some top level appointments from the ranks of the progressives—in foreign as well as domestic affairs. . . .

(d) Portrait of a President. A crucial—but easy—step forward to November 1948 is to create in the public mind a vote-getting picture of President Truman. The men around the President, naturally the most devoted of his followers, are inevitably so immersed in the details and execution of his day-to-day orders that they do not "see him whole." They cannot see the forest for the trees. Possibly it is helpful if the impress[ion] President Truman makes on the public is summa-rized from a more distant, and therefore more objective, perspective. . . .

The press must print news of the President; so he controls his publicity by his own whim. One or two non-political personages a week should be the tar-get. The need for conferences with labor leaders has already been emphasized for other reasons. This technique of summons to the White House has the added virtue, besides publicity, of building good will. An organization is flat-tered that its leader is considered important enough to be consulted. This takes that most important of commodities—Presidential Time—but it is well worth its expenditure. It is worth it because of the American's inordinate cu-riosity—he will watch that lunch with a new interest, even a sense of personal participation, if the other participant is someone other that a Government ad-ministrator or Congressman. . . .

2. The Program Level.

The suggestions made on the political level go almost wholly to "form", the manner and method with which things that need doing are to be done. But it is the things that are to be done—the "substance"—that determines the outcome of elections.

The issues are there for anyone to see. What remains is only the decision how and when they are to be handled, so their advantages are politically exploited to the utmost, their disadvantages politically minimized as much as possible.

How does the opposition plan to handle them? It is hardly a secret.

Having performed yeoman service for those interests (e.g. the "Real Estate Lobby") which provide the financial sinews for political warfare, the Republican strategists proclaimed their intentions to swing "left" in the next session.

Senator Taft, their leader on domestic policy, has three strings to his bow: Housing, Education (relief for teachers) and Health. The people, including the veterans, are stirred up about housing and rents, and the teachers have votes. The Republicans plan to raise the minimum wage level, do what they can for the DP's and give the Negro his FEPC and civil rights legislation, or try to.

All this means they are chasing votes in earnest. And it emphasizes the only tenable Democratic strategy, which is to swing further "left" that they do. . . .

(a) Housing. . . .

In the four months before Congress returns the Administration has time to devise its own housing bill. . . . This Bill can be worked out in all its detail by housing experts in and out of the Government; probably it should be designed particularly for the unhoused group just below the buyers and tenants who are getting what little is being built today. . . .

(b) High Prices. . . .

Something must be done. As time goes on this cry for action from the salaried people and from labor (no better off than in "real" "take-home pay" than in 1939 according to BLS statistics), who feel the squeeze more and more, will rise to a roar. It may well be as vital an issue in the 1948 campaign as were the irritations caused by OPA controls which, ironically enough today, were the major contribution to the crushing Democratic defeat in 1946. . . .

To say "something must be done" is much easier than to do it. The only real solution is to go back to the OPA controls system—and there is no way of dodging that conclusion. But despite the howls of anguish, the nation is far from educated for such drastic steps. It should be educated, as fast as possible because they are inevitable. . . .

The President—after a long and careful study by the technicians—should ask the Congress anyway for price control, and possibly rationing. . . .

(c) <u>Foreign Reconstruction—The Marshall Plan.</u> If the European nations can agree on a program after revision and suggestion by the State Department, it will probably be accepted by the Congress after much public debate and a long fight.

At that stage, the President becomes responsible for its efficient administration. . . .

The relevance of the Marshall Plan here is that if this planning <u>now</u> is not of a higher quality than any seen in Washington during the war years, its poor execution can and, may well be, the <u>hottest</u> political issue for 1948 that the Republicans can have.

(d) <u>The West—and "America's Needs and Resources."</u> In the land of Electoral Votes, the West is the "Number One Priority" for the Democrats. Its people are more liberal because they need the economic help of government and in the years of the New Deal have come to understand how it functions. Even the Chambers of Commerce of the West rarely prate of governmental economy; they learned better long ago.

There is no need for an extended discussion here about what should be done politically for the Western States. They know their needs—less discrimination in freight rates, reclamation projects and lots of them, better roads (their road system suffered from lack of maintenance in the war years), public power, help in the development and protection of their resources, and so forth. Their needs are not hard to understand. The Administration, which in the last year or two has at least budget-wise not shown much sympathy (although far more than the Republicans), must display a constant and increasing interest in these Western needs. . . .

. . . The appeal of Wallace to the young voters during his western swing several months ago was because he dared to talk in an idealistic strain. No other American figure (not even Stassen, who leads Truman almost 2–1 among the independent and western voters, according to the <u>Fortune</u> poll) has had the imagination to "pitch" his arguments at that level.

Yet it is just that level, other things being equal, that has always had more appeal to the American people than any other. A planning program for the United States, with 1960 as the target-date, may well have that kind of political glamour. It might catch on. . . .

C. <u>The Mechanics for 1948</u>

This memorandum has made two points—(A) It is "probable" certain things will happen in 1948; and (B) A certain "course of action" must be followed to shape those probabilities to bring about the President's election.

The question remains how to create the necessary machinery. . .

What kind of mechanism will work?

Some sort of a <u>small</u> "working committee" (or "think" group) should set up. Its function would be to coordinate the political program in and out of the Administration. (This does <u>not</u> mean it would run all over the departments; indeed, if it works right, no one in any of the agencies will ever hear of it.)

The members of such a committee would be imaginative men with understanding of and experience in government, and with some knowledge, even if only a theoretical one of the folkways, the give-and-take of politics. To put it bluntly (although it is poor semantics to do so) they would be the counterpart of Roosevelt's "Brain Trust" and "The Team" of Dewey.

They would be close-mouthed (the hardest requisite of all!). . . .

What sort of work would [a] "working committee" do?

It would, even at this early date, start the preparation of memoranda looking toward the drafting of the 1948 Platform.

It would begin assembling material for approximately ten major <u>political</u> speeches—the campaign speeches after the Convention. As part of this project it would draw up tentative plans for the campaign itinerary, including folders on the cities and towns to be visited, information on the industries, personages, their occupations and the past voting habits of the inhabitants.

It would create a functioning political intelligence. . . .

It would do research on the "availability" and the disadvantages of the numerous Vice-Presidential candidates. . . .

It would present to the President a "Monthly Estimate of the Situation" (somewhat similar to this memorandum, but scientifically based on reports and statistics and polls), informing him of recent political trends, the rise or fall of the leading Republican candidates, the disaffection or conciliation of any large social group or potent political or fraternal organization, the weakness in certain geographical areas, and so forth. . . .

It would do research on the various personalities to be involved in the campaign. . . .

The White House leader of this group would be in charge of "riding herd" on the Administration programs on housing, prices, taxes and foreign policy. . . .

The "working committee" would set up its own private polling system similar to one used with some success in the 1940 campaign. . . .

Another badly neglected function the "working committee" would take on is preparing answers to Republican charges. Its performance must be <u>efficient</u> enough so the answer will be carried in newspaper stories the same day, and not on the back pages a week or so later. . . .

These are illustrative of what a good "working committee" can do. Someone must do them if there is to be success in 1948. The Presidential election is being determined <u>now</u> by the day-to-day events of 1947. . . .

In national politics the American people normally make up their minds irrevocably about the two Presidential candidates by the end of July.

If the program discussed here can be properly executed it may be of help in getting them to make up their minds <u>the right way.</u>

[signed]
James Rowe, Jr.
September 18, 1947

❦ 36 ❧

The First Kennedy-Nixon Debate*

(1960)

1. How important are debates to winning presidential elections? Specifically, what strategies did future presidential nominees learn from the Kennedy-Nixon debates?
2. How do presidential debates differ today from Kennedy and Nixon's first televised debate? In what ways are they similar?

IN THE 1960 PRESIDENTIAL ELECTION Democratic senator John Kennedy won the popular vote by just over one hundred thousand votes and the Electoral College by only eighty-four votes. If five thousand votes had shifted from the Democratic to the Republican column in the state of Illinois and twenty-four thousand Texans had voted differently, then Republican Vice President Richard Nixon would have been inaugurated as the thirty-fifth president of the United States. Although never proven, it was widely believed that the Democratic political machines in those two states delivered the election to Kennedy through fraudulent methods.

Many factors affect the outcome of elections, but in close campaigns everything plays a role in who wins. Easily the most prominent new feature of the 1960 election was the use of television to broadcast four

*www.debates.org/pages/trans60a.html

debates between Kennedy and Nixon. These were the first-ever presidential debates between the Democratic and Republican nominees, and they were nationally televised. An estimated 66.4 million viewers watched the first debate on September 26, 1960, and that number only slipped slightly for the remaining three.

The first debate was moderated by Howard K. Smith of CBS News. A panel of four journalists asked the candidates questions on issues of domestic politics. Afterward, many news outlets considered the debate a draw; a few thought that Kennedy had performed slightly better. (The *New York Times* reported, "Kennedy on first by a fielder's choice.") Most campaign professionals from both parties, on the other hand, saw it as a home run for the Massachusetts senator. Nixon had successfully countered Kennedy's rhetorical punches point by point, but he had lacked Kennedy's style in connecting with the audience.

The Kennedy-Nixon debates marked the role that television would have in the presidential selection process. For the first time, voters saw both candidates on the same stage, and the visuals proved very influential. During the two weeks prior to the debate, Kennedy had campaigned outdoors, which left him looking very healthy and tan. On the weekend of the first debate, Kennedy rested and met with his advisers periodically to prepare.

In contrast, Nixon was hospitalized for two weeks in August for an infection that developed in his knee after banging it into a car door. By late September, he had still not completely recovered. When he arrived in Chicago the evening before the debate, he found that Republican leaders had scheduled five rallies where he was to make an appearance, which allowed him little sleep that night. The afternoon of the debate Nixon made a campaign appearance before the Carpenters Union before taking a few hours to read and reflect upon the materials that his staff had prepared for the debate. By the time he arrived at the site of the debate, he looked generally weak and fatigued. He wore a gray suit and a shirt that fit poorly around the neck because he had lost weight while hospitalized. He refused to wear makeup that would improve his pale complexion on camera, but did allow his staff to apply a powder called "Lazy Shave" to cover up his five o'clock shadow. The result was that his skin tone looked even paler on black and white television and his beard stubble still showed up prominently. Nixon later reported in his memoirs that his campaign advisers were unanimous that he had won the debate on substance, but overall they felt he lost it by his appearance because "a picture is worth a thousand words." In preparation for the remaining debates, Nixon regained the weight he had lost by drinking two milkshakes per day, he wore a darker suit, and he applied television makeup. Unfortunately, his efforts came too late: viewership had been highest for the first debate.

Incumbents and front-runners could not be convinced to return to the debate podium until 1976. Both Lyndon Johnson and Richard Nixon used Section 315 of the Federal Communications Act of 1934 to justify their refusal to participate. Known as the Equal Time Provision, it required that when airtime was provided to one candidate it had to be provided to all candidates, including those of third-parties. (Congress had suspended the equal time provision in 1959 to allow for debate between the major party candidates.) In 1975, the Federal Communications Commission classified presidential debates as bona fide news events, which are not subject to the equal time provision. Wasting no time, President Gerald Ford challenged his opponent, former Georgia governor Jimmy Carter, to a debate in his acceptance of the Republican presidential nomination in August 1976. Carter accepted immediately.

HOWARD K. SMITH, MODERATOR: Good evening. The television and radio stations of the United States and their affiliated stations are proud to provide facilities for a discussion of issues in the current political campaign by the two major candidates for the presidency. The candidates need no introduction. The Republican candidate, Vice President Richard M. Nixon, and the Democratic candidate, Senator John F. Kennedy. According to rules set by the candidates themselves, each man shall make an opening statement of approximately eight minutes' duration and a closing statement of approximately three minutes' duration. In between the candidates will answer, or comment upon answers to questions put by a panel of correspondents. In this, the first discussion in a series of four uh—joint appearances, the subject-matter has been agreed, will be restricted to internal or domestic American matters. And now for the first opening statement by Senator John F. Kennedy.

SENATOR KENNEDY: Mr. Smith, Mr. Nixon. In the election of 1860, Abraham Lincoln said the question was whether this nation could exist half-slave or half-free. In the election of 1960, and with the world around us, the question is whether the world will exist half-slave or half-free, whether it will move in the direction of freedom, in the direction of the road that we are taking, or whether it will move in the direction of slavery. I think it will depend in great measure upon what we do here in the United States, on the kind of society that we build, on the kind of strength that we maintain. We discuss tonight domestic issues, but I would not want that to be any implication to be given that this does not involve directly our struggle with Mr. Khrushchev for survival. Mr. Khrushchev is in New York, and he maintains the Communist offensive throughout the world because of the productive power of the Soviet Union itself. The Chinese Communists have always had a large population. But they are important and dangerous now because they are mounting a major effort within their own country. The kind of country we have here, the kind of society we have, the kind of strength we build in the United States will be the defense of freedom. If we do well here, if we meet our obligations, if we're moving ahead, then I think freedom will be secure around the world. If we fail, then freedom fails. Therefore, I think the question before the American people is: Are we doing as much as we can do? Are we as strong as we should be? Are we as strong as we must be if we're going to maintain our independence, and if we're going to maintain and hold out the hand of friendship to those who look to us for assistance, to those who look to us for survival? I should make it very clear that I do not think we're doing enough, that I am not satisfied as an American with the progress that we're making. This is a great country, but I think it could be a greater country; and this is a powerful country, but I think it could be a more powerful country. I'm not satisfied to have fifty percent of our steel-mill capacity unused. I'm not satisfied when the United States had last year the lowest rate of economic growth of any major industrialized society in the world. Because economic growth means strength and vitality; it means we're able to sustain our defenses; it means we're able to meet our commitments abroad. I'm not satisfied when we have over nine billion dollars worth of food—some of it rotting—even though there is a hungry world, and even though four million Americans wait every month for a food package from the government, which averages five cents a day per individual. I saw cases in West Virginia, here in the United States, where children took home part of their school lunch in order to feed their families because I don't think we're meeting our obligations toward these Americans. I'm not satisfied when the Soviet Union is turning out twice as many scientists and engineers as we are. I'm not satisfied when many of our teachers are inadequately paid, or when our children go to school [in] part-time shifts. I think we should have an educational system second to none. I'm not satisfied when I see men like Jimmy Hoffa—in charge of the largest union in the United States—still free. I'm not satisfied when we are failing to develop the natural resources of the United States to the fullest. Here in the United States, which developed the Tennessee Valley and which built the Grand Coulee and the other dams in the Northwest United States at the present rate of hydropower production—and that is the hallmark of an industrialized society—the Soviet Union by 1975 will be producing more power than we are. These are all the things, I think, in this country that can make our society strong, or can mean that it stands still. I'm not satisfied until every American enjoys his full constitutional rights. If a Negro baby is born—and this is true also of Puerto Ricans and Mexicans in some of our cities—he has about one-half as much chance to get through high school as a white baby. He has one-third as much chance to get through college as a white student. He has about a third as much chance to be a professional man, about half as much chance to own a house. He has about uh—four times as much chance that he'll be out of work in his life as the white baby. I think we can do better. I don't want the talents of any American to go to waste. I know that there are those who want to turn everything over to the government. I don't at all. I want the individuals to meet their responsibilities. And I want the states to meet their responsibilities. But I think there is also a national responsibility. The argument has been used against every piece of social legislation in the last twenty-five years. The people of the United States individually could not have developed the Tennessee Valley; collectively they could have. A cotton farmer in Georgia or a peanut farmer or a dairy farmer in Wisconsin and Minnesota, he cannot protect himself against the forces of supply and demand in the market place; but working together in effective governmental programs he can do so. Seventeen million Americans, who live over sixty-five on an average Social Security check of about seventy-eight dollars a month, they're not able to sustain themselves individually, but they can sustain themselves through the social security system. I don't believe in big government, but I believe in effective governmental action. And I think that's the only way that the United States is going to maintain its freedom. It's the only way that we're going to move ahead. I think we can do a better job. I think we're going to have to do a better job if we are going to meet the responsibilities which time and events have placed upon us. We cannot turn the job over to anyone else. If the United States fails, then the whole cause of freedom fails. And I think it depends in great measure on what we do here in this country. The reason Franklin Roosevelt was a good neighbor in Latin America was because he was a good neighbor in the United States. Because they felt that the American society was moving again. I want us to recapture that image. I want people in Latin America and Africa and Asia to start to look to America; to see how we're doing things;

to wonder what the resident of the United States is doing; and not to look at Khrushchev, or look at the Chinese Communists. That is the obligation upon our generation. In 1933, Franklin Roosevelt said in his inaugural that this generation of Americans has a rendezvous with destiny. I think our generation of Americans has the same rendezvous. The question now is: Can freedom be maintained under the most severe tack—attack it has ever known? I think it can be. And I think in the final analysis it depends upon what we do here. I think it's time America started moving again.

MR. SMITH: And now the opening statement by Vice President Richard M. Nixon.

MR. NIXON: Mr. Smith, Senator Kennedy. The things that Senator Kennedy has said many of us can agree with. There is no question but that we cannot discuss our internal affairs in the United States without recognizing that they have a tremendous bearing on our international position. There is no question but that this nation cannot stand still; because we are in a deadly competition, a competition not only with the men in the Kremlin, but the men in Peking. We're ahead in this competition, as Senator Kennedy, I think, has implied. But when you're in a race, the only way to stay ahead is to move ahead. And I subscribe completely to the spirit that Senator Kennedy has expressed tonight, the spirit that the United States should move ahead. Where, then, do we disagree? I think we disagree on the implication of his remarks tonight and on the statements that he has made on many occasions during his campaign to the effect that the United States has been standing still. We heard tonight, for example, the statement made that our growth in national product last year was the lowest of any industrial nation in the world. Now last year, of course, was 1958. That happened to be a recession year. But when we look at the growth of G.N.P. this year, a year of recovery, we find that it's six and nine-tenths per cent and one of the highest in the world today. More about that later. Looking then to this problem of how the United States should move ahead and where the United States is moving, I think it is well that we take the advice of a very famous campaigner: Let's look at the record. Is the United States standing still? Is it true that this Administration, as Senator Kennedy has charged, has been an Administration of retreat, of defeat, of stagnation? Is it true that, as far as this country is concerned, in the field of electric power, in all of the fields that he has mentioned, we have not been moving ahead. Well, we have a comparison that we can make. We have the record of the Truman Administration of seven and a half years and the seven and a half years of the Eisenhower Administration. When we compare these two records in the areas that Senator Kennedy has—has discussed tonight, I think we find that America has been moving ahead. Let's take schools. We have built more schools in these last seven and a half years than we built in the previous seven and a half, for that matter in the previous twenty years. Let's take hydroelectric power. We have developed more hydroelectric power in these seven and a half years than was developed in any previous administration in history. Let us take hospitals. We find that more have been built in this Administration than in the previous Administration. The same is true of highways. Let's put it in terms that all of us can understand. We often hear gross national product discussed and in that respect may I say that when we compare the growth in this Administration with that of the previous Administration that then there was a total growth of eleven per cent over seven years; in this Administration there has been a total growth of nineteen per cent over seven years. That shows that there's been more growth in this Administration than in its predecessor. But let's not put it there; let's put it in terms of the average family. What has happened to you? We find that your wages have gone up five times as much in the Eisenhower Administration as they did in the Truman Administration. What about the prices you pay? We find that the prices you pay went up five times as much in the Truman Administration as they did in the Eisenhower Administration. What's the net result of this? This means that the average family income went up fifteen per cent in the Eisenhower years as against two per cent in the Truman years. Now, this is not standing still. But, good as this record is, may I emphasize it isn't enough. A record is never something to stand on. It's something to build on. And in building on this record, I believe that we have the secret for progress, we know the way to progress. And I think, first of all, our own record proves that we know the way. Senator Kennedy has suggested that he believes he knows the way. I respect the sincerity which he m- which he makes that suggestion. But on the other hand, when we look at the various programs that he offers, they do not seem to be new. They seem to be simply retreads of the programs of the Truman Administration which preceded it. And I would suggest that during the course of the evening he might indicate those areas in which his programs are new, where they will mean more progress than we had then. What kind of programs are we for? We are for programs that will expand educational opportunities, that will give to all Americans their equal chance for education, for all of the things which are necessary and dear to the hearts of our people. We are for programs, in addition, which will see that our medical care for the aged are—is—are much—is much better handled than it is at the present time. Here again, may I indicate that Senator

Kennedy and I are not in disagreement as to the aims. We both want to help the old people. We want to see that they do have adequate medical care. The question is the means. I think that the means that I advocate will reach that goal better than the means that he advocates. I could give better examples, but for—for whatever it is, whether it's in the field of housing, or health, or medical care, or schools, or the eh- development of electric power, we have programs which we believe will move America, move her forward and build on the wonderful record that we have made over these past seven and a half years. Now, when we look at these programs, might I suggest that in evaluating them we often have a tendency to say that the test of a program is how much you're spending. I will concede that in all the areas to which I have referred Senator Kennedy would have the spe- federal government spend more than I would have it spend. I costed out the cost of the Democratic platform. It runs a minimum of thirteen and two-tenths billions dollars a year more than we are presently spending to a maximum of eighteen billion dollars a year more than we're presently spending. Now the Republican platform will cost more too. It will cost a minimum of four billion dollars a year more, a maximum of four and nine-tenths billion dollar[s] a year more than we're presently spending. Now, does this mean that his program is better than ours? Not at all. Because it isn't a question of how much the federal government spends; it isn't a question of which government does the most. It is a question of which administration does the right thing. And in our case, I do believe that our programs will stimulate the creative energies of a hundred and eighty million free Americans. I believe the programs that Senator Kennedy advocates will have a tendency to stifle those creative energies, I believe in other words, that his program would lead to the stagnation of the motive power that we need in this country to get progress. The final point that I would like to make is this: Senator Kennedy has suggested in his speeches that we lack compassion for the poor, for the old, and for others that are unfortunate. Let us understand throughout this campaign that his motives and mine are sincere. I know what it means to be poor. I know what it means to see people who are unemployed. I know Senator Kennedy feels as deeply about these problems as I do, but our disagreement is not about the goals for America but only about the means to reach those goals.

MR. SMITH: Thank you, Mr. Nixon. That completes the opening statements, and now the candidates will answer questions or comment upon one another's answers to questions, put by correspondents of the networks. The correspondents: [introducing themselves: "I'm Sander Vanocur, NBC News;" "I'm Charles Warren, Mutual News;" "I'm Stuart Novins, CBS News;" "Bob Fleming, ABC News."] The first question to Senator Kennedy from Mr. Fleming.

MR. FLEMING: Senator, the Vice President in his campaign has said that you were naive and at times immature. He has raised the question of leadership. On this issue, why do you think people should vote for you rather than the Vice President?

MR. KENNEDY: Well, the Vice President and I came to the Congress together 1946; we both served in the Labor Committee. I've been there now for fourteen years, the same period of time that he has, so that our experience in uh—government is comparable. Secondly, I think the question is uh—what are the programs that we advocate, what is the party record that we lead? I come out of the Democratic party, which in this century has produced Woodrow Wilson and Franklin Roosevelt and Harry Truman, and which supported and sustained these programs which I've discussed tonight. Mr. Nixon comes out of the Republican party. He was nominated by it. And it is a fact that through most of these last twenty-five years the Republican leadership has opposed federal aid for education, medical care for the aged, development of the Tennessee Valley, development of our natural resources. I think Mr. Nixon is an effective leader of his party. I hope he would grant me the same. The question before us is: which point of view and which party do we want to lead the United States?

MR. SMITH: Mr. Nixon, would you like to comment on that statement?

MR. NIXON: I have no comment.

MR. SMITH: The next question: Mr. Novins.

MR. NOVINS: Mr. Vice President, your campaign stresses the value of your eight year experience, and the question arises as to whether that experience was as an observer or as a participant or as an initiator of policy-making. Would you tell us please specifically what major proposals you have made in the last eight years that have been adopted by the Administration?

MR. NIXON: It would be rather difficult to cover them in eight and- in two and a half minutes. I would suggest that these proposals could be mentioned. First, after each of my foreign trips I have made recommendations that have been adopted. For example, after my first trip abroad—abroad, I strongly recommended that we increase our exchange programs particularly as they related to exchange of persons of leaders in the labor field and in the information field. After my trip to South America, I made recommendations that a separate inter-American lending agency be set up which the South American nations would like much better than a lend- than to participate in the lending agencies which treated all the countries of the world the same. Uh—I have made other recommendations after each of the other trips; for example, after my trip abroad to Hungary I made some recommendations with regard to the Hungarian refugee situation which were adopted, not only by the President but some of them were enacted into law by the Congress. Within the Administration, as a chairman of the President's Committee on Price Stability and Economic Growth, I have had the opportunity to make recommendations which have been adopted within the Administration and which I think have been reasonably effective. I know Senator Kennedy suggested in his speech at Cleveland yesterday that that committee had not been particularly effective. I would only suggest that while we do not take the credit for it—I would not presume to—that since that committee has been formed the price line has been held very well within the United States.

MR. KENNEDY: Well, I would say in the latter that the—and that's what I found uh—somewhat unsatisfactory about the figures uh—Mr. Nixon, that you used in your previous speech, when you talked about the Truman Administration. You—Mr. Truman came to office in nineteen uh—forty-four and at the end of the war, and uh—difficulties that were facing the United States during that period of transition—1946 when price controls were lifted—so it's rather difficult to use an overall figure taking those seven and a half years and comparing them to the last eight years. I prefer to take the overall percentage record of the last twenty years of the Democrats and the eight years of the Republicans to show an overall period of growth. In regard to uh—price stability uh—I'm not aware that that committee did produce recommendations that ever were certainly before the Congress from the point of view of legislation in regard to controlling prices. In regard to the exchange of students and labor unions, I am chairman of the subcommittee on Africa and I think that one of the most unfortunate phases of our policy towards that country was the very minute number of exchanges that we had. I think it's true of Latin America also. We did come forward with a program of students for the Congo of over three hundred which was more than the federal government had for all of Africa the previous year, so that I don't think that uh—we have moved at least in those two areas with sufficient vigor. . . .

MR. SMITH: The next question to Vice President Nixon from Mr. Vanocur.

MR. VANOCUR: Uh—Mr. Vice President, since the question of executive leadership is a very important campaign issue, I'd like to follow Mr. Novins' question. Now, Republican campaign slogans—you'll see them on signs around the country as you did last week—say it's experience that counts—that's over a picture of yourself; sir uh—implying that you've had more governmental executive decision-making uh—experience than uh—your opponent. Now, in his news conference on August twenty-fourth, President Eisenhower was asked to give one example of a major idea of yours that he adopted. His reply was, and I'm quoting; "If you give me a week I might think of one. I don't remember." Now that was a month ago, sir, and the President hasn't brought it up since, and I'm wondering, sir, if you can clarify which version is correct—the one put out by Republican campaign leaders or the one put out by President Eisenhower?

MR. NIXON: Well, I would suggest, Mr. Vanocur, that uh—if you know the President, that was probably a facetious remark. Uh—I would also suggest that insofar as his statement is concerned, that I think it would be improper for the President of the United States to disclose uh—the instances in which members of his official family had made recommendations, as I have made them through the years to him, which he has accepted or rejected. The President has always maintained and very properly so that he is entitled to get what advice he wants from his cabinet and from his other advisers without disclosing that to anybody—including as a matter of fact the Congress. Now, I can only say this. Through the years I have sat in the National Security Council. I have been in the cabinet. I have met with the legislative leaders. I have met with the President when he made the great decisions with regard to Lebanon, Quemoy and Matsu, other matters. The President has asked for my advice. I have given it. Sometimes my advice has been taken. Sometimes it has not. I do not say that I have made the decisions. And I would say that no president should ever allow anybody else to make the major decisions, [sic] The president only makes the decisions. All that his advisers do is to give counsel when he asks for it. As far as what experience counts and whether that is experience that counts, that isn't for me to say. Uh—I can only say that my experience is there for the people to consider; Senator Kennedy's is there for the people to consider. As he pointed out, we came to the Congress in the same year. His experience has been different from mine. Mine has been in the executive branch. His has been in the legislative branch. I would say that the people now have the opportunity to evaluate his as against mine and I think both he and I are going to abide by whatever the people decide.

MR. SMITH: Senator Kennedy.

MR. KENNEDY: Well, I'll just say that the question is of experience and the question also is uh—what our judgment is of the future, and what our goals are for the United States, and what ability we have to implement those goals.

Abraham Lincoln came to the presidency in 1860 after a rather little known uh—session in the House of Representatives and after being defeated for the Senate in fifty-eight and was a distinguished president. There's no certain road to the presidency. There are no guarantees that uh—if you take uh—one road or another that you will be a successful president. I have been in the Congress for fourteen years. I have voted in the last uh—eight years uh—and the Vice President was uh—presiding over the Senate and meeting his other responsibilities. I have met met uh—decisions over eight hundred times on matters which affect not only the domestic security of the United States, but as a member of the Senate Foreign Relations Committee. The question really is: which candidate and which party can meet the problems that the United States is going to face in the sixties? . . .

MR. SMITH: The next question to Vice President Nixon fa- from Mr. Fleming.

MR. FLEMING: Mr. Vice President, do I take it then you believe that you can work better with Democratic majorities in the House and Senate than Senator Kennedy could work with Democratic majorities in the House and Senate?

MR. NIXON: I would say this: that we, of course, expect to pick up some seats in both in the House and the Senate. Uh—We would hope to control the House, to get a majority in the House uh—in this election. We cannot, of course, control the Senate. I would say that a president will be able to lead—a president will be able to get his program through—to the effect that he has the support of the country, the support of the people. Sometimes we—we get the opinion that in getting programs through the House or the Senate it's purely a question of legislative finagling and all that sort of thing. It isn't really that. Whenever a majority of the people are for a program, the House and the Senate responds to it. And whether this House and Senate, in the next session is Democratic or Republican, if the country will have voted for the candidate for the presidency and for the proposals that he has made, I believe that you will find that the president, if it were a Republican, as it would be in my case, would be able to get his program through that Congress. Now, I also say that as far as Senator Kennedy's proposals are concerned, that, again, the question is not simply one of uh—a presidential veto stopping programs. You must always remember that a president can't stop anything unless he has the people behind him. And the reason President Eisenhower's vetoes have been sustained—the reason the Congress does not send up bills to him which they think will be vetoed—is because the people and the Congress, the majority of them, know the country is behind the President.

MR. SMITH: Senator Kennedy.

MR. KENNEDY: Well, now let's look at these bills that the Vice President suggests were too extreme. One was a bill for a dollar twenty-five cents an hour for anyone who works in a store or company that has a million dollars a year business. I don't think that's extreme at all; and yet nearly two-thirds to three-fourths of the Republicans in the House of Representatives voted against that proposal. Secondly was the federal aid to education bill. It—it was a very uh—because of the defeat of teacher salaries, it was not a bill that uh—met in my opinion the need. The fact of the matter is it was a bill that was less than you recommended, Mr. Nixon, this morning in your proposal. It was not an extreme bill and yet we could not get one Republican to join, at least I think four of the eight Democrats voted to send it to the floor of the House—not one Republican—and they joined with those Democrats who were opposed to it. I don't say the Democrats are united in their support of the program. But I do say a majority are. And I say a majority of the Republicans are opposed to it. The third is medical care for the aged which is tied to Social Security, which is financed out of Social Security funds. It does not put a deficit on the Treasury. The proposal advanced by you and by Mr. Javits would have cost six hundred millions of dollars—Mr. Rockefeller rejected it in New York, said he didn't agree with the financing at all, said it ought to be on Social Security. So these are three programs which are quite moderate. I think it shows the difference between the two parties. One party is ready to move in these programs. The other party gives them lip service. . . .

MR. SMITH: Can I have the summation time please? We've completed our questions and our comments, and in just a moment, we'll have the summation time.

VOICE: This will allow three minutes and twenty seconds for the summation by each candidate.

MR. SMITH: Three minutes and twenty seconds for each candidate. Vice President Nixon, will you make the first summation?

MR. NIXON: Thank you, Mr. Smith. Senator Kennedy. First of all, I think it is well to put in perspective where we really do stand with regard to the Soviet Union in this whole matter of growth. The Soviet Union has been moving faster than we have. But the reason for that is obvious. They start from a much lower base. Although they have been moving faster in growth than we have, we find, for example, today that their total gross national product is only forty-four per cent of our total gross national product. That's the same percentage that it was twenty years ago. And as far as the absolute gap is concerned, we find that the United States is even further ahead than it was twenty years ago. Is this any reason for complacency? Not at all. Because these are determined men. They are fanatical men. And we have to get the very most of uh—out uh—out of our economy. I agree with Senator Kennedy completely on that score. Where we disagree is in the means that we would use to get the most out of our economy. I respectfully submit that Senator Kennedy too often would rely too much on the federal government, on what it would do to solve our problems, to stimulate growth. I believe that when we examine the Democratic platform, when we examine the proposals that he has discussed tonight, when we compare them with the proposals that I have made, that these proposals that he makes would not result in greater growth for this country than would be the case if we followed the programs that I have advocated. There are many of the points that he has made that I would like to comment upon. The one in the field of health is worth mentioning. Our health program—the one that Senator Javits and other Republican Senators, as well as I supported—is one that provides for all people over sixty-five who want health insurance, the opportunity to have it if they want it. It provides a choice of having either government insurance or private insurance. But it compels nobody to have insurance who does not want it. His program under Social Security, would require everybody who had Social Security to take government health insurance whether he wanted it or not. And it would not cover several million people who are not covered by Social Security at all. Here is one place where I think that our program does a better job than his. The other point that I would make is this: this downgrading of how much things cost I think many of our people will understand better when they look at what happened when—during the Truman Administration when the government was spending more than it took in—we found savings over a lifetime eaten up by inflation. We found the people who could least afford it—people on retired incomes uh—people on fixed incomes—we found them unable to meet their bills at the end of the month. It is essential that a man who's president of this country certainly stand for every program that will mean for growth. And I stand for programs that will mean growth and progress. But it is also essential that he not allow a dollar spent that could be better spent by the people themselves.

MR. SMITH: Senator Kennedy, your conclusion.

MR. KENNEDY: The point was made by Mr. Nixon that the Soviet production is only forty-four percent of ours. I must say that forty-four percent and that

**Memorandum on Television Debate
with Vice President Nixon, September 26th**

To: Senator John F. Kennedy
From: Clark M. Clifford

Your time is so limited, I shall make my comments as brief as possible.

1) You clearly came out the winner. You were clear, concise and very convincing.

2) You kept Nixon on the defensive. This kept him off balance and was a great plus for you.

3) Unquestionably this appearance made you votes. I feel sure the other three will do the same.

Suggestions.

1) Nixon is making a determined effort to convince the American people your and his goals are the same. That the only difference lies in the means to attain those goals.
   This is false. The goals are very different, and he must not be permitted to create the illusion that you and he are working toward the same end.
   Be prepared the next time to point out specifically the positive differences that exist in goals, i.e., minimum wage, housing, etc.
   If Nixon can convince the people that his and your philosophies are the same, then he will rob you of one of your greatest strengths.

2) Attention must be given to adding greater warmth to your image. If you can retain the technical brilliance and obvious ability, but also project the element of warm, human understanding, you will possess an unbeatable combination.
   Give illustrations based upon contacts with service personnel when you were in the Navy. Also conversations you have had with ordinary people who have discussed their problems with you during the campaign.

3) Take advantage of every opportunity to appear with Nixon. You are better than he is.

                                                    C.M.C.

September 27, 1960

SOURCE: "Memorandum on Television Debate with Vice President Nixon September 26th," Clark M. Clifford to Sen. John F. Kennedy, September 27, 1960, Personal Papers of Robert F. Kennedy, Pre-Administration Political Files 1952–1960, Kennedy-Nixon Debate Folder, Box 36, John F. Kennedy Library.

Soviet country is causing us a good deal of trouble tonight. I want to make sure that it stays in that relationship. I don't want to see the day when it's sixty percent of ours, and seventy and seventy-five and eighty and ninety percent of ours, with all the force and power that it could bring to bear in order to cause our destruction. Secondly, the Vice President mentioned medical care for the aged. Our program was an amendment to the Kerr bill. The Kerr bill provided assistance to all those who were not on Social Security. I think it's a very clear contrast. In 1935, when the Social Security Act was written, ninety-four out of ninety-five Republicans voted against it. Mr. Landon ran in 1936 to repeal it. In August of 1960, when we tried to get it again, but this time for medical care, we received the support of one Republican in the Senate on this occasion. Thirdly, I think the question before the American people is: as they look at this country and as they look at the world around them, the goals are the same for all Americans. The means are at question. The means are at issue. If you feel that everything that is being done now is satisfactory, that the relative power and prestige and strength of the United States is increasing in relation to that of the Communists; that we've b- gaining more security, that we are achieving everything as a nation that we should achieve, that we are achieving a better life for our citizens and greater strength, then I agree. I think you should vote for Mr. Nixon. But if you feel that we have to move again in the sixties, that the function of the president is to set before the people the unfinished business of our society as Franklin Roosevelt did in the thirties, the agenda for our people—what we must do as a society to meet our needs in this country and protect our security and help the cause of freedom. As I said at the beginning, the question before us all, that faces all Republicans and all Democrats, is: can freedom in the next generation conquer, or are the Communists going to be successful? That's the great issue. And if we meet our responsibilities I think freedom will conquer. If we fail, if we fail to move ahead, if we fail to develop sufficient military and economic and social strength here in this country, then I think that uh—the tide could begin to run against us. And I don't want historians, ten years from now, to say, these were the years when the tide ran out for the United States. I want them to say these were the years when the tide came in; these were the years when the United States started to move again. That's the question before the American people, and only you can decide what you want, what you want this country to be, what you want to do with the future. I think we're ready to move. And it is to that great task, if we're successful, that we will address ourselves.

MR. SMITH: Thank you very much, gentlemen. This hour has gone by all too quickly. Thank you very much for permitting us to present the next president of the United States on this unique program. I've been asked by the candidates to thank the American networks and the affiliated stations for providing time and facilities for this joint appearance. Other debates in this series will be announced later and will be on different subjects. This is Howard K. Smith. Good night from Chicago.

≈ *37* ≈

*Baker v. Carr**

(1962)

1. Under what circumstances, if any, should the courts become involved in cases of legislative redistricting?
2. What impact does legislative redistricting have on how candidates campaign for office?

FOR DECADES PEOPLE had been moving off the farm to the city, but in many states electoral districts had not been changed to reflect that migration. Thus, city voters selected lawmakers, but rural voters selected proportionately more. In one example, a Vermont legislator represented forty-nine people while another represented more than thirty thousand.

In the 1960s the U.S. Supreme Court fundamentally changed the process of legislative apportionment in the United States through a series of cases that began with *Baker v. Carr* (369 U.S. 186). The plaintiff in that case was Charles W. Baker, chair of the Shelby County Quarterly Court, the fiscal and legislative body for the county that included the city of Memphis, Tennessee. Baker felt that Memphis was underrepresented in the state legislature and that such underrepresentation meant that it did not receive the attention or revenue that it needed and deserved. On

---

*http://supreme.justia.com/us/369/186/case.html

behalf of the League of Women Voters, which was interested in promoting free, honest, and fair elections, Baker filed suit, complaining that whereas the Tennessee General Assembly was required by law to pass a plan for reapportioning legislative districts every ten years, it had not done so since 1901. He argued that the significant population shifts from rural to urban areas and the failure of the General Assembly to reapportion the districts effectively diluted his vote, depriving him of the "equal protection of the law" required by the Fourteenth Amendment.

The defendant in the case was Secretary of State Joe C. Carr, who was responsible for administering the state's elections. Carr and the state of Tennessee argued that relief from legislative malapportionment should come through the legislative, not the judicial, process. This argument was consistent with the earlier majority opinion of the Supreme Court in *Colegrove v. Green,* 328 U.S. 549 (1946).

When no clear majority emerged in the initial conference between the justices, the litigants were called back to argue again. The Court eventually ruled in March 1962 that issues of legislative reapportionment could be judicial in nature and therefore could be decided by the federal courts. Justice William Brennan wrote the Court's majority opinion, essentially concluding that there were sufficient issues related to equal protection in *Baker* to merit judicial evaluation. So, the case was remanded back to the district court to be decided.

The case also produced three concurring opinions and two dissenting opinions. Justices Felix Frankfurter and John Marshall Harlan vigorously dissented. They felt that their colleagues had set aside historical precedent, failed to practice judicial restraint, and violated the principle of separation of powers by interjecting the courts into what they considered to be a political question best left to the legislature.

By November 1962, voters in thirty states had initiated lawsuits to reapportion voting districts. In 1964, the Supreme Court provided a new standard for evaluating malapportionment claims in *Reynolds v. Sims,* 377 U.S. 533 (1964). In ruling on this case, the Court went beyond *Baker v. Carr* and actually applied the standard of "one person, one vote" to drawing legislative districts in Alabama. As Chief Justice Earl Warren wrote in the majority opinion, "Legislators represent people, not trees or acres. Legislators are elected by voters, not farms or cities or economic interests." This ruling further obligated states with bicameral legislatures to apportion both houses using the one person, one vote standard, which effectively voided provisions of many state constitutions that required the selection of a specific number of state senators from each county. Illinois senator Everett Dirksen fought to pass an amendment to the Constitution that would have allowed malapportioned legislative districts, but the standard was ultimately applied to federal congressional districts as well in *Wesberry v. Sanders*, 36 U.S. 1 (1964).

These cases required almost every state to reapportion legislative districts at least once during the 1960s; many had to do so several times. This widespread reapportionment resulted in a shift in political power from rural to urban America.

<hr>

BAKER v. CARR, 369 U.S. 186 (1962)

JUSTICE BRENNAN delivered the opinion of the Court:

This civil action was brought under 42 U.S.C. §§ 1983 and 1988 to redress the alleged deprivation of federal constitutional rights. The complaint, alleging that by means of a 1901 statute of Tennessee apportioning the members of the General Assembly among the State's 95 counties, "these plaintiffs and others similarly situated, are denied the equal protection of the laws accorded them by the Fourteenth Amendment to the Constitution of the United States by virtue of the debasement of their votes," was dismissed by a three-judge court convened under 28 U.S.C. § 2281 in the Middle District of Tennessee. The court held that it lacked jurisdiction of the subject matter and also that no claim was stated upon which relief could be granted. . . . We noted probable jurisdiction of the appeal. . . . We hold that the dismissal was error, and remand the cause to the District Court for trial and further proceedings consistent with this opinion. . . .

. . . Tennessee's standard for allocating legislative representation among her counties is the total number of qualified voters resident in the respective counties, subject only to minor qualifications. Decennial reapportionment in compliance with the constitutional scheme was effected by the General Assembly each decade from 1871 to 1901. The 1871 apportionment was preceded by an 1870 statute requiring an enumeration. The 1881 apportionment involved three statutes, the first authorizing an enumeration, the second enlarging the

Senate from 25 to 33 members and the House from 75 to 99 members, and the third apportioning the membership of both Houses. In 1891 there were both an enumeration and an apportionment. In 1901 the General Assembly abandoned separate enumeration in favor of reliance upon the Federal Census and passed the Apportionment Act here in controversy. In the more than 60 years since that action, all proposals in both Houses of the General Assembly for reapportionment have failed to pass. . . .

II. Jurisdiction of the Subject Matter

The District Court was uncertain whether our cases withholding federal judicial relief rested upon a lack of federal jurisdiction or upon the inappropriateness of the subject matter for judicial consideration—what we have designated "nonjusticiability." The distinction between the two grounds is significant. In the instance of nonjusticiability, consideration of the cause is not wholly and immediately foreclosed; rather, the Court's inquiry necessarily proceeds to the point of deciding whether the duty asserted can be judicially identified and its breach judicially determined, and whether protection for the right asserted can be judicially molded. In the instance of lack of jurisdiction the cause either does not "arise under" the Federal Constitution, laws or treaties (or fall within one of the other enumerated categories of Art. III, §2), or is not a "case or controversy" within the meaning of that section; or the cause is not one described by any jurisdictional statute. Our conclusion . . . that this cause presents no nonjusticiable "political question" settles the only possible doubt that it is a case or controversy. Under the present heading of "Jurisdiction of the Subject Matter" we hold only that the matter set forth in the complaint does arise under the Constitution and is within 28 U.S.C. § 1343.

Article III, §2, of the Federal Constitution provides that "The judicial Power shall extend to all Cases, in Law and Equity, arising under this Constitution, the Laws of the United States, and Treaties made, or which shall be made, under their Authority. . . ." It is clear that the cause of action is one which "arises under" the Federal Constitution. The complaint alleges that the 1901 statute effects an apportionment that deprives the appellants of the equal protection of the laws in violation of the Fourteenth Amendment. . . .

The appellees refer to *Colegrove v. Green,* 328 U.S. 549, as authority that the District Court lacked jurisdiction of the subject matter. Appellees misconceive the holding of that case. The holding was precisely contrary to their reading of it. Seven members of the Court participated in the decision. Unlike many other cases in this field which have assumed without discussion that there was jurisdiction, all three opinions filed in *Colegrove* discussed the question. Two of the opinions expressing the views of four of the Justices, a majority, flatly held that there was jurisdiction of the subject matter. Mr. Justice Black joined by Mr. Justice Douglas and Mr. Justice Murphy stated: "It is my judgment that the District Court had jurisdiction . . . ." Mr. Justice Rutledge, writing separately, expressed agreement with this conclusion. . . .

We hold that the District Court has jurisdiction of the subject matter of the federal constitutional claim asserted in the complaint. . . .

IV. Justiciability

. . [T]he mere fact that the suit seeks protection of a political right does not mean it presents a political question. Such an objection "is little more than a play upon words." . . .

Our discussion, even at the price of extending this opinion, requires review of a number of political question cases, in order to expose the attributes of the doctrine—attributes which, in various settings, diverge, combine, appear, and disappear in seeming disorderliness. . . . That review reveals that in the *Guaranty Clause* cases and in the other "political question" cases, it is the relationship between the judiciary and the coordinate branches of the Federal Government, and not the federal judiciary's relationship to the States, which gives rise to the "political question."

We have said that "In determining whether a question falls within [the political question] category, the approriateness under our system of government of attributing finality to the action of the political departments and also the lack of satisfactory criteria for a judicial determination are dominant considerations." *Coleman v. Miller,* 307 U.S. 433, 454–455. The nonjusticiability of a political question is primarily a function of the separation of powers. Much confusion results from the capacity of the "political question" label to obscure the need for case-by-case inquiry. Deciding whether a matter has in any measure been committed by the Constitution to another branch of government, or whether the action of that branch exceeds whatever authority has been committed, is itself a delicate exercise in constitutional interpretation, and is a responsibility of this Court as ultimate interpreter of the Constitution. To demonstrate this requires no less than to analyze representative cases and to infer from them the analytical threads that make up the political question doctrine. . . .

We come, finally, to the ultimate inquiry whether our precedents as to what constitutes a nonjusticiable "political question" bring the case before us under the umbrella of that doctrine. A natural beginning is to note whether any of the common characteristics which we have been able to identify and label descriptively are present. We find none: The question here is the consistency of state action with the Federal Constitution. We have no question decided, or to be decided, by a political branch of government coequal with this Court. Nor do we risk embarrassment of our government abroad, or grave disturbance at home if we take issue with Tennessee as to the constitutionality of her action here challenged. Nor need the appellants, in order to succeed in this action, ask the Court to enter upon policy determinations for which judicially manageable standards are lacking. Judicial standards under the Equal Protection Clause are well developed and familiar, and it has been open to courts since the enactment of the Fourteenth Amendment to determine, if on the particular facts they must, that a discrimination reflects no policy, but simply arbitrary and capricious action. . . .

We conclude that the complaint's allegations of a denial of equal protection present a justiciable constitutional cause of action upon which appellants are entitled to a trial and a decision. The right asserted is within the reach of judicial protection under the Fourteenth Amendment.

The judgment of the District Court is reversed and the cause is remanded for further proceedings consistent with this opinion. . . .

JUSTICE FRANKFURTER, whom Justice Harlan joins, dissenting:

The Court today reverses a uniform course of decision established by a dozen cases, including one by which the very claim now sustained was unanimously rejected only five years ago. The impressive body of rulings thus cast aside reflected the equally uniform course of our political history regarding the relationship between population and legislative representation—a wholly different matter from denial of the franchise to individuals because of race, color, religion or sex. Such a massive repudiation of the experience of our whole past in asserting destructively novel judicial power demands a detailed analysis of the role of this Court in our constitutional scheme. Disregard of inherent limits in the effective exercise of the Court's "judicial Power" not only presages the futility of judicial intervention in the essentially political conflict of forces by which the relation between population and representation has time out of mind been, and now is, determined. It may well impair the Court's position as the ultimate organ of "the supreme Law of the Land" in that vast range of legal problems, often strongly entangled in popular feeling, on which this Court must pronounce. The Court's authority—possessed of neither the purse nor the sword—ultimately rests on sustained public confidence in its moral sanction. Such feeling must be nourished by the Court's complete detachment, in fact and in appearance, from political entanglements and by abstention from injecting itself into the clash of political forces in political settlements.

A hypothetical claim resting on abstract assumptions is now for the first time made the basis for affording illusory relief for a particular evil even though it foreshadows deeper and more pervasive difficulties in consequence. The claim is hypothetical and the assumptions are abstract because the Court does not vouchsafe the lower courts—state and federal—guidelines for formulating specific, definite, wholly unprecedented remedies for the inevitable litigations that today's umbrageous disposition is bound to stimulate in connection with politically motivated reapportionments in so many States. In such a setting, to promulgate jurisdiction in the abstract is meaningless. It is as devoid of reality as "a brooding omnipresence in the sky," for it conveys no intimation what relief, if any, a District Court is capable of affording that would not invite legislatures to play ducks and drakes with the judiciary. For this Court to direct the District Court to enforce a claim to which the Court has over the years consistently found itself required to deny legal enforcement and at the same time to find it necessary to withhold any guidance to the lower court [on] how to enforce this turnabout, new legal claim, manifests an odd—indeed an esoteric—conception of judicial propriety. One of the Court's supporting opinions, as elucidated by commentary, unwittingly affords a disheartening preview of the mathematical quagmire (apart from divers judicially inappropriate and elusive determinants) into which this Court today catapults the lower courts of the country without so much as adumbrating the basis for a legal calculus as a means of extrication. Even assuming the indispensable intellectual disinterestedness on the part of judges in such matters, they do not have accepted legal standards or criteria or even reliable analogies to draw upon for making judicial judgments. To charge courts with the task of accommodating the incommensurable factors of policy that underlie these mathematical puzzles is to attribute, however flatteringly, omnicompetence to judges. The Framers of the Constitution persistently rejected a proposal that embodied this assumption and Thomas Jefferson never entertained it. . . .

38

The "Peace, Little Girl" Television Advertisement (The Daisy Girl Ad)*

(1964)

1. Why is the "Peace, Little Girl" ad considered to have been so effective? How is this success manifest in political advertising today?
2. Republicans were critical of the Johnson campaign for running the "Peace, Little Girl" ad. Was their criticism justified? Why or why not?

IN 1948, THE ADVERTISING EXECUTIVE who developed the "Eisenhower Answers American" campaign tried to persuade the Republican presidential candidate, Thomas Dewey, to produce a small number of televised political advertisements. Given that he expected to defeat incumbent president Harry S. Truman handily, Dewey dismissed the idea. Two years later, the first televised political advertisements were aired by Democratic senator William Benton of Connecticut in his successful reelection campaign. By 1952 the number of televisions in the United States was rapidly increasing, and Dwight Eisenhower and Adlai Stevenson used television advertising to reach American voters. Since then, the reliance on television advertising at all levels of campaigning has grown exponentially.

Doyle, Dane and Bernbach (DDB), the most highly regarded advertising firm of the 1960s was hired by Lyndon Johnson's reelection campaign in 1964 to produce its political advertisements. At the time, DDB was best known for its 1959 Volkswagen campaign (voted the best advertising campaign of the twentieth century in 2000). One of the advertisements the firm developed for Johnson's campaign was a "news" ad officially titled "Peace, Little Girl"; today, it is commonly known as "The Daisy Girl Ad." A news ad is not intended to be aired repeatedly,

*http://conelrad.com/daisy/daisy_001.pdf

but rather to encourage a response provocative enough to generate news coverage of the advertisement itself. The ad itself may not appear credible, but the news coverage that it generates does.

The Daisy Girl Ad opens on a little girl in a field counting the petals as she picks them off of a daisy. When she reaches nine the frame freezes and an adult male voice that sounds like it is broadcast over a loudspeaker counts backward from ten to one—at which time the little girl is replaced on screen with footage of a nuclear explosion. The ad concludes with carefully chosen, instructive sentiments expressed by Johnson and an announcer's voiceover reminding viewers to vote for Johnson on November 3 because "The stakes are too high for you to stay home."

Aired only once as a paid advertisement during the movie *David and Bathsheba* on NBC, the ad reached an estimated fifty million viewers on the evening of Monday, September 7, 1964. Given that the ad ran later in the week on all of the major network news broadcasts for free, its cost of between $24,000–$30,000 turned out to be quite a bargain. A photo of the little girl even appeared on the cover of *Time* magazine on September 25, 1964.

The target of the advertisement was the Republican presidential candidate, Sen. Barry Goldwater of Arizona. Goldwater, however, was never identified in the advertisement. The goal instead was to reinforce a perception perpetuated by Goldwater's mis-statements on the campaign trail and perpetuated by the news media that he was more willing to use nuclear weapons than most candidates for office. Understandably, Republicans were infuriated by the Daisy Girl Ad, but their efforts to control the damage caused to Senator Goldwater's presidential candidacy may have attached the negative "nuclear" message to the party even more securely.

Today, the Daisy Girl Ad is considered so effective that many televised political ads copy the technique pioneered by DDB. (For an example, see www.factcheck.org/article457.html.)

TRANSCRIPT OF "PEACE, LITTLE GIRL"
1964 Democratic Campaign Spot

Picture	Sound
Little girl in field, picking petals off a daisy.	(little girl's voice:) "One. . two. . three. . four. . five. . seven. . six. . eight. . nine. . nine. ."
Girl looks up, startled; freeze frame on girl; move into extreme CU of her eye.	(very loud man's voice, as if heard over a loudspeaker at a test site:) "Ten. . nine. . eight. . seven. . six. . five. . four. . three. . two. . one. ."
Atom bomb exploding.	(Sound of explosion.)
Move into CU of explosion.	(LBJ voiceover:) "These are the stakes—to make a world in which all of God's children can live, or to go into the dark. We must either love each other, or we must die."
"Vote for President Johnson on November 3." (White letters on black bkgrnd)	(announcer's voice:) "Vote for President Johnson on November 3. The stakes are too high for you to stay home."

END

39

Lyndon Johnson's Message to Congress on the Voting Rights Act*

(1965)

1. How was President Johnson successful in getting Congress to pass meaningful voting rights legislation when previous efforts had failed?
2. How has the growing number of black and Latino voters affected the electoral and political agendas of the Democratic and Republican Parties?

P RIOR TO THE CIVIL WAR the qualifications for voting imposed by the different states were not considered matters of federal law. Many states imposed various methods to ensure that only specific members of the population could vote, mostly prosperous white men. The Fifteenth Amendment, ratified in 1870, superseded state laws that prohibited blacks from voting and granted blacks the franchise. Resistance to the enfranchisement of blacks was vigorous in the former slave-holding states, but the Enforcement Act of 1870 and the Force Act of 1871 allowed for oversight of state elections in the South by the federal government. The result of these actions was that blacks registered to vote and elected people to federal, state, and local political offices. Not long after, however, the Compromise of 1877 allowed Rutherford B. Hayes to take the presidency but brought an end to the reforms of Reconstruction. Union troops pulled out, oversight ended, and efforts began to disenfranchise the vote of blacks through gerrymandering of electoral districts, poll taxes, literacy tests, and other methods. The Supreme Court's ruling in *Plessy v. Ferguson* in 1896, which stated that "separate but equal" was constitutional, further hindered the voting rights of blacks.

Proponents of the enfranchisement of black voters adopted a dual strategy of amending public policy through litigation and lobbying. Slowly,

---

*Lyndon B. Johnson. *Special Message to the Congress: The American Promise.* March 15, 1965, John Wooley and Gerhard Peters, The American Presidency Project (online) (Santa Barbara: University of California [hosted], Gerhard Peters [database]). Available at www.presidency. ucsb.edu/ws/print.php?pid=26805.

but surely, their efforts bore fruit. The Supreme Court found in *Guinn v. United States* (1915) that "grandfather clauses," or provisions requiring that voter registration depend on whether the applicant descended from someone enfranchised before 1867, violated the Fifteenth Amendment. Later, the Court found in *Smith v. Allwright* (1944) that a "white primary" in Texas also violated the amendment. Such a primary prohibited the participation of voters in the state who were not white from voting in the Democratic primary, effectively blocking those voters from voting since the Democratic Party controlled most political offices in the South.

Unfortunately, the strategy of case-by-case litigation failed to prompt voluntary compliance in states and communities that were not sued. Lobbying legislators from the South also achieved few results because most federal and state legislators were white and had little vested interest in changing the status quo. By the late 1950s and the early 1960s, however, Congress had passed three pieces of legislation with provisions that made it more difficult for states to keep blacks from registering to vote. Despite these efforts, registration rates of black voters remained negligible in the Deep South and well below the registration rates of whites in the remainder of the South.

The tide began to turn with passage of the Voting Rights Act of 1965, widely considered the most important piece of civil rights legislation ever passed by Congress. In it Congress intervened in matters previously left to the states, providing statutory guarantees that Congress would fulfill the spirit of the Fifteenth Amendment. The measure passed because of President Lyndon Johnson's leadership in the wake of the assassination of President John Kennedy and compelling evidence of continued interference with attempts by blacks to vote in the South.

President Johnson introduced the bill to a joint session of Congress on March 15, 1965, and was able to sign it a few months later on August 6, 1965. The legislation was opposed by Southern senators, but it passed with substantial support from both parties due to the bipartisan support of individuals like Majority Leader Mike Mansfield, D-Mont., and Minority Leader Everett Dirksen, R-Ill. A year later, the Supreme Court upheld the act's constitutionality in *South Carolina v. Katzenbach*, 383 U.S. 301, 327–328 (1966) after the state challenged the pre-clearance provision. Congress has since passed and the president has extended various provisions of the act in 1970, 1975, 1982, and 2006.

At the time that the Voting Rights Act was passed, blacks were virtually excluded from public office in the South. Approximately two-thirds of white voters were registered to vote compared to one-third of eligible black voters. Today, black and Latino voter registration rates are closing the gap on whites in relation to the percentage of each group in the overall population, and enforcement of the Voting Rights Act has increased the opportunity for black and Latino voters to elect black and Latino representatives.

[As delivered in person before a joint session at 9:02 p.m.]
Mr. Speaker, Mr. President, Members of the Congress:

I speak tonight for the dignity of man and the destiny of democracy.

I urge every member of both parties, Americans of all religions and of all colors, from every section of this country, to join me in that cause.

At times history and fate meet at a single time in a single place to shape a turning point in man's unending search for freedom. So it was at Lexington and Concord. So it was a century ago at Appomattox. So it was last week in Selma, Alabama.

There, long-suffering men and women peacefully protested the denial of their rights as Americans. Many were brutally assaulted. One good man, a man of God, was killed.

There is no cause for pride in what has happened in Selma. There is no cause for self-satisfaction in the long denial of equal rights of millions of Americans. But there is cause for hope and for faith in our democracy in what is happening here tonight.

For the cries of pain and the hymns and protests of oppressed people have summoned into convocation all the majesty of this great Government—the Government of the greatest Nation on earth.

Our mission is at once the oldest and the most basic of this country: to right wrong, to do justice, to serve man.

In our time we have come to live with moments of great crisis. Our lives have been marked with debate about great issues; issues of war and peace, issues of prosperity and depression. But rarely in any time does an issue lay bare the secret heart of America itself. Rarely are we met with a challenge, not to our growth or abundance, our welfare or our security, but rather to the values and the purposes and the meaning of our beloved Nation.

The issue of equal rights for American Negroes is such an issue. And should we defeat every enemy, should we double our wealth and conquer the stars, and still be unequal to this issue, then we will have failed as a people and as a nation.

For with a country as with a person, "What is a man profited, if he shall gain the whole world, and lose his own soul?"

There is no Negro problem. There is no Southern problem. There is no Northern problem. There is only an American problem. And we are met here tonight as Americans—not as Democrats or Republicans—we are met here as Americans to solve that problem.

This was the first nation in the history of the world to be founded with a purpose. The great phrases of that purpose still sound in every American heart, North and South: "All men are created equal"—"government by consent of the governed"—"give me liberty or give me death." Well, those are not just clever words, or those are not just empty theories. In their name Americans have fought and died for two centuries, and tonight around the world they stand there as guardians of our liberty, risking their lives.

Those words are a promise to every citizen that he shall share in the dignity of man. This dignity cannot be found in a man's possessions; it cannot be found in his power, or in his position. It really rests on his right to be treated as a man equal in opportunity to all others. It says that he shall share in freedom, he shall choose his leaders, educate his children, and provide for his family according to his ability and his merits as a human being.

To apply any other test—to deny a man his hopes because of his color or race, his religion or the place of his birth—is not only to do injustice, it is to deny America and to dishonor the dead who gave their lives for American freedom.

The Right to Vote

Our fathers believed that if this noble view of the rights of man was to flourish, it must be rooted in democracy. The most basic right of all was the right to choose your own leaders. The history of this country, in large measure, is the history of the expansion of that right to all of our people.

Many of the issues of civil rights are very complex and most difficult. But about this there can and should be no argument. Every American citizen must have an equal right to vote. There is no reason which can excuse the denial of that right. There is no duty which weighs more heavily on us than the duty we have to ensure that right.

Yet the harsh fact is that in many places in this country men and women are kept from voting simply because they are Negroes.

Every device of which human ingenuity is capable has been used to deny this right. The Negro citizen may go to register only to be told that the day is wrong, or the hour is late, or the official in charge is absent. And if he persists, and if he manages to present himself to the registrar, he may be disqualified because he did not spell out his middle name or because he abbreviated a word on the application.

And if he manages to fill out an application he is given a test. The registrar is the sole judge of whether he passes this test. He may be asked to recite the entire Constitution, or explain the most complex provisions of State law. And even a college degree cannot be used to prove that he can read and write.

For the fact is that the only way to pass these barriers is to show a white skin.

Experience has clearly shown that the existing process of law cannot overcome systematic and ingenious discrimination. No law that we now have on the books—and I have helped to put three of them there—can ensure the right to vote when local officials are determined to deny it.

In such a case our duty must be clear to all of us. The Constitution says that no person shall be kept from voting because of his race or his color. We have all sworn an oath before God to support and to defend that Constitution. We must now act in obedience to that oath.

Guaranteeing the Right to Vote

Wednesday I will send to Congress a law designed to eliminate illegal barriers to the right to vote.

The broad principles of that bill will be in the hands of the Democratic and Republican leaders tomorrow. After they have reviewed it, it will come here formally as a bill. I am grateful for this opportunity to come here tonight at the invitation of the leadership to reason with my friends, to give them my views, and to visit with my former colleagues.

I have had prepared a more comprehensive analysis of the legislation which I had intended to transmit to the clerk tomorrow but which I will submit to the clerks tonight. But I want to really discuss with you now briefly the main proposals of this legislation,

This bill will strike down restrictions to voting in all elections—Federal, State, and local—which have been used to deny Negroes the right to vote.

This bill will establish a simple, uniform standard which cannot be used, however ingenious the effort, to flout our Constitution.

It will provide for citizens to be registered by officials of the United States Government if the State officials refuse to register them.

It will eliminate tedious, unnecessary lawsuits which delay the right to vote.

Finally, this legislation will ensure that properly registered individuals are not prohibited from voting.

I will welcome the suggestions from all of the Members of Congress—I have no doubt that I will get some—on ways and means to strengthen this law and to make it effective. But experience has plainly shown that this is the only path to carry out the command of the Constitution.

To those who seek to avoid action by their National Government in their own communities; who want to and who seek to maintain purely local control over elections, the answer is simple:

Open your polling places to all your people.

Allow men and women to register and vote whatever the color of their skin.

Extend the rights of citizenship to every citizen of this land.

The Need for Action

There is no constitutional issue here. The command of the Constitution is plain.

There is no moral issue. It is wrong—deadly wrong—to deny any of your fellow Americans the right to vote in this country.

There is no issue of States [r]ights or national rights. There is only the struggle for human rights.

I have not the slightest doubt what will be your answer.

The last time a President sent a civil rights bill to the Congress it contained a provision to protect voting rights in Federal elections. That civil rights bill was passed after 8 long months of debate. And when that bill came to my desk from the Congress for my signature, the heart of the voting provision had been eliminated.

This time, on this issue, there must be no delay, no hesitation and no compromise with our purpose.

We cannot, we must not, refuse to protect the right of every American to vote in every election that he may desire to participate in. And we ought not and we cannot and we must not wait another 8 months before we get a bill. We have already waited a hundred years and more, and the time for waiting is gone.

So I ask you to join me in working long hours—nights and weekends, if necessary—to pass this bill. And I don't make that request lightly. For from the window where I sit with the problems of our country I recognize that outside this chamber is the outraged conscience of a nation, the grave concern of many nations, and the harsh judgment of history on our acts.

We Shall Overcome

But even if we pass this bill, the battle will not be over. What happened in Selma is part of a far larger movement which reaches into every section and State of America. It is the effort of American Negroes to secure for themselves the full blessings of American life.

Their cause must be our cause too. Because it is not just Negroes, but really it is all of us, who must overcome the crippling legacy of bigotry and injustice. And we shall overcome.

As a man whose roots go deeply into Southern soil I know how agonizing racial feelings are. I know how difficult it is to reshape the attitudes and the structure of our society.

But a century has passed, more than a hundred years, since the Negro was freed. And he is not fully free tonight.

It was more than a hundred years ago that Abraham Lincoln, a great President of another party, signed the Emancipation Proclamation, but emancipation is a proclamation and not a fact.

A century has passed, more than a hundred years, since equality was promised. And yet the Negro is not equal.

A century has passed since the day of promise. And the promise is unkept.

The time of justice has now come. I tell you that I believe sincerely that no force can hold it back. It is right in the eyes of man and God that it should come. And when it does, I think that day will brighten the lives of every American.

For Negroes are not the only victims. How many white children have gone uneducated, how many white families have lived in stark poverty, how many white lives have been scarred by fear, because we have wasted our energy and our substance to maintain the barriers of hatred and terror?

So I say to all of you here, and to all in the Nation tonight, that those who appeal to you to hold on to the past do so at the cost of denying you your future.

This great, rich, restless country can offer opportunity and education and hope to all: black and white, North and South, sharecropper and city dweller. These are the enemies: poverty, ignorance, disease. They are the enemies and not our fellow man, not our neighbor. And these enemies too, poverty, disease and ignorance, we shall over, come.

An American Problem

Now let none of us in any sections look with prideful righteousness on the troubles in another section, or on the problems of our neighbors. There is really no part of America where the promise of equality has been fully kept. In Buffalo as well as in Birmingham, in Philadelphia as well as in Selma, Americans are struggling for the fruits of freedom.

This is one Nation. What happens in Selma or in Cincinnati is a matter of legitimate concern to every American. But let each of us look within our own hearts and our own communities, and let each of us put our shoulder to the wheel to root out injustice wherever it exists.

As we meet here in this peaceful, historic chamber tonight, men from the South, some of whom were at Iwo Jima, men from the North who have carried Old Glory to far corners of the world and brought it back without a stain on it, men from the East and from the West, are all fighting together without regard to religion, or color, or region, in Viet-Nam. Men from every region fought for us across the world 20 years ago.

And in these common dangers and these common sacrifices the South made its contribution of honor and gallantry no less than any other region of the great Republic—and in some instances, a great many of them, more.

And I have not the slightest doubt that good men from everywhere in this country, from the Great Lakes to the Gulf of Mexico, from the Golden Gate to the harbors along the Atlantic, will rally together now in this cause to vindicate the freedom of all Americans. For all of us owe this duty; and I believe that all of us will respond to it.

Your President makes that request of every American.

Progress through the Democratic Process

The real hero of this struggle is the American Negro. His actions and protests, his courage to risk safety and even to risk his life, have awakened the conscience of this Nation. His demonstrations have been designed to call attention to injustice, designed to provoke change, designed to stir reform.

He has called upon us to make good the promise of America. And who among us can say that we would have made the same progress were it not for his persistent bravery, and his faith in American democracy.

For at the real heart of battle for equality is a deep-seated belief in the democratic process. Equality depends not on the force of arms or tear gas but upon the force of moral right; not on recourse to violence but on respect for law and order.

There have been many pressures upon your President and there will be others as the days come and go. But I pledge you tonight that we intend to fight this battle where it should be fought: in the courts, and in the Congress, and in the hearts of men.

We must preserve the right of free speech and the right of free assembly. But the right of free speech does not carry with it, as has been said, the right to hol[l]er fire in a crowded theater. We must preserve the right to free assembly, but free assembly does not carry with it the right to block public thorough-fares to traffic.

We do have a right to protest, and a right to march under conditions that do not infringe the constitutional rights of our neighbors. And I intend to pro-tect all those rights as long as I am permitted to serve in this office.

We will guard against violence, knowing it strikes from our hands the very weapons which we seek—progress, obedience to law, and belief in American values.

In Selma as elsewhere we seek and pray for peace. We seek order. We seek unity. But we will not accept the peace of stifled rights, or the order imposed by fear, or the unity that stifles protest. For peace cannot be purchased at the cost of liberty.

In Selma tonight, as in every—and we had a good day there—as in every city, we are working for just and peaceful settlement. We must all remember that after this speech I am making tonight, after the police and the FBI and the Marshals have all gone, and after you have promptly passed this bill, the peo-ple of Selma and the other cities of the Nation must still live and work to-gether. And when the attention of the Nation has gone elsewhere they must try to heal the wounds and to build a new community.

This cannot be easily done on a battleground of violence, as the history of the South itself shows. It is in recognition of this that men of both races have shown such an outstandingly impressive responsibility in recent days—last Tuesday, again today,

Rights Must Be Opportunities

The bill that I am presenting to you will be known as a civil rights bill. But, in a larger sense, most of the program I am recommending is a civil rights pro-gram. Its object is to open the city of hope to all people of all races.

Because all Americans just must have the right to vote. And we are going to give them that right.

All Americans must have the privileges of citizenship regardless of race. And they are going to have those privileges of citizenship regardless of race.

But I would like to caution you and remind you that to exercise these privi-leges takes much more than just legal right. It requires a trained mind and a healthy body. It requires a decent home, and the chance to find a job, and the opportunity to escape from the clutches of poverty.

Of course, people cannot contribute to the Nation if they are never taught to read or write, if their bodies are stunted from hunger, if their sickness goes untended, if their life is spent in hopeless poverty just drawing a welfare check.

So we want to open the gates to opportunity. But we are also going to give all our people, black and white, the help that they need to walk through those gates.

The Purpose of This Government

My first job after college was as a teacher in Cotulla, Tex., in a small Mexican-American school. Few of them could speak English, and I couldn't speak much Spanish. My students were poor and they often came to class without breakfast, hungry. They knew even in their youth the pain of prejudice. They never seemed to know why people disliked them. But they knew it was so, because I saw it in their eyes. I often walked home late in the afternoon, after the classes were finished, wishing there was more that I could do. But all I knew was to teach them the little that I knew, hoping that it might help them against the hardships that lay ahead.

Somehow you never forget what poverty and hatred can do when you see its scars on the hopeful face of a young child.

I never thought then, in 1928, that I would be standing here in 1965. It never even occurred to me in my fondest dreams that I might have the chance to help the sons and daughters of those students and to help people like them all over this country.

But now I do have that chance—and I'll let you in on a secret—I mean to use it. And I hope that you will use it with me.

This is the richest and most powerful country which ever occupied the globe. The might of past empires is little compared to ours. But I do not want to be the President who built empires, or sought grandeur, or extended dominion.

I want to be the President who educated young children to the wonders of their world. I want to be the President who helped to feed the hungry and to prepare them to be taxpayers instead of taxeaters.

I want to be the President who helped the poor to find their own way and who protected the right of every citizen to vote in every election.

I want to be the President who helped to end hatred among his fellow men and who promoted love among the people of all races and all regions and all parties.

I want to be the President who helped to end war among the brothers of this earth.

And so at the request of your beloved Speaker and the Senator from Montana; the majority leader, the Senator from Illinois; the minority leader, Mr. McCulloch, and other Members of both parties, I came here tonight—not as

President Roosevelt came down one time in person to veto a bonus bill, not as President Truman came down one time to urge the passage of a railroad bill— but I came down here to ask you to share this task with me and to share it with the people that we both work for. I want this to be the Congress, Republicans and Democrats alike, which did all these things for all these people.

Beyond this great chamber, out yonder in 50 States, are the people that we serve. Who can tell what deep and unspoken hopes are in their hearts tonight as they sit there and listen. We all can guess, from our own lives, how difficult they often find their own pursuit of happiness, how many problems each little family has. They look most of all to themselves for their futures. But I think that they also look to each of us.

Above the pyramid on the great seal of the United States it says—in Latin—"God has favored our undertaking."

God will not favor everything that we do. It is rather our duty to divine His will. But I cannot help believing that He truly understands and that He really favors the undertaking that we begin here tonight.

Alabama Literacy Test

At the time the Voting Rights Act of 1965 was passed, the state of Alabama required all applicants to vote to fill out a lengthy application (reprinted on pages 262–265) and then pass a test to determine whether the individual was literate or not. Applicants were asked to choose randomly from a hundred different versions of the test in order to make it more difficult to study for the exam. The test itself was composed of three parts. The first part of the exam required applicants to read aloud, write an excerpt from the U.S. Constitution as it was dictated by the registrar, or both. Second, applicants were required to answer four questions based on the excerpt they had just written. For example, one version of the test asked applicants, "What officer is designated by the Constitution to be President of the Senate of the United States?" (The answer is the vice president.) Finally, applicants were asked to answer four questions about state or national government. For example, the same version of the test asked applicants to name "The only legal tender which may be authorized by states for payment of debts. . . ." (The answer is U.S. currency.) Applications were reviewed later by a three-person board of registrars, which permitted subjective assessment of what was already a very difficult test.

APPLICATION FOR REGISTRATION, QUESTIONNAIRE AND OATHS

PART I

(This is to be filled in by a member of the Board of Registrars or a duly authorized clerk of the board. If applicant is a married woman, she must state given name by which she is known, maiden surname, and married surname, which shall be recorded as her full name.)

Full Name:_____

        Last   First   Middle

Date of Birth:_____ Sex_____ Race_____

Residence Address:_____

Mailing Address:_____

Voting Place: Precinct_____ Ward_____ District_____

Length of Residence: In State_____ County_____

    Precinct, ward or district_____

Are you a member of the Armed Forces?_____

Are you the wife of a member of the Armed Forces?_____

Are you a college student?_____ If so, where_____

Have you ever been registered to vote in any other state or in any other county in Alabama?_____ If so, when and in

    what state and county and, if in Alabama, at what place did you vote in such county?_____

_____

Highest grade, 1 to 12, completed_____Where_____

Years college completed_____Where_____

PART II

(To be filled in by the applicant in the presence of the Board of Registrars without assistance.)   **MONTGOMERY**

I,_____, do hereby apply to the Board of Registrars of_____

County, State of Alabama, to register as an elector under the Constitution and laws of the State of Alabama and do herewith submit my answers to the interrogatories propounded to me by the board.

_____

                              (Signature of Applicant)

1. Are you a citizen of the United States?_____

2. Where were you born?_____

3. If you are a naturalized citizen, give number appearing on your naturalization papers and date of issuance_____

_____

4. Have you ever been married?_____If so, give the name, residence and place of birth of your husband or wife_____

    Are you divorced?_____

5. List the places you have lived the past five years, giving town or county and state_____

_____

_____

6. Have you ever been known by any name other than the one appearing on this application?____If so, state what name

_____

7. Are you employed?____If so, state by whom. (If you are self-employed, state this.)_____

_____

8. Give the address of your present place of employment_____

9. If, in the past five years, you have been employed by an employer other than your present employer, give name of all employers and cities and states in which you worked_____

_____

10. Has your name ever been stricken for any reason from any list of persons registered to vote?____If so, where, when, and why?_____

_____

11. Have you previously applied for and been denied registration as a voter?____ If so, when and where?_____

_____

12. Have you ever served in the Armed Forces?_____If so, give dates, branch of service, and serial number

_____

13. Have you ever been dishonorably discharged from military service?_____

14. Have you ever been declared legally insane?____If so, give details_____

_____

15. Give names and addresses of two persons who know you and can verify the statements made above by you relative to your residence in this state, county and precinct, ward or district_____

_____

16. Have you ever seen a copy of this registration application form before receiving this copy today?____If so, when and where? _____

17. Have you ever been convicted of any offense or paid any fine for violation of the law?____ (Yes or No) If so, give the following information concerning each fine or conviction; charge, in what court tried, fine imposed, sentence, and, if paroled, state when, and if pardoned, state when. (If fine is for traffic violation only, you need write below only the words "traffic violation only.")_____

_____

_____

_____

(Remainder of this form is to be filled out only as directed by an individual member of the Board of Registrars.)

PART III

Part III of this questionnaire shall consist of one of the forms which are Insert Part III as herein below set out. The insert shall be fastened to the questionnaire. The questions set out on the insert shall be answered according to the instructions therein set out. Each applicant shall demonstrate ability to read and write as required by the Constitution of Alabama, as amended, and no person shall be considered to have completed this application, nor shall the name of any applicant be entered upon the list of registered voters of any county until after such inserted Part III of the questionnaire has been satisfactorily completed and signed by the applicant.

PLEASE INSERT PART III HERE

PART IV

OATHS

STATE OF ALABAMA

_____COUNTY

Before me,_____

a registrar in and for said county and state, personally appeared_____,

an applicant for registration as an elector, who being first duly sworn deposes and says:

"I do solemnly swear (or affirm) that the foregoing answers to the interrogatories are true and correct to the best of my knowledge, information and belief. I do further personally swear (or affirm) that I will support and defend the Constitution of the United States and the Constitution of the State of Alabama; that I do not believe in nor am I affiliated with any group or party which advocated or advocates the overthrow of the United States or the State of Alabama by unlawful means. I do further solemnly swear (or affirm) that in the matter of this application for registration I have spoken the truth, the whole truth and nothing but the truth, so help me God."

_____

(Signature of Applicant)

Sworn to and subscribed before me this the_____day of_____, 19____.)

_____

(Signature of Board Member)

EXPLANATION AND REMARKS

(Board members interviewing applicants may place here any special explanations, such as of residence status, or other remarks for purposes of clarification. If person is blind or is otherwise physically handicapped to such an extent that he cannot fill out this application form, the circumstances are to be recorded here, along with an explanation of the method used to determine if the person is, in fact, literate and can spell words and recognize those spelled to him, or can read large block letters and words in the case of persons with sight handicaps._____

_____

_____

PART V

ACTION OF THE BOARD

STATE OF ALABAMA

_____COUNTY

The applicant_____ appeared before the board of registrars for said state and county in a regular session and executed the foregoing application in the manner prescribed by law. The Board, having further examined said applicant under oath, touching his qualifications under Section 181, Constitution of Alabama, as amended, and having fully considered the foregoing application for registration, questionnaire and oaths, adjudges said applicant entitled to

be registered and he was duly registered this the_____day of_____ _____, 19_____.

Signed:_____
                                        Chairman

_____
                                        Member

_____
                                        Member

(NOTE: The act of actually determining an applicant entitled to be registered is judicial. A majority of the Board must concur. A majority must be present. The power cannot be delegated. Each member must vote on each application. Not until this is done may a certificate be issued the applicant.)

The Applicant,_____, due to failure to meet the requirements of state law for registration as an elector, is hereby rejected on this the_____day of_____, 19_____.

Signed:_____
                                        Chairman

_____
                                        Member

_____
                                        Member

PART VI

EXAMINATION OF SUPPORTING WITNESS

(The witness shall be placed under oath to tell the truth, the person administering the oath being a Board member or other person authorized to administer oaths and acting under the direction of the Board.)

Name of Witness_____

Address_____

Place of Voting_____

"I have known the applicant_____ for_____years and_____months

and I have personal knowledge that his place of residence is_____

_____

and that he has resided in the State of Alabama at least one year and in_____County for at least six months."

_____
                                        Signature of Witness

Sworn to and subscribed before me this the_____day of_____, 19_____.

_____
                                        (Person Administering Oath)

Date_____

❧ 40 ❧
The McGovern-Fraser Commission Report*
(1971)

1. How is winning the party nomination through a presidential primary system different than winning the nomination through a party convention? Which alternative promotes stronger political parties?
2. How does mandating that the racial, gender, and age composition of state party delegations mirror states' racial, gender, and age makeups affect political parties?

THE 1968 DEMOCRATIC NATIONAL CONVENTION, held that year in Chicago, Illinois, was one of the most controversial in the history of party politics. Selection of the presidential nominee was particularly difficult. Earlier in the year President Lyndon Johnson, frustrated with U.S. progress in the Vietnam War, had chosen not to run for reelection. Both Sen. Robert Kennedy and Dr. Martin Luther King Jr. had been assassinated. To make matters worse, outside the convention hall Chicago police were clashing on national television with thousands of protesters calling for an end to U.S. participation in the war. The Democrats were taking a public relations beating that they could not afford in an election year.

At the convention, the two leading contenders for the nomination were split over the issue of the Vietnam War. Sen. Eugene McCarthy of Minnesota ran for president campaigning against the war and called for the United States to withdraw militarily from Southeast Asia. Vice President Hubert Humphrey, on the other hand, chose to follow a policy closely associated with the Johnson administration's efforts to make the reduction of troops contingent on concessions obtained through peace negotiations in Paris.

While Humphrey entered the race very late and obviously lacked the grassroots organization of McCarthy, he was supported by the political

*Congressional Record, 92nd Congress, 1st Sess., September 22, 1971 (Washington, D.C.: Government Printing Office, 1971), 13–18.

266

bosses of many states and with that influence was able to win the Democratic nomination. This led to McCarthy's supporters declaring that they had been excluded from meaningful participation in the process of delegate selection to the convention. They called for and were granted the promise of an examination of how delegates were selected and the relationship between the national party and the state parties.

The chair of the Democratic National Committee, Sen. Fred Harris of Oklahoma, appointed a committee to evaluate the party's presidential selection process and make recommendations for reform. The official designation of this group was the Committee on Party Structure and Delegate Selection. Initially, the committee was led by Sen. George McGovern of South Dakota; Rep. Donald Fraser of Minnesota took over later. In all, the McGovern-Fraser Commission held seventeen regional meetings between 1969 and 1972, that eventually resulted in the report *Mandate for Reform.*

This effectively revised the delegate selection rules of the Democratic Party by making them consistent with two guidelines. The first was that the rules and procedures of the national Democratic Party should take precedence over state and local party rules and procedures. Second, the selection of delegates to the convention should fall to party activists and candidates rather than to state and local party officials. The report also recommended many other changes to the party's presidential selection process. Among the most important were the following:

• State and local parties should follow written, clearly defined, easily accessible rules and procedures.

• Party meetings should be publicized well in advance, held on uniform dates at uniform times, and in public places with access to all.

• All interested Democrats should have the right to participate on full and equal terms.

• The "unit rule" for allocating delegates should be abolished and a proportional allocation rule adopted.

• Delegate selection procedures should be held during the year of the election.

• Race, gender, and age (under 30) composition of state delegations should mirror a state's race, gender, and age makeup.

The consequences of the reforms were not evident from the technical language adopted by the commission in the resolution, however, the Democratic Party continued to reform its selection process over the next two decades in response to the requests of state and local party officials. States found that binding preference primaries, in which convention delegates are legally bound to vote for the candidate(s) preferred by the state's voters, were the easiest method by which to fully comply with the recommendations of the commission. By the mid-1980s almost 90 percent of the states were holding presidential primaries.

Around the same time, the Republican Party organized a similar commission called the Delegates and Organization Committee. This group made similar recommendations, and eventually many of the reforms were codified in state laws.

On November 19 and 20, 1969, the Commission, meeting in open session in Washington, D.C., adopted the following Guidelines to delegate selection. . . .

A-1 Discrimination on the basis of race, color, creed, or national origin

The 1964 Democratic National Convention adopted a resolution which conditioned the seating of delegations at future conventions on the assurance that discrimination in any State Party affairs on the grounds of race, color, creed or national origin did not occur. The 1968 Convention adopted the 1964 Convention resolution for inclusion in the Call to the 1972 Convention. In 1966, the Special Equal Rights Committee, which had been created in 1964, adopted six . . . anti-discrimination standards—designated as the "six basic elements"—for the State Parties to meet. These standards were adopted by the Democratic National Committee in January 1968 as its official policy statement.

These actions demonstrate the intention of the Democratic Party to ensure a full opportunity for all minority group members to participate in the delegate selection process. To supplement the requirements of the 1964 and 1968 Conventions, the Commission requires that:

1. State Parties add the six basic elements of the Special Equal Rights Committee to their Party rules and take appropriate steps to secure their implementation;

2. State Parties overcome the effects of past discrimination by affirmative steps to encourage minority group participation, including representation of minority groups on the national convention delegation in reasonable relationship to the group's presence in the population of the State.

A-2 Discrimination on the basis of age or sex

The Commission believes that discrimination on the grounds of age or sex is inconsistent with full and meaningful opportunity to participate in the delegate selection process. Therefore, the Commission requires State Parties to eliminate all vestiges of discrimination on these grounds. Furthermore, the Commission requires State Parties to overcome the effects of past discrimination by affirmative steps to encourage representation on the national convention delegation of young people—defined as people of not more than thirty nor less than eighteen years of age—and women in reasonable relationship to their presence in the population of the State. Moreover, the Commission requires State Parties to amend their Party rules to allow and encourage any Democrat of eighteen years or more to participate in all party affairs.

When State law controls, the Commission requires State Parties to make all feasible efforts to repeal, amend, or otherwise modify such laws to accomplish the stated purpose. . . .

A-3 Voter registration

The purpose of registration is to add to the legitimacy of the electoral process, not to discourage participation. Democrats do not enjoy an opportunity to participate fully in the delegate selection process in States where restrictive voter registration laws and practices are in force, preventing their effective participation in primaries, caucuses, conventions and other Party affairs. These restrictive laws and practices include annual registration requirements, lengthy residence requirements, literacy tests, short and untimely registration periods, and infrequent enrollment sessions.

The Commission urges each State Party to assess the burdens imposed on a prospective participant in the Party's delegate selection processes by State registration laws, customs and practices, as outlined in the report of the Grass Roots Subcommittee of the Commission on Party Structure and Delegate Selection, and use its good offices to remove or alleviate such barriers to participation.

A-4 Costs and fees; petition requirements

The Commission believes that costs, fees, or assessments and excessive petition requirements made by State law and Party rule or resolutions impose a financial burden on (1) national convention delegates and alternates; (2) candidates for convention delegates and alternates; and (3) in some cases, participants. Such costs, fees, assessments or excessive petition requirements discouraged full and meaningful opportunity to participate in the delegate selection process.

The Commission urges the State Parties to remove all costs and fees involved in the delegate selection process. . . .

A-5 Existence of party rules

In order for rank-and-file Democrats to have a full and meaningful opportunity to participate in the delegate selection process, they must have access to the substantive and procedural rules which govern the process. In some States the process is not regulated by law or rule, but by resolution of the State Committee and by tradition. In other States, the rules exist, but generally are inaccessible. In still others, rules and laws regulate only the formal aspects of the selection process (e.g., date and place of the State convention) and leave to Party resolution or tradition the more substantive matters (e.g., intrastate apportionment of votes; rotation of alternates; nomination of delegates).

The Commission believes that any of these arrangements is inconsistent with the spirit of the Call in that they permit excessive discretion on the part of Party officials, which may be used to deny or limit full and meaningful opportunity to participate. Therefore, the Commission requires State Parties to adopt and make available readily accessible statewide Party rules and statutes which prescribe the State's delegate selection process with sufficient details and clarity. . . .

B-1 Proxy voting

When a Democrat cannot, or chooses not to, attend a meeting related to the delegate selection process, many States allow that person to authorize another to act in his name. This practice—called proxy voting—has been a significant source of real or felt abuse of fair procedure in the delegate selection process.

The Commission believes that any situation in which one person is given the authority to act in the name of the absent Democrat, on any issue before the meeting, gives such person an unjustified advantage in affecting the outcome of the meeting. Such a situation is inconsistent with the spirit of equal participation. Therefore, the Commission requires State Parties to add to their explicit written rules provisions which forbid the use of proxy voting in all procedures involved in the delegate selection process.

B-2 Clarity of purpose

An opportunity for full participation in the delegate selection process is not meaningful unless each Party member can clearly express his preference for candidates for delegates to the National Convention, or for those who will select such delegates. In many States, a Party member who wishes to affect the selection of the delegation must do so by voting for delegates or Party officials who will engage in many activities unrelated to the delegate selection process.

Whenever other Party business is mixed, without differentiation, with the delegate selection process, the Commission requires State Parties to make it clear to voters how they are participating in a process that will nominate their Party's candidate for President. Furthermore, in States which employ a convention or committee system, the Commission requires State Parties to clearly designate the delegate selection procedures as distinct from other Party business. . . .

B-3 Quorum provisions

Most constituted bodies have rules or practices which set percentage or number minimums before they can commence their business. Similarly, Party committees which participate in the selection process may commence business only after it is determined that this quorum exists. In some States, however, the quorum requirement is satisfied when less than 40% of committee members are in attendance.

The Commission believes a full opportunity to participate is satisfied only when a rank-and-file Democrat's representative attends such committee meetings. Recognizing, however, that the setting of high quorum requirements may impede the selection process, the Commission requires State Parties to adopt rules setting quorums at not less than 40% for all party committees involved in the delegate selection process.

B-4 Selection of alternates; filling of delegate and alternate vacancies

The Call to the 1972 Convention requires that alternates be chosen by one of the three methods sanctioned for the selection of delegates—i.e., by primary, convention or committee. In some States, Party rules authorize the delegate himself or the State Chairman to choose his alternate. The Commission requires State Parties to prohibit these practices—and other practices not specifically authorized by the Call—for selecting alternates. . . .

B-5 Unit rule

In 1968, many States used the unit rule at various stages in the processes by which delegates were selected to the National Convention. The 1968 Convention defined unit rule, did not enforce the unit rule on any delegate in 1968, and added language to the 1972 Call requiring that "the unit rule not be used in any stage of the delegate selection process." In light of the Convention action, the Commission requires State Parties to add to their explicit written rules provisions which forbid the use of the unit rule or the practice of instructing delegates to vote against their stated preferences at any stage of the delegate selection process.

B-6 Adequate representation of minority views on presidential candidates at each stage in the delegate selection process

The Commission believes that a full and meaningful opportunity to participate in the delegate selection process is precluded unless the presidential preference of each Democrat is fairly represented at all levels of the process. Therefore, the Commission urges each State Party to adopt procedures which will provide fair representation of minority views on presidential candidates and recommends that the 1972 Convention adopt a rule requiring State Parties to provide for the representation of minority views to the highest level of the nominating process.

The Commission believes that there are at least two different methods by which a State Party can provide for such representation. First, in at-large elections it can divide delegate votes among presidential candidates in proportion to their demonstrated strength. Second, it can choose delegates from fairly apportioned districts no larger than congressional districts. . . .

B-7 Apportionment

The Commission believes that the manner in which votes and delegates are apportioned within each State has a direct bearing on the nature of participation. If the apportionment formula is not based on Democratic strength and/or population the opportunity for some voters to participate in the delegate selection process will not be equal to the opportunity of others. Such a situation is inconsistent with a full and meaningful opportunity to participate.

Therefore, the Commission requires State Parties which apportion their delegation to the National Convention to apportion on a basis of representation which fairly reflects the population and Democratic strength within the State. The apportionment is to be based on a formula giving equal weight to total population and to the Democratic vote in the previous presidential election. . . .

C-1 Adequate public notice

The Call to the 1968 convention required State Parties to assure voters an opportunity to "participate fully" in party affairs. The Special Equal Rights Committee interpreted this opportunity to include adequate public notice. The Committee listed several elements—including publicizing of the time, places and rules for the conduct of all public meetings of the Democratic Party and holding such meetings in easily accessible places—which comprise adequate public notice. These elements were adopted by the Democratic National Committee in January 1968 as its official policy statement and are binding on the State Parties. . . .

Accordingly, the Commission requires State Parties to give every candidate for delegate (and candidate for committee, where appropriate) the opportunity to state his presidential preferences on the ballot at each stage of the delegate selection process. The Commission requires the State Parties to add the word "uncommitted" or like term on the ballot next to the name of every candidate for delegate who does not wish to express a presidential preference. . . .

C-2 Automatic (ex-officio) delegates (see also C-4)

In some States, certain public or Party officeholders are delegates to county, State and National Conventions by virtue of their official position. The Commission believes that State laws, Party rules and Party resolutions which so provide are inconsistent with the Call to the 1972 Convention for three reasons:

1. The Call requires all delegates to be chosen by primary, convention or committee procedures. Achieving delegate status by virtue of public or Party office is not one of the methods sanctioned by the 1968 Convention.

2. The Call requires all delegates to be chosen by a process which begins within the calendar year of the Convention. Ex-officio delegates usually were elected (or appointed) to their positions before the calendar year of the Convention.

3. The Call requires all delegates to be chosen by a process in which all Democrats have a full and meaningful opportunity to participate. Delegate selection by a process in which certain places on the delegation are not open to competition among Democrats is inconsistent with a full and meaningful opportunity to participate.

Accordingly, the Commission requires State Parties to repeal Party rules or resolutions which provide for ex-officio delegates. When State law controls, the Commission requires State Parties to make all feasible efforts to repeal, amend or otherwise modify such laws to accomplish the stated purpose. . . .

C-3 Open and closed processes

The Commission believes that Party membership, and hence opportunity to participate in the delegate selection process, must be open to all persons who wish to be Democrats and who are not already members of another political party; conversely, a full opportunity for all Democrats to participate is diluted if members of other political parties are allowed to participate in the selection of delegates to the Democratic National Convention.

The Commission urges State Parties to provide for party enrollment that (1) allows non-Democrats to become Party members, and (2) provides easy access and frequent opportunity for unaffiliated voters to become Democrats.

C-4 Premature delegate selection (timeliness)

The 1968 Convention adopted language adding to the Call to the 1972 Convention the requirement that the delegate selection process must begin within the calendar year of the Convention. In many States, Governors, State Chairmen, State, district and county committees who are chosen before the calendar year of the Convention, select—or choose agents to select—the delegates. These practices are inconsistent with the Call.

The Commission believes that the 1968 Convention intended to prohibit any untimely procedures which have any direct bearing on the process by which National Convention delegates are selected. The process by which delegates are nominated is such a procedure. Therefore, the Commission requires State Parties to prohibit any practices by which officials elected or appointed before the calendar year choose nominating committees or propose or endorse a slate of delegates—even when the possibility for a challenge to such slate or committee is provided.

When State law controls, the Commission requires State Parties to make all feasible efforts to repeal, amend, or modify such laws to accomplish the stated purposes.

C-5 Committee selection process

The 1968 Convention indicated no preference between primary, convention, and committee systems for choosing delegates. The Commission believes, however, that committee systems by virtue of their indirect relationship to the delegate selection process, offer fewer guarantees for a full and meaningful opportunity to participate than other systems.

The Commission is aware that it has no authority to eliminate committee systems in their entirety. However, the Commission can and does require State Parties which elect delegates in this manner to make it clear to voters at the time the Party committee is elected or appointed that one of its function will be the selection of National Convention delegates.

Believing, however, that such selection system is undesirable even when adequate public notice is given, the Commission requires State Parties to limit the national Convention delegation chosen by committee procedure to not more than 10 percent of the total number of delegates and alternates.

Since even this obligation will not ensure an opportunity for full and meaningful participation, the Commission recommends that State Parties repeal rules or resolutions which require or permit Party committees to select any part of the State's delegation to the National Convention. When State law controls, the Commission recommends that State Parties make all feasible efforts to repeal, amend, or otherwise modify such laws to accomplish the stated purpose.

C-6 Slate-making

In mandating a full and meaningful opportunity to participate in the delegate selection process, the 1968 Convention meant to prohibit any practice in the process of selection which made it difficult for Democrats to participate. Since the process by which individuals are nominated for delegate positions and slates of potential delegates are formed is an integral and crucial part of the process by which delegates are actually selected, the Commission requires State Parties to extend to the nominating process all guarantees of full and meaningful opportunity to participate in the delegate selection process. When State law controls, the Commission requires State Parties to make all feasible efforts to repeal, amend, or otherwise modify such laws to accomplish the stated purpose. . . .

Conclusion

The Guidelines that we have adopted are designed to open the door to all Democrats who seek a voice in their Party's most important decision: the choice of its presidential nominee. We are concerned with the opportunity to participate, rather than the actual level of participation, although the number of Democrats who vote in their caucuses, meetings and primaries is an important index of the opportunities available to them. As members of the Commission, we are less concerned with the product of the meetings than the process, although we believe that the product will be improved in the give and take of open and fairly conducted meetings.

We believe that popular participation is more than a proud heritage of our party, more even than a first principle. We believe that popular control of the Democratic Party is necessary for its survival.

We do not believe this is an idle threat. When we view our past history and present policies alongside that of the Republican Party, we are struck by one unavoidable fact: our Party is the only major vehicle for peaceful, progressive change in the United States.

If we are not an open party; if we do not represent the demands of change, then the danger is not that people will go to the Republican Party; it is that there will no longer be a way for people committed to orderly change to fulfill their needs and desires within our traditional political system. It is that they will turn to third and fourth party politics or the anti-politics of the street.

We believe that our Guidelines offer an alternative for these people. We believe that the Democratic Party can meet the demands for participation with their adoption. We trust that all Democrats will give the Guidelines their careful consideration.

We are encouraged by the response of state Parties to date. In 40 states and territories the Democratic Party has appointed reform commissions (or sub-committees of the state committee) to investigate ways of modernizing party procedures. Of these, 17 have already issued reports and recommendations. In a number of states, party rules and state laws have already been revised, newly written or amended to insure the opportunity for participation in Party matters by all Democratics. . . .

All of these efforts lead us to the conclusion that the Democratic Party is bent on meaningful change. A great European statesman once said, "All things are possible, even the fact that an action in accord with honor and honesty ultimately appears to be a prudent political investment." We share this sentiment. We are confident that party reform, dictated by our Party's heritage and principles, will insure a strong, winning and united Party.

❧ 41 ❧
*Buckley v. Valeo**
(1976)

1. The Federal Election Campaign Act required candidates, political action committees, and political parties to file reports that fully disclosed contributions and expenditures. Is the disclosure requirement beneficial to preventing corruption in U.S. elections? Why or why not?
2. In *Buckley v. Valeo* the Supreme Court concluded that Congress could not limit political spending by a campaign or by a candidate. If Congress could pass a law limiting spending that could survive judicial scrutiny, what effect, if any, would it have on campaigns and elections?

DESPITE THE REFORMS in the first half of the twentieth century, campaign finance was still effectively unregulated by the 1960s. As written, reform laws were unenforceable because of loopholes and the need for a more effective enforcement administration. When, in the 1960s, radio and television advertising became the principal campaign methods for federal office and the cost of political campaigns skyrocketed, concern over how campaigns raised that additional revenue grew. In addition, the influence of corporate and labor money in federal elections and the abuses uncovered during the Watergate scandal led Congress to spend a decade creating the first comprehensive system of campaign finance reform.

The Federal Election Campaign Act (FECA) was passed by Congress in 1971 to address the rising costs of campaigning for federal office and to strengthen disclosure requirements on federal campaigns. When signed into law by President Nixon on February 7, 1972, FECA changed campaign finance in three ways. First, it limited the amount of money candidates could personally contribute to their own campaigns. Second, it limited the amount of money candidates could spend on advertising.

*http://supreme.justia.com/us/424/1/case.html

Third, it required candidates, political action committees (PACs), and political parties to file quarterly reports that fully disclosed contributions and expenditures.

Amendments to FECA were signed into law by President Gerald Ford on October 14, 1974. Added in response to the Watergate scandal and the continued rise in campaign spending during the 1972 election, these amendments supplemented the original act to create a comprehensive system of campaign finance. The amended law placed tougher limits on contributions, replaced spending limits on advertising with overall spending limits, strengthened disclosure requirements, limited what political parties could spend on behalf of their nominees, amended the system of public funding created under the Revenue Act of 1971, and created the Federal Election Commission (FEC) to administer and enforce federal campaign finance laws.

In 1976, the constitutionality of the major provisions of FECA were tested by the U.S. Supreme Court in *Buckley v. Valeo* (424 U.S. 1). The Court concluded that Congress did not have the right to create a more equal campaign finance system by limiting political spending either by the campaign or by the candidate except when presidential candidates accepted matching funds. It did, however, have the authority to regulate campaign contributions to prevent corruption or the appearance of corruption. Congress was forced to enact additional amendments to address this new development.

FECA was revised again in 1979 to streamline reporting requirements and ease restrictions on spending by political parties. To ease passage, Congress addressed only those reforms acceptable to both the House and the Senate; as a result, the bill was signed into law by President Jimmy Carter on January 8, 1980.

The new rules allowed state and local party committees to spend unlimited amounts on voter registration; get-out-the-vote events; and other volunteer materials, such as buttons, bumper stickers, posters, and brochures. The purpose of this exception was to encourage political parties to promote grassroots activities at the state and local level rather than focus political advertising on such things as broadcast media.

. . . The statutes at issue summarized in broad terms, contain the following provisions: (a) individual political contributions are limited to $1,000 to any single candidate per election, with an overall annual limitation of $25,000 by any contributor; independent expenditures by individuals and groups "relative to a clearly identified candidate" are limited to $1,000 a year; campaign spending by candidates for various federal offices and spending for national conventions by political parties are subject to prescribed limits; (b) contributions and expenditures above certain threshold levels must be reported and publicly disclosed; (c) a system for public funding of Presidential campaign activities is established by Subtitle H of the Internal Revenue Code; and (d) a Federal Election Commission is established to administer and enforce the legislation. . . .

A. General Principles

The Act's contribution and expenditure limitations operate in an area of the most fundamental First Amendment activities. Discussion of public issues and debate on the qualifications of candidates are integral to the operation of the system of government established by our Constitution. The First Amendment affords the broadest protection to such political expression in order "to assure [the] unfettered interchange of ideas for the bringing about of political and social changes desired by the people." . . . The First Amendment protects political association as well as political expression. . . .

It is with these principles in mind that we consider the primary contentions of the parties with respect to the Act's limitations upon the giving and spending of money in political campaigns. Those conflicting contentions could not more sharply define the basic issues before us. Appellees contend that what the Act regulates is conduct, and that its effect on speech and association is incidental at most. Appellants respond that contributions and expenditures are at the very core of political speech, and that the Act's limitations thus constitute restraints on First Amendment liberty that are both gross and direct.

In upholding the constitutional validity of the Act's contribution and expenditure provisions on the ground [424 U.S. 1, 16] that those provisions should be viewed as regulating conduct, not speech, the Court of Appeals relied upon *United States v. O'Brien* (1968). . . .

We cannot share the view that the present Act's contribution and expenditure limitations are comparable to the restrictions on conduct upheld in *O'Brien.* The expenditure of money simply cannot be equated with such conduct as destruction of a draft card. Some forms of communication made possible by the giving and spending of money involve speech alone, some involve conduct primarily, and some involve a combination of the two. Yet this Court has never suggested that the dependence of a communication on the expenditure of money operates itself to introduce a non speech element or to reduce the exacting scrutiny required by the First Amendment. . . .

A restriction on the amount of money a person or group can spend on political communication during a campaign necessarily reduces the quantity of expression by restricting the number of issues discussed, the depth of their exploration, and the size of the audience reached. This is because virtually every means of communicating ideas in today's mass society requires the expenditure of money. The distribution of the humblest handbill or leaflet entails printing, paper, and circulation costs. Speeches and rallies generally necessitate hiring a hall and publicizing the event. The electorate's increasing dependence on television, radio, and other mass media for news and information has made these expensive modes of communication indispensable instruments of effective political speech.

The expenditure limitations contained in the Act represent substantial, rather than merely theoretical, restraints on the quantity and diversity of political speech. The $1,000 ceiling on spending "relative to a clearly identified candidate," would appear to exclude all citizens and groups except candidates, political parties, and the institutional press from any significant use of the most effective modes of communication. Although the Act's limitations on expenditures by campaign organizations and political parties provide substantially greater room for discussion and debate, they would have required restrictions in the scope of a number of past congressional and Presidential campaigns and would operate to constrain campaigning by candidates who raise sums in excess of the spending ceiling.

By contrast with a limitation upon expenditures for political expression, a limitation upon the amount that any one person or group may contribute to a candidate or political committee entails only a marginal restriction upon the contributor's ability to engage in free communication. A contribution serves as a general expression of support for the candidate and his views, but does not communicate the underlying basis for the support. The quantity of communication by the contributor does not increase perceptibly with the size of his contribution, since the expression rests solely on the undifferentiated, symbolic act of contributing. At most, the size of the contribution provides a very rough index of the intensity of the contributor's support for the candidate. A limitation on the amount of money a person may give to a candidate or campaign organization thus involves little direct restraint on his political communication, for it permits the symbolic expression of support evidenced by a contribution but does not in any way infringe the contributor's freedom to discuss candidates and issues. While contributions may result in political expression if spent by a candidate or an association to present views to the voters, the transformation of contributions into political debate involves speech by someone other than the contributor.

. . . The overall effect of the Act's contribution [424 U.S. 1, 22] ceilings is merely to require candidates and political committees to raise funds from a greater number of persons and to compel people who would otherwise contribute amounts greater than the statutory limits to expend such funds on direct political expression, rather than to reduce the total amount of money potentially available to promote political expression. . . .

In sum, although the Act's contribution and expenditure limitations both implicate fundamental First Amendment interests, its expenditure ceilings impose significantly more severe restrictions on protected freedoms of political expression and association than do its limitations on financial contributions.

B. Contribution Limitations

. . . It is unnecessary to look beyond the Act's primary purpose—to limit the actuality and appearance of corruption resulting from large individual financial contributions—in order to find a constitutionally sufficient justification for the $1,000 contribution limitation. Under a system of private financing of elections, a candidate lacking immense personal or family wealth must depend on financial contributions from others to provide the resources necessary to conduct a successful campaign. The increasing importance of the communications media and sophisticated mass-mailing and polling operations to effective campaigning make the raising of large sums of money an ever more essential ingredient of an effective candidacy. To the extent that large contributions are given to secure a political quid pro quo from current and potential office holders, the integrity of our system of representative democracy is undermined. Although the scope of such pernicious practices can never be reliably ascertained, the deeply disturbing examples surfacing after the 1972 election demonstrate that the problem is not an illusory one.

Of almost equal concern as the danger of actual quid pro quo arrangements is the impact of the appearance of corruption stemming from public awareness of the opportunities for abuse inherent in a regime of large individual financial contributions. . . .

Appellants contend that the contribution limitations must be invalidated because bribery laws and narrowly drawn disclosure requirements constitute a less restrictive means of dealing with "proven and suspected quid pro quo arrangements." But laws making criminal the giving and taking of bribes deal with only the most blatant and specific attempts of those with money to influence governmental action. And while disclosure requirements serve the many salutary purposes discussed elsewhere in this opinion, Congress was surely entitled to conclude that disclosure was only a partial measure, and that contribution ceilings were a necessary legislative concomitant to deal with the reality or appearance of corruption inherent in a system permitting unlimited financial contributions, even when the identities of the contributors and the amounts of their contributions are fully disclosed.

The Act's $1,000 contribution limitation focuses precisely on the problem of large campaign contributions—the narrow aspect of political association where the actuality and potential for corruption have been identified—while leaving persons free to engage in independent political expression, to associate actively through volunteering their services, and to assist to a limited but nonetheless substantial extent in supporting candidates and committees with financial resources. Significantly, the Act's contribution limitations in themselves do not undermine to any material degree the potential for robust and effective discussion of candidates and campaign issues by individual citizens, associations, the institutional press, candidates, and political parties.

We find that, under the rigorous standard of review established by our prior decisions, the weighty interests served by restricting the size of financial contributions to political candidates are sufficient to justify the limited effect upon First Amendment freedoms caused by the $1,000 contribution ceiling. . . .

C. Expenditure Limitations

. . . 1. The $1,000 Limitation on Expenditures "Relative to a Clearly Identified Candidate"

Section 608(e)(1) provides that "[n]o person may make any expenditure . . . relative to a clearly identified candidate during a calendar year which, when added to all other expenditures made by such person during the year advocating the election or defeat of such candidate, exceeds $1,000." The plain effect of §608(e)(1) is to prohibit all individuals, who are neither candidates nor owners of institutional press facilities, and all groups, except political parties and campaign organizations, from voicing their views "relative to a clearly identified candidate" through means that entail aggregate expenditures of more than $1,000 during a calendar year. The provision, for example, would make it a federal criminal offense for a person or association to place a single one-quarter page advertisement "relative to a clearly identified candidate" in a major metropolitan newspaper.

Before examining the interests advanced in support of §608(e)(1)'s expenditure ceiling, consideration must be given to appellants' contention that the provision is unconstitutionally vague. . . .

. . . We agree that, in order to preserve the provision against invalidation on vagueness grounds, §608(e)(1) must be construed to apply only to expenditures for communications that in express terms advocate the election or defeat of a clearly identified candidate for federal office.

We turn then to the basic First Amendment question—whether §608(e)(1), even as thus narrowly and explicitly construed, impermissibly burdens the constitutional right of free expression. . . .

We find that the governmental interest in preventing corruption and the appearance of corruption is inadequate to justify §608(e)(1)'s ceiling on independent expenditures. First, assuming, arguendo, that large independent expenditures pose the same dangers of actual or apparent quid pro quo arrangements as do large contributions, §608(e)(1) does not provide an answer that sufficiently relates to the elimination of those dangers. Unlike the contribution limitations' total ban on the giving of large amounts of money to candidates, §608(e)(1) prevents only some large expenditures. So long as persons and groups eschew expenditures that in express terms advocate the election or defeat of a clearly identified candidate, they are free to spend as much as they want to promote the candidate and his views. . . . It would naively underestimate the ingenuity and resourcefulness of persons and groups desiring to buy influence to believe that they would have much difficulty devising expenditures that skirted the restriction on express advocacy of election or defeat but nevertheless benefited the candidate's campaign. Yet no substantial societal interest would be served by a loophole-closing provision designed to check corruption that permitted unscrupulous persons and organizations to expend unlimited sums of money in order to obtain improper influence over candidates for elective office.

Second, . . . the independent advocacy restricted by the provision does not presently appear to pose dangers of real or apparent corruption comparable to those identified with large campaign contributions. . . . Section 608(b)'s contribution ceilings rather than §608(e)(1)'s independent expenditure limitation prevent attempts to circumvent the Act through prearranged or coordinated expenditures amounting to disguised contributions. . . .

It is argued, however, that the ancillary governmental interest in equalizing the relative ability of individuals and groups to influence the outcome of elections serves to justify the limitation on express advocacy of the election or defeat of candidates imposed by §608(e)(1)'s expenditure ceiling. But the concept that government may restrict the speech of some elements of our society in order to enhance the relative voice of others is wholly foreign to the First Amendment, which was designed "to secure 'the widest possible dissemination of information from diverse and antagonistic sources,'" and "'to assure unfettered interchange of ideas for the bringing about of political and social changes desired by the people.'"...

For the reasons stated, we conclude that §608(e)(1)'s independent expenditure limitation is unconstitutional under the First Amendment.

2. Limitation on Expenditures by Candidates from Personal or Family Resources

The Act also sets limits on expenditures by a candidate "from his personal funds, or the personal funds of his immediate family, in connection with his campaigns during any calendar year." §608(a)(1)....

The ceiling on personal expenditures by candidates on their own behalf, like the limitations on independent expenditures contained in §608(e)(1), imposes a substantial restraint on the ability of persons to engage in protected First Amendment expression. The candidate, no less than any other person, has a First Amendment right to engage in the discussion of public issues and vigorously and tirelessly to advocate his own election and the election of other candidates. Indeed, it is of particular importance that candidates have the unfettered opportunity to make their views known so that the electorate may intelligently evaluate the candidates' personal qualities and their positions on vital public issues before choosing among them on election day....

The primary governmental interest served by the Act—the prevention of actual and apparent corruption of the political process—does not support the limitation on the candidate's expenditure of his own personal funds....

The ancillary interest in equalizing the relative financial resources of candidates competing for elective office, therefore, provides the sole relevant rationale for §608(a)'s expenditure ceiling. That interest is clearly not sufficient to justify the provision's infringement of fundamental First Amendment rights....

3. Limitations on Campaign Expenditures

Section 608(c) places limitations on overall campaign expenditures by candidates seeking nomination for election and election to federal office....

No governmental interest that has been suggested is sufficient to justify the restriction on the quantity of political expression imposed by §608(c)'s campaign expenditure limitations. The major evil associated with rapidly increasing campaign expenditures is the danger of candidate dependence on large contributions. The interest in alleviating the corrupting influence of large contributions is served by the Act's contribution limitations and disclosure provisions, rather than by §608(c)'s campaign expenditure ceilings. . . .

The campaign expenditure ceilings appear to be designed primarily to serve the governmental interests in reducing the allegedly skyrocketing costs of political campaigns. . . . In any event, the mere growth in the cost of federal election campaigns in and of itself provides no basis for governmental restrictions on the quantity of campaign spending and the resulting limitation on the scope of federal campaigns. The First Amendment denies government the power to determine that spending to promote one's political views is wasteful, excessive, or unwise. In the free society ordained by our Constitution it is not the government, but the people—individually as citizens and candidates and collectively, as associations and political committees—who must retain control over the quantity and range of debate on public issues in a political campaign.

For these reasons, we hold that §608(c) is constitutionally invalid.

II. Reporting and Disclosure Requirements

A. General Principles

Unlike the overall limitations on contributions and expenditures, the disclosure requirements impose no ceiling on campaign-related activities. But we have repeatedly found that compelled disclosure, in itself, can seriously infringe on privacy of association and belief guaranteed by the First Amendment. . . . Since *NAACP v. Alabama,* we have required that the subordinating interests of the State must survive exacting scrutiny. We also have insisted that there be a "relevant correlation" or "substantial relation" between the governmental interest and the information required to be disclosed.

. . . But we have acknowledged that there are governmental interests sufficiently important to outweigh the possibility of infringement, particularly when the "free functioning of our national institutions" is involved. *Communist Party v. Subversive Activities Control Bd.,* 367 U.S. 1, 97 (1961).

The governmental interests sought to be vindicated by the disclosure requirements are of this magnitude. They fall into three categories. First, disclosure provides the electorate with information "as to where political campaign money comes from and how it is spent by the candidate" in order to aid the voters in evaluating those who seek federal office. It allows voters to place each candidate in the political spectrum more precisely than is often possible solely on the basis of party labels and campaign speeches. The sources of a candidate's financial support also alert the voter to the interests to which a candidate is

most likely to be responsive and thus facilitate predictions of future performance in office.

Second, disclosure requirements deter actual corruption and avoid the appearance of corruption by exposing large contributions and expenditures to the
light of publicity. . . .

Third, and not least significant, recordkeeping, reporting, and disclosure
requirements are an essential means of gathering the data necessary to detect
violations of the contribution limitations described above. . . .

It is undoubtedly true that public disclosure of contributions to candidates
and political parties will deter some individuals who otherwise might contribute. In some instances, disclosure may even expose contributors to harassment or retaliation. These are not insignificant burdens on individual rights,
and they must be weighed carefully against the interests which Congress has
sought to promote by this legislation. In this process, we note and agree with
appellants' concession that disclosure requirements—certainly in most applications—appear to be the least restrictive means of curbing the evils of campaign ignorance and corruption that Congress found to exist. . . .

B. Application to Minor Parties and Independents
Appellants contend that the Act's requirements are overbroad insofar as they
apply to contributions to minor parties and independent candidates because
the governmental interest in this information is minimal, and the danger of
significant infringement on First Amendment rights is greatly increased.

In *NAACP v. Alabama* the organization had "made an uncontroverted
showing that on past occasions revelation of the identity of its rank-and-file
members [had] exposed these members to economic reprisal, loss of employment, threat of physical coercion, and other manifestations of public hostility,"
and the State was unable to show that the disclosure it sought had a "substantial bearing" on the issues it sought to clarify. Under those circumstances, the
Court held that "whatever interest the State may have in [disclosure] has not
been shown to be sufficient to overcome petitioner's constitutional objections."

The Court of Appeals rejected appellants' suggestion that this case fits into
the *NAACP v. Alabama* mold. It concluded that substantial governmental interests in "informing the electorate and preventing the corruption of the political process" were furthered by requiring disclosure of minor parties and independent candidates, and therefore found no "tenable rationale for assuming
that the public interest in minority party disclosure of contributions above a
reasonable cutoff point is uniformly outweighed by potential contributors' as-

sociational rights." The court left open the question of the application of the disclosure requirements to candidates (and parties) who could demonstrate injury of the sort at stake in *NAACP v. Alabama.* . . .

Appellants agree that "the record here does not reflect the kind of focused and insistent harassment of contributors and members that existed in the *NAACP* cases." They argue, however, that a blanket exemption for minor parties is necessary lest irreparable injury be done before the required evidence can be gathered. . . .

We recognize that unduly strict requirements of proof could impose a heavy burden, but it does not follow that a blanket exemption for minor parties is necessary. Minor parties must be allowed sufficient flexibility in the proof of injury to assure a fair consideration of their claim. . . . Where it exists, the type of chill and harassment identified in *NAACP v. Alabama* can be shown. We cannot assume that courts will be insensitive to similar showings when made in future cases. We therefore conclude that a blanket exemption is not required. . . .

III. Public Financing of Presidential Election Campaigns

A series of statutes for the public financing of Presidential election campaigns produced the scheme now found in §6096 and Subtitle H of the Internal Revenue Code of 1954. Both the District Court and the Court of Appeals sustained Subtitle H against a constitutional attack. Appellants renew their challenge here, contending that the legislation violates the First and Fifth Amendments. We find no merit in their claims and affirm.

A. Summary of Subtitle H

. . . establishes a Presidential Election Campaign Fund, financed from general revenues in the aggregate amount designated by individual taxpayers, who on their income tax returns may authorize payment to the Fund of one dollar of their tax liability in the case of an individual return or two dollars in the case of a joint return. The Fund consists of three separate accounts to finance (1) party nominating conventions, (2) general election campaigns, and (3) primary campaigns. . . . A major party is defined as a party whose candidate for President in the most recent election received 25% or more of the popular vote. A minor party is defined as a party whose candidate received at least 5% but less than 25% of the vote at the most recent election. All other parties are new parties, including both newly created parties and those receiving less than 5% of the vote in the last election.

REPORT OF RECEIPTS AND DISBURSEMENTS

1/1331
02/20/2000   19:67

BY AN AUTHORIZED COMMITTEE OF A CANDIDATE FOR THE OFFICE OF PRESIDENT OR VICE-PRESIDENT

1. NAME OF COMMITTEE (in full)
McCain 2000, Inc

ADDRESS (number and street)
PO Box 25382

☐ Check if different then previously reported

2. IDENTIFICATION NUMBER
CO0342154

CITY, STATE, and ZIP CODE
Alexandria   VA   22313

3. IS THIS REPORT FOR:
☐ Primary election   ☐ General election

4. TYPE OF REPORT

☐ April 15 Quarterly Report
☐ July 15 Quarterly Report
☐ October 15 Quarterly Report
☐ January 31 Year End Report

Monthly Report Due On:

☒ February 20
☐ March 20
☐ April 20
☐ May 20

☐ June 20
☐ July 20
☐ August 20
☐ September 20

☐ October 20
☐ November 20
☐ December 20
☐ January 31

☐ Twelfth day report preceding ___Primary___
(election type)

election on _____ in the State of _____

☐ Thirtieth day report following the General Election
on _____

IS THIS REPORT AN AMENDMENT   ☐ YES   ☒ NO

5. COVERING PERIOD

	FROM	THROUGH
	01/01/2000	01/31/2000

SUMMARY

6. CASH ON HAND AT BEGINNING OF THE REPORTING PERIOD		1497622.20
7. TOTAL RECEIPTS THIS PERIOD (from Line 22, Column A, Page 2)		5641513.83
8. SUBTOTAL (Lines 6 and 7)		7139236.03
9. TOTAL DISBURSEMENTS THIS PERIOD (from Line 30, Column A, Page 2)		6797433.77
10. CASH ON HAND AT CLOSE OF REPORTING PERIOD (Subtract Line 9 from 8)		341802.26
11. DEBTS AND OBLIGATIONS OWED TO THE COMMITTEE (Itemize All on Schedule C-P or Schedule D-P)		3845431.22
12. DEBTS AND OBLIGATIONS OWED BY THE COMMITTEE (Itemize All on Schedule C-P or Schedule D-P)		2844535.24
13. EXPENDITURES SUBJECT TO LIMITATION		17288571.44

NEXT YEAR-TO-DATE CONTRIBUTIONS AND EXPENDITURES

14. NET CONTRIBUTIONS (other than loans) (Subtract Line 28d, Column B from 17a. Column B, Page 2)		2503092.21
15. NET OPERATING EXPENDITURES (Subtract Line 20a, Column B from 23, Column B, Page 2)		4974122.04

I certify that I have examined this Report and to the best of my knowledge and belief it is true, correct, and complete.

Type or Print Name of Treasurer	Date
Max Fose	02/20/2000

Signature of Treasurer

NOTE: Submissions of false, erroneous, or incomplete information may subject the person signing this Report to the penalties of 2 U.S.C. 5437g.
ALL PREVIOUS VERSIONS OF FEC FORM 3P ARE OBSOLETE AND SHOULD NO LONGER BE USED

For further information contact: Federal Election Commission
999 E Street, NW • Washington, DC 20483
Toll Free 800-424-9530 • Local 202-219-3420

FEC FORM 3P
(5/95)

The three pages shown here are the summary pages of a 1,331-page report submitted to the FEC by John McCain's 2000 presidential campaign. Note that not every candidate is able to focus on every state—McCain's campaign had to decide where to invest its limited resources.

DETAILED SUMMARY OF RECEIPTS AND DISBURSEMENTS
(PAGE 2 FEC FORM 3P)

2/1331

Name of committee (in full) McCain 2000, Inc	Report Covering the Period From: 01/01/2000 To: 01/31/2000	
I. RECEIPTS	**COLUMN A** this period	**COLUMN B** Calendar year-to-date
16. FEDERAL FUNDS (Itemize on Schedule A-P)	2098785.54	2098785.54
17. CONTRIBUTIONS (other than loans) FROM: (a) Individuals/Persons Other Than Political Parties	2520915.87	2520915.87
(b) Political Party Committees	0.00	0.00
(c) Other Political Committees	6300.00	6300.00
(d) The Candidate	0.00	0.00
(e) TOTAL CONTRIBUTIONS (other than loans) (17(a) + 17(b) + 17(c) + 17(d))	2527215.97	2527215.97
18. TRANSFERS FROM OTHER AUTHORIZED COMMITTEES	0.00	0.00
19. LOANS RECEIVED (a) Loans Received from or Guaranteed by Candidate	0.00	0.00
(b) Other Loans	1000000.00	1000000.00
(c) TOTAL LOANS (19(a) + 19 (b))	1000000.00	1000000.00
20. OFFSETS TO EXPENDITURES (Refunds, Rebates, etc.): (a) Operating	13151.62	13151.62
(b) Fundraising	0.00	0.00
(c) Legal and Accounting	0.00	0.00
(d) TOTAL OFFSETS TO OPERATING EXPENDITURES (20(a) + 20(b) + 20(c))	13151.62	13151.62
21. OTHER RECEIPTS (Dividend, Interest, etc.)	2460.00	2460.00
22. TOTAL RECEIPTS (16 + 17(e) + 18 + 19(c) + 20(d) + 21)	5641613.83	5641613.83
II. DISBURSEMENTS		
23. OPERATING EXPENDITURES	4967273.00	4967273.00
24. TRANSFERS TO OTHER AUTHORIZED COMMITTEES	11482.00	11482.00
25. FUNDRAISING DISBURSEMENTS	1774574.45	1774574.45
26. EXEMPT LEGAL AND ACCOUNTING DISBURSEMENTS	0.00	0.00
27. LOAN REPAYMENTS MADE: (a) Repayment of Loans made or Guaranteed by Candidate	0.00	0.00
(b) Other Repayments	0.00	0.00
(c) TOTAL LOAN REPAYMENTS MADE (27(a) + 27(b))	0.00	0.00
28. REFUNDS OF CONTRIBUTIONS TO: (a) Individuals/Persons Other Than Political Parties	24123.66	24123.66
(b) Political Party Committees	0.00	0.00
(c) Other Political Committees	0.00	0.00
(d) TOTAL CONTRIBUTION REFUNDS (28(a) + 28(b) + 28(c))	24123.66	24123.66
29. OTHER DISBURSEMENTS	0.00	0.00
30. TOTAL DISBURSEMENTS (23 + 24 + 25 + 26 + 27(c) + 28(d) + 29)	6707433.77	6707433.77
III. CONTRIBUTED ITEMS (Stock, Art Objects, etc.)		
31. ITEMS ON HAND TO BE LIQUIDATED (attach list)	0.00	

ALLOCATION OF PRIMARY EXPENDITURES BY STATE FOR A PRESIDENTIAL CANDIDATE   3/1331
(Used Only by Primary Committees Receiving or Expecting to Receive Federal Funds)
(PAGE 3, FEC FORM 3P)

1. NAME OF COMMITTEE (in full)
McCain 2000, Inc

ADDRESS (number and street)
PO Box 25382

CITY, STATE, and ZIP CODE
Alexandria   VA   22313

2. IDENTIFICATION NUMBER
CO0342154

ALLOCATION BY STATE

STATE	ALLOCATION THIS PERIOD	TOTAL ALLOCATION TO DATE	STATE	ALLOCATION THIS PERIOD	TOTAL ALLOCATION TO DATE
Alabama	0.00	0.00	Nebraska	0.00	7091.45
Alaska	0.00	0.00	Nevada	0.00	0.00
Arizona	111233.24	432427.70	New Hampshire	275765.01	618860.05
Arkansas	0.00	0.00	New Jersey	0.00	0.00
California	8012.07	93021.43	New Mexico	0.00	0.00
Colorado	0.00	4047.72	New York	55155.63	129944.10
Connecticut	8897.92	12358.59	North Carolina	0.00	0.00
Delaware	0.00	0.00	North Dakota	0.00	0.00
District of Columbia	0.00	28022.52	Ohio	26.73	4788.18
Florida	4382.24	15758.12	Oklahoma	2500.00	2500.00
Georgia	0.00	88.12	Oregon	0.00	0.00
Hawaii	0.00	1489.33	Pennsylvania	2345.57	5345.11
Idaho	0.00	0.00	Rhode Island	120.81	120.81
Illinois	0.00	12803.76	South Carolina	495057.43	868693.33
Indiana	2800.00	2800.00	South Dakota	0.00	0.00
Iowa	0.00	580.84	Tennessee	0.00	0.00
Kansas	0.00	1657.74	Texas	0.00	0.00
Kentucky	1000.00	1000.00	Utah	500.00	680.00
Louisiana	1025.00	4594.92	Vermont	5149.72	12694.72
Maine	0.00	0.00	Virginia	0.00	36032.26
Maryland	0.00	350.00	Washington	11697.87	31576.97
Massachusetts	0.00	4071.42	West Virginia	4000.00	0.00
Michigan	1022488.26	1130425.87	Wisconsin	0.00	0.00
Minnesota	0.00	0.00	Wyoming	0.00	0.00
Mississippi	0.00	0.00	Puerto Rico	0.00	0.00
Missouri	0.00	3709.15	Guam	0.00	0.00
Montana	0.00	0.00	Virgin Islands	0.00	0.00
			TOTALS	0.00	3598046.16

❦ 42 ❧

Birch Bayh's Resolution to Amend the Constitution to Provide for Direct Popular Election of the President*

(1977)

1. What impact would amending the Constitution to elect the president and vice president by popular vote have on political parties?
2. How would elimination of the Electoral College system in favor of the popular election of the president and vice president affect how presidential candidates campaign for the Oval Office?

IN THE UNITED STATES the president and vice president are selected by "electors," public officials elected by voters to the position that chooses the president. Today, electors in forty-eight states are required to abide by the "unit rule," that is, they must either by law or by political affiliation vote for the candidate who wins the popular vote within the state. The two remaining states, Maine and Nebraska, require electors to vote for the candidate who wins the popular vote within the congressional district that the elector represents, or, in the case of the at-large electors, the candidate who wins the popular vote within the state. Critics of the Electoral College system argue that less populous states are better represented; that the unit rule disenfranchises those who did not vote for the candidate who won a state's popular vote; and that, under the system, candidates who fail to win the popular vote still can be elected president.

Since the 1960s the Electoral College's most outspoken critic has been Democrat Birch Bayh, who represented Indiana in the U.S. Senate from 1963 until 1981. Bayh was chair of the Subcommittee on Constitutional

*Hearings before the Subcommittee on the Constitution of the Committee on the Judiciary, U.S. Senate, 96th Congress, 1st Sess., March 27, 30, April 3, 9, 1979 (Washington, D.C.: Government Printing Office, 1979).

Amendments and the principal architect of three proposals to amend the Constitution. The first, the Twenty-fifth Amendment, established the rules for presidential succession and disability, and the second, the Twenty-sixth Amendment, lowered the minimum age for voting to eighteen. The third was the Equal Rights Amendment, which was approved by Congress but was not ratified by the necessary number of states within the time limit imposed by the Constitution.

Bayh's Subcommittee on Constitutional Amendments held its first hearing on Electoral College reform on February 28, 1966. Three years later, in 1969, the House of Representatives passed S.J. Res. 1, which proposed abolishing the Electoral College in favor of the direct election of the president and vice president by the voting public. That resolution was blocked by a filibuster in the Senate, but on January 10, 1977, Bayh brought a similar resolution, S.J. Res. 28, to the floor of the Ninety-sixth Congress for a vote. Before doing so, his subcommittee held five days of hearings on Electoral College reform, during which members listened to thirty-eight witnesses and read additional statements by witnesses and other academic reports. This new resolution was approved by fifty-one senators; however, it failed to gain the two-third majority needed to approve an amendment to the Constitution. Since then, Congress has not held congressional hearings on reforming the Electoral College beyond hearings related to the potential effect of Ross Perot's third-party candidacy on the outcome of the 1992 presidential election.

Then in 2006, former Senator Bayh joined National Popular Vote, a coalition whose purpose is to effectively eliminate the Electoral College through a compact among state legislatures. Since the Constitution allows state legislatures to determine how they will select presidential electors, state legislators may bind themselves by statute to appoint electors who will vote for the candidate who wins the national popular vote. If any number of states that represent a majority of the Electoral College—270 votes—form such a coalition, then the direct election of the president becomes law without amending the Constitution.

So far, the only state in which the National Popular Vote Plan has been passed by the legislature and signed into law by the governor is Maryland (for updates see www.nationalpopularvote.com). Critics argue that such a plan will neutralize the federal and majoritarian elements of presidential selection, destabilize the two-party system, and increase the already skyrocketing cost of presidential campaigns because it would encourage presidential candidates to compete for votes in states that are otherwise dominated by one of the two major political parties. Many politicians and news columnists and editors, however, support the plan or other types of reform to the current system.

S.J. Res. 28

Proposing an amendment to the Constitution
to provide for the direct popular election of
the President and Vice President of the United States.

Resolved by the Senate and House of Representatives of the United States of America in Congress assembled (two-thirds of each House concurring therein), That the following article is proposed as an amendment to the Constitution of the United States, which shall be valid to all intents and purposes as part of the Constitution when ratified by the legislatures of three-fourths of the several States within seven years from the date of its submission by the Congress:

"ARTICLE—

"SECTION 1. The people of the several States and the District constituting the seat of government of the United States shall elect the President and Vice President. Each elector shall cast a single vote for two persons who shall have consented to the joining of their names as candidates for the offices of President and Vice President. No candidate shall consent to the joinder of his name with that o[f] more than one other person.

"SEC. 2. The electors of President and Vice President in each State shall have the qualifications requisite for electors of the most numerous branch of the State legislature, except that for electors of President and Vice President the legislature of any State may prescribe less restrictive residence qualifications and for electors of President and Vice President the Congress may establish uniform residence qualifications.

"SEC. 3. The persons joined as candidates for President and Vice President having the greatest number of votes shall be elected President and Vice President, if such number be at least 40 per centum of the whole number of votes cast.

"If, after any such election, none of the persons joined as candidates for President and Vice President is elected pursuant to the preceding paragraph, a runoff election shall be held in which the choice of President and Vice President shall be made from the two pairs of persons joined as candidates for President and Vice President who received the highest numbers of votes cast in the election. The pair of persons joined as candidates for President and Vice President receiving the greater number of votes in such runoff election shall be elected President and Vice President.

"SEC. 4. The times, places, and manner of holding such elections and entitlement to inclusion on the ballot shall be prescribed in each State by the legislature thereof; but the Congress may at any time by law make or alter such regulations. The days for such elections shall be determined by Congress and shall be uniform throughout the United States. The Congress shall prescribed by law the times, places, and manner in which the results of such elections shall be ascertained and declared. No such election, other than a runoff election, shall be held later than the first Tuesday after the first Monday in November, and the results thereof shall be declared no later than the thirtieth day after the date on which the election occurs.

"SEC. 5. The Congress may by law provide for the case of the death, inability, or withdrawal of any candidate for President or Vice President before a President and Vice President have been elected, and for the case of the death of both the President-elect and Vice-President-elect.

"SEC. 6. Sections 1 through 4 of this article shall take effect two years after the ratification of this article.

"SEC. 7. The Congress shall have power to enforce this article by appropriate legislation."

Bill Clinton's Remarks on Signing the National Voter Registration Act*

(1993)

1. What effect, if any, does improving the accessibility of voter registration have on political parties? How could each party respond to more accessible registration in a way that benefits the party?
2. Despite the passage of the "Motor Voter" bill, many adults still are not registered to vote. How could the government improve voter registration further? Is higher voter registration advantageous? Disadvantageous?

ACCESS TO THE ELECTORAL PROCESS is an important part of representative government. Recognizing this, efforts to pass legislation making voter registration more accessible began in the 1970s. Many states, beginning with Michigan in 1975, voluntarily adopted "Motor Voter" programs, which allow individuals to register to vote at public or private agencies that provide government services and by mail.

These programs turned out to be a highly partisan issue by the late 1980s. Democrats in Congress sponsored a bill for a national voter registration act to make easier voter registration mandatory nationwide, but Republicans were highly critical of the measure for a number of reasons. First, they argued that it cost too much to enact and protested that the administrative burden of complying with the provisions of the new law would cost states millions of dollars. Second, they were concerned that the new law invited the manipulation of elections in that easier voter registration laws would encourage the formation of new political machinery designed to steal elections through fraudulent voting practices. Third, the GOP was not pleased at the likelihood that the number of registered Democratic voters would expand significantly as core

*Reprinted on John T. Woolley and Gerhard Peters, The American Presidency Project (online) (Santa Barbara: University of California [hosted], Gerhard Peters [database]). Available at www.presidency.ucsb.edu/ws/?pid=46583.

Democratic constituencies would be permitted to register to vote at social service offices. While Democrats disagreed with Republicans on the first two points, they generally allowed that the "Motor Voter" bill primarily benefited groups from lower socioeconomic backgrounds who, historically, tend to vote Democratic.

The House of Representatives did pass the National Voter Registration Act (NVRA) in 1990 during the 101st Congress, but the Senate refused to bring the measure to the floor for debate. The House and Senate both finally passed the NVRA during the 102nd Congress, but President George Bush vetoed it in 1992. (The Senate was five votes shy of the two-thirds necessary to override his veto.) In the presidential election that same year more than 120 million individuals were registered to vote, but almost 60 million eligible adults were not. Democratic presidential nominee, Arkansas governor Bill Clinton, supported the NVRA measure during his campaign, and when the NVRA passed the House of Representatives (259–160) and the Senate (62–36) along party lines, now President Clinton signed it into law on May 20, 1993. It took effect in 1995.

The NVRA requires states to develop procedures that permit individuals to register to vote by mail, in person, or when applying for or renewing their driver's license. Nine in ten adult Americans are eligible to register through one of these methods. The remaining 10 percent can register at other government offices, as the act requires that states designate specific agencies for voter registration. States also must designate a chief election official and establish criminal penalties for persons attempting to manipulate the voter registration process. Finally, the legislation prohibits states from repealing a voter's registration for failure to vote or for moving without first providing due notice.

Thirty-two states and the District of Columbia implemented the NVRA by May 1995. Four states are exempt from the law: Minnesota, Wisconsin, and Wyoming allow voter registration on election day, and North Dakota does not require voter registration in order to vote. Arkansas, Vermont, and Virginia were permitted extra time to resolve conflicts between the new law and their state constitutions. Other states, including California, initially refused to implement the law. They claimed it was an unfunded mandate imposed by the federal government on their state budgets. In the end, however, each was forced by the courts to comply with the NVRA.

❦

Remarks on Signing the National Voter Registration Act of 1993

May 20th, 1993

Thank you very much. Joel, thank you for the T-shirt. In a few moments I'll give out bill-signing pens, but I'd rather have the T-shirt. [Laughter]

Getting to know the young people across this country, beginning in New Hampshire, who pushed the motor voter bill, was one of the most rewarding parts of the 1992 campaign. But the effort that we come here to celebrate today has a long and venerable heritage.

A few moments ago, you heard the voice of President Johnson crossing the chasm of time back to 1965 as he signed the Voting Rights Act into law. As a southerner and as President, his words have special significance to me. During my childhood, no family's dinner table, no church congregation, no community, and no place of work was immune from the searing struggle for civil rights. To hear Johnson's voice is to make vivid for me once again those difficult, yet glorious years of struggle, difficult and terrible because so many people gave their lives moving the stone of freedom up the side of a mountain, glorious because the years of contention eventually gave way to an overdue season of reconciliation and renewal, and gave our region and our country a second chance to fulfill our promise.

The victory we celebrate today is but the most recent chapter in the overlapping struggles of our Nation's history to enfranchise women and minorities, the disabled, and the young with the power to affect their own destiny and our common destiny by participating fully in our democracy. When blacks and women won the right to vote, when we outlawed the poll tax and literacy test, when the voting age was lowered to 18, and when finally we recognized the rights of disabled Americans, it was because the forces of change overcame the indifference of the majority and the resistance by the guardians of the status quo. And who prevailed? Brave people working at the grass roots, impatient with an always imperfect democracy and dedicated to widening the circle of liberty to encompass more and more of our fellow citizens.

I have said many times in many places that in this country we don't have a person to waste. Surely the beginning of honoring that pledge is making sure the franchise is extended to and used by every eligible American. Today we celebrate our noble tradition by signing into law our newest civil rights law, the National Voter Registration Act of 1993, which all of us know and love as "motor voter."

An extraordinary coalition of organizations, many of whom played historic roles in our expanding democratic rights, joined many years ago with the hope that they would see this day come. I'm honored to share this podium with representatives with three fighters for freedom: the NAACP, the League of Women Voters, and Human Serve. I want to pay special tribute to Disabled and Able To Vote, to Project Vote, and to Rock the Vote, and literally, the scores of other groups for whom the goal of full voter participation has been a durable and lasting dream. I want to pay special tribute to the young people who lobbied me personally for motor voter and who voted with renewed energy and conviction for their own futures in the election last November.

They all labored hard because this bill was necessary. As many as 35 percent of otherwise eligible voters in our Nation are not registered, and the failure to register is the primary reason given by eligible citizens for their not voting. The principle behind this legislation is clear: Voting should be about discerning the will of the majority, not about testing the administrative capacity of a citizen.

The State of Washington instituted a similar measure during the 1992 election, and their motor voter program registered in that State alone an additional 186,000 people. Motor voter works at registering voters and people who register vote.

With this law and its appropriate implementation by States, voters can register by applying for a driver's license, through uniform mail application, or by applying in person at various agencies designated by the States. As a result, registration for Federal election will become as accessible as possible, while the integrity of the electoral process is clearly preserved.

As I said, I have long supported the idea of motor voter. More than a year ago, I promised as President that I would sign H.R. 2 and fight for its passage. I'm pleased to be able to keep the promise today that I made on this Rock the Vote card which still has my signature back in New Hampshire.

I also want to point out that all the President does is lobby for and sign laws. If the Congress doesn't pass them, they don't get passed. The Rock the Vote card that I signed here says, "Why don't politicians want you to vote?" Well, there are a lot of Members of the Congress here from both parties who do want you to vote, and I want to thank not only those on the platform here but all of those out in the audience who, after all, passed this bill into law. It was their votes that made this day possible.

This bill in its enactment is a sign of a new vibrancy in our democracy. With all the challenges and difficulties, with the years of accumulated economic problems we face, with all the divisions among our people, there is a new determination to make progress. You can see it in many ways: Voter participation was up in November, and after the election it didn't stop. Here at the White House, mail has climbed to unprecedented levels. After I had been in office 14 weeks, the White House had received more mail than was received in all of 1992. We have had the switchboards jammed, the E-mail system full. And if you haven't gotten an answer to your letter, we're working on it. [Laughter]

This country is pulsing with the power of individual citizens' ideas in their determination to get something done. The legislators who worked so hard to adopt this bill, the organizations that gave themselves so completely to its endeavor, the young people, the activists, MTV, all of them tapped a powerful current of energy that is still flowing in this country.

The Congress has responded in other ways: the United States Senate passing just a few days ago a lobbying bill requiring registration by all lobbyists and requiring the disclosure of lobbyists' spending on Members of Congress is an example of that. The campaign finance reform which has been presented, dramatically trying to lower the costs of campaigns and reduce the influence of special interest groups, is an example of that.

The current of reform is moving in this country. And those of you who helped to bring this bill to pass can take a large share of credit not only for this bill but for the general movement and energy and involvement and determination of all of our fellow citizens. It was never right to sit on the sidelines of our democracy. And now with motor voter, there will be fewer and fewer excuses for anyone to do so.

Let us remember this in closing: Voting is an empty promise unless people vote. Now there is no longer the excuse of the difficulty of registration. It is the right of every American to vote. It is also the responsibility of every American to vote. We have taken an important step this morning to protect that right. And I want to challenge Joel and all the young people who did so much to register voters for the last election, and all of you who did so much to bring this voting rights bill to law and all the ones that preceded it, to make sure now that we keep the rights alive by making sure that the responsibility to exercise it is exercised by every eligible American.

When we leave here today, we ought to say: This voting rights bill and the others will not be in vain. Every year from now on, we're going to have more registered voters and more people voting. We're going to make the system work. The law empowers us to do it. It's now up to us to assume the responsibility to see that it gets done.

Thank you very much.

❧ 44 ❧
The Contract with America*
(1994)

1. How important is it for Democratic and Republican leaders in Congress to develop a clear, coherent policy agenda to present to voters in election years? What effect, if any, do such agendas have on campaigns and elections?
2. How should voters respond during an election cycle if the majority party has not accomplished its policy agenda from the previous election? Under what circumstances, if any, should the majority party be held accountable and to what degree?

B Y THE 1994 MIDTERM congressional elections Republicans had not held control of both the House and Senate simultaneously in more than forty years. Minority Whip Newt Gingrich and other conservative Republican leaders hoped to win control of the House in November. To that end, they encouraged Republican candidates to align themselves with a policy platform called the Contract with America. This "contract" represented the legislative agenda Republicans would pursue in the House if they won control of the chamber.

Unveiled on September 27, 1994, the contract was signed by 367 Republican candidates for the House of Representatives on the steps of the U.S. Capitol. Its premise was to present voters with a clear, coherent policy agenda that could be accomplished quickly if the Republicans won the majority. The issues included in it were selected because while they were important policy concerns they also were not overly controversial or contentious. And polling had revealed that more than 60 percent of the American public supported each of the ten items found in the contract, even though a majority of those polled had not heard of it.

It proved to be the right move at the right time. After the 1992 election Democrats held majorities in both houses of Congress and had

*www.house.gov/house/Contract/CONTRACT.html

elected a Democratic president for the first time in twelve years. President Bill Clinton had campaigned on substantive policy change on many issues, the most prominent of which was health care reform. Ultimately, however, he had been unable to deliver on all of his campaign promises. So, by 1994, the public's disenchantment with the Democratic-controlled Congress, coupled with Clinton's low approval ratings, helped the Republicans sweep the midterm election, winning fifty-two more seats in the House than the Democrats and eight more in the Senate.

When the Republicans took control of the House in January 1995, Gingrich was selected as the new Speaker. His hope was that the Contract with America might enjoy the same success of President Franklin Roosevelt's New Deal, most of the legislation of which had passed in Congress within Roosevelt's first one hundred days in office in 1933. In order to transform the ideas espoused in the contract into reality, Republican House members were organized into working groups to draft appropriate legislation. Overall, it was relatively easy to build support for most of the program because many of the issues had broad, sometimes bipartisan, backing.

But while the Republicans may have claimed a mandate upon taking office, Clinton was still the president and still a Democrat. The divided partisan control of the federal government clearly limited how quickly and how extensively the Republicans could act in early 1995. Yet within the first one hundred days after taking office nine of the ten items in the contract had been passed by the House, and the constitutional amendment to limit the terms of legislators had been defeated only because it required a two-thirds vote for passage. A majority of the legislation also passed in the Senate, but many measures were either defeated or tied up procedurally. For example, the balanced budget amendment was defeated when it fell one vote short of the two-thirds necessary for passage. In the end, Clinton signed legislation to make Congress accountable, provide for a presidential line-item veto, and prohibit unfunded federal mandates to the states. Other issues listed in the contract were addressed in subsequent congressional terms.

Fast forward twelve years, to before the 2006 midterm congressional elections. House Minority Leader Nancy Pelosi rallied Democrats around a similar strategy dubbed the "100 Hour Plan." (The time period refers to legislative business hours and not actual time.) On January 18, 2007, with approximately a dozen legislative business hours to spare, the House of Representatives passed the last of the plan's measures.

❦

Republican Contract with America

As Republican Members of the House of Representatives and as citizens seeking to join that body we propose not just to change its policies, but even more important, to restore the bonds of trust between the people and their elected representatives.

That is why, in this era of official evasion and posturing, we offer instead a detailed agenda for national renewal, a written commitment with no fine print.

This year's election offers the chance, after four decades of one-party control, to bring to the House a new majority that will transform the way Congress works. That historic change would be the end of government that is too big, too intrusive, and too easy with the public's money. It can be the beginning of a Congress that respects the values and shares the faith of the American family.

Like Lincoln, our first Republican president, we intend to act "with firmness in the right, as God gives us to see the right." To restore accountability to Congress. To end its cycle of scandal and disgrace. To make us all proud again of the way free people govern themselves.

On the first day of the 104th Congress, the new Republican majority will immediately pass the following major reforms, aimed at restoring the faith and trust of the American people in their government:

• FIRST, require all laws that apply to the rest of the country also apply equally to the Congress;

• SECOND, select a major, independent auditing firm to conduct a comprehensive audit of Congress for waste, fraud or abuse;

• THIRD, cut the number of House committees, and cut committee staff by one-third;

• FOURTH, limit the terms of all committee chairs;

• FIFTH, ban the casting of proxy votes in committee;

• SIXTH, require committee meetings to be open to the public;

• SEVENTH, require a three-fifths majority vote to pass a tax increase;

• EIGHTH, guarantee an honest accounting of our Federal Budget by implementing zero base-line budgeting.

Thereafter, within the first 100 days of the 104th Congress, we shall bring to the House Floor the following bills, each to be given full and open debate, each to be given a clear and fair vote and each to be immediately available this day for public inspection and scrutiny.

1. THE FISCAL RESPONSIBILITY ACT: A balanced budget/tax limitation amendment and a legislative line-item veto to restore fiscal responsibility to an out-of-control Congress, requiring them to live under the same budget constraints as families and businesses.

2. THE TAKING BACK OUR STREETS ACT: An anti-crime package including stronger truth-in-sentencing, "good faith" exclusionary rule exemptions, effective death penalty provisions, and cuts in social spending from this summer's "crime" bill to fund prison construction and additional law enforcement to keep people secure in their neighborhoods and kids safe in their schools.

3. THE PERSONAL RESPONSIBILITY ACT: Discourage illegitimacy and teen pregnancy by prohibiting welfare to minor mothers and denying increased AFDC for additional children while on welfare, cut spending for welfare programs, and enact a tough two-years-and-out provision with work requirements to promote individual responsibility.

4. THE FAMILY REINFORCEMENT ACT: Child support enforcement, tax incentives for adoption, strengthening rights of parents in their children's education, stronger child pornography laws, and an elderly dependent care tax credit to reinforce the central role of families in American society.

5. THE AMERICAN DREAM RESTORATION ACT: A $500 per child tax credit, begin repeal of the marriage tax penalty, and creation of American Dream Savings Accounts to provide middle class tax relief.

6. THE NATIONAL SECURITY RESTORATION ACT: No U.S. troops under U.N. command and restoration of the essential parts of our national security funding to strengthen our national defense and maintain our credibility around the world.

7. THE SENIOR CITIZENS FAIRNESS ACT: Raise the Social Security earnings limit which currently forces seniors out of the work force, repeal the 1993 tax hikes on Social Security benefits and provide tax incentives for private long-term care insurance to let Older Americans keep more of what they have earned over the years.

8. THE JOB CREATION AND WAGE ENHANCEMENT ACT: Small business incentives, capital gains cut and indexation, neutral cost recovery, risk assessment/cost-benefit analysis, strengthening the Regulatory Flexibility Act and unfunded mandate reform to create jobs and raise worker wages.

9. THE COMMON SENSE LEGAL REFORM ACT: "Loser pays" laws, reasonable limits on punitive damages and reform of product liability laws to stem the endless tide of litigation.

10. THE CITIZEN LEGISLATURE ACT: A first-ever vote on term limits to replace career politicians with citizen legislators.

Further, we will instruct the House Budget Committee to report to the floor and we will work to enact additional budget savings, beyond the budget cuts specifically included in the legislation described above, to ensure that the Federal budget deficit will be less than it would have been without the enactment of these bills.

Respecting the judgment of our fellow citizens as we seek their mandate for reform, we hereby pledge our names to this Contract with America.

❧ 45 ☙
*Bush v. Gore**
(2000)

1. Under what circumstances, if any, is it appropriate to use exit polls to declare the winner of an election before all the votes are tallied?
2. When an election is very close and a recount is mandated by law, how long should election officials be permitted to conduct the recount? Specifically, how long and how much leeway should election officials be given to ascertain the will of the voters?

VOTERS WHO WENT to the polls to choose a president on November 7, 2000, had to do more than just wait in line—the outcome of this election was not known until December 12, more than a month after the initial balloting. The Constitution requires that the winning presidential candidate receive a majority of the votes in the Electoral College. Today there are 538 electors selected in each presidential election; the votes of 270 of these electors are needed to win the presidency.

*www.law.cornell.edu/supct/html/00-949.ZPC.html

Forty-eight states administer federal elections for president under the "unit rule," meaning that all of the electors representing the winner of the popular vote in that state are assigned to cast their vote for president. (Maine and Nebraska assign electors to the presidential candidates who win within specific congressional districts.)

Such a "winner take all" system makes it possible for a candidate to lose the nationwide popular vote and still be elected president. This is most likely to happen when the candidate winning the Electoral College vote loses some of the more populous states by large popular vote margins but still wins a few of the more populous states and a larger number of states overall. In the 2000 presidential election Bush won thirty states and Gore won twenty (plus the District of Columbia). It was one of three elections in U.S. history (the others were in 1876 and 1888) in which the presidential candidate receiving a majority of votes in the Electoral College did not receive a majority of the popular vote.

Typically, election outcomes are not this close and the victors are known on election night. Exit polls conducted by the Voter News Service (VNS) allow news organizations to project the winner of each state once its polls close. On the night of November 7, 2000, however, VNS and most major news organizations declared Gore the winner of Florida at 7:00 P.M. Eastern Standard Time, which contradicted traditional practice because voters in the Florida panhandle are in the Central Time Zone. They had until 8:00 P.M. EST to cast their votes. Then VNS was forced to change its declaration of the winner—twice—from Gore to Bush, then from Bush to "too close to call." In addition, the election results in many other states, particularly Iowa, New Mexico, Oregon, and Wisconsin, were also close. Recounts were necessary, and the distribution of the electoral votes of these states was not known for many days.

The most important state, however, was Florida. Bush needed the state's twenty-five votes to receive a majority in the Electoral College, and thus the presidency. The Florida Division of Elections reported on November 8 that he had won the state by 1,784 votes. Since that made his margin of victory less than 0.5 percent, state law mandated a recount, which was finished on November 10. This time the margin of victory had decreased to 327 votes.

Under Florida law, candidates may request that counties conduct manual recounts. Gore's campaign requested that Broward, Miami-Dade,

Palm Beach, and Volusia counties do so. Each county granted the request, but Broward, Miami-Dade, and Palm Beach were unable to fulfill it before Florida law required that certified election returns be delivered to Secretary of State Katherine Harris. The Florida Circuit Court had ruled earlier on November 10 that the deadline for certifying returns was mandatory, but that any county could submit an amendment to its return at a later date.

The court further ruled that the secretary of state had the discretion to accept amended returns. At 5:00 P.M. on the date of the deadline, Harris announced that she had received the certified returns from each county even though Broward, Miami-Dade, and Palm Beach were still recounting their votes manually. Four counties, the fourth being Volusia, had in fact submitted statements to Harris requesting permission to make late filings. In each case, she had decided that an extension of the filing was not warranted; after she received the returns of overseas absentee ballots, the election was certified on November 18, 2000. Harris then declared Bush the winner, but the manual recount of votes continued while the courts heard appeals from the Democrats.

The controversy surrounding the election soon found its way to the nation's highest court. On December 11, 2000, the U.S. Supreme Court heard oral arguments in *Bush v. Gore*, 531 U.S. 98 (2000). Using the Equal Protection Clause of the Fourteenth Amendment as the basis for its ruling, the Court decided in a per curiam opinion that the proposal for recounting ballots that had been issued by the Florida Supreme Court was unconstitutional and that it was impossible to establish a uniform recount procedure and properly recount the contested votes within the time limit established under Florida law.

The ruling was not without disagreement. Several justices wrote opinions differing slightly from the Court's judgment. Justices Rehnquist, Scalia, and Thomas argued that the recount procedure developed by the Florida Supreme Court effectively created a new election law, which only the state legislature was authorized to do. Justices Breyer and Souter maintained that a recount method could still have been developed that would have met the state's constitutional requirements. Justices Ginsburg and Stevens argued that due to the federal nature of the U.S. system the decision of the Florida Supreme Court should stand.

Once the Court's decision was issued, the manual recount stopped, and the previous certification of George W. Bush as the winner stood. Bush was awarded Florida's twenty-five electoral votes, giving him a total of 271.

❦

Per Curiam.

I

On December 8, 2000, the Supreme Court of Florida ordered that the Circuit Court of Leon County tabulate by hand 9,000 ballots in Miami-Dade County. It also ordered the inclusion in the certified vote totals of 215 votes identified in Palm Beach County and 168 votes identified in Miami-Dade County for Vice President Albert Gore, Jr., and Senator Joseph Lieberman, Democratic Candidates for President and Vice President. The Supreme Court noted that petitioner, Governor George W. Bush asserted that the net gain for Vice President Gore in Palm Beach County was 176 votes, and directed the Circuit Court to resolve that dispute on remand. The court further held that relief would require manual recounts in all Florida counties where so-called "undervotes" had not been subject to manual tabulation. The court ordered all manual recounts to begin at once. Governor Bush and Richard Cheney, Republican Candidates for the Presidency and Vice Presidency, filed an emergency application for a stay of this mandate. On December 9, we granted the application, treated the application as a petition for a writ of certiorari, and granted certiorari.

. . . On November 8, 2000, the day following the Presidential election, the Florida Division of Elections reported that petitioner, Governor Bush, had received 2,909,135 votes, and respondent, Vice President Gore, had received 2,907,351 votes, a margin of 1,784 for Governor Bush. Because Governor Bush's margin of victory was less than "one-half of a percent . . . of the votes cast," an automatic machine recount was conducted under §102.141(4) of the election code, the results of which showed Governor Bush still winning the race but by a diminished margin. Vice President Gore then sought manual recounts in Volusia, Palm Beach, Broward, and Miami-Dade Counties, pursuant to Florida's election protest provisions. A dispute arose concerning the deadline for local county canvassing boards to submit their returns to the Secretary of State (Secretary). The Secretary declined to waive the November 14 deadline imposed by statute. The Florida Supreme Court, however, set the deadline at November 26. We granted certiorari and vacated the Florida Supreme Court's decision, finding considerable uncertainty as to the grounds on which it was based. On December 11, the Florida Supreme Court issued a decision on remand reinstating that date.

On November 26, the Florida Elections Canvassing Commission certified the results of the election and declared Governor Bush the winner of Florida's 25 electoral votes. On November 27, Vice President Gore, pursuant to Florida's contest provisions, filed a complaint in Leon County Circuit Court contesting the certification. He sought relief . . . that "[r]eceipt of a number of illegal votes or rejection of a number of legal votes sufficient to change or place in doubt the result of the election" shall be grounds for a contest. The Circuit Court denied relief, stating that Vice President Gore failed to meet his burden of proof. He appealed to the First District Court of Appeal, which certified the matter to the Florida Supreme Court.

Accepting jurisdiction, the Florida Supreme Court affirmed in part and reversed in part. *Gore v. Harris,* (2000). The court held that the Circuit Court had been correct to reject Vice President Gore's challenge to the results certified in Nassau County and his challenge to the Palm Beach County Canvassing Board's determination that 3,300 ballots cast in that county were not, in the statutory phrase, "legal votes."

The Supreme Court held that Vice President Gore had satisfied his burden of proof . . . with respect to his challenge to Miami-Dade County's failure to tabulate, by manual count, 9,000 ballots on which the machines had failed to detect a vote for President ("undervotes"). Noting the closeness of the election, the Court explained that "[o]n this record, there can be no question that there are legal votes within the 9,000 uncounted votes sufficient to place the results of this election in doubt." A "legal vote," as determined by the Supreme Court, is "one in which there is a 'clear indication of the intent of the voter.' " The court therefore ordered a hand recount of the 9,000 ballots in Miami-Dade County. Observing that the contest provisions vest broad discretion in the circuit judge to "provide any relief appropriate under such circumstances," . . . the Supreme Court further held that the Circuit Court could order "the Supervisor of Elections and the Canvassing Boards, as well as the necessary public officials, in all counties that have not conducted a manual recount or tabulation of the undervotes . . . to do so forthwith, said tabulation to take place in the individual counties where the ballots are located."

The Supreme Court also determined that both Palm Beach County and Miami-Dade County, in their earlier manual recounts, had identified a net gain of 215 and 168 legal votes for Vice President Gore. Rejecting the Circuit Court's conclusion that Palm Beach County lacked the authority to include the 215 net votes submitted past the November 26 deadline, the Supreme Court explained that the deadline was not intended to exclude votes identified after that date through ongoing manual recounts. As to Miami-Dade County, the Court concluded that although the 168 votes identified were the result of a partial recount, they were "legal votes [that] could change the outcome of the election." The Supreme Court therefore directed the Circuit Court to include those totals in the certified results, subject to resolution of the actual vote total from the Miami-Dade partial recount.

The petition presents the following questions: whether the Florida Supreme Court established new standards for resolving Presidential election contests, thereby violating Art. II, §1, cl. 2, of the United States Constitution and . . . whether the use of standardless manual recounts violates the Equal Protection and Due Process Clauses. With respect to the equal protection question, we find a violation of the Equal Protection Clause.

II

A

The closeness of this election, and the multitude of legal challenges which have followed in its wake, have brought into sharp focus a common, if heretofore unnoticed, phenomenon. Nationwide statistics reveal that an estimated 2% of ballots cast do not register a vote for President for whatever reason, including deliberately choosing no candidate at all or some voter error, such as voting for two candidates or insufficiently marking a ballot. . . . In certifying election results, the votes eligible for inclusion in the certification are the votes meeting the properly established legal requirements.

This case has shown that punch card balloting machines can produce an unfortunate number of ballots which are not punched in a clean, complete way by the voter. After the current counting, it is likely legislative bodies nationwide will examine ways to improve the mechanisms and machinery for voting.

B

The individual citizen has no federal constitutional right to vote for electors for the President of the United States unless and until the state legislature chooses a statewide election as the means to implement its power to appoint members of the Electoral College. This is the source for the statement in *McPherson v. Blacker* (1892), that the State legislature's power to select the manner for appointing electors is plenary; it may, if it so chooses, select the electors itself, which indeed was the manner used by State legislatures in several States for many years after the Framing of our Constitution. History has now favored the voter, and in each of the several States the citizens themselves vote for Presidential electors. When the state legislature vests the right to vote for President in its people, the right to vote as the legislature has prescribed is fundamental; and one source of its fundamental nature lies in the equal weight accorded to each vote and the equal dignity owed to each voter. The State, of course, after granting the franchise in the special context of Article II, can take back the power to appoint electors. . . .

The right to vote is protected in more than the initial allocation of the franchise. Equal protection applies as well to the manner of its exercise. Having once granted the right to vote on equal terms, the State may not, by later arbitrary and disparate treatment, value one person's vote over that of another. . . . It must be remembered that "the right of suffrage can be denied by a debasement or dilution of the weight of a citizen's vote just as effectively as by wholly prohibiting the free exercise of the franchise."

There is no difference between the two sides of the present controversy on these basic propositions. Respondents say that the very purpose of vindicating the right to vote justifies the recount procedures now at issue. The question before us, however, is whether the recount procedures the Florida Supreme Court has adopted are consistent with its obligation to avoid arbitrary and disparate treatment of the members of its electorate.

Much of the controversy seems to revolve around ballot cards designed to be perforated by a stylus but which, either through error or deliberate omission, have not been perforated with sufficient precision for a machine to count them. In some cases a piece of the card—a chad—is hanging, say by two corners. In other cases there is no separation at all, just an indentation.

The Florida Supreme Court has ordered that the intent of the voter be discerned from such ballots. For purposes of resolving the equal protection challenge, it is not necessary to decide whether the Florida Supreme Court had the authority under the legislative scheme for resolving election disputes to define what a legal vote is and to mandate a manual recount implementing that definition. The recount mechanisms implemented in response to the decisions of the Florida Supreme Court do not satisfy the minimum requirement for nonarbitrary treatment of voters necessary to secure the fundamental right. Florida's basic command for the count of legally cast votes is to consider the "intent of the voter." This is unobjectionable as an abstract proposition and a starting principle. The problem inheres in the absence of specific standards to ensure its equal application. The formulation of uniform rules to determine intent based on these recurring circumstances is practicable and, we conclude, necessary.

The law does not refrain from searching for the intent of the actor in a multitude of circumstances; and in some cases the general command to ascertain intent is not susceptible to much further refinement. In this instance, however, the question is not whether to believe a witness but how to interpret the marks or holes or scratches on an inanimate object, a piece of cardboard or paper which, it is said, might not have registered as a vote during the machine count. The factfinder confronts a thing, not a person. The search for intent can be confined by specific rules designed to ensure uniform treatment.

The want of those rules here has led to unequal evaluation of ballots in various respects. . . . As seems to have been acknowledged at oral argument, the standards for accepting or rejecting contested ballots might vary not only from county to county but indeed within a single county from one recount team to another. . . .

The State Supreme Court ratified this uneven treatment. It mandated that the recount totals from two counties, Miami-Dade and Palm Beach, be included in the certified total. The court also appeared to hold *sub silentio* that the recount totals from Broward County, which were not completed until after the original November 14 certification by the Secretary of State, were to be considered part of the new certified vote totals even though the county certification was not contested by Vice President Gore. Yet each of the counties used varying standards to determine what was a legal vote. Broward County used a more forgiving standard than Palm Beach County, and uncovered almost three times as many new votes, a result markedly disproportionate to the difference in population between the counties.

In addition, the recounts in these three counties were not limited to so-called undervotes but extended to all of the ballots. The distinction has real consequences. A manual recount of all ballots identifies not only those ballots which show no vote but also those which contain more than one, the so-called overvotes. Neither category will be counted by the machine. This is not a trivial concern. At oral argument, respondents estimated there are as many as 110,000 overvotes statewide. As a result, the citizen whose ballot was not read by a machine because he failed to vote for a candidate in a way readable by a machine may still have his vote counted in a manual recount; on the other hand, the citizen who marks two candidates in a way discernable by the machine will not have the same opportunity to have his vote count, even if a manual examination of the ballot would reveal the requisite indicia of intent. Furthermore, the citizen who marks two candidates, only one of which is discernable by the machine, will have his vote counted even though it should have been read as an invalid ballot. The State Supreme Court's inclusion of vote counts based on these variant standards exemplifies concerns with the remedial processes that were under way.

That brings the analysis to yet a further equal protection problem. The votes certified by the court included a partial total from one county, Miami-Dade.

The Florida Supreme Court's decision thus gives no assurance that the recounts included in a final certification must be complete. Indeed, it is respondent's submission that it would be consistent with the rules of the recount procedures to include whatever partial counts are done by the time of final certification, and we interpret the Florida Supreme Court's decision to permit this. . . . This accommodation no doubt results from the truncated contest period established by the Florida Supreme Court in *Bush {v. Palm Beach County Canvassing Bd.}*, at respondents' own urging. The press of time does not diminish the constitutional concern. A desire for speed is not a general excuse for ignoring equal protection guarantees.

In addition to these difficulties the actual process by which the votes were to be counted under the Florida Supreme Court's decision raises further concerns. That order did not specify who would recount the ballots. The county canvassing boards were forced to pull together ad hoc teams comprised of judges from various Circuits who had no previous training in handling and interpreting ballots. Furthermore, while others were permitted to observe, they were prohibited from objecting during the recount.

The recount process, in its features here described, is inconsistent with the minimum procedures necessary to protect the fundamental right of each voter in the special instance of a statewide recount under the authority of a single state judicial officer. Our consideration is limited to the present circumstances, for the problem of equal protection in election processes generally presents many complexities.

The question before the Court is not whether local entities, in the exercise of their expertise, may develop different systems for implementing elections. Instead, we are presented with a situation where a state court with the power to assure uniformity has ordered a statewide recount with minimal procedural safeguards. When a court orders a statewide remedy, there must be at least some assurance that the rudimentary requirements of equal treatment and fundamental fairness are satisfied.

Given the Court's assessment that the recount process underway was probably being conducted in an unconstitutional manner, the Court stayed the order directing the recount so it could hear this case and render an expedited decision. The contest provision, as it was mandated by the State Supreme Court, is not well calculated to sustain the confidence that all citizens must have in the outcome of elections. The State has not shown that its procedures include the necessary safeguards. The problem, for instance, of the estimated 110,000 overvotes has not been addressed, although Chief Justice Wells called attention to the concern in his dissenting opinion.

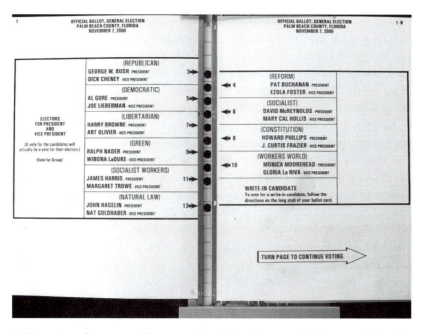

Ballots such as the one seen here caused confusion for many Florida voters during the 2000 election and resulted in the creation of the National Commission on Federal Election Reform and passage of the Help America Vote Act of 2002 (see pages 315–319).

Upon due consideration of the difficulties identified to this point, it is obvious that the recount cannot be conducted in compliance with the requirements of equal protection and due process without substantial additional work. It would require not only the adoption (after opportunity for argument) of adequate statewide standards for determining what is a legal vote, and practicable procedures to implement them, but also orderly judicial review of any disputed matters that might arise. In addition, the Secretary of State has advised that the recount of only a portion of the ballots requires that the vote tabulation equipment be used to screen out undervotes, a function for which the machines were not designed. If a recount of overvotes were also required, perhaps even a second screening would be necessary. Use of the equipment for this purpose, and any new software developed for it, would have to be evaluated for accuracy by the Secretary of State, as required by Fla. Stat. §101.015 (2000).

The Supreme Court of Florida has said that the legislature intended the State's electors to "participat[e] fully in the federal electoral process." . . . That statute, in turn, requires that any controversy or contest that is designed to lead to a conclusive selection of electors be completed by December 12. That date is upon us, and there is no recount procedure in place under the State Supreme Court's order that comports with minimal constitutional standards. Because it is evident that any recount seeking to meet the December 12 date will be unconstitutional for the reasons we have discussed, we reverse the judgment of the Supreme Court of Florida ordering a recount to proceed.

Seven Justices of the Court agree that there are constitutional problems with the recount ordered by the Florida Supreme Court that demand a remedy. . . . The only disagreement is as to the remedy. Because the Florida Supreme Court has said that the Florida Legislature intended to obtain the safe-harbor benefits of JUSTICE BREYER's proposed remedy—remanding to the Florida Supreme Court for its ordering of a constitutionally proper contest until December 18—contemplates action in violation of the Florida election code, and hence could not be part of an "appropriate" order authorized by Fla. Stat. §102.168(8) (2000).

* * *

None are more conscious of the vital limits on judicial authority than are the members of this Court, and none stand more in admiration of the Constitution's design to leave the selection of the President to the people, through their legislatures, and to the political sphere. When contending parties invoke the process of the courts, however, it becomes our unsought responsibility to resolve the federal and constitutional issues the judicial system has been forced to confront.

The judgment of the Supreme Court of Florida is reversed, and the case is remanded for further proceedings not inconsistent with this opinion.

❦ 46 ❦
Report of the National Commission on Federal Election Reform*
(2001)

1. The Help America Vote Act has significantly increased the federal government's role in administering elections. Was it important for the federal government to more actively participate in federal elections? Should these responsibilities have remained at the state and local level?
2. Is it important that the U.S. electoral system be a source of "national pride" and a "model to all the world"? Why or why not?

A LMOST TWO MILLION BALLOTS were disqualified in the 2000 presidential election. Most registered in voting machines as either "undervotes" (no vote for an office) or "overvotes" (multiple votes for an office). And while the disqualification of votes is both necessary and normal, the disqualification of these particular votes was brought to the public's attention largely by the difficulty in recounting punch-card ballots in Florida, where George W. Bush defeated Al Gore by only 537 votes of the nearly six million votes cast. (The butterfly-style punch card ballot used by Palm Beach County, Florida, is shown on page 313.)

In response to the outcry generated by the Florida recount and in reaction to the growing number of problems in the administration of elections nationwide, the National Commission on Federal Election Reform was formed in 2001. Co-chaired by former presidents Gerald Ford and Jimmy Carter, the commission was comprised of public leaders from both political parties organized into task forces that held four public hearings to assist in the commission's analysis of the relevant research on election reform and offer policy alternatives to Congress and the president. Its final report, "To Assure Pride and Confidence in the Electoral Process," was released on July 31, 2001.

*www.tcf.org/Publications/ElectionReform/99_full_report.pdf

The Help America Vote Act (HAVA) was signed into law by President Bush on October 29, 2002. Passed with bipartisan support, the new law relied heavily on the commission's final report. Ford and Carter said of HAVA, "The bill represents a delicate balance of shared responsibilities between levels of government. This comprehensive bill can ensure that America's electoral system will again be a source of national pride and a model to all the world."

HAVA represents a significant increase of federal authority over the election process, which traditionally and legally has been the domain of state and local government. The goals of HAVA include the replacement of punch-card voting systems, establishment of minimum election administration standards, and the creation of the Election Assistance Commission (EAC) to assist in the administration of federal elections. The principal responsibilities of the EAC are to serve as a clearinghouse of information for election administration, test and certify voting machines, and assist states in complying with federal election guidelines. The commission also provides grants to states to assist in compliance with HAVA and conducts research on different voting policies, such as voting by mail or how military service personnel vote properly.

States have responded to HAVA in different ways, but many have attempted to comply with it by purchasing electronic voting machines to automate and simplify the voting process. However, these machines are often criticized because of their unreliability and poor security, and many of them are not compliant with HAVA's standards. These include machines sold after the 2000 presidential election, but before the requirements of HAVA were in place. They also include noncompliant machines sold to unsuspecting states and communities who believed the machines were compliant with the new law. Much of the equipment purchased in recent years has required either disposal or refurbishing at taxpayer expense to become compliant with HAVA.

Some critics of the act argue that the errors produced by punch-card voting machines in Florida in the 2000 election were merely replaced by those produced by expensive electronic voting machines that do not offer a voter verified paper audit trail (VVPAT). Under HAVA all voting systems were required by January 1, 2006, to produce a permanent paper record that can be audited in the event a recount needs to be conducted.

Finally, Republicans who were concerned by high estimates of persons voting fraudulently insisted that HAVA include stronger voter identification requirements. Democrats argued that the Republican rates are exaggerated and that laws requiring voters to produce identification when voting actually reduce rather than expand the voting electorate. But while they believed that poor and less informed voters may be more easily confused or intimidated, the stronger laws were put in place to ensure bipartisan support for the legislation.

❧

Letter to the American People

In 2000 the American electoral system was tested by a political ordeal unlike any in living memory. From November 7 until December 12 the outcome of the presidential election was fought out in bitter political and legal struggles that ranged throughout the state of Florida and ultimately extended to the Supreme Court of the United States. The American political system proved its resilience. But we must think about the future.

The ordinary institutions of election administration in the United States, and specifically Florida, just could not readily cope with an extremely close election. Many aspects of the election process were put under a microscope and viewed by an anxious nation. With dismay and growing anger we saw controversial ballot design; antiquated and error-prone voting machines; subjective and capricious processes for counting votes; voter rolls that let unqualified voters vote in some counties and turned away qualified voters in others; confusion in the treatment of overseas military ballots; and a political process subjected to protracted litigation.

Stepping back from Florida, the picture is no more encouraging. The chief election official of Georgia, Cathy Cox, testified to our Commission that: "As the presidential election drama unfolded in Florida last November, one thought was foremost in my mind: there but for the grace of God go I. Because the truth is, if the presidential margin had been razor thin in Georgia and if our election systems had undergone the same microscopic scrutiny that Florida endured, we would have fared no better. In many respects, we might have fared even worse." Across America, we have heard from official after official who feels the same way.

There is good news, though. In the last few years, and now spurred by the events last year, election reform has returned to the legislative agenda in many states. In much of the country cadres of able and dedicated election administrators are in place who can show what is possible and carry reforms into practice. In a world of problems that often defy any solution, the weaknesses in election administration are, to a very great degree, problems that government actually can solve.

In this report we and our colleagues offer very specific recommendations on what should be done. In other words, Americans can and should expect their electoral system to be a source of national pride and a model to all the world.

[Signed]

Gerald R. Ford	Jimmy Carter
Robert H. Michel	Lloyd N. Cutler

Co-chairs of the National Commission on Federal Election Reform

Policy Recommendation[s]

1. Every state should adopt a system of statewide voter registration. . . .

2. Every state should permit provisional voting by any voter who claims to be qualified to vote in that state. . . .

3. Congress should enact legislation to hold presidential and congressional elections on a national holiday. . . .

4. Congress should adopt legislation that simplifies and facilitates absentee voting by uniformed and overseas citizens. . . .

5. Each state should allow for restoration of voting rights to otherwise eligible citizens who have been convicted of a felony once they have fully served their sentence, including any term of probation or parole. . . .

6. The state and federal governments should take additional steps to assure the voting rights of all citizens and to enforce the principle of one person, one vote. . . .

7. Each state should set a benchmark for voting system performance, uniform in each local jurisdiction that conducts elections. The benchmark should be expressed as a percentage of residual vote (the combination of overvotes, spoiled votes, and undervotes) in the contest at the top of the ballot and should take account of deliberate decisions of voters not to make a choice. . . .

8. The federal government should develop a comprehensive set of voting equipment system standards for the benefit of state and local election administration. . . .

9. Each state should adopt uniform statewide standards for defining what will constitute a vote on each category of voting equipment certified for use in that state. Statewide recount, election certification, and contest procedures should take account of the timelines for selection of presidential electors. . . .

10. News organizations should not project any presidential election results in any state so long as polls remain open elsewhere in the 48 contiguous states. If necessary, Congress and the states should consider legislation, within First Amendment limits, to protect the integrity of the electoral process. . . .

11. The federal government, on a matching basis with the governments of the 50 states, should provide funds that will add another $300–400 million to the level of annual spending on election administration in the United States. The federal share will require a federal contribution totaling $1–2 billion spread out over two or three years to help capitalize state revolving funds that will provide long-term assistance. . . .

12. The federal responsibilities envisioned in this report should be assigned to a new agency, an Election Administration Commission (EAC). . . .

13. Congress should enact legislation that includes federal assistance for election administration, setting forth policy objectives for the states while leaving the choice of strategies to the discretion of the states. . . .

❧ 47 ❧

Russ Feingold's Speech Supporting the Bipartisan Campaign Reform Act and Mitch McConnell's Speech Opposing the Bipartisan Campaign Reform Act*

(2002)

1. Has the prohibition on raising and spending soft money affected political parties? If so, how? Are the two major parties weaker or stronger today as a result of BCRA?
2. What impact, if any, have the changes to "electioneering communications" under BCRA had on campaigns and elections?

THE FEDERAL ELECTION CAMPAIGN ACT (FECA), passed in 1971 and amended in 1974, 1976, and 1979, brought campaign finance law under the same comprehensive legal umbrella for the first time. By

*Congressional Record, 107th Congress, 2nd Sess., March 20, 2002 (Washington, D.C.: Government Printing Office, 2002), 3555–3655.

the 1990s the nature of campaign finance in federal elections had changed dramatically, however, and many legislators felt that the provisions of FECA were in need of review.

On September 7, 1995, Republican John McCain of Arizona and Democrat Russell Feingold of Wisconsin introduced the first version of a campaign finance reform bill that eventually became known as the Bipartisan Campaign Reform Act of 2002 (BCRA). Over the next few years different versions of the McCain-Feingold bill were debated and filibustered on the Senate floor. Efforts to end these debates were unsuccessful, and each time the bill was eventually withdrawn. It took the revelation of a number of financial scandals involving "soft" money donated to both major parties during 2000 election cycle to get the Senate to finally approve the McCain-Feingold bill in the spring of 2001.

The Senate's companion bill in the House of Representatives was sponsored by Republican Chris Shays of Connecticut and Democrat Martin Meehan of Massachusetts. During the 107th Congress the Republican leadership refused to bring the bill to the floor, but its sponsors eventually acquired the necessary 218 signatures on a discharge petition to force a floor vote. The Shays-Meehan bill was approved by the House on February 14, 2002, by a vote of 240–189. To avoid the need for a conference committee in which important provisions of the bill might be changed, the Senate simply approved the House version of the legislation on March 20, 2002, by a vote of 60–40. President George W. Bush signed the Bipartisan Campaign Reform Act of 2002 a week later on March 27.

BCRA is a very complex piece of legislation, but it was essentially designed to reform how political parties raise and spend soft money and to regulate issue advocacy. BCRA bans national political parties from raising soft money and restricts how political parties at the state level can spend it. In contrast to "hard" money, which is raised and spent according to legal limits, prohibitions, and disclosure requirements, "soft" money is raised and spent outside the regulatory framework of federal campaign finance law and may directly or indirectly influence election to federal office. These types of donations by individuals to political parties were not subject to the hard money contribution limits. Much of the soft money that the Democratic and Republican Parties raised was spent on so-called issue advertising. Such ads could not expressly advocate the election or defeat of a candidate, but they could link the candidate with issue positions that might be popular or unpopular with voters.

Second, BCRA defines "electioneering communications" in order to regulate issue advocacy. Electioneering communications refer to broadcast advertisements that reference a clearly identified candidate for federal office within thirty days of a primary or caucus or within sixty days of a general election. Individuals and groups that finance such communications are required to disclose their contributors and expenses with the Federal Election Commission (FEC) and unions and corporations are generally prohibited from spending treasury funds on them.

The act is not without its detractors. Among its most vocal opponent has been Republican Mitch McConnell of Kentucky, formerly Senate majority whip (and current Senate minority leader). In 2003, McConnell challenged the implementation of BCRA in federal court. On December 10, 2003, however, in *McConnell v. FEC,* 540 U.S. 93 (2003) the U.S. Supreme Court found the principal provisions of BCRA related to political party soft money and electioneering communications constitutional by a vote of 5–4.

During the 2004 election cycle a number of Democratic and Republican "watchdog" groups filed complaints with the FEC arguing that 527 organizations were effectively raising and spending soft money. These organizations were able to avoid registering as political committees with the FEC by registering as tax-exempt political organizations under Section 527 of the Internal Revenue Code. As such, they were not subject to the fundraising, spending, and disclosure requirements of BCRA.

Initially, the FEC refused to apply the law to 527s because after holding public hearings in 2004, it determined that the campaign finance laws did not cover 527s unless they expressly advocated the election or defeat of a candidate. In late 2006, however, the commission determined that a few of the larger 527s had expressly advocated the election or defeat of candidates during the 2004 election cycle, and these were fined for failing to register as political committees with the FEC and for failing to abide by campaign finance regulations.

MR. FEINGOLD: Mr. President, on September 7, 1995, 6½ years ago, the senior Senator from Arizona and I introduced the first version of the McCain-Feingold campaign finance reform bill. It was a different bill from the bill we are about to pass today, but it was a different world then. The Senate that year was controlled by the Republican party. The Majority Leader was Bob Dole. The occupant of the White House was a Democrat, Bill Clinton, still in his first term. Still far in the future, unimaginable to any of us then, were an impeachment trial, an impossibly close Presidential election, and of course, September 11.

The world of campaign finance was much different too. Still to come was the 1996 Presidential campaign with campaign finance abuses that by now we refer to in shorthand—the White House coffees, the Lincoln Bedroom, the Buddhist temple fundraiser, Roger Tamraz. Still ahead were the extraordinary revelations of the Thompson investigation concerning fundraising abuses by both political parties. Still in the future was the explosion of phony issue ads by outside groups and by the political parties—hundreds of millions of dollars spent to influence elections through a loophole that assumes that the advertising is not meant to influence elections.

Most amazing, as I look back on these many years, is the growth since then of the soft money outrage, which has become the central focus of our campaign finance reform effort over the past several years. When we introduced our first bill—I have to be honest about this—soft money was still in, if not its infancy, then, at the most, it was in its adolescence.

When we introduced the bill in 1995, banning soft money was on our list of provisions, but we listed it, actually, as the sixth component of the bill, coming after, believe it or not, the problem of reforming the congressional franking privilege. I noted in that speech, with some sense of emerging outrage, that the political parties had raised—I kid you not—"tens of millions of dollars" in 1995 alone, a figure that, of course, is absolutely nothing compared to what we see today.

The soft money loophole surely came of age in the 1996 elections, and has only kept growing since then. In the 1992 election cycle, the parties raised a total of $86 million. In 1996, that number more than tripled to $262 million. And in 2000, soft money receipts nearly doubled again to $495 million, nearly half a billion dollars.

As the world of campaign finance has changed, so has the McCain-Feingold bill. In late 1997, in the wake of the Thompson investigation, we reluctantly concluded that we needed to first focus our efforts on closing the biggest loopholes in the system: the soft money and the phony issue ads. But narrowing the bill, obviously, did not make it easy to pass. As those two loopholes have grown in importance, and more and more money has flowed through them into our elections, the commitment of the major players in the political system to protect them has only increased.

Indeed, there was a time when the opponents of campaign finance reform called soft money "sewer money" and proposed banning it in their own alternative bill. Now, instead, they champion soft money as essential to the health and stability of the political parties and that it is somehow protected by the first amendment, even though they wanted to eliminate it and called it "sewer money" before.

But a few things have not changed a bit since Senator McCain and I began this journey together. One is our commitment to bipartisan reform. Both Senator McCain and I mentioned this in our first speeches in 1995. We knew then that a partisan effort on this issue would be doomed to failure.

In my speech, I noted that we were both speaking to Members of both parties about our bill, and that "we are not dividing up the Senate because this has to be a product of the Senate." This had to be a product of the whole Senate, both parties.

That hope was put to the test last year when this body engaged in an extraordinary 2-week floor debate on campaign finance reform, with an open amendment process and a vote on final passage for first time since 1993. We had 27 roll call votes in that debate. Thirty-eight amendments to the bill were offered and 17 were adopted. This bill is truly the work product of the Senate as a whole. That is a major reason why it will soon be headed to the President for signature.

Another thing that has not changed since 1995, of course, is the need for reform. If anything, it has increased as much as the amount of soft money contributed to the parties has increased. In 1995, I noted that the public had reason for concern when big money was being poured into legislative efforts such as the telecommunications bill and regulatory reform legislation. Since then, the list of legislative battles where money has seemed to call the shots has gotten longer and longer: the bankruptcy bill, product liability legislation, the tobacco wars, financial services modernization, the Patients' Bill of Rights, China MFN. I could, obviously, go on and on.

I have called the bankroll on this floor more than 30 times since June 1999. These days, major legislation almost never comes to this floor without interests, often on both sides, that have made major soft money contributions to the political parties. We need look no further than the work we do on this Senate floor to see the appearance of corruption—the appearance of corruption—that justifies banning soft money.

A few years ago, an advocacy group unveiled a huge "FOR SALE" sign and held it up for an afternoon on the steps on the east front of the Capitol. We have seen similar images for years in political cartoons. A constituent once wrote to me that perhaps Senators should wear jackets with corporate logos on them like race cars. We laugh at these images, but inside we cringe, because this great center of democracy is truly tainted by money. Particularly after September 11, all of us in this Chamber hope the public will look to the Capitol and look to the Senate with reverence and pride, not with derision. Our task today is to restore some of that pride. I believe we can undertake that task with our own sense of pride, because we know it is the right thing to do, and we know it has to be done.

Another thing that has not changed since we first introduced the McCain-Feingold bill in 1995 is the determination of the opposition to defeat reform. Early in 1996, when we were approaching our first vote on the McCain-Feingold bill and the first filibuster against our bill, a coalition began to meet to plot our defeat. The Washington Post described the coalition as "an unusual alliance of unions, businesses, and liberal and conservative groups."

I called them at the time—and continue to call them—the Washington gatekeepers: the major players in politics and policy in this town for whom campaign money is the currency of influence.

The National Association of Business PACs even began to run ads against House members who cosponsored the bill, and they threatened to withhold financial support in the next election. Even before our bill had seen its first debate, the status quo had organized to kill it. And their efforts have continued unabated throughout the last 6½ years.

The opposition has plainly made our task more difficult, but it also now makes our victory more satisfying. Because as we stand on the verge of enacting this major accomplishment, we in the Congress who have supported this effort know we have acted not out of self interest, and not for the special interests, but for the public interest. This bill is for the American people, for our democracy, and for the future of our country.

When a previous effort to reform the campaign finance system failed in an end-of-session filibuster in late 1994, then-Majority Leader George Mitchell said this on the floor:

> The fact of the matter is, Mr. President, every Senator knows this system stinks. Every Senator who participates in it knows this system stinks. And the American people are right when they mistrust this system, where what matters most in seeking public office is not integrity, not ability, not judgment, not reason, not responsibility, not experience, not intelligence, but money.

This bill won't fix every problem in our campaign finance system. The Presiding Officer and I have talked about this throughout the years of his steadfast support for our efforts. This bill will not miraculously erase distrust and suspicion of the Congress overnight. It will not completely end the primacy of money in politics that so disturbed Senator Mitchell. But the bill is a step in the right direction. It is a step in the right direction.

After so many years of effort, and so many disappointments, the public has reason to be gratified by what we are about to do, and to look with hope to what we can accomplish together when the monkey of soft money is finally lifted off our backs.

As elated as we are about finally finishing this long battle for reform, I cannot leave the floor without noting that the war is not over. We must be vigilant as the Federal Election Commission promulgates regulations to implement the legislation. And, of course, we face a certain court challenge by opponents of reform who will argue that it violates the Constitution.

I assure my colleagues of two things. First, we have had one eye on the eventual court challenge ever since we started this process. This bill has been carefully crafted to take account of the Supreme Court's decisions in this area. Can I guarantee that every provision will survive a court challenge? Of course not. But I can tell you that we have done our very best to design these reforms in a constitutional manner.

Second, we plan to be active participants in the legal fight that will undoubtedly end in the Supreme Court of the United States, perhaps as early as a year from now.

We will be similarly active in pressing the FEC to promulgate regulations that fulfill—that fulfill, not frustrate—the intent of the Congress in passing this bill. The Senator from Arizona and I did not fight for 6½ years to pass these reforms only to see them undone by a hostile FEC. The role of the FEC is to carry out the will of the Congress, to implement and enforce the law, not to undermine it.

I call on each of the Commissioners, regardless of political party or personal views on our reform effort, to be true to that role and to the oaths of office they took.

I urge my colleagues to join with us in overseeing the crucial work of the FEC and to participate in its rulemaking proceedings where appropriate.

In addition, even after we have enacted this law, there will be other reforms to do. We need to look at the cost of broadcast advertising and consider whether those having a license to use the public airwaves ought to be required to provide free airtime to promote democratic discourse during election campaigns.

In my opinion, we need to again consider the possibility of public funding of congressional elections, following the very successful experience with clean money systems in Maine and Arizona.

Finally, we must remain vigilant to guard against the next abuse of the campaign finance system when it comes, as it surely will.

I thank all of my colleagues for their patience and their support. I know this battle has been difficult for many of them. The pressure to preserve the status quo was intense. Inertia is a powerful force against change. We have all compromised at least a little in order to achieve this final result. Many members have cast difficult votes. They have sometimes followed Senator McCain and me down a path without knowing exactly where it would lead. I am grateful for the trust they have shown in us, and I thank them from the bottom of my heart.

Before I close, I pay special tribute to my partner in this effort, the Senator from Arizona. When Senator McCain called me shortly after the 1994 elections and asked me to join with him in bipartisan reform efforts, I could never have imagined that we would be standing here together on this day on the verge of a great victory for the American people. He just didn't tell me how long it would take. I truly believe his courage and dedication, demonstrated in so many ways over so many years, are the reasons the Bipartisan Campaign Reform Act of 2002 will soon become the law of the land.

My respect for him has grown with every challenge we have faced together. He is a great legislator, a great leader, and, above all, a great friend.

Our work on this bill, John McCain, has been the highlight of my professional life. Your friendship means more to me than you will ever know. Thanks, John.

* * *

MR. MCCONNELL. Madam President, I begin by citing the ultimate campaign reform: The first amendment to our Constitution. It says Congress shall make no law—no law—abridging freedom of speech or of the press. I refer to the freedom of the press because it is the robust exercise of that freedom which has brought us today to assault the freedom of speech. Over the past 5 years, the New York Times and the Washington Post have joined forces to publish an editorial an average of every 5½ days on campaign finance reform. . . . Of course, that type of corporate, big media, soft money expenditure will not be regulated in this new law.

Why is the press, the institution that has unlimited free speech, so interested in restricting the speech of everyone else? Let's take a closer look. The unconstitutional issue ad restrictions in this bill purport to limit advertising within proximity to an election. However, it does not, interestingly enough, apply to newspaper ads. So the already powerful corporations that control the news—and, in many instances, the public policy—in America will get more power and more money under this new law. . . .

Outside groups such as Common Cause have devoted years and millions of dollars to lobbying this issue in the House and Senate. Why not? Their fundraising will explode if this bill passes. They no longer have to compete with party committees for soft dollars. Shays-Meehan permits every Member of the House and the Senate to raise soft money for these outside groups. . . .

Although the facts about the provisions of this bill are almost always misrepresented, the driving mantra behind the entire movement is that we are all corrupt or that we appear to be corrupt.

We have explored corruption and the appearance of corporation [sic] before in this Chamber. You cannot have corruption unless someone is corrupt. At no time has any Member of either body offered evidence of even the slightest hint of corruption by any Member of either body. As for the appearance of corruption, our friends in the media who are part and parcel of the reform industry continue to make broad and baseless accusations.

. . . These are all soft dollar expenditures used to fuel negative perceptions of Federal officeholders and candidates. Scandal, or perceived scandal, sells papers and gets viewers. In the nonstop competition to be the next Woodward and Bernstein, the reform industry relentlessly works to raise questions in our minds.

In short, I believe that the appearance of corruption is whatever the New York Times says it is. Add to that, cash-strapped, scandal-hungry newspapers and unlimited foundation donations to the reform industry, and you are in full-scale corruption mode. The actual facts are rarely relevant. . . .

With no basis in fact or reality, the media consistently and repeatedly alleges that our every decision can be traced back to money given to support a political party. I trust that every member in the Chamber recognizes how completely absurd, false, and insulting these charges are. We have been derelict in refuting these baseless allegations. I doubt we will ever see a headline that says 99 percent of Congress has never been under an ethics cloud. That is a headline we simply will not see.

Each Member is elected to represent our constituents. We act in what we believe is the best interest of the country and, obviously, of our home States. Does representing the interests of our State and our constituents lead to corruption or the appearance of corruption? These allegations are not an attack on us, they are an attack on representative democracy.

What we are talking about today is speech: the Government telling people how, when, and how much speech they are allowed. This wholesale regulation of every action of every American anytime there is a Federal election is truly unprecedented.

The courts have consistently upheld the free speech rights of individuals and of parties. Even in the most recent case . . . , the Court made clear that parties are not to be treated any worse than any other organization in the protection of constitutional rights. This legislation falls far short of that charge. The Shays-Meehan bill weaves a bizarre web of restrictions and prohibitions around parties and candidates while simultaneously strengthening the power of outside groups and the corporations that own newspapers.

This legislation is remarkable in its scope. Indeed, this legislation seeks no less than a fundamental reworking of the American political system. Our Nation's two-party system has for centuries brought structure and order to our electoral process. This legislation seeks, quite literally, to eliminate any prominence for the role of political parties in American elections. This legislation favors special interests over parties and favors some special interests over other special interests. It treads on the associational rights of groups by compelling them to disclose their membership lists to a greater extent than ever before contemplated. It hampers the ability of national and State parties to support State and local candidates. It places new limits on the political parties' ability to make independent and coordinated expenditures supporting their candidates.

Many of these provisions are directly contrary to existing Supreme Court precedent. . . .

Equally remarkable is the patchwork manner in which this legislation achieves its virtual elimination of political parties from the electoral process. It seeks to achieve a pernicious goal via a haphazard means, and the real loser under this legislation is the American voter, who no longer can rely on the support of a major political party as an indicia of what that candidate stands for.

So let me walk you through how this legislation will affect all of us. First, let's look at the national parties. Shays-Meehan will eliminate nearly 50 percent of the fundraising receipts of the national parties. National parties will be forced to conduct their wide array of Federal and State party activities with only half the revenue. Shays-Meehan will eliminate 90 percent of the cash on hand of the national parties. If Shays-Meehan were law in 2001 the total cash on hand for all six national parties would have dropped from $66 million to $6 million. . . .

What does that all mean? That means this bill eviscerates the national party committees. It singles out six national committees out of all the committees that may exist in America and takes away a huge percentage of their receipts. By eliminating so-called soft money, or non-Federal money, national party support for State parties and local candidates will be dramatically reduced if not entirely eliminated in the next cycle. . . .

It is going to go to outside groups. We, the Members of Congress, will be able to raise it for them. The soft money will also go to the newspapers because they can sell advertising in proximity to the election when no one else can. . . .

Now let's look at issue ad restrictions. The Shays-Meehan issue ad provision muzzles political speech based solely upon the timing of the speech. A person or a group must report to the Government whenever they mention the name of a candidate in any broadcast, cable, or satellite communication within 30 days of a primary or 60 days of a general election. Corporations and labor unions are totally censored during that period. The censorship extends to nonprofit corporations such as the Sierra Club and the NAACP on the left, and the National Right to Life Committee and the NRA on the right. . . .

If this legislation is passed today, the radio ad falls within the issue ad prohibitions and restrictions, so it could not be run, however, the newspaper ad is not affected. . . .

This kind of arbitrary and capricious stifling of political speech is the essence of the issue ad restrictions in this bill. Both advertisements are issue speech. . . . However, only one advertisement invokes the jurisdiction of a newly created speech police. . . .

Reformers are apparently not concerned by the fact that this provision flies in the face of more than a quarter of a century of court decisions striking down such attempts to restrict issue speech. . . .

Although this legislation will pass today, I am confident the Supreme Court will step in to defend the Constitution. . . .

Today is a sad day for our Constitution, a sad day for our democracy, and for our political parties. We are all now complicit in a dramatic transfer of power from challenger-friendly, citizen-action groups known as political parties to outside special interest groups, wealthy individuals, and corporations that own newspapers.

After a decade of making my constitutional arguments to this body, I am eager to become the lead plaintiff in this case and take my argument to the branch of Government charged with the critical task of interpreting our Constitution.

Today is not a moment of great courage for the legislative branch. We have allowed a few powerful editorial pages to prod us into infringing the First Amendment rights of everybody but them. Fortunately, this is the very moment for which the Bill of Rights was enacted. The Constitution is most powerful when our courage is most lacking. . . .

In conclusion, this may be the end of the legislative chapter of this bill, but a new and exciting phase lies ahead as we go to court to seek to uphold the Constitution and protect the rights of individuals, parties and outside groups to comment and engage in political discourse in our country. . . .

❧ 48 ❧

Colorado Amendment 36, Allocating Presidential Electors Proportionally[*]

(2004)

1. Does the "winner-take-all" nature of U.S. elections disenfranchise those individuals who voted for the losing candidate? Does the proportional allocation of presidential electors address this issue?
2. What impact, if any, would a state's allocating its presidential electors on a proportional basis have on how presidential campaigns are conducted in the state?

O N NOVEMBER 2, 2004, Colorado voters rejected an amendment proposed to the state constitution that would have altered the method by which the state assigns presidential electors. The state's constitution may be amended by popular vote if a sufficient number of voters sign petitions to place the proposed amendment on the ballot and a majority of those voting approve. Like all other states (except Maine and Nebraska), Colorado allocates presidential electors using the "unit rule," which means that the presidential candidate receiving the most popular votes in the state wins all of the state's presidential electors.

Amendment 36 would have changed Colorado's system to one that allocated electors based on the proportion of the vote in the state that each presidential or vice presidential candidate received. More specifically, the percentage of the vote that each candidate received would be multiplied by nine and then rounded to the nearest whole number. When the sum of the total exceeded nine, the candidate receiving the fewest popular votes (but at least one electoral vote) would have his or her electoral vote total reduced by one. When the sum of the total was less than nine, the candidate with the most popular votes would have his or her electoral vote total increased by one.

*www.lawanddemocracy.org/pdffiles/COamend36.pdf

Proponents of the amendment argued that the proportional plan ended the disenfranchisement of those who had voted for a losing candidate. Opponents argued that without the winner-take-all nature of electoral allocation, the importance of the state in an election is significantly reduced.

In the end, the amendment failed to pass, getting only 355,712 or 34 percent of the more than one million votes cast. Its failure is easily attributable to the provision that, if passed, Amendment 36 be applied to the 2004 presidential vote in Colorado. The state typically leans Republican in presidential elections—since Lyndon Johnson swept the 1964 election, the only Democrat to win there has been Bill Clinton in 1992 and 1996. By changing the method of allocating electors, Democrats in Colorado could have ensured that John Kerry would receive some electoral votes at the expense of President George W. Bush. As election day grew closer, however, it appeared that Kerry could win the state of Colorado anyway. Thus, many Democrats who initially supported Amendment 36 withdrew their support, deciding to take their chances that Kerry could win all of Colorado's electoral votes (he did not). But even if the amendment had passed, it is highly likely that it would have been challenged in the courts.

Going back four years, if the proportional method had been in place in Colorado in 2000 the outcome of that year's presidential election might have been decided by the House of Representatives. George W. Bush won 50.8 percent of the vote in Colorado; Al Gore won 42.4 percent. Under the plan proposed in Amendment 36, Bush would have received five electoral votes instead of eight. Gore would have led the Electoral College tally by a vote of 269–268, but neither candidate would have received the 270 majority necessary to win outright. However, things could have turned out very differently. If Barbara Lett-Simmons, an Al Gore elector from the District of Columbia, had cast her vote for Gore instead of protesting the District of Columbia's lack of representation in Congress, Al Gore would have won the Electoral College with 270 votes—the minimum needed to win the Electoral College.

Amendment 36
Selection of Presidential Electors

Be it enacted by the People of the State of Colorado:

ARTICLE VII OF THE CONSTITUTION is amended BY THE ADDITION OF A NEW SECTION, to read:

Section 13. Popular proportional selection of presidential electors.

(1)   The People of the state of Colorado hereby find and declare that:

     (a)   The United States Constitution delegates to each state the method of choosing presidential electors who are charged with casting votes in the Electoral College for the offices of president and vice president of the United States;

     (b)   The Colorado Constitution reserves to the people of this state the right to act in the place of the state legislature in any legislative matter, and through enactment of this section, the people do hereby act as the legislature of Colorado for the purpose of changing the manner of electing presidential electors in accordance with the provisions of Article II, Section 1 of the United States Constitution;

     (c)   The right to vote for president of the United States is a fundamental right and each person's vote is entitled to equal dignity and should count equally;

     (d)   The present winner-take-all method of awarding presidential electors in Colorado permits a presidential ticket to receive all of this state's electoral votes even though it wins less than a majority of the ballots cast in this state;

     (e)   The will of the Colorado electorate is best reflected by the popular proportional allocation of Electoral College representatives, based on the number of ballots cast for the respective presidential tickets in this state; and

     (f)   In the strongest possible terms, the voters of Colorado declare that, by approving this initiative, they understand, desire, and expect that the popular proportional selection of presidential electors is intended to apply retroactively and thus determine the manner in which our state's presidential electors are chosen and our state's electoral votes are cast for the general election of 2004.

(2)   The total number of electoral votes to which Colorado is entitled shall be divided among the presidential tickets on the general election bal-

lot, based upon the popular proportional share of the total statewide ballots cast for each presidential ticket, subject to subsections (3) and (4) of this section. Each presidential elector shall vote for the presidential candidate and, by separate ballot, vice-presidential candidate on the presidential ticket of the political party or political organization that nominated that presidential elector.

(3) The allocation of a presidential ticket's popular proportion of this state's electoral votes shall be in whole numbers and shall be made in the following manner:

(a) The total number of ballots cast in this state for each presidential ticket at a general election shall be divided by the total number of ballots cast for all presidential tickets that receive votes at that general election; and

(b) The proportion of a presidential ticket's popular vote, as determined in paragraph (a) of this subsection, shall be multiplied by the number of electoral votes to which Colorado is entitled.

(4) The number of electoral votes that is attributable to the ballots cast for any presidential ticket, as determined in subsection (3) of this section, shall be rounded to the nearest whole number, subject to the following limitations.

(a) No presidential ticket shall receive any electoral votes from this state if its proportion of the total ballots cast for all presidential tickets would reflect less than a full electoral vote after rounding to the nearest whole number.

(b) If the sum of electoral votes allocated pursuant to paragraph (a) of this subsection is greater than the number of electoral votes to which Colorado is entitled:

(I) The allocation of electoral votes to the presidential ticket receiving at least one electoral vote and the fewest number of ballots cast shall be reduced by whole electoral votes until only that number of electoral votes to which Colorado is entitled have been allocated; and

(II) The process set forth in subparagraph (I) of this paragraph shall be repeated if, after the reduction of electoral votes as set forth in subparagraph (I) of this paragraph, the total number of electoral votes allocated to all presidential tickets remains greater than the total number of electoral votes to which this state is entitled, and such process shall be applied to the presidential ticket receiving at least one electoral vote and the next fewest number of ballots cast until the total number of electoral votes allocated to all presidential tickets is equal to the total number of electoral votes to which this state is entitled.

(c) If the sum of all electoral votes allocated would be less than the number of electoral votes to which Colorado is entitled, the presidential ticket receiving the greatest number of ballots cast shall receive any unallocated electoral votes until all of the electoral votes to which Colorado is entitled have been allocated.

(d) If two or more presidential tickets receive the identical total number of ballots cast for all presidential tickets and the allocation of electoral votes to which Colorado is entitled cannot be proportionally allocated in whole electoral votes to these presidential tickets, the secretary of state shall determine by lot which of these presidential tickets will have their number of electoral votes increased or decreased by a whole electoral vote until all of the electoral votes to which Colorado is entitled have been allocated.

(5) (a) A recount of ballots cast for and against this initiative shall be ordered by the secretary of state if the difference between the number of ballots cast for and against this initiative is less than or equal to one-half of one percent of the highest number of ballots cast in the election on this initiative. Where the difference between the number of ballots cast for and against this initiative is greater than one-half of one percent of the highest number of ballots cast in the election on this initiative, a recount in connection with this initiative may be requested by a petition representative identified with this initiative or the registered agent of an issue committee opposing this initiative; provided, however, that any such person or the committee with which he or she is associated shall pay the cost of such recount before the secretary may begin the recount, but if the prevailing side in the election is changed thereby, such amount shall be refunded.

(b) A recount shall be ordered by the secretary of state if:

(I) The difference between the number of ballots cast for any two presidential tickets is less than or equal to one-half of one percent of the ballots cast for the ticket that received the most votes of the two presidential tickets in question; and

(II) At least one of the two presidential tickets, as a result of such recount, could qualify for one or more additional electoral votes.

Where the difference between the number of ballots cast for the two presidential tickets in question is greater than one-half of one percent of the ballots cast for the ticket that received the most votes as between those two tickets, a recount for presidential electors may be requested by a presidential ticket or the political party or political organization associated with such ticket; provided, however, that any such ticket or political party or organization with which it is associated shall pay the cost of such recount before the secretary may begin the recount, but if the election result is changed thereby and an additional electoral vote or votes is awarded to that presidential ticket, such amount shall be refunded.

(c) Any recount authorized pursuant to this subsection shall be ordered or requested not later than 5:00 P.M. on the twenty-third day after the general election at which such ballots are cast and shall be completed and the result shall be certified by the secretary of state not later than close of business on the thirtieth day after the general election at which such ballots are cast.

(6) For purposes of this section only and notwithstanding any other provision of this constitution:

(a) The results of the election on this initiative shall be officially declared by proclamation of the governor which shall be issued after the votes thereon have been canvassed but before noon on:

(i)   The twenty-fourth day following the general election, if no recount is ordered or requested; or

(ii) The thirty-first day following the general election, if a recount is ordered or requested.

(b) The secretary of state shall certify the election of presidential electors, as determined pursuant to this section, but in no event shall such certification be issued later than 2:00 P.M. on:

(i)   The twenty-fourth day following the general election, if no recount is ordered or requested as to such election; or

(ii) The thirty-first day following the general election, if a recount is ordered or requested as to such election.

(c) The election certification process referred to in paragraph (b) of this subsection shall apply to the ballots cast for presidential tickets at the November 2, 2004 general election and at general elections held after 2004 at which presidential tickets are on the statewide ballot.

(7)   The secretary of state shall determine by lot which presidential electors, nominated in conjunction with a presidential ticket that quali-
fies for at least one electoral vote pursuant to this section, shall be entitled to cast electoral votes. For each presidential ticket, the secretary
of state shall then determine by lot the order of nominated presidential electors for that presidential ticket to serve as alternates if any vacancies occur in the office of presidential elector for that presidential
ticket because of death, refusal to act, absence or other cause. Such determinations by lot performed by the secretary of state shall be made
before 3:00 P.M. of the twenty-fourth day following the election if no
recount is ordered or requested and before 3:00 P.M. of the thirty-first
day following such election if a recount is ordered or requested. If the
number of nominated presidential electors for a presidential ticket is
insufficient to allow the secretary of state to fill a vacancy in the office
of presidential elector by lot, the political party or political organization of the presidential ticket for which the vacancy remains shall
nominate the number of additional presidential electors necessary to
fill the vacancy. The secretary of state shall prepare a certificate of
election for each presidential elector entitled to cast an electoral vote.
The governor shall sign and affix the seal of the state to the certificates
and deliver one certificate to each elector on the first Monday after the
second Wednesday of December following a general election.

(8)   The Supreme Court shall have original jurisdiction for the adjudica-
tion of all contests concerning presidential electors and shall prescribe
rules for practice and proceedings for such contests. Contests concerning the election of presidential electors shall be given the highest priority on the court's calendar and shall be expedited in all respects, including hearing and decision. The court shall render its final decision
in any contest concerning presidential electors not later than the first
Friday after the second Wednesday of December following a general
election. No justice of the court who is a contestor in the election
shall be permitted to hear and determine the matter.

(9)   This section shall be effective on and after November 3, 2004.

(10)   This section shall be liberally construed to achieve popular proportional allocation of presidential electors at the 2004 general election.

(11)   The general assembly may enact legislation to change the manner of
selecting presidential electors or any of the procedures related thereto.

(12)   For purposes of this section:

(a) "Presidential ticket" means candidates for president and vice
president of the United States who run for their respective offices
jointly in Colorado.

    (b) "Rounded to the nearest whole number" means:

        (I) Increased to the next whole number if the fractional proportion of an electoral vote allocated is equal to or greater than .5; and

        (II) Decreased to the preceding whole number if the fractional proportion of an electoral vote allocated is less than .5.

    (c) "This initiative" means the voter-initiated constitutional amendment, approved at the November 2, 2004 general election, providing for popular proportional selection of presidential electors.

    (d) "Whole number" means a positive integer, including zero.

(13) If any provision of this section or any part thereof is, for any reason, held to be invalid or unconstitutional, the remaining provisions shall not be affected, but shall remain in full force and effect, and to this end, the provisions of this section are severable.

❧ 49 ❧
Memo of Understanding Regarding the Presidential Debates between George W. Bush and John Kerry*
(2004)

1. Would an independent, nonpartisan debate sponsor accomplish a more meaningful dialogue than that negotiated by the two major parties? If so, how?

2. Should third-party candidates be included in presidential debates? If so, under what circumstances?

IN THE 1976, 1980, AND 1984 ELECTIONS the League of Women Voters (LWV) served as the nonpartisan sponsor of presidential debates. As such, it was responsible for issuing invitations to the candidates, determining the debate format, and securing moderators and panelists.

*www.c-span.org/pdf/memounderstanding.pdf

Everything worked well in the 1976 election. In the 1980 presidential election, however, the LWV met resistance from President Jimmy Carter's campaign over the inclusion of independent candidate John Anderson. Carter perceived Anderson's candidacy as a greater threat to his own than it did to Governor Reagan, so when Carter refused to debate Anderson, the LWV sponsored two debates: John Anderson and the Republican nominee, Ronald Reagan, participated in the first; Reagan and Carter participated in the second. In 1984, both campaigns rejected most of the LWV's recommendations for panelists, arguing they were either too biased or too incompetent. As a result, the LWV was forced to change its selection process for moderators and panelists.

In 1986, Charles Mannat, chair of the Democratic National Committee, and Frank Fahrenkopf, chair of the Republican National Committee, formed the bipartisan Commission on Presidential Debates (CPD). The purpose of the CPD was to implement joint sponsorship of general election presidential and vice-presidential debates between nominees of the Democratic and Republican Parties starting in 1988.

The LWV and the CPD agreed to sponsor one debate each in 1988. As the LWV was preparing to negotiate with the campaigns over the format of its debate, each campaign provided a Memorandum of Understanding between the two campaigns effectively dictating specific details of the debate negotiated by the campaigns and without the input of the LWV. The leadership of the LWV decided to withdraw its sponsorship and issued a press release critical of the two campaign organizations. Thus, the CPD became the only sponsor of debates after 1988.

Since then, representatives from the two major parties meet to negotiate the details of the presidential debates for each election cycle. These documents outline guidelines that govern the preparation for and conduct of the presidential and vice-presidential debates. The principal criticisms of this approach are that candidates of minor parties are excluded (with the exception of Ross Perot, who received substantial support in the polls in 1992), and the format provides for less meaningful deliberation between the candidates than could be achieved by an independent, nonpartisan sponsor.

The memorandum of understanding for the 2004 presidential debates was negotiated by Democrat Vernon Jordan and Republican James Baker and was issued on September 20, 2004. In the negotiation each campaign got what they wanted from the other. The Bush campaign wanted viewers to know when Senator Kerry was taking too much time. So the Kerry team conceded to allowing colored lights and audio beeps to appear on camera. The Bush team conceded to having three debates instead of two—Kerry's campaign advisers recognized that the more often the challenger appears on stage with an incumbent president the better.

***

Memorandum of Understanding

This Memorandum of Understanding constitutes an agreement between Kerry-Edwards, '04, Inc. and Bush-Cheney, '04, Inc. (the "campaigns") regarding the rules that will govern debates in which the campaigns participate in 2004. This agreement shall be binding upon the Bush-Cheney and Kerry-Edwards Campaigns and, provided it agrees to sponsor the debates by executing this agreement on or before September 22, 2004, upon the Commission on Presidential Debates (the "Commission").

1. Number, Dates, Time, Locations, Topics
   (a) Presidential Debates

Date	Location
Thursday, September 30	University of Miami
	Coral Gables, Florida
Friday, October 8	Washington University in St. Louis
	St. Louis, Missouri
Wednesday, October 13	Arizona State University
	Tempe, Arizona

   (b) Vice Presidential Debate

Date	Location
Tuesday, October 5	Case Western Reserve University
	Cleveland, Ohio

   (c) Each debate shall begin at 9 p.m., Eastern Daylight Time.
   (d) The parties agree that they will not (1) issue any challenges for additional debates, (2) appear at any other debate or adversarial forum with any other presidential or vice presidential candidate, or (3) accept any television or radio air time offers that involve a debate format or otherwise involve the simultaneous appearance of more than one candidate.

(e) The topic of the September 30 debate shall be foreign policy and homeland security. The topic of the October 13 debate shall be economic and domestic policy. The October 5 vice presidential debate and the October 8 presidential debate shall not be limited by topic and shall include an equal number of questions related to foreign policy and homeland security on the one hand and economic and domestic policy on the other.

2. Sponsorship

The two campaigns will participate in four debates sponsored by the Commission. . . .

3. Participants

If one or more candidates from campaigns other than the two (2) signatories is invited to participate pursuant to those Selection Criteria, those candidates shall be included in the debates, if those candidates accept the terms of this agreement. . . .

4. Moderator

(a) Each debate will have a single moderator.

(b) The parties have accepted the Commission's recommendations of the below listed moderators, provided that each proposed moderator executes a copy of this agreement at least seven (7) days prior to the debate that individual is to moderate in order to evidence his or her understanding and acceptance of, and agreement to, the provisions hereof pertaining to moderators. . . .

  (i) Jim Lehrer for the first presidential debate, September 30, 2004 at the University of Miami;

  (ii) Charles Gibson for the second presidential debate, October 8, 2004 at Washington University in St. Louis;

  (iii) Bob Schieffer for the third presidential debate, October 13, 2004 at Arizona State University, and;

  (iv) Gwen Ifill for the vice presidential debate, October 5, 2004 at the Case Western Reserve University.

5. Rules Applicable to All Debates

The following rules shall apply to each of the four debates:

(a) Each debate shall last for ninety (90) minutes.

(b) For each debate there shall be no opening statements, but each candidate may make a two (2) minute closing statement.

(c) No props, notes, charts, diagrams, or other writings or other tangible things may be brought into the debate by any candidate. Neither candidate may reference or cite any specific individual sitting in a debate audience at any time during a debate. . . .

(d) Notwithstanding subparagraph 5(c), the candidates may take notes during the debate on the size, color, and type of paper each prefers and using the type of pen or pencil that each prefers. . . .

(e) Neither film footage nor video footage nor any audio excerpts from the debates may be used publicly by either candidate's campaign through any means, including but not limited to, radio, television, internet, or videotapes, whether broadcast or distributed in any other manner.

(f) The candidates may not ask each other direct questions, but may ask rhetorical questions.

(g) The order of questioning and closing statements shall be determined as follows: The Commission will conduct a coin toss. . . .

(h) Each candidate shall determine the manner by which he prefers to be addressed by the moderator and shall communicate this to the Commission, at least forty eight (48) hours before the September 30 debate.

(i) Whether or not a debate runs beyond the planned ending time, each candidate shall be entitled to make a closing statement in accordance with subparagraph (b). The Commission shall use its best efforts to ensure that the TV networks carry the entire debate even if it runs past the specified ending time.

(j) No question shall be asked of a candidate by the moderator if less than six (6) minutes remain in the scheduled time of the debate.

(k) The candidates shall not address each other with proposed pledges.

(l) In each debate, the moderator shall:

  (i) open and close the debate and enforce all time limits. In each instance where a candidate exceeds the permitted time for comment, the moderators shall interrupt and remind both the candidate and the audience of the expiration of the time limit and call upon such candidate to observe the strict time limits which have been agreed upon herein by stating, "I am sorry . . . [Senator Kerry or President Bush as the case may be] . . . your time is up";

  (ii) use his or her best efforts to ensure that the questions are reasonably well balanced in all debates and within the designated subject matter areas of the September 30 and October 13 debates in terms of addressing a wide range of issues of major public interest facing the United States and the world;

(iii)   vary the topics on which he or she questions the candidates and ensure that the topics of the questions are fairly apportioned between the candidates;

(iv)   use best efforts to ensure that the two candidates speak for approximately equal amounts of time during the course of each debate, and;

(v)   use any reasonable method to ensure that the agreed-upon format is followed by the candidates and the audience.

6.   Additional Rules Applicable to September 30 and October 13 Debates
For the September 30 and October 13 debates, the candidates will appear at podiums. The September 30 and October 13 debates shall be governed by the rules set forth in section 5 and the following additional rules:

(a)   There shall be no audience participation in the September 30 and October 13 debates. . . . The moderator shall direct the first question to the candidate determined by the procedure set forth in subparagraph 5(g). The candidate receiving the question shall be entitled to give an opening response not to exceed two (2) minutes, and thereafter the other candidate shall be permitted to comment on the question and/or the first candidate's answer for up to one and one-half (1½) minutes. Thereafter the moderator in his discretion may extend the discussion for a period of time not to exceed sixty (60) seconds, but the moderator shall begin each such discussion by calling upon the candidate who first received the question. To the extent that the moderator opens extended discussion, the moderator shall use best efforts to ensure that each candidate has a maximum of approximately thirty (30) seconds to comment in the extended discussion period.

(b)   The moderator shall then ask a question of the other candidate, and the answer, comments by the other candidate, and extension of discussion by the moderator shall be conducted as set out in paragraph 6(a) above for the first question. Thereafter the moderator shall follow the procedure in paragraph 6(a) above by asking a question of the first candidate and shall continue with questions of the candidates in rotation until the time for closing statements occurs.

(c)   During the extended discussion of a question, no candidate may speak for more than thirty (30) seconds.

(d) The moderator shall manage the debate so that the candidates address at least sixteen (16) questions.

(e) At no time during these debates shall either candidate move from their designated area behind their respective podiums.

7. Additional Rules Applicable to October 8 Debate
The October 8 debate will be conducted in an audience participation ("town hall") format. This debate shall be governed by the rules set forth in section 5 and the following additional rules:

(a) There shall be no audience participation in the October 8 debate other than as described below. . . . The moderator shall facilitate audience members in asking questions to each of the candidates, beginning with the candidate determined by the procedure set forth in subparagraph 5(h). The candidate to whom the question is initially directed shall have up to two (2) minutes to respond, after which the other candidate shall have up to one and one-half (1½) minutes to respond to the question and/or to comment on the first candidate's answer. Thereafter, the moderator, in his or her discretion, may extend the discussion of that question for sixty (60) seconds, but the moderator shall begin each such discussion by calling upon the candidate who first received the question. The moderator shall balance additional discussion of the question with the interest in addressing a wide range of topics during the debate. To the extent that the moderator opens extended discussion, the moderator shall use best efforts to ensure that each candidate has a maximum of approximately thirty (30) seconds to comment in the extended discussion period.

(b) After completion of the discussion of the first question, the moderator shall call upon an audience member to direct a question to the candidate to whom the first question was not directed, and follow the procedure outlined in paragraph 7(a) above. Thereafter, the moderator shall follow the procedures in this paragraph by calling upon another audience member to ask a question of the first candidate and shall continue facilitating questions of the candidates in rotation until the time for closing statements occurs.

(c) During the extended discussion of a question, no candidate may speak for more than thirty (30) seconds.

(d) The audience members shall not ask follow-up questions or otherwise participate in the extended discussion, and the audience member's microphone shall be turned off after he or she completes asking the question.

(e) Prior to the start of the debate, audience members will be asked to submit their questions in writing to the moderator. No third party, including both the Commission and the campaigns, shall be permitted to see the questions. The moderator shall approve and select all questions to be posed by the audience members to the candidates. The moderator shall ensure that the audience members pose to the candidates an equal number of questions on foreign policy and homeland security on the one hand and economic and domestic policy on the other. The moderator will further review the questions and eliminate any questions that the moderator deems inappropriate. At least seven (7) days before the October 8 debate the moderator shall develop, and describe to the campaigns, a method for selecting questions at random while assuring that questions are reasonably well balanced in terms of addressing a wide range of issues of major public interest facing the United States and the world. Each question selected will be asked by the audience member submitting that question. If any audience member poses a question or makes a statement that is in any material way different than the question that the audience member earlier submitted to the moderator for review, the moderator will cut-off the questioner and advise the audience that such non-reviewed questions are not permitted. . . .

(f) The debate will take place before a live audience of between 100 and 150 persons who shall be seated and who describe themselves as likely voters who are "soft" Bush supporters or "soft" Kerry supporters as to their 2004 presidential vote. The number of "soft" Bush supporters shall equal the number of "soft" Kerry supporters in the audience. The moderator shall ensure that an equal number of "soft" Bush supporters and "soft" Kerry supporters pose questions to the candidates. These participants will be selected by the Gallup organization ("Gallup"). Gallup shall have responsibility for selecting the nationally demographically representative group of voters. At least fourteen (14) days prior to October 8, Gallup shall provide a comprehensive briefing on the selection methodology to the campaigns, and both the Kerry-Edwards Campaign and the Bush-Cheney Campaign shall approve the methodology. Either campaign may raise objections on the methodology to Gallup and to the Commission within twenty-four (24) hours of the briefing. . . .

8. Additional Rules Applicable to October 5 Debate

For the October 5 vice presidential debate, the candidates will be seated at a table with the moderator. This debate shall be governed by the rules set forth in sections 5 and 6. There shall be no audience participation in the October 5 vice presidential debate. At the start of the October 5 debate and in the event of and in each instance whereby an audience member(s) attempts to participate in the debate by any means thereafter, the moderator shall instruct the audience to refrain from any participation in the debate as described in section 9(a) (viii) below.

9. Staging

   (a) The following rules apply to each of the four debates:

       (i)   All staging arrangements for the debates not specifically addressed in this agreement shall be jointly addressed by representatives of the two campaigns.

       (ii) The Commission will conduct a coin toss at least seventy-two hours before the September 30 debate. At that time, the winner of the coin toss shall have the option of choosing stage position for the September 30 debate; The loser of the coin toss will have first choice of stage position for the October 8 debate. . . . The stage position for the October 13 debate will be determined by a coin toss to take place at least seventy-two (72) hours before the debate. The stage position for the October 5 vice presidential debate will be determined by a separate coin toss to take place at least seventy-two (72) hours before the debate.

       (iii) For the September 30, October 8, and October 13 debates, the candidates shall enter the stage upon a verbal cue by the moderator after the program goes on the air, proceed to center stage, shake hands, and proceed directly to their positions behind their podiums or their stools in the case of the October 8 debate. For the October 5 vice presidential debate, the candidates shall be pre-positioned before the program goes on the air, and immediately after the program goes on the air the candidates shall shake hands.

       (iv) Except as provided in subparagraph (d) (viii) of this paragraph 9, TV cameras will be locked into place during all debates. They may, however, tilt or rotate as needed.

(v) Except as provided in subparagraph (d) (viii), TV coverage during the question and answer period shall be limited to shots of the candidates or moderator and in no case shall any television shots be taken of any member of the audience (including candidates' family members) from the time the first question is asked until the conclusion of the closing statements. When a candidate is speaking, either in answering a question or making his closing statement, TV coverage will be limited to the candidate speaking. There will be no TV cut-aways to any candidate who is not responding to a question while another candidate is answering a question or to a candidate who is not giving a closing statement while another candidate is doing so.

(vi) The camera located at the rear of the stage shall be used only to take shots of the moderator.

(vii) For each debate each candidate shall have camera-mounted, timing lights corresponding to the timing system described in section 9(b) (vi) below positioned in his line of sight. For each debate additional timing lights, corresponding to the timing system described in section 9(b) (vi) below, shall be placed such that they are visible to the debate audiences and television viewers.

(viii) All members of the debate audiences will be instructed by the moderator before the debate goes on the air and by the moderator after the debate goes on the air not to applaud, speak, or otherwise participate in the debate by any means other than by silent observation. . . .

(ix) The Commission shall use best efforts to maintain an appropriate temperature according to industry standards for the entire debate.

(x) Each candidate shall be permitted to have a complete, private production and technical briefing and walk-through ("Briefing") at the location of the debate on the day of the debate. . . .

(xi) The color and style of the backdrop will be recommended by the Commission and mutually determined by representatives of the campaigns. . . .

(xii) The set will be completed and lit no later than 3 p.m. at the debate site on the day before the debate will occur.

(xiii) Each candidate may use his own makeup person, and adequate facilities shall be provided at the debate site for makeup.

(xiv) In addition to Secret Service personnel, the President's military aide, and the President's physician and the Vice President's military aide and the Vice President's physician, each candidate will be permitted to have one (1) pre-designated staff member in the wings or in the immediate backstage area during the debate at a location to be mutually agreed upon by representatives of the campaigns at each site. All other staff must vacate the wings or immediate backstage areas no later than five (5) minutes before the debate commences. A PL phone line will be provided between each candidate's staff work area and the producer.

(xv) Other than security personnel not more than two (2) aides will accompany each candidate on the stage before the program begins.

(xvi) Each candidate shall be allowed to have one (1) professional still photographer present on the stage before the debate begins and in the wings during the debate as desired and on the stage immediately upon the conclusion of the debate. No photos shall be taken from the wings by these photographers during the debate. Photos taken by these photographers may be distributed to the press as determined by each candidate.

(b) In addition to the rules in subparagraph (a) the following rules apply to the September 30 and October 13 debates:

(i) The Commission shall construct the podiums and each shall be identical to view from the audience side. The podiums shall measure fifty (50) inches from the stage floor to the outside top of the podium facing the audience and shall measure forty-eight (48) inches from the stage floor to the top of the inside podium writing surface facing the respective candidates, and otherwise shall be constructed in the style and specifications recommended by the Commission, shown in attachment A. There shall be no writings or markings of any kind on the fronts of the podiums. No candidate shall be permitted to use risers or any other device to create an impression of elevated height, and no candidate shall be permitted to use chairs, stools, or other seating devices during the debate.

(ii)   Each podium shall have installed a fixed hardwired micro-
       phone, and an identical microphone to be used as backup per
       industry standards.

(iii) The podiums will be equally canted toward the center of the
       stage at a degree to be determined by the Commission's pro-
       ducer. The podiums shall be ten (10) feet apart; such distance
       shall be measured from the left-right center of a podium to
       the left-right center of the other podium.

(iv)   The moderator will be seated at a table so as to be positioned
       in front, between, and equidistant from the candidates, and
       between the cameras to which the candidates direct their
       answers.

(v)   As soon as possible, the Commission shall submit for joint
       consultation with the campaigns a diagram for camera
       placement.

(vi)   At least seven (7) days before the September 30 debate the
       Commission shall recommend a system, to be used as a
       model for each successive debate, of visible and audible time
       cues and placement subject to approval by both campaigns.
       Such a system shall be comprised of camera mounted timing
       lights placed in the line of sight of each candidate and addi-
       tional timing lights that are clearly visible to both the de-
       bate audiences and television viewers. Time cues in the form
       of colored lights will be given to the candidates and the
       moderator when there are thirty (30) seconds remaining, fif-
       teen (15) seconds remaining, and five (5) seconds remaining,
       respectively for the two (2) minute, one and one-half (1½)
       minute, and sixty (60) second response times permitted un-
       der section 6(a). Pursuant to Section 5(l) (i) the moderators
       shall enforce the strict time limits described in this agree-
       ment. The Commission shall provide for an audible cue an-
       nouncing the end of time for each of the candidate's re-
       sponses, rebuttals and rejoinder time periods to be used in
       the event the moderator(s) fail to take action to enforce the
       strict time limits described in this Agreement. The audible
       cue shall be clearly audible to both candidates, the debate
       audiences and television viewers. The Commission shall
       commence the use of the audible cue and continue its use
       through the conclusion of any debate where a moderator

fails to take the action described in Section 5(l) (i) after two (2) instances in which either candidate has exceeded the time for responses, rebuttals, or rejoinders described in this Agreement.

(c) In addition to the rules in subparagraph (a), the following rules apply to the October 5 vice presidential debate:

    (i) The Commission shall construct the table according to the style and specifications proposed by the Commission in consultation with each campaign. The moderator shall be facing the candidates with his or her back to the audience.

    (ii) The chairs shall be swivel chairs that can be locked in place, and shall be of equal height.

    (iii) Each candidate and the moderator shall have a wireless lapel microphone, and an identical microphone to be used as a backup per industry standards.

    (iv) At least seven (7) days before the October 5 debate the Commission shall recommend a system of time cues and placement subject to approval by both campaigns and consistent with the visual and audible time cues described in section 9(b) (vi).

    (v) As soon as possible, the Commission shall submit for joint consultation with each campaign a diagram for camera placement.

    (vi) The candidates shall remain seated throughout the debate.

(d) In addition to the rules in subparagraph (a), the following rules apply to the October 8 debate:

    (i) The candidates shall be seated on stools before the audience, which shall be seated in approximately a horseshoe arrangement as symmetrically as possible around the candidates. . . .

    (ii) The stools shall be identical and have backs and a footrest. . . .

    (iii) Each candidate shall have a place to put a glass of water and paper and pens or pencils for taking notes (in accordance with subparagraph 5(d)) of sufficient height to allow note taking while sitting on the stool, . . .

    (iv) Each candidate may move about in a predesignated area, as proposed by the Commission in consultation with each campaign, and may not leave that area while the debate is underway. The pre-designated areas of the candidates may not overlap.

(v) Each candidate shall have a choice of either wireless hand held microphone or wireless lapel microphone to allow him to move about as provided for in subparagraph (iv) above and to face different directions while responding to questions from the audience.

(vi) As soon as possible, the Commission shall submit for joint consultation by the campaigns a diagram for camera placement.

(vii) At least seven (7) days before the October 8 debate the Commission shall recommend a system of time cues subject to approval by both campaigns, and consistent with the visual and audible cues described in sections 9(b) (vi).

(viii) Notwithstanding sections 9(a) (iv) and 9(a) (v) a roving camera may be used for shots of an audience member only during the time that audience member is asking a question.

(ix) Prior to the start of the debate neither the moderator nor any other person shall engage in a "warm up" session with the audience by engaging in a question or answer session or by delivering preliminary remarks.

10. Ticket Distribution and Seating Arrangements

(a) The Commission shall be responsible for printing and ensuring security of all tickets to all debates. Each campaign shall be entitled to receive directly from the Commission one-third of the available tickets (excluding those allocated to the participating audience in the October 8 debate), with the remaining one-third going to the Commission.

(b) In the audience participation debate, the participating audience shall be separated from any nonparticipating audience, and steps shall be taken to ensure that the participating audience is admitted to the debate site without contact with the campaigns, the media, or the nonparticipating audience.

(c) The Commission shall allocate tickets to the two (2) campaigns in such a manner to ensure that supporters of each candidate are interspersed with supporters of the other candidate. . . .

(d) Any media seated in the auditorium shall be accommodated only in the last two (2) rows of the auditorium farthest from the stage. Two (2) still photo stands may be positioned near either side of the television camera stands located in the audience. . . .

(e) Tickets will be delivered by the Commission to the chairman of each candidate's campaign or his designated representative by 12:00 noon on the day preceding each debate. . . .

11. Dressing Rooms/Holding Rooms
   (a) Each candidate shall have a dressing room available of adequate size so as to provide private seclusion for that candidate and adequate space for the staff the candidate desires to have in this area. The two (2) dressing rooms shall be comparable in size and in quality and in proximity and access to the debate stage.
   (b) An equal number of other backstage rooms will be available for other staff members of each candidate. Each candidate shall have a minimum of eight (8) such rooms, five (5) of which shall be in the debate facility itself, and three (3) of which shall be located next to the press center. The rooms located next to the media center shall be located so that each campaign has equal proximity and ease of access to the media center. . .
   (c) The number of individuals allowed in these rooms or trailers shall be determined by each candidate. The Commission shall issue backstage passes (if needed) to the candidates' representatives as requested.
   (d) The Commission shall provide each candidate with a direct television feed from the production truck to two (2) monitors placed in the candidate's dressing room and staff holding rooms as requested by the candidates' representatives. . . .

12. Media
   (a) Each candidate will receive not fewer than thirty (30) press passes for the Media Center during the debate and more if mutually agreed upon by the campaigns.
   (b) Each candidate will be allowed to have an unlimited number of people in the Media Center upon the conclusion of the debate.
   (c) The Commission will be responsible for all media credentialing.

13. Survey Research
   The sponsor of the debates agrees that it shall not, prior to two days after the Presidential Inauguration of 2005, release publicly or to the media or otherwise make publicly available any survey research (including polls or focus group results or data) concerning the performance of the

candidates in the debate or the preferences of the individuals surveyed for either candidate.

14. Complete Agreement

This memorandum of understanding constitutes the entire agreement between the parties concerning the debates in which the campaigns will participate in 2004.

15. Amendments

This Agreement will not be changed or amended except in writing signed by those persons who signed this Agreement or their designees.

16. Ratification and Acknowledgement

The undersigned moderators selected by the Commission agree to the terms contained herein and agree to fulfill their responsibilities as described in the Agreement.

≈§ 50 §≈

The Price-Herman Commission Report[*]

(2005)

1. What effect, if any, does a front-loaded primary calendar have on the presidential nomination process? Are the political parties strengthened or weakened by moving primaries and caucuses forward?
2. Does permitting Iowa to hold its caucuses first and New Hampshire to hold its primary first affect the outcome of the presidential nomination process? Are there alternatives to this precedent that should be considered?

IT CAN BE DIFFICULT to keep voters' attention during many months of campaigning. To keep them focused, candidates must spend money and a lot of it. In addition, expensive, divisive nomination campaigns

---

*Report of the Commission on Presidential Nomination Timing and Scheduling, Democratic National Committee, December 10, 2005.

can weaken a party's prospects of winning the presidency come November. As a result, political parties prefer to create an environment in which it is easier to find consensus among voters and wrap up the party's presidential nomination as quickly as possible. In 1980 the Democratic Party established a time period, or "window," in which state parties are allowed to schedule presidential primaries and caucuses. And since primary and caucus dates are set by the legislature in many states, Republicans are often obligated to adopt the same or a similar date.

When the Democrats adopted their rules establishing the window for holding primaries and caucuses, they also informally permitted Iowa and New Hampshire to continue their tradition of holding the first caucus and primary, respectively, and formally exempted them from this requirement in 1984. To attain the same level of influence in the presidential nomination process, many other states moved their primaries or caucuses to earlier dates within the permitted time period (or even earlier). The principal reason for "frontloading" the primary calendar was that most, if not all, candidates are forced to withdraw from the nomination process before most states hold their primaries or caucuses because of a lack of support among partisan voters or a lack of campaign funds. States that held early primaries and caucuses enjoyed a disproportionate influence over who became the party's nominee.

Things got even more complicated when, in an effort to secure a nominee early in the calendar year, the Republican Party established its own window for holding primaries and caucuses. This window opened a month before the Democratic window was scheduled to open in 2000. The Democrats, in response, advanced the opening of their window by a month in 2004. The result that year was a presidential nomination cycle that began earlier and was over faster than any before it.

After the Democratic National Committee (DNC) adopted rules for delegate selection in the 2004 presidential nomination cycle in January 2002, the Democratic leadership in Michigan objected very strongly to the exceptions to the rules that had been made for Iowa and New Hampshire. The following year the Michigan Democratic Party indicated that it would submit a plan for selecting delegates to the national convention that provided for the Michigan primary to be held the same day as the New Hampshire primary. This proposal generated a strong reaction from the Democratic leaders in Iowa and New Hampshire, along with intense coverage from the news media. Michigan finally relented and agreed to hold its 2004 primary within the time period permitted by the DNC, but in return the DNC agreed to review the scheduling of primaries and caucuses in preparation for the 2008 nomination calendar.

On July 25, 2004, delegates at the Democratic National Convention passed a resolution sponsored by Sen. Carl Levin of Michigan, former DNC chair Terry McAuliffe, and National Committeewoman Debbie Dingell of Michigan to create a commission for the purpose of studying the timing and scheduling of Democratic primaries and caucuses. The co-chairs of this Commission on Presidential Nomination Timing and Scheduling were Rep. David Price of North Carolina and Alexis Herman, secretary of labor under President Bill Clinton. The Price-Herman Commission was charged with examining the presidential primary and caucus schedule and recommending changes for the 2008 nomination cycle. After holding five public meetings from March 12, 2005, until mid-December in Washington, D.C., the commission submitted its final report to the chair of the Democratic National Committee, former Vermont governor Howard Dean, on December 10, 2005.

In this report, the commission recommended that in addition to Iowa and New Hampshire two states be permitted to hold primaries or caucuses before the window starts on February 5. The Democrats decided to generate greater regional representation by allowing Nevada to schedule its caucuses early and South Carolina to schedule its primary early. However, both Michigan and Florida scheduled their primaries before February 5 as well, despite the possibility that the DNC could impose the substantial penalty of losing 50 percent of their delegates to the convention. Ultimately, the leadership of the Democratic National Committee's Rules and Bylaws Committee did decide to strip both states of their delegates to the national nominating convention. While each state may still petition at the convention to have its delegates seated, the Democratic candidates are not campaigning in either state.

Findings and Recommendations

Pre-Window Period

The questions considered by the Commission with respect to the pre-window period, initially, were whether any contests should be permitted within that period; if so, whether the Iowa caucuses and New Hampshire primary should be designated in the rules; whether other state contests should be allowed to take place within that period; and, if so, how many and when. The Commission examined and discussed a number of different scenarios and alternatives relative to these questions.

With respect to these issues, the Commission found that:

1. There was consensus among its members that the goal of the nominating process should be to produce the best and strongest Democratic presidential nominee; and that that goal is best achieved by devising a system that gives Democratic candidates an opportunity to present themselves and their views to a broad range of voters and gives voters an opportunity to see, hear and question the candidates and measure them against one another.

2. Commission members understand and appreciate the valuable role the Iowa caucuses and New Hampshire primary have played in the Democratic nominating process over many election cycles. These are key swing states whose caucus participants and primary voters are informed and engaged. The processes in these states subject candidates to "retail politics" involving extensive face to face discussions with voters in addition to the pervasive influence of money and media. The presentations made on behalf of Iowa and New Hampshire state parties were thoughtful, detailed and persuasive in this regard.

3. At the same time, a majority of the Commission members expressed serious concerns that Iowa and New Hampshire are not fully reflective of the Democratic electorate or the national electorate generally—and therefore do not place Democratic candidates before a representative range of voters in the critical early weeks of the process.

First, Iowa and New Hampshire together account for only about 1.4% of the nation's population as of 2004. New Hampshire ranks 41st out of 50 states in population. Together they select a total of just 11 of the 540 electors in the Electoral College.

Second, Iowa and New Hampshire do not represent the racial and ethnic diversity of the Party or of the Nation. It has been often noted that the African

American community is the most loyal constituency of the Party, and that the Hispanic/Latino vote—for which the Republicans competed strongly in 2004—is a growing share of the total electorate and a key to the Party's future. Yet, according to the U.S. Census Bureau 2004 American Community Survey, 2.2% of Iowa's population is African American and 0.8% of New Hampshire's population is African American, compared to 12.2% for the nation as a whole. In terms of African American population, Iowa ranks 40th out of 50 states and New Hampshire ranks 43rd.

The 2004 Census data indicate that the Hispanic/Latino population of Iowa was 3.7% and that of New Hampshire was 2.1% compared to 14.2% for the nation as a whole.

Third, these two states alone cannot and do not represent the geographic diversity that is increasingly critical to the future of the Democratic Party. As matters stand, no Western or Southern state has any role in the pre-window period. The Commission heard substantial testimony—from Rep. Solis, from Mr. Pineda, from the Democrats for the West group, from a Nebraska DNC member and others—that the Party has made significant inroads in state and local elections in the Western states, that the Western states are critical to the Party's future, and that it is imperative that Western states be given a greater role in the process. A similar logic applies to the South, where the DNC has given priority to rebuilding State Parties.

4. Commission members' concerns were reinforced by the testimony of numerous presenters. . . .

5. From different perspectives, a number of presenters also expressed the view, shared by many Commission members, that the disproportionate influence of Iowa and New Hampshire means that, even apart from considerations of diversity and representation, too few voters, too small a slice of the electorate, truly get to participate in the nominating process in a meaningful way. . . .

In balancing these considerations, the Commission considered a number of alternatives. One way to redress the disproportionate influence of Iowa and New Hampshire would be simply to include them in the regular window period, which is exactly how these states' contests are treated under the current Republican Party rules. This alternative would address many of the concerns noted above and would have the advantage of matching the Democratic calendar to that of the Republicans.

Another alternative would be to allow one or more states to hold caucuses prior to, or on the same day as, Iowa, and/or to allow one or more states to hold primaries prior to, or on the same day as, New Hampshire.

In the end, a majority of Commission members favored an approach that would preserve the first in the nation status of Iowa and New Hampshire but address the diversity, representation and participation issues in a meaningful way by including other states in the pre-window period, in a schedule in which they would play an important role alongside Iowa and New Hampshire. . . .

Accordingly, the Commission recommends for the 2008 nominating process:

a. That the first caucus be held in Iowa and the first primary be held in New Hampshire.

b. That there be an additional one or two first-tier caucuses between the Iowa caucus and the New Hampshire primary.

c. That following the New Hampshire primary, and prior to the opening of the regular window on February 5, 2008, there be one or two presidential preference primaries.

d. That the Rules and Bylaws Committee select the appropriate date on which the pre-window period shall begin, which date shall under no circumstances be earlier than January 14, 2008.

e. That the Rules and Bylaws Committee determine the states (other than Iowa and New Hampshire) whose contests may occur during the pre-window period, applying the following criteria: racial and ethnic diversity; regional diversity; and economic diversity including union density.

In making these recommendations, the Commission emphasizes the following additional points:

The Commission desires to ensure, to the greatest extent possible, that the inclusion of additional contests in the pre-window period not exacerbate the problem of front-loading (a problem described in more detail in the next section). The Commission urges the Rules and Bylaws Committee, in selecting the states (in addition to Iowa and New Hampshire), whose contests will be allowed to occur in the pre-window period, to consider an appropriate means to limit the aggregate number of delegates allocated through pre-window contests.

Commission members desire that there be an orderly process of establishing and implementing the Delegate Selection Rules for 2008 and that there be clarity and certainty for state parties called upon to develop and submit their delegate selection plans. The Commission urges the Rules and Bylaws Committee to adopt a process for determination of the additional states whose contests will be allowed to occur during the pre-window period, a process in which state parties may apply to the RBC for consideration and in which the RBC will expeditiously consider such applications and make its determination early in 2006. Prior to completion of that process, and the determination of the RBC, no state party should take or permit any action, and no state's legislature should take any action, to schedule the date of that state's contest for any time prior to the start of the regular window (February 5, 2008).

The Commission desires and expects that, to the extent these recommendations are incorporated into the 2008 Delegate Selection Rules developed by the RBC and adopted by the DNC, the RBC will vigorously enforce those Rules. In this regard, the Commission notes that under current Rule 19.C(1) of the 2004 Delegate Selection Rules, if a state's delegate selection plan violates the timing rules, the number of pledged delegates from that state is automatically reduced by 50% and none of the states' DNC members or other unpledged delegates shall be credentialed as voting delegates at the Convention. It should be further noted that, as explained above, under the Republican Party rules, a state whose event is held outside the regular Republican window (beginning February 5, 2008, with no exceptions for any state) automatically suffers a 50% loss of delegates if delegates are elected before the call to the Convention is issued, and a cut of 90% if delegates are elected after the call is issued. The penalty is automatic and the chairman of the RNC is to impose it automatically. There is no appeal from these penalties.

Inside the Window Period

The continued front-loading of the nominating process has been steady and inexorable. Not only has the process started even earlier; it has also concluded ever earlier; as increasing percentages of delegates are effectively selected earlier in the process. . . .

In 1992, by the end of the second Tuesday of the window (March 10), 40% of the delegates had been allocated and almost exactly half had been allocated by the end of March. In 1996, by the second Tuesday of the window (March 12), 54% of the pledged delegates had been allocated. In 2000, by the second Tuesday (March 14) 66.67%, two-thirds, of the delegates had been allocated. In 2004, with the regular window opening earlier, by the second Tuesday in March (March 9), 71.4% of the delegates had been allocated.

Commission members and presenters from virtually all sides of the calendar issue expressed serious concerns about the front-loading trend. In this regard, representatives of Michigan and other states were joined by party leaders from Iowa and New Hampshire. . . .

To address these concerns, the Commission recommends that the DNC, through its Rules and Bylaws Committee, make every effort to schedule no more than five contests in any one week, and that it consult with state parties and political leaders to further this result.

The Commission also recommends a system that would encourage state parties to schedule their events later in the process, or that at least would

2008 Presidential Caucus and Primary Dates

Date	Caucuses	Primaries
January 3	Iowa	
January 5	Wyoming (R)	
January 8		New Hampshire
January 15		Michigan
January 19	Nevada	South Carolina (D)
January 25–February 7	Hawaii (R)	
January 26		South Carolina (R)
January 29		Florida
February 1	Maine (R)	
February 5	Alaska	Alabama
	Colorado	Arizona
	Idaho (D)	Arkansas
	Kansas (D)	California
	Minnesota	Connecticut
	New Mexico (D)	Delaware
	North Dakota	Georgia
		Illinois
		Massachusetts
		Missouri
		New Jersey
		New York
		Oklahoma
		Tennessee
		Utah
February 9	Kansas (R)	Louisiana
	Nebraska (D)	
February 10	Maine (D)	
February 12		District of Columbia
		Maryland
		Virginia
February 19	Hawaii (D)	Washington
		Wisconsin
March 4		Ohio
		Rhode Island
		Texas
		Vermont
March 8	Wyoming (D)	
March 11		Mississippi
April 22		Pennsylvania
May 6		Indiana
		North Carolina
May 13		Nebraska
		West Virginia
May 20		Kentucky
		Oregon
May 27		Idaho
June 3		Montana
		New Mexico (R)
		South Dakota
August 25–28	Democratic National Convention, Denver, Colo.	
September 1–4	Republican National Convention, Minneapolis-St. Paul, Minn.	

SOURCE: Adapted from the Federal Election Commission, www.fec.gov/pubrec/2008pdates.pdf; accessed December 6, 2007.

discourage them from moving earlier than they were in 2000 or 2004. The Commission noted that the bonus delegate system attempted by the Republican Party for 2000, with bonuses ranging from 5% to 10%, was not remotely sufficient to induce state parties to schedule their events later in the process. Accordingly, the Commission recommends a program of considerably stronger incentives. Specifically, the Commission proposes that:

The calendar be divided into the following four time stages:

Stage I: March 4 through March 17, inclusive
Stage II: March 18 through April 7, inclusive
Stage III: April 8 through April 28, inclusive
Stage IV: April 29 through June 10, inclusive

A state would be awarded additional delegates to the 2008 Democratic National Convention equal to the following percentages, applied to the total number of pledged delegates otherwise allocated by the *Charter* and Call to the Convention, and based on the time period in which the state's first determining step in the delegate selection process is scheduled to occur in 2008:

Stage I: 15 percent
Stage II: 20 percent
Stage III: 30 percent
Stage IV: 40 percent

The Commission believes that only a system of strong and meaningful incentives, such as the proposed system outlined above, can mitigate against continued front-loading of the process. In that regard, the Commission suggests that the Rules and Bylaws Committee consider and discuss the issue of whether any system of disincentives (i.e., loss of delegates for moving contests earlier) should be incorporated into the process. . . .

Topical Guide to the Documents

Topic	Year	Origin and History of Political Parties	Party in Government	Party Organization	Party and the Electorate	Nomination Campaigns	The General Election Campaign	Campaign Finance	Parties and the Press	Third Parties
1. The Constitution: Provisions Concerning Elections	1787	X					X			
2. *The Federalist Papers*, No. 10	1787	X		X	X					
3. Alexander Hamilton's Letter to Edward Carrington	1792	X	X						X	
4. George Washington's Letter to Thomas Jefferson and Jefferson's Response to Washington	1792	X	X						X	
5. Thomas Jefferson's Letter to Philip Mazzei and George Washington's Letter to Jefferson	1796	X	X						X	
6. John Beckley's Letters to William Irvine	1796	X	X	X			X			
7. George Washington's Farewell Address	1796	X	X							
8. Thomas Jefferson's First Inaugural Address	1801	X	X							

(guide continues)

Topical Guide to the Documents (*continued*)

Topic	Year	Origin and History of Political Parties	Party in Government	Party Organization	Party and the Electorate	Nomination Campaigns	The General Election Campaign	Campaign Finance	Parties and the Press	Third Parties
9. The Tennessee General Assembly's Protest Against the Caucus System	1823	×	×	×		×				
10. Martin Van Buren's Letter to Thomas Ritchie	1827	×	×						×	
11. Henry Clay's Speech Concerning the Whig Party and Henry Clay's Letter to the Whig Party Convention	1834 1839	×		×						
12. Alexis de Tocqueville's "Parties in the United States"	1835	×	×	×	×					
13. The Declaration of Sentiments and Resolutions from the Seneca Falls Women's Rights Convention	1848				×					
14. Abraham Lincoln's "A House Divided" Speech	1858	×				×	×			
15. The Wade-Davis Manifesto	1864			×		×				
16. Thomas Nast's Cartoons of William "Boss" Tweed	1871			×					×	

No. & Document	Year								
17. Abram Hewitt's "Secret History of the Disputed Election, 1876–77"	1878				×			×	×
18. John McPherson's Speech Opposing the Pendleton Act	1882							×	×
19. Woodrow Wilson's "Wanted—A Party"	1886			×			×	×	×
20. The Massachusetts Australian Ballot Law	1888				×			×	×
21. The Omaha Platform	1892	×							
22. William Jennings Bryan's "Cross of Gold" Speech	1896				×		×		
23. Robert LaFollette's "Peril in the Machine" Speech	1897					×		×	
24. William Riordan's "The Strenuous Life of the Tammany District Leader"	1905		×				×	×	
25. The Tillman Act	1907			×					
26. George Norris's Resolution to Change the Membership of the House Rules Committee	1910				×				
27. The Publicity Act of 1910	1910			×					
28. Theodore Roosevelt's "Confession of Faith" Speech	1912	×							
29. Franklin Roosevelt's "Commonwealth Club" Speech	1932		×		×			×	×

(guide continues)

Topical Guide to the Documents (*continued*)

Topic	Year	Origin and History of Political Parties	Party in Government	Party Organization	Party and the Electorate	Nomination Campaigns	The General Election Campaign	Campaign Finance	Parties and the Press	Third Parties
30. George Norris's "The Model Legislature" Address	1934		X	X						
31. Huey Long's "Every Man a King" Radio Address	1934								X	X
32. The *Literary Digest* Poll	1936				X		X		X	
33. Franklin Roosevelt's Message to Congress on the Hatch Act	1939		X	X			X			
34. The Taft-Hartley Act	1947							X		
35. James Rowe's Memorandum to Harry Truman	1947			X			X			
36. The First Kennedy-Nixon Debate	1960						X		X	
37. *Baker v. Carr*	1962				X					
38. The "Peace, Little Girl" Television Advertisement	1964						X		X	
39. Lyndon Johnson's Message to Congress on the Voting Rights Act	1965				X					

#	Document	Year							
40.	The McGovern-Fraser Commission Report	1971							
41.	*Buckley v. Valeo*	1976							X
42.	Birch Bayh's Resolution to Amend the Constitution to Provide for Direct Popular Election of the President	1977					X		X
43.	Bill Clinton's Remarks on Signing the National Voter Registration Act	1993			X	X		X	
44.	The Contract with America	1994	X						
45.	*Bush v. Gore*	2000					X		X
46.	Report of the National Commission on Federal Election Reform	2001					X		
47.	Russ Feingold's Speech Supporting the Bipartisan Campaign Reform Act and Mitch McConnell's Speech Opposing the Bipartisan Campaign Reform Act	2002				X			
48.	Colorado Amendment 36, Allocating Presidential Electors Proportionally	2004		X			X	X	
49.	Memo of Understanding Regarding the Presidential Debates between George W. Bush and John Kerry	2004		X			X		X
50.	The Price-Herman Commission Report	2005			X	X			